T0341505

Engaging with
Martyn Lloyd-Jones

For
future generations yet to discover 'the Doctor'

Engaging with
Martyn Lloyd-Jones

The life and legacy of 'the Doctor'

Edited by
Andrew Atherstone & David Ceri Jones

APOLLOS (an imprint of Inter-Varsity Press)
Norton Street, Nottingham NG7 3HR, England
Website: www.ivpbooks.com
Email: ivp@ivpbooks.com

This collection © Inter-Varsity Press, 2011

All rights reserved. No part of this publication may be reproduced, stored in a retrieval system, or transmitted, in any form or by any means, electronic, mechanical, photocopying, recording or otherwise, without the prior permission of the publisher or the Copyright Licensing Agency.

First published 2011

British Library Cataloguing in Publication Data
A catalogue record for this book is available from the British Library.

ISBN: 978-1-84474-553-1

Set in Monotype Garamond 11/13pt
Typeset in Great Britain by Servis Filmsetting Ltd, Stockport, Cheshire

CONTENTS

Contributors   7

Foreword   9
J. I. Packer

Introduction: Lloyd-Jones and his biographers   11
Andrew Atherstone and David Ceri Jones

1. Lloyd-Jones and the interwar Calvinist resurgence   38
David W. Bebbington

2. Lloyd-Jones and Wales   59
David Ceri Jones

3. Lloyd-Jones and revival   91
Ian M. Randall

4. Lloyd-Jones and the charismatic controversy   114
Andrew Atherstone, David Ceri Jones and William K. Kay

5. Lloyd-Jones and the demise of preaching   156
   Ben Bailie

6. Lloyd-Jones and ministerial education   176
   Philip H. Eveson

7. Lloyd-Jones and fundamentalism   197
   Robert Pope

8. Lloyd-Jones and Karl Barth   220
   Robert Strivens

9. Lloyd-Jones and Roman Catholicism   232
   John Maiden

10. Lloyd-Jones and the Anglican secession crisis   261
    Andrew Atherstone

11. Lloyd-Jones and the Protestant past   293
    John Coffey

   Bibliography: Lloyd-Jones and his writings   326
   Andrew Atherstone and David Ceri Jones

   Index   363

CONTRIBUTORS

Andrew Atherstone is Tutor in History and Doctrine, and Latimer Research Fellow, at Wycliffe Hall, Oxford. His books include *Oxford's Protestant Spy: The Controversial Career of Charles Golightly* (2007) and *The Reformation: Faith and Flames* (2011).

Ben Bailie is a research student at Southern Baptist Theological Seminary in Louisville, Kentucky, and is currently completing a doctoral dissertation on the preaching of Martyn Lloyd-Jones. He also serves as pastor of Corn Creek Baptist Church.

David W. Bebbington has taught since 1976 at the University of Stirling, where since 1999 he has been Professor of History. His publications include *Evangelicalism in Modern Britain: A History from the 1730s to the 1980s* (1989; 2nd ed., 1993), *Victorian Nonconformity* (1992; 2nd ed., 2011), *The Dominance of Evangelicalism: The Age of Spurgeon and Moody* (2005) and *Baptists through the Centuries: A History of a Global People* (2010).

John Coffey is Professor of Early Modern History at the University of Leicester. He is the author of *Politics, Religion and the British Revolutions: The Mind of Samuel Rutherford* (2002) and *John Goodwin and the Puritan Revolution: Religion* *and Intellectual Change in Seventeenth-Century England* (2006). He has also recently co-edited *The Cambridge Companion to Puritanism* (2008).

Philip H. Eveson retired as Principal of London Theological Seminary in 2009, but is still involved in teaching Old Testament exegesis and theology. His publications include *The Great Exchange* (1996) and *Travel with Lloyd-Jones* (2004), a travel guide to the life of Martyn Lloyd-Jones.

David Ceri Jones is a Lecturer in History at Aberystwyth University. He is the author of '*A Glorious Work in the World': Welsh Methodism and the International Evangelical Revival, 1735–1750* (2004) and *The Elect Methodists: Calvinistic Methodism in England and Wales, 1735–1811* (2011).

William K. Kay is Professor of Theology at Glyndwr University, Wrexham, and has written extensively on Pentecostalism, including *Pentecostals in Britain* (2000), *Apostolic Networks in Britain* (2007) and *Pentecostalism: A Very Short Introduction* (2011).

John Maiden is Lecturer in Religious Studies at the Open University. An historian of religion, with a particular interest in evangelicalism, he is author of *National Religion and the Prayer Book Controversy, 1927–1928* (2009).

Robert Pope is Reader in Theology at University of Wales, Trinity St David, based in Lampeter, Ceredigion. He is the author of *Building Jerusalem: Nonconformity, Labour and the Social Question in Wales, 1906–1939* (1997), *Seeking God's Kingdom: Nonconformity and the Social Gospel* (1999) and *Lloffion ym Maes Crefydd: Ysgrifau ar Bynciau Diwinyddol y Byd Cyfoes* (2007).

Ian M. Randall is a Senior Research Fellow at the International Baptist Theological Seminary, Prague, and Spurgeon's College, London. He is the author of a number of books on aspects of evangelical history, including *Evangelical Experiences: A Study in the Spirituality of English Evangelicalism, 1918–1939* (1999) and *Rhythms of Revival: The Spiritual Awakening of 1857–1863* (2010).

Robert Strivens is the Principal of London Theological Seminary, where he teaches New Testament, Greek and Contemporary Issues. He is currently completing a doctoral dissertation on the thought of eighteenth-century Nonconformist minister Philip Doddridge at the University of Stirling.

FOREWORD

The greatness of great men boils down to the conjunction in them of two things: great visionary power in formulating objectives, and great leadership power expressed in a masterful, indeed magnetic persuasiveness, linked with full personal consistency in pursuing what is envisioned. Martyn Lloyd-Jones was a great man, and still today, a generation after his death, his objectives (faithful preaching, faithful churches and revival) and the inspiring force of his advocacy for them remain powerful influences on many Christian minds. He was a titan: though physically small, apart from his oversized, domed head, he dominated any circle in which he was involved and it is no wonder that the first attempts to appreciate him in print should have been more than a little hagiographical and uncritical. Thirty to fifty years usually proves to be the first really adequate viewing distance for looking at persons and events of the recent past, and that is reason enough to welcome the present book, with its broader learning and more carefully nuanced perspectives, to which I am now privileged to contribute this foreword.

What are my qualifications for so doing? you may ask. Well, for twenty years I was the organizer of the annual Puritan Studies Conference which Dr Lloyd-Jones hosted and chaired; I actively supported him in fostering area preaching meetings around England, each of which he would himself visit every year; and I helped edit the now regrettably defunct *Evangelical Magazine*, which sought to give his type of Christianity a commanding voice at pastoral level. He, I think, saw me in those days as a kind of Timothy to his Paul; at all events, we were quite close and during our years of working together I gained enormously from the relationship. To be sure, our ways parted abruptly when he realized that on the question of local church alignment I, a would-be reforming Anglican, was not with him nor was ever likely to be. But I have never ceased to regard him as a great man and indeed to celebrate him as the greatest I have ever known.

I am old now, a retired expatriate academic anchored in Canada, and this symposium is the work of younger scholars benefiting from, among other things, fresh thought and debate about all the fields of faith and practice on which Dr Lloyd-Jones expressed his mind and thereby offered leadership to the evangelical world of his day. As he was a generation ahead of me, and on some matters seemed to me to be quite old-fashioned, so no doubt my own thinking on some of the topics covered here might seem old-fashioned to some of the contributors to this book. But it will be clear, I think, that we are all together in regarding Dr Lloyd-Jones as, warts and all, one of the greatest Christian men of the twentieth century, a man whom God used powerfully to recall British evangelicals, both individually and corporately, to their true roots in the Bible, in the gospel and in theology – in other words, in Christ – at a time when such a recall was badly needed. Seeing him so, we join in honouring his memory, and in hoping that English-speaking evangelicals will continue to honour him as he deserves long after we ourselves are gone.

Professor J. I. Packer
Regent College, Vancouver

INTRODUCTION: LLOYD-JONES AND HIS BIOGRAPHERS

Andrew Atherstone and David Ceri Jones

The figure of Martyn Lloyd-Jones dominates the history of British evangelicalism in the twentieth century. He was perhaps the greatest Nonconformist statesman of his generation, best known as a magnetic preacher and a mentor of young preachers. From the pulpit of Westminster Chapel, near Buckingham Palace in central London, and from the platforms of his many wider networks, he called the evangelical movement back to a robust Reformed Christianity, with a passion for biblical conviction and Spirit-empowered revival. Lloyd-Jones's impact upon evangelicalism was immense and his legacy remains deeply influential.

Lloyd-Jones was born in Cardiff on 20 December 1899 and his life kept almost exact pace with all but the last two decades of the twentieth century. His formative years were spent at Llangeitho in Cardiganshire, the village made famous by the long ministry in the eighteenth century of Daniel Rowland, who had been expelled from the Church of England, and Lloyd-Jones attended Rowland's old chapel. He was educated at the nearby Tregaron County School, but following a devastating fire in the family home and shop in 1910 from which the business never recovered, the Lloyd-Joneses, like many others in Wales seeking a better life for themselves, relocated to London in 1914. Two years later Martyn began medical training at St Bartholomew's Hospital and by the age of twenty-three he had earned the London MD (doctorate of medicine), having already become chief clinical assistant to the king's physician, Sir

Thomas Horder. Hence throughout his life, even as a preacher, he was known affectionately as 'the Doctor'. A glittering career seemed to beckon, but in 1927 Lloyd-Jones quit the medical profession altogether and took up the pastorate of Bethlehem Forward Movement Mission at Sandfields in the South Wales industrial town of Port Talbot.

Lloyd-Jones's early ministry was a resounding success. A struggling church was transformed into a bustling and thriving enterprise, largely through his preaching gifts, and sizeable congregations flocked to listen to him throughout the region, helped by the celebrity status he achieved in the Welsh press. On the eve of the Second World War, an exhausted Lloyd-Jones left Wales to serve as assistant to the ageing G. Campbell Morgan at Westminster Chapel, and he became sole pastor when Campbell Morgan retired in 1943. Having guided the chapel through the dark days of Hitler's aerial bombardment of London, Lloyd-Jones quickly saw the congregation begin to grow, so that by the time he started his major expository series on Jesus' Sermon on the Mount in October 1950 his reputation as the most gifted preacher of his generation was all but secured. More ambitious series on Paul's letters to the Ephesians and the Romans occupied much of his energies from the mid-1950s until his retirement from the Westminster Chapel pulpit in 1968.

From this secure base in Westminster, Lloyd-Jones, together with his younger Anglican contemporaries John Stott and J. I. Packer, exerted an enormous influence over postwar British evangelicalism. That influence was felt largely through Lloyd-Jones's involvement in a number of strategic parachurch agencies. In 1939 he became president of the Inter-Varsity Fellowship, a role which enabled him to introduce generations of students to serious theological engagement, and he was chairman of the International Fellowship of Evangelical Students from 1947. At a similar period he was instrumental in the founding of Tyndale House in Cambridge, to promote evangelical Bible scholarship, and the Evangelical Library in London, dedicated to the revival of Reformed and Puritan theology. In his native Wales a new network of evangelical students, to be known as the Evangelical Movement of Wales, received his blessing and encouragement, and in 1950 the annual Puritan Conferences began at Westminster Chapel.

Yet from the early 1960s onwards Lloyd-Jones became increasingly perturbed at the direction of the evangelical movement which he had done so much to resuscitate. In an address to the second National Assembly of Evangelicals in October 1966, against the backdrop of the ambitious ecumenical movement, he controversially called evangelicals, otherwise dispersed among many of the traditional denominations, to stand together in a new network of independent congregations. The response to his appeal polarized

British evangelicals between those who acted on his vision and those, especially within the Church of England, who chose to fight for the reform of their denominations from within. In many respects this was the defining moment of Lloyd-Jones's ministry. Following serious illness in 1968, he retired from Westminster Chapel and devoted much of his final decade to itinerant preaching, especially among those churches that had heeded his call to secede from their denominations, and to editing his sermons for publication. He preached for the last time at Barcombe Baptist Chapel near Lewes, East Sussex, in June 1980 and died, appropriately for such a passionate Welshman, on St David's Day 1981. In the decades following his death his voice has continued to be heard through the work of the Martyn Lloyd-Jones Recordings Trust and the frequent publication of new volumes of his sermons.

Although the basic narrative of Lloyd-Jones's life and ministry is well known, several areas of his theology and legacy remain hotly contested. The purpose of this introductory chapter is to survey the trends within Lloyd-Jones scholarship in the first three decades after his death. It will focus on the perspectives of four biographers – Iain Murray, Christopher Catherwood, Gaius Davies and John Brencher – each of whom has made a significant contribution to the debate. Their writings on Lloyd-Jones have all been controversial in different ways and generated a literature of their own. Each has provoked fresh thinking about the Doctor, establishing a substantial and diverse historiography upon which this present volume of essays seeks to build.

Iain Murray and Christopher Catherwood

Iain H. Murray (born 1931) was closely involved with Martyn Lloyd-Jones for a quarter of a century. The two men shared a common passion for the revival of Reformed and evangelical theology, and Lloyd-Jones invited Murray to work as his assistant at Westminster Chapel from 1956 to 1959 while he continued his early researches in church history.[1] Murray became the editor of *The Banner of Truth* magazine from its first issue in September 1955 and two years later was a co-founder of the Banner of Truth Trust, which sought to disseminate Reformed literature worldwide and became Lloyd-Jones's publisher

---

1. London, Westminster Chapel Archives, Church Meeting Minute Book (January 1929 – November 1958), 12 July 1956; Church Meeting Minute Book (January 1959 – May 1977), 9 July 1959.

of choice during the 1970s for his sermon series on Romans and Ephesians.[2] Murray himself specialized in popular Christian biography, including studies of Charles Spurgeon, A. W. Pink, John Murray, Jonathan Edwards, John Wesley and many other Christian worthies.[3]

From the early 1960s, Murray began collecting material for a biography of Lloyd-Jones. Although the Doctor had previously quashed two biographies written by admirers, preventing their publication, he consented to help Murray during the last year of his life.[4] Murray was granted unique access to Lloyd-Jones's personal papers, correspondence and sermon notes, and to numerous press cuttings gathered over more than half a century by his wife, Bethan Lloyd-Jones. He interviewed his subject at length, sometimes tape-recorded, and they discussed together the basic framework and approach of the work. Murray acknowledged that 'the general interpretation which it gives of his career is his own'.[5] He added, 'While I have not sought to produce an uncritical life – an exercise of which he would not have approved – I have tried to give the reader, as closely as possible, and often in his own words, his thinking on the issues which arose.'[6] The extensive quotations from Lloyd-Jones's many sermons, addresses and letters gave the biography an autobiographical flavour. The first volume was published in 1982, taking the narrative up to the eve of the Second World War, and a second volume appeared in 1990, running to a combined total of nearly 1,200 pages, excluding appendices. Murray's *magnum opus* will never be surpassed for the sheer volume of invaluable source material it brought into the public domain. It remains the first port of call for every student of Lloyd-Jones.

Murray's biography met with high praise. The *Gospel Magazine* enjoyed its

---

2. See especially John J. Murray, *Catch the Vision: Roots of the Reformed Recovery* (Darlington: Evangelical Press, 2007), ch. 7.

3. Iain Murray's biographical studies include *The Forgotten Spurgeon* (London: Banner of Truth, 1966); *Arthur W. Pink: His Life and Thought* (Edinburgh: Banner of Truth, 1981); 'Life of John Murray', in *Collected Writings of John Murray*, vol. 3 (Edinburgh: Banner of Truth, 1982), pp. 1–158; *Jonathan Edwards: A New Biography* (Edinburgh: Banner of Truth, 1987); *Wesley and the Men Who Followed* (Edinburgh: Banner of Truth, 2003); *Heroes* (Edinburgh: Banner of Truth, 2009); and *John MacArthur: Servant of the Word and Flock* (Edinburgh: Banner of Truth, 2011).

4. Iain H. Murray, *D. Martyn Lloyd-Jones: The First Forty Years 1899–1939* (Edinburgh: Banner of Truth, 1982), p. xii.

5. Ibid., p. xiii.

6. Iain H. Murray, *D. Martyn Lloyd-Jones: The Fight of Faith 1939–1981* (Edinburgh: Banner of Truth, 1990), p. xx.

'very gripping narrative', while the *Church of England Newspaper* found it 'spiritually powerful', containing 'much food for thought and fuel for prayer'.[7] *Peace and Truth* considered it 'outstanding . . . destined to take its place among the most significant Evangelical biographies of the Twentieth Century'.[8] Another reviewer called the work 'an inspiration' which should be compulsory reading for every Bible college student.[9] For some it was life-changing. One young theology graduate, Michael Haykin (later a prominent professor of church history), acknowledged that Murray's first volume 'was used by God to initiate a profound revolution in his theological perspective and to spark an unquenchable love for the doctrines of grace'.[10] Written soon after Lloyd-Jones's death by one of his close admirers, the biography inevitably leaned 'in the hagiographic direction'[11] and was, in the words of two commentators, an 'outstanding tribute' and a 'noble memorial'.[12] Murray himself proclaimed:

> Those who stood close to Dr Lloyd-Jones and who revered him as a leader, indeed father, in Christ, may well find that these pages give but a faint impression of what he was. It is true to say that his ministry, his friendship, his thought, became part of the very lives of those who knew and loved him. For many he was more than anything which print can convey . . . The truth is that we have lost a leader who, in our generation at least, cannot be replaced.[13]

One reader observed that Murray was 'virtually "one" with his subject theologically', so those hoping for 'coolly dispassionate' biography would be disappointed.[14] Another feared that his skills in critical evaluation were hindered by

7. Review by Maurice Handford, *Gospel Magazine*, no. 1510 (May – June 1983), p. 138; review by Tony Baker, *Church of England Newspaper* (4 February 1983), p. 12.

8. Review by Peter D. Johnson, *Peace and Truth*, no. 4 (1990), p. 12.

9. Review by Alexander Barkley, *Reformed Theological Review*, vol. 50 (September – December 1991), p. 106.

10. Michael A. G. Haykin, 'Jonathan Edwards: A Review of the New Biography', *Reformation Today*, no. 100 (November – December 1987), p. 30.

11. Hugh L. Williams, 'Martyn Lloyd-Jones Warts and All', *British Reformed Review*, no. 37 (Spring 2003), p. 34.

12. Review by Arthur Bennett, *Churchman*, vol. 105 (1991), p. 279; review by Peter Lewis, *Evangelicals Now* (January 1991), p. 11.

13. Murray, *Lloyd-Jones: First Forty Years*, pp. xiv–xv.

14. Review by Joseph H. Hall, *Presbyterian: Covenant Seminary Review*, vol. 9 (Spring – Fall 1983), p. 106.

his 'mammoth respect' for Lloyd-Jones.[15] Nevertheless, Professor F. F. Bruce insisted, 'A man is no worse a biographer for being a wholehearted admirer of his subject.'[16]

Densil Morgan described Murray's two volumes as 'massive and wholly adulatory'.[17] Yet there were some places where gentle criticism of Lloyd-Jones peeked through – admittedly only a handful of pages amongst nearly 1,200. Murray described the Doctor's complex personality and his sometimes unpredictable attitudes which could seem at times 'contradictory'. He was by nature 'too impatient, too vigorous, too prone to "crack a nut with a sledgehammer"'. According to Murray, Lloyd-Jones did not always speak his full mind in personal conversation, so individuals were sometimes misled as to his true views. In contrast, his love of debating sometimes carried him too far in order to win a point against his opponent. He was 'guilty of exaggeration and even misrepresentation. He was scarcely ever indefinite or undecided. The authority with which he spoke . . . did at times betray him into a dogmatism which was not well founded'. Murray also observed that Lloyd-Jones's lack of organizational skills meant that he failed to train co-workers at Westminster Chapel, which grew too dependent on him as a solitary individual and was left with a leadership vacuum when he suddenly retired.[18] These character weaknesses were explored at greater length by later biographers, as will be seen, but it was Murray who began to map the terrain. Nevertheless, it remained his conviction, as he explained elsewhere, that 'True Christian biography should . . . concentrate on what is edifying and for the praise of Christ.' He was glad to reclaim the category of 'hagiography', believing that Christian biographies should present godly models for readers to imitate.[19]

The fruit of Murray's research into Lloyd-Jones's life did not end with his biography. His detailed knowledge of Lloyd-Jones's manuscripts also resulted in the publication of a large body of primary source material, including two volumes of evangelistic sermons and a volume of letters.[20] Murray also encouraged Bethan Lloyd-Jones to publish her memoir of Sandfields, and saw

15. Review by John H. Armstrong, *Trinity Journal*, vol. 12 (Spring 1991), p. 97.

16. Review by F. F. Bruce, *Evangelical Quarterly*, vol. 57 (January 1985), p. 91.

17. Review by D. Densil Morgan, *Journal of Welsh Religious History*, vol. 3 (2003), p. 98.

18. See especially, Murray, *Lloyd-Jones: Fight of Faith*, pp. 755–758, 769–770.

19. Murray, *Heroes*, pp. ix–xi.

20. D. M. Lloyd-Jones, *Evangelistic Sermons at Aberavon* (Edinburgh: Banner of Truth, 1983); D. M. Lloyd-Jones, *Old Testament Evangelistic Sermons* (Edinburgh: Banner of

through the press two further volumes of Lloyd-Jones's collected addresses, first delivered at the Puritan and Westminster Conferences and on other occasions.[21] His contribution to our understanding of Lloyd-Jones's public ministry and teaching is considerable.

While Murray focused on Lloyd-Jones as a public figure, a more intimate portrait was provided by the Doctor's eldest grandchild, Christopher Catherwood, son of Sir Frederick and Lady Elizabeth Catherwood. With his family he attended Westminster Chapel from birth in 1955 until he left home in 1973 to read modern history at Balliol College, Oxford. Catherwood was converted aged eleven through listening to his grandfather's preaching on the book of Acts,[22] and was baptized at the chapel three years later, shortly after Lloyd-Jones's retirement.[23] After his grandfather's death, Catherwood invested considerable energy in editing his sermons for publication. Between 1984 and 1992 he was responsible for seeing eleven volumes through the press, mostly with Kingsway and none with the Banner of Truth Trust.[24] The first two in the series, *Joy Unspeakable: The Baptism with the Holy Spirit* (1984) and *Prove All Things: The Sovereign Work of the Spirit* (1985) were highly controversial and provoked extensive debate about Lloyd-Jones's relationship with the

---

Truth, 1995); *D. Martyn Lloyd-Jones: Letters 1919–1981* (Edinburgh: Banner of Truth, 1994).

21. Bethan Lloyd-Jones, *Memories of Sandfields 1927–1938* (Edinburgh: Banner of Truth, 1983); D. M. Lloyd-Jones, *The Puritans: Their Origins and Successors: Addresses Delivered at the Puritan and Westminster Conferences 1959–1978* (Edinburgh: Banner of Truth, 1987); D. M. Lloyd-Jones, *Knowing the Times: Addresses Delivered on Various Occasions 1942–1977* (Edinburgh: Banner of Truth, 1989).

22. Christopher Catherwood, *Martyn Lloyd-Jones: A Family Portrait* (Eastbourne: Kingsway, 1995), pp. 162–163.

23. London, Westminster Chapel Archives, Church Meeting Minute Book (January 1959 – May 1977), 24 April 1969.

24. The volumes of sermons edited by Catherwood were *Joy Unspeakable* (Eastbourne: Kingsway, 1984); *Prove All Things* (Eastbourne: Kingsway, 1985); *I Am Not Ashamed* (London: Hodder and Stoughton, 1986); *The Cross* (Eastbourne: Kingsway, 1986); *Saved in Eternity* (Eastbourne: Kingsway, 1988); *Safe in the World* (Eastbourne: Kingsway, 1988); *Sanctified Through the Truth* (Eastbourne: Kingsway, 1989); *Growing in the Spirit* (Eastbourne: Kingsway, 1989); *Enjoying the Presence of God* (Eastbourne: Crossway, 1991); *The Heart of the Gospel* (Eastbourne: Crossway, 1991); and *The Kingdom of God* (Cambridge: Crossway, 1992). He also edited a compilation volume, *The Best of Martyn Lloyd-Jones* (Eastbourne: Kingsway, 1992).

charismatic movement, which will be considered elsewhere.[25] Catherwood also edited *Martyn Lloyd-Jones: Chosen by God* (1986), a collection of tributes, some written as obituaries after his grandfather's death or delivered at his memorial service. He described his subject as 'a truly remarkable man . . . a man of many talents', and maintained, 'We have not known anyone of such spiritual stature or personal qualities such as he possessed. We may never in our lifetimes see his like again.'[26]

Catherwood was not only Lloyd-Jones's literary editor, but also made a significant contribution as a biographer, offering a more tender portrayal than Murray's *magnum opus*. He began to sketch out his interpretative framework in *Five Evangelical Leaders* (1984), expanded to a full-length study in *Martyn Lloyd-Jones: A Family Portrait* (1995). Woven into the narrative were many personal anecdotes, showing Lloyd-Jones from a new aspect, far removed from the popular impression of an austere preacher clad in black Geneva gown. Instead he was shown to be a warm-hearted grandfather with an impish sense of humour, enjoying a relaxed and close-knit relationship with his family, devoted to his grandchildren who knew him affectionately as 'Dacu'.[27] Catherwood gladly acknowledged that Lloyd-Jones was 'someone with whom I enjoyed the warmest and most formative of relationships all my conscious life'.[28] Much of his language was adulatory. Lloyd-Jones was a 'spiritual giant' at whose 'superlative preaching' the congregation was 'transported into the presence of heaven'. He was a 'loving pastor' with a 'wonderfully incisive mind', a 'fount of wisdom' for perplexed ministers. He was a 'prophetic genius', with 'a rare combination of great intellect and fiery emotion'. His fifty-four-year marriage was 'lyrically happy'.[29]

Catherwood's sole criticism of his grandfather was reserved for the one area where Murray defended him most robustly – the appeal to evangelical separatism in the late 1960s. Catherwood appreciated Lloyd-Jones's 'magnificent vision' of gospel unity, but concluded that the appeal to separate from doctrinally mixed denominations was 'mistaken', well motivated but a sign of

---

25. See in this volume, Andrew Atherstone, David Ceri Jones and William Kay, 'Lloyd-Jones and the charismatic controversy', pp. 114–155.

26. Christopher Catherwood (ed.), *Martyn Lloyd-Jones: Chosen by God* (Crowborough: Highland Books, 1986), pp. 10, 279.

27. See especially, Catherwood, *Lloyd-Jones: Family Portrait*, pp. 68, 103, 156–182.

28. Christopher Catherwood, *Five Evangelical Leaders* (London: Hodder and Stoughton, 1984), p. 10.

29. Ibid., p. 106; Catherwood, *Lloyd-Jones: Family Portrait*, pp. 30, 37, 68, 74, 78, 82, 104.

impatience, and 'drove a wedge' between British evangelicals.[30] Catherwood wrote sympathetically of evangelicals within the Church of England, while his sternest words fell upon Lloyd-Jones's disciples. He described some of them as 'hot-headed zealots' who had turned their hero into a talisman:

> When he died, and was no longer there to contradict, some of those followers tended to be very dogmatic about what he would and would not have said, always quoting him as being on their own side. Ironically, some of them were anti-Catholic, yet their method of quoting the Doctor as some infallible source reminded some of us strongly of unreformed Catholic appeals to tradition and the invocation of saints![31]

Catherwood's interpretation of the controversial events of the 1960s and 1970s was soon picked up by his Oxford friend and contemporary, Professor Alister McGrath, in *To Know and Serve God: A Biography of James I. Packer* (1997). In this volume McGrath did for Packer what Murray had done for Lloyd-Jones, by providing an engaging but largely uncritical defence of his subject. Inevitably, McGrath's sympathy for Packer shaped his attitude to Lloyd-Jones. He asserted that Lloyd-Jones's separatist ecclesiology was 'a sure-fire recipe for civil war' amongst evangelicals and that he was responsible for shattering the movement's 'peaceful coexistence'. He declared that the Doctor became 'a voice in the wilderness', while Packer was 'frozen out' by 'the Lloyd-Jones faction'.[32] Nevertheless, McGrath was at pains to shift the burden of blame from Lloyd-Jones himself onto his disciples. He emphasized that it was the 'rather harsh and strident circle of supporters and advisers' gathered around Lloyd-Jones who were responsible for the 'hard-line attitude' towards Packer.[33]

One sceptical reviewer, Professor Gerald Bray, complained that McGrath's biography left readers with the impression that Lloyd-Jones was 'manipulated by a coterie of lesser individuals'.[34] Nevertheless, this viewpoint was widely accepted. For example, Robert Letham criticized McGrath's 'hagiography', but readily adopted his verdict on the Lloyd-Jones circle:

---

30. Catherwood, *Lloyd-Jones: Family Portrait*, pp. 106, 146.
31. Ibid., p. 144.
32. Alister McGrath, *To Know and Serve God: A Biography of James I. Packer* (London: Hodder and Stoughton, 1997), pp. 123, 127, 157, 161, 234.
33. Ibid., pp. 127, 158.
34. Gerald Bray, '*To Know and Serve God: A Biography of James I. Packer* by Alister McGrath: An Extended Review', *Churchman*, vol. 111 (1997), p. 359.

This is an uncritical biography. Not an adverse word is passed about the hero. Yes, people ganged up on him, not least the nasty acolytes of Martyn Lloyd-Jones. But Packer emerges from these pages lilywhite-pure . . . McGrath is correct that Lloyd-Jones was surrounded and influenced by his minions . . .[35]

Yet Geoffrey Thomas (pastor of Alfred Place Baptist Church, Aberystwyth from 1965) was clear that none who knew Lloyd-Jones could come to such a conclusion. He maintained that Lloyd-Jones's break with Packer was the result of serious theological reflection and replied to the 'silly' suggestions of Letham and McGrath:

> But as for some yokel underlings stirring the easy-going and gullible Doctor into a course of action he would have been wiser to have avoided – men who write that simply do not know the Doctor. He had friends and supporters whom he patiently taught whose blindness he sometimes groaned over, but we acolytes could no more influence him than the moon give light to the sun.[36]

Thomas observed that the interpretative framework of Catherwood and McGrath concerning the disputes of the 1960s and 1970s had quickly become 'received tradition'.[37] Likewise Murray warned that McGrath's perspective was being 'blindly followed' rather than subjected to proper scrutiny.[38] He insisted that 'Lloyd-Jones was never "advised" by men thirty years his junior, and the younger men closest to him were often slow to accept a break with Packer because, unlike Lloyd-Jones, they had some personal indebtedness to him in the recovery of Reformed and Puritan beliefs.' Murray maintained that the split with Packer was not in fact marked by any 'bitterness' on the Nonconformist side, but was on the contrary 'a parting of friends'.[39]

---

35. Review by Robert Letham, *Westminster Theological Journal*, vol. 61 (Fall 1999), pp. 309–310.
36. Geoffrey Thomas, 'Dr Lloyd-Jones and his "Minions"' (1999), www.banneroftruth.org (accessed 17 February, 2011). For a personal tribute, see Geoffrey Thomas, 'The Doctor', *Reformation Today*, no. 61 (May – June 1981), pp. 3–12.
37. Thomas, 'Dr Lloyd-Jones and his "Minions"'.
38. Iain H. Murray, *Lloyd-Jones: Messenger of Grace* (Edinburgh: Banner of Truth, 2008), p. 187.
39. Iain H. Murray, *Evangelicalism Divided: A Record of Crucial Change in the Years 1950 to 2000* (Edinburgh: Banner of Truth, 2000), pp. 110–111.

Murray's defence of Lloyd-Jones's position was hammered home in *Evangelicalism Divided* (2000), a devastating protest at the doctrinal degeneration of the evangelical movement in the last half of the twentieth century. His central argument was that the gospel had been fatally compromised by evangelical involvement in the ecumenical movement, which had led to collaboration with liberals and Roman Catholics, even in evangelism. By working hand in hand with unbelievers, evangelicals had blurred their distinctives and jettisoned their traditional answer to the vital question, 'What is a Christian?' According to Murray, the villains of the piece in North America were Billy Graham, Fuller Theological Seminary and *Christianity Today*, while his main British targets were evangelicals in the Church of England, chiefly John Stott, J. I. Packer, Colin Buchanan and Alister McGrath. By contrast, the blameless hero was Martyn Lloyd-Jones, portrayed as a solitary and prophetic voice against these trends.[40]

Evangelicalism Divided was published to wide acclaim on both sides of the Atlantic. R. C. Sproul declared, 'Murray's critique is as kind and gracious as it is revealing and devastating. The icons of modern evangelicalism are shown as falling into egregious strategic errors that have weakened the evangelical faith at its very core.'[41] John F. MacArthur celebrated, 'It's one of the best and most eye-opening books I have read in years.'[42] *Evangelicals Now* called it a 'vital warning' which must be heeded.[43] David Searle (warden of Rutherford House, Edinburgh) acknowledged, 'By any standards, this is an extremely impressive work and reformed Christians will be deeply indebted to Iain Murray for his immense scholarship, inexorable logic and clear passion for the purity of the church and the glory of God.'[44] Nevertheless, Murray's historical *cri de coeur* was open to criticism at a number of significant points. His fulsome praise notwithstanding, Searle believed *Evangelicalism Divided* to be guilty of 'astonishing selectivity', a criticism echoed by Anglican evangelicals like Christopher Idle and Melvin Tinker.[45] The very few Anglicans applauded in the book were almost all dead, like J. C. Ryle and Alan Stibbs. There was little or no mention of Anglican

---

40. Ibid., pp. 44–49, 94–98, 278–293.

41. R. C. Sproul, 'The Roots of Division', *Tabletalk*, vol. 25 (January 2001), p. 61.

42. Iain H. Murray, *The Unresolved Controversy: Unity with Non-Evangelicals* (Edinburgh: Banner of Truth, 2001), p. 32.

43. Review by John E. Benton, *Evangelicals Now* (September 2000), p. 18.

44. Review by David C. Searle, *Scottish Bulletin of Evangelical Theology*, vol. 19 (Spring 2001), p. 87.

45. Ibid., p. 88. See also review by Christopher Idle, *New Directions*, no. 71 (April 2001), p. 26; review by Melvin Tinker, *Churchman*, vol. 115 (Spring 2001), pp. 79–80.

evangelical organizations such as Reform, the Fellowship of Word and Spirit, Oak Hill Theological College or Crosslinks, nor of the ministry of Dick Lucas at St Helen's, Bishopsgate and his Proclamation Trust. The impression, according to Tinker, was that Anglican evangelicalism had 'sold the pass and is being led lemming-like towards ecumenical oblivion'. He feared that such a 'one-sided' presentation of history would merely accentuate evangelical divisions rather than help to heal them.[46] Stott's and Packer's positive contributions to evangelical theology were largely ignored under the weight of Murray's 'heavy lash of criticism', as Gaius Davies wryly noted: 'Perhaps in the light of earlier Christian infighting – let us say between the Wesleys and their Calvinistic friends in the eighteenth century – his criticisms of Packer and Stott are mild. But it gives substance to the ironic comment "see how these Christians love one another".'[47]

Several commentators also challenged Murray's unwavering defence of Lloyd-Jones. Searle complained at his lack of objectivity, while Tinker believed the credibility of Murray's analysis was weakened by his refusal to acknowledge any fault on Lloyd-Jones's part in the divisions of the 1960s and 1970s. He warned that Murray had painted 'an all too glowing picture' of the Lloyd-Jones circle and was guilty of 'special pleading' in his revisionist interpretation of Lloyd-Jones's call to evangelical unity.[48] Likewise Roger Beckwith asked, 'If Lloyd-Jones was so deeply misunderstood, one wonders why he did not do more in his lifetime to put the record straight.'[49] David F. Wright (Professor of Patristic and Reformed Christianity at New College, Edinburgh) also argued that Murray 'patently misreads' Lloyd-Jones's crucial address to the National Assembly of Evangelicals in 1966.[50] While sharing Murray's 'lament over the weakness and incoherence of much evangelical ecclesiology', he concluded that *Evangelicalism Divided* contained 'too many half-truths and overstatements'.[51] Professor Wright was particularly concerned at a style of historical writing which treated Lloyd-Jones as an unimpeachable icon:

---

46. Tinker, ibid., pp. 79–80.
47. Gaius Davies, *Genius, Grief and Grace: A Doctor Looks at Suffering and Success* (Fearn: Christian Focus, 2001), p. 367.
48. Review by Melvin Tinker, pp. 78–79.
49. Roger Beckwith, '*Evangelicalism Divided*: An Extended Review', *Churchman*, vol. 116 (Summer 2002), p. 160.
50. Review by David F. Wright, *Reformation and Revival*, vol. 10 (Spring 2001), p. 129. For Murray's response to Wright on this point, see Iain H. Murray, 'Who is Misrepresenting Lloyd-Jones?', *Evangelicals Now* (November 2001), p. 21.
51. Wright, ibid., pp. 134–135.

This book would be a more humanly sympathetic exercise if only it betrayed some
slight recognition that Lloyd-Jones, too, had feet of clay. If only it acknowledged
that, for example, like the consummate orator he was, in the classic mold of great
preachers from Chrysostom and Augustine onward, he was given to overstatement.
. . . Hyperbole and superlatives were part of his stock-in-trade! . . . North American
readers ought also to be aware of some unease, not least among senior evangelical
brethren in Scotland, that Lloyd-Jones pursued some unwise causes in his latter years,
to the detriment of his core ministry. The idolizing of our leaders has been one of the
unhealthier marks of modern evangelicalism . . . I suspect that behind such inflated
deference lurks a defective pneumatology – one that works with an Old Testament
prophet-model to the despite of that democratizing of the Spirit which, according to
Acts 2:16–18, characterizes the heart of the new covenant.[52]

Gaius Davies and John Brencher

If Iain Murray, and to a certain extent Christopher Catherwood, saw Lloyd-Jones
as the heroic figure *par excellence* of modern British evangelicalism, there has been
another stream of historiography more willing to question the Doctor's legacy.
An early pioneer was Professor Donald Macleod of the Free Church College in
Edinburgh, not far from the headquarters of the Banner of Truth Trust. He was
editor of the *Monthly Record of the Free Church of Scotland* which lamented Lloyd-
Jones on his death as 'an extraordinary man and an extraordinary preacher'.[53]
Writing two years later, in October 1983, Macleod continued:

It is curious that in a day of small things God gave the church a preacher such as Dr
Martyn Lloyd-Jones. It was not simply that in an age of pygmies he towered above
the others. He would have towered in any age. Indeed he was arguably the greatest
British preacher since the Reformation, rivalled only by Whitefield, Spurgeon and
Chalmers.[54]

Nevertheless, Macleod was alarmed at the way in which Lloyd-Jones was so
quickly canonized by his disciples, beyond the reach of any criticism:

---

52. Ibid., pp. 128–129.
53. Donald Macleod, 'The Passing of Dr Lloyd-Jones', *Monthly Record of the Free Church
of Scotland* (April 1981), p. 84.
54. Donald Macleod, 'The Lloyd-Jones Legacy', *Monthly Record of the Free Church of
Scotland* (October 1983), p. 207.

While the Doctor lived, he bestrode English and Welsh evangelicalism like a colossus and his death was a traumatic event for the whole movement. In fact many felt, despairingly, that his passing had left a gaping void; and although they did not quite say that God would have difficulty in filling it the thought was probably in their hearts. Whether such a judgment is right or wrong, its very existence causes problems.

The most obvious is the emergence of a Doctor-cult. This is not a mere danger. It is a reality. Brethren vie with one another in recounting Doctor anecdotes, indulge in open hagiography and refrain from all critical evaluation. Indeed this present article probably contains more criticism than has appeared in all other evangelical magazines put together. The thing just is not done.

This puts us in a very difficult position. Our personal debt to the Doctor is immeasurable. But not even John Calvin was infallible and we must keep a sense of proportion. We can follow no man implicitly and we certainly cannot stand idly by while blind loyalty to one man's vision becomes a barrier to further evangelical progress. In some matters – notably his view of the sealing of the Spirit, his concept of Christian unity and his attitude to evangelical Anglicanism – the Doctor was quite simply wrong.[55]

Macleod mocked the tendency in some quarters to promote Lloyd-Jones's style of preaching as the only valid method of biblical exposition. Naïve imitation of Lloyd-Jones's 'microscopic analysis of the Pauline epistles', Macleod suggested, had led many a young preacher to lose his congregation half way through Ephesians 1. He described Lloyd-Jones as 'the Cardinal Archbishop of evangelicalism', participating in the Westminster Fellowship, the Puritan Conference, the British Evangelical Council and the Evangelical Movement of Wales 'not as an ordinary minister but as a different order of being', always treated with special deference. Macleod commented:

> This was not something he sought. It was thrust upon him. But he was wrong to accept it. He should have borne testimony by his example to the parity of ministers. He should have given others an opportunity to develop their gifts of leadership (for example, by chairing the Westminster Fellowship). He should have taken positive steps to minimise evangelicalism's dependence on himself.[56]

Professor Macleod did not develop his thesis. It seemed initially that this more critical angle of interpretation would end in an historiographical cul-de-sac, buried in a Scottish magazine. Nevertheless, others slowly began to

---

55. Ibid., p. 209.
56. Ibid.

come forward to offer extended comment on Lloyd-Jones's weaknesses. For example, in 1999 Densil Morgan from Bangor University in Wales gave a brief but critical assessment:

> There is no doubt about Lloyd-Jones's place among the great . . . His greatness, though, was flawed. The older he got, the more sectarian he became . . . Not only did this curtail his effectiveness as a Christian leader but ensured that his name would be linked with schism and contention rather than unity and peace. Which was a pity for the gifts which 'the Doctor' possessed were profuse and his potential for good, though squandered, was immense.[57]

Elsewhere Morgan described Lloyd-Jones's influence as 'overbearing', his brand of evangelicalism as 'highly sectarian' and his legacy as 'strangely flawed'.[58] It was not, however, until the turn of the new millennium, two decades after Lloyd-Jones's death, that his character and legacy were subjected to sustained scrutiny in the controversial writings of Gaius Davies and John Brencher.

Gaius Davies (born 1929) was a medical student at St Bartholomew's Hospital from 1947 to 1953, during which time he was a member of Westminster Chapel and sat under Lloyd-Jones's preaching, a deeply formative experience. He remained a devoted follower for many years. As a GP (family doctor) at Conway in North Wales from 1957 to 1969, Davies was closely involved in the Evangelical Movement of Wales, serving as one of the editors of its Welsh-language magazine, *Y Cylchgrawn Efengylaidd*, from 1964. To mark the occasion of Lloyd-Jones's retirement from Westminster Chapel, Davies published a eulogy which he later admitted was 'a panegyric . . . full of praise, with no critical assessment'.[59] He described Lloyd-Jones as 'a prophet', 'a voice crying in the wilderness of the evangelical world', 'a contemporary Puritan' and 'a father to his people'.[60] With this pedigree, Davies was one of five men chosen to offer tributes at Lloyd-Jones's memorial service at Westminster Chapel in April 1981.[61]

---

57. D. Densil Morgan, 'Giants of Faith Against a Secular Tide', *New Welsh Review*, no. 43 (Winter 1998–9), p. 37.

58. D. Densil Morgan, *The Span of the Cross: Christian Religion and Society in Wales, 1914–2000* (Cardiff: University of Wales Press, 1999), pp. 144, 249–250.

59. Davies, *Genius, Grief and Grace*, p. 336.

60. Translation of Gaius Davies, 'Dr D. Martyn Lloyd-Jones', *Y Cylchgrawn Efengylaidd*, cyf. 9, rhif 6 (Gorfennaf – Medi 1968), pp. 164–169.

61. A revised version of the memorial tribute was published as Gaius Davies, 'The Doctor as a Doctor', in Catherwood (ed.), *Lloyd-Jones: Chosen by God*, pp. 59–74.

Davies had returned from Wales to London in 1969 to train at the Institute of Psychiatry and then worked for two decades as a consultant psychiatrist at King's College Hospital. He put his specialist knowledge to use in *Genius and Grace: Sketches from a Psychiatrist's Notebook* (1992), nine biographical vignettes on Christian personalities ranging from Martin Luther and John Bunyan through to C. S. Lewis and J. B. Phillips. The book's dominant theme was that even great Christian heroes have obvious frailties and character flaws, but God's grace transforms human weakness. One reviewer observed, 'In a harsher hand these warts-and-all portraits could read as character assassinations, but Davies has an affection for them all and the psychiatrist's strong sense that God loves to use his imperfect sons and daughters.'[62] Nevertheless, a furore blew up when Davies added Lloyd-Jones into the mix. An expanded edition was published by Christian Focus in 2001 under the title *Genius, Grief and Grace*, with two new chapters, on Frances Ridley Havergal and Martyn Lloyd-Jones, additions made at the suggestion of J. I. Packer.[63]

Davies was fulsome in praise of his former mentor. He spoke of Lloyd-Jones's kindness, generosity, courage, wisdom, humour and skill as a debater. Lloyd-Jones was 'great fun to be with'. He was godly and devout, a man of remarkable intelligence who preached with 'great spiritual power'.[64] Nine times in the chapter Davies called his subject a 'genius'.[65] Yet Davies also offered a frank assessment of Lloyd-Jones's character and temperament. He was 'a confirmed hypochondriac' with many 'foibles' about his health and diet. He was guilty of perfectionism, inflexibility and 'a great need to be *in control*'. His continual emphasis on revival revealed an 'obsessive-compulsive' tendency. Moreover, some of the important theological decisions he took in the late 1960s may have been influenced by his suffering with colonic cancer, Davies speculated.[66] As a psychiatrist, Davies diagnosed the root cause of Lloyd-Jones's defensiveness and drive for success as profound grief experienced in adolescence – especially the fire which engulfed the family home in Llangeitho, the bankruptcy of his father and the untimely death of his older brother. Davies asked, 'Why did he always have to be right about everything, and why was he so combative,

---

62. Review by Peter Comont, *Evangelicals Now* (April 2002), p. 23.

63. Davies, *Genius, Grief and Grace*, preface.

64. Ibid., pp. 342, 373.

65. Ibid., pp. 334–335, 342, 375–376.

66. Ibid., pp. 360, 365, 373.

so aggressive? It was the only way he could cope with all that had happened, in my view.'[67]

Especially polemical were Davies' comments about Lloyd-Jones's split with Packer after the publication of the ecumenical tract *Growing into Union* in 1970. He wrote of Packer's 'very scurvy treatment by Dr Lloyd-Jones and his like-minded colleagues . . . he was cold shouldered and rejected by people with whom he had worked closely'.[68] He claimed that Packer had been ousted by a '*putsch*',[69] and criticized Iain Murray for having airbrushed this contentious history from *Evangelicalism Divided*:

> For me it makes sad reading, since Murray's agendas are evident, and he wishes to justify everything that Dr Lloyd-Jones did as right, and infallibly correct. Many who loved and honoured him thought he was not always right, and believe that his treatment of Dr J. I. Packer was shabby in the extreme.[70]

Even more stringent were Davies' observations on the circle of disciples who gathered around Lloyd-Jones. He portrayed the Doctor as a dominant character who surrounded himself with lesser men and brooked no opposition:

> Whether he required submission consciously is immaterial: that is what he obtained from any true follower. The forming of a party leads to party spirit. For Dr Lloyd-Jones the first chapter of the First Letter to Corinthians was very important. Why did he not then do more to prevent such party spirit developing? 'I am of Paul, I am of Apollos' soon became 'I am of Lloyd-Jones'. The fact that this was never stated, except by implication, made it all the more menacing for the future healthy development of his followers. All followers of great men, all of us who give in to the natural impulse to hero-worship, should never forget the last verse of the apostle John's first letter: '*Little children, keep yourselves from idols*'.
>
> The sad thing is that so many seemed unaware that such a great man, when acting as a politician in church matters, lost something of his greatness by becoming the head of a party. He would speak of the men who followed him as 'his boys'. Of course one knows that calling them his boys was a real mark of affection, but it was also something else perhaps more sinister. To be a true boy meant never being allowed to grow up or to challenge effectively what the father said or did. It also

---

67. Ibid., p. 373. See also pp. 338–339.
68. Ibid., p. 366.
69. Ibid., p. 368.
70. Ibid., p. 367.

meant, for a great many, idolising Dr Lloyd-Jones as I did when I was a medical student. I once said, speaking rather lightly, to a person close to the great Doctor, that there was a time in my teens that I thought he not only knew everything, but was *right* about everything. The serious reply to my frivolous remark was: 'But I still believe that.'

It is one thing to believe in the infallible Word of God, quite another to believe that the words of a leader are infallible, or his conduct always right. The best men make mistakes, but I doubt if the true follower of Dr Lloyd-Jones ever attributed any mistake or misjudgment to the hero that they loved and worshipped.[71]

These stern strictures were as much a critical exposé of attitudes within Lloyd-Jones's fan club as an expression of Davies' personal trajectory away from those circles. Subjecting his own youthful attitudes to mature reflection, after half a century of life experience, the psychiatrist recalled the time he fell under Lloyd-Jones's 'spell':[72]

Such was his personality, his power and influence that we were given to much excessive adulation. We not only thought like him but talked and gestured like him. It was a process of adolescent identification which may now be easily understood and forgiven. As young hero-worshippers we were sometimes called *martinets* . . . It was a long time before I and many of my generation who experienced the teaching of Dr Lloyd-Jones could take some steps in the direction of independence of thought. It was hard for many of us who knew and loved a great teacher and preacher of genius to move on from slavish imitation to a more critical appreciation of the man and his genius . . . Those whom we idolise in adolescence often have feet of clay which we are unwilling to notice.[73]

Genius, Grief and Grace was welcomed by many evangelical reviewers. *Reformation Today* found it 'very encouraging. It reminds us of the folly of idolising men', while the chapter on Lloyd-Jones was 'fascinating and helpful'.[74] *Y Cylchgrawn Efengylaidd* applauded this 'truly gripping book' and reflected, 'Perhaps we are too unwilling at times to observe what goes on in life's dark corners. Certainly there is a great need for evangelicals, more than anyone, to be self-critical at

---

71. Ibid., pp. 371–372.
72. Ibid., p. 332.
73. Ibid., pp. 335–336.
74. Review by Sharon James, *Reformation Today*, no. 186 (March – April 2002), pp. 31–32.

all times. Self-examination can be cleansing and healing.'[75] Christopher Idle applauded Davies' 'kind but probing touch',[76] and the *Evangelical Times* appreciated his 'deep sympathy' for his subjects, though with some concern about his chapter on Lloyd-Jones.[77] Likewise *The Banner of Truth* found it 'a deeply moving book, written with real love for these men and women in which God's strength was made perfect in their human weakness', though it also warned of 'deep reservations' over Davies' treatment of Lloyd-Jones.[78] The most outspoken commentary came in the *Evangelical Magazine* from Stephen Clark (pastor of Free School Court Evangelical Church, Bridgend) who sought to 'put the record straight'.[79] He dismissed Davies' verdict on Lloyd-Jones as a 'false account' and insisted, 'The idea that Packer was treated in a "scurvy" and "shabby" way by a bunch of bigots who could not withstand Lloyd-Jones's tyranny is a terrible misrepresentation of the facts.' In particular, Clark argued that to explain serious theological controversy in terms of psychology was to trivialize it – like attributing Luther's spiritual crisis to his constipation or Spurgeon's stand against doctrinal downgrade to his gout and depression. Clark maintained that Lloyd-Jones's break with Packer was a matter of principle, not personality. He may have had 'camp followers who were harsh and unloving', but many others also felt obliged to cut their ties with Packer, 'not out of loyalty to Lloyd-Jones but out of faithfulness to Scripture'. Clark speculated that in fact it was Davies' own psychological make-up and personal friendship with Packer which had distorted the biographer's perspective, so he issued the stark challenge, 'Physician, heal thyself!'

This controversy was renewed some years later on the publication of *J. I. Packer and the Evangelical Future* (2009), the fruit of a symposium held in Packer's honour at Beeson Divinity School in Birmingham, Alabama. The paper by Professor Carl Trueman of Westminster Theological Seminary explored the relationship between Lloyd-Jones and Packer, especially their clash in the late 1960s, but it relied on Gaius Davies for some of its argumentation. Trueman spoke of 'suspicion' and 'bile' directed towards Packer, who received 'shoddy

75. Translation of Bobi Jones, 'Athrylith Galar a Gras', *Y Cylchgrawn Efengylaidd*, cyf. 38, rhif. 4 (Tymor y Gaeaf 2002), p. 29.

76. Review by Christopher Idle, *Hymn Society of Great Britain and Ireland Bulletin*, no. 231 (April 2002), p. 252.

77. Review by Dennis Hill, *Evangelical Times* (April 2003), p. 23.

78. Review by Hywel Roberts, *The Banner of Truth*, no. 465 (June 2002), pp. 31–32.

79. Stephen Clark, 'Physician, Heal Thyself!', *Evangelical Magazine*, vol. 42 (September – October 2003), pp. 20–22; vol. 43 (January – February 2004), pp. 29–30.

treatment by the Lloyd-Jones faction'. He suggested that the falling-out between the two men was inevitable because in Packer, Lloyd-Jones had 'met his intellectual and theological match' and could not tolerate this challenge to his 'iconic guru status'.[80] Iain Murray was unimpressed and published an unfavourable review in *The Banner of Truth*, chastising Trueman for his dependence on the 'unworthy opinions' and 'slander' circulated by Davies.[81] Such sharp criticism provoked the professor into a fierce riposte, in which he defended the right of historians to speak freely about Lloyd-Jones without their motives being impugned:

> Given that Mr Murray managed to write a massive two volume biography of MLJ which contained virtually no criticism whatsoever, I suspect (and here I speculate again) that the problem with Davies is not that he makes this particular criticism of Lloyd-Jones, but rather that he makes any criticism at all. The world is full of Lloyd-Jones fans who keep telling us that the man had his faults, but who never specify exactly what they were or what impact they had, and who are merciless with those who attempt so to do.

Trueman continued:

> In sum, the reaction of Mr Murray to my review [sic] typifies the problem surrounding the legacy of MLJ: those who knew him best have signally failed to engage critically with his life and thought, preferring simply to burnish the edifice and deride all who do not buy the party line. The result is that, instead of a genuine assessment of his strengths and weaknesses which might have been of real value to the contemporary church, what we have is a personality cult, supported by a body of hagiography, and maintained by a defensive mentality, where all critics are dismissed as unworthy slanderers and mediocre historians . . . But he was not right on everything, and especially not on matters relating to ecclesiology. It is surely time that this was acknowledged by those who seem to claim the exclusive right to comment upon his life and ministry.[82]

---

80. Carl R. Trueman, 'J. I. Packer: An English Nonconformist Perspective', in Timothy George (ed.), *J. I. Packer and the Evangelical Future: The Impact of his Life and Thought* (Grand Rapids, MI: Baker, 2009), pp. 124, 126.

81. Iain H. Murray, 'J. I. Packer and the Evangelical Future: The Impact of his Life and Thought', *The Banner of Truth*, no. 558 (March 2010), p. 18.

82. Carl Trueman, 'On the Gloucestershire Way of Identifying Sheep: A Response to Iain Murray' (March 2010), www.reformation21.org (accessed 3 December 2010).

Reflecting on Iain Murray's 1,200-page tribute to Lloyd-Jones, Gaius Davies pleaded for 'an *unauthorised* biography' which would take a fresh look at the evangelical turmoil of the 1960s.[83] He did not have to wait long for this wish to be granted. Just a year after Davies had entered the fray, Paternoster published *Martyn Lloyd-Jones (1899–1981) and Twentieth-Century Evangelicalism*, by John Brencher, the fruit of his doctoral research. It was the first full-length critical assessment of Lloyd-Jones's career and influence.

John F. Brencher (born 1936) was introduced to Westminster Chapel as a young teenager in 1950 by his Bible class leader at Stroud Green Baptist Church in north London. Attracted by Lloyd-Jones's preaching, he transferred his membership to the chapel from 1954 to 1959, where he attended regularly on Sunday mornings and Friday evenings before moving to Nottinghamshire as a school teacher. He acknowledged that these years sitting at the feet of Lloyd-Jones had 'an extraordinary effect upon my life and ministry'.[84] After retraining at London Bible College, Brencher served as pastor of Bethel Church, Liverpool from 1968 to 1987 and was national president of the Fellowship of Independent Evangelical Churches (FIEC) from 1984 to 1985, in succession to Leith Samuel. After retiring from the pastorate, he retrained again as an historian and completed a doctorate on Lloyd-Jones at Sheffield University in 1997 under the supervision of Professor Clyde Binfield, a leading authority on British Nonconformity.[85]

Brencher's research uncovered much new material not available in Murray's or Catherwood's volumes. His approach was thematic rather than chrono-logical, examining Lloyd-Jones's ministry as a preacher, his oversight of Westminster Chapel, his attitudes to ecumenism and separatism, the impact of his Welsh heritage, his leadership gifts and the extent of his influence. Brencher sought to provide 'a critical assessment without being destructive', though he acknowledged his conclusions were 'less soothing' than some would like.[86] He explained his rationale as a biographer and the difficulties of the task:

> It has not been my intention either to safeguard or enhance the reputation of Lloyd-Jones. I have looked upon him neither as icon nor object of scorn. Some information has not been easy to come by. Such was his stature and influence that few people

---

83. Davies, *Genius, Grief and Grace*, p. 368.

84. John Brencher, *Martyn Lloyd-Jones (1899–1981) and Twentieth-Century Evangelicalism* (Carlisle: Paternoster, 2002), p. 5.

85. John Brencher to Andrew Atherstone, 25 February 2011.

86. Brencher, *Lloyd-Jones*, pp. 2, 4.

even now are prepared to express their criticisms in print and the overwhelming view
among evangelicals who knew him is still adulatory. Much of the source material
lies hidden in the minds of people who have much to say but are unwilling to do so
... Thus, twenty years after his death, there is still a strong interest in preserving a
particular view of the man and for many it is a case of 'Touch not mine anointed, and
do my prophets no harm.'[87]

Brencher agreed that Lloyd-Jones was one of the best preachers of the
twentieth century, but was unembarrassed to offer some sharp criticisms. He
argued that Lloyd-Jones's views on church government were 'uncertain if not
random', his baptism policy was 'confused', and pastoral care at Westminster
Chapel was 'a marginal affair'.[88] In theory Lloyd-Jones recognized the variety
of ministry gifts in the local church, but in practice he functioned as a 'benevolent dictator'.[89] He had a 'coterie of admirers who hung on his every word' at
the British Evangelical Council and the Bala Conference, some of whom were
guilty of 'sycophancy'.[90] His disciples looked on him as 'an oracle of the faith',
which fostered his 'papal tendencies'. Brencher claimed that there was 'a touch
of arrogance' in Lloyd-Jones's make-up and that he had 'an unnecessarily
inflated view' of his own ministry: 'Being the corrector of error and signpost
of the truth became habitual and the danger was that, in the end, for all practical purposes Lloyd-Jones came to assume his own infallibility.'[91] Moreover,
he could be 'economical with the truth', was guilty of 'double standards' and
had 'an irresistible urge to dominate'. His treatment of opponents in public
meetings was harsh; what some might see as 'the pursuit of truth', others saw
as 'bullying'.[92] When it came to the ecumenical controversy of the late 1960s,
Brencher concluded that Lloyd-Jones's call to separation was 'a political
mistake', leading to a decline of influence amidst bitterness and polarization,
'a retreat into self-imposed marginalization'. He 'marooned himself ecclesiasti-
cally' and had little impact outside a small minority of like-minded people.[93]
Moreover, according to Brencher, Lloyd-Jones's Welsh roots created a 'blind
spot' where the Church of England was concerned, and 'his anti-Anglicanism

---

87. Ibid., p. 2.
88. Ibid., pp. 68, 70, 72.
89. Ibid., pp. 77–78, 222.
90. Ibid., p. 42.
91. Ibid., pp. 177–179.
92. Ibid., pp. 192, 195, 224.
93. Ibid., pp. 131, 135, 197, 233.

. . . was essentially a Welsh view of the English'.[94] Brencher had certainly managed to restrain any hagiographic impulse in this forthright analysis. One disappointed reader, Peter Milsom (director from 2010 of Affinity, the successor of the British Evangelical Council), was left with the abiding impression of Lloyd-Jones as 'a deeply flawed character who stubbornly isolated himself from those who understood the times better than he did and who were committed to living in the real world'.[95]

Brencher's monograph was widely applauded and was shortlisted for the 2003 John Pollock Award for Christian Biography. It received laudatory reviews and commendations from evangelical historians working in the secular academy. Professor Binfield praised the book for managing to convey Lloyd-Jones's stature 'without lapsing either into hagiography or denigration. It is authoritative because it is both admiring and critical.'[96] Professor Richard Carwardine called it 'sometimes sympathetic, sometimes trenchant, but always fair-minded'.[97] Another welcomed the volume as 'a full and balanced picture . . . remarkably fair'.[98] From the United States of America, Professor Mark Noll observed that amongst the ample literature concerning Lloyd-Jones there was an obvious lack of 'analytical, contextual, or critical assessment'. Brencher therefore provided significant new perspectives, because he

> dares to question if Lloyd-Jones always made the right choices . . . while it may irritate the disciples of Lloyd-Jones, it is neither vindictive or reductionist in its assessments. The book, in other words, should be read by anyone who takes seriously the important work of unusually blessed preachers, but who also wants to move beyond either simple praise or blame in assessing the long-term impact of such ministry.[99]

Closer to home and with a sharper polemical edge, Professor Densil Morgan warmly approved of Brencher's 'illuminating and perceptive' study as a 'cautionary tale' of a great Christian leader who made significant errors of

---

94. Ibid., p. 172.

95. Review by Peter Milsom, *Evangel: The British Evangelical Review*, vol. 23 (Spring 2005), p. 31.

96. Clyde Binfield, 'Foreword', in Brencher, *Lloyd-Jones*, p. xi.

97. Brencher, *Lloyd-Jones*, back cover.

98. Review by Robert W. Bernard, *Southwestern Journal of Theology*, vol. 47 (Fall 2004), pp. 106–107.

99. Mark Noll, 'Diagnosing the Doctor', *Christianity Today*, vol. 47 (March 2003), www.christianitytoday.com (accessed 4 March 2011).

judgment. He praised Brencher for having 'gone a considerable way in demystifying Lloyd-Jones in order to appreciate the man in his weakness as well as his manifold strengths. The cult, it seems, is being subjected to objective scrutiny, and not before time.'[100] Anticipating the hostile reactions the book would provoke in some quarters, Derek Tidball of London Bible College simply called it 'brave'.[101]

The chief criticism of Brencher's monograph by friends of Lloyd-Jones was not that it was too critical, but that it was not critical enough, in the sense of dispassionate objectivity and careful weighing of sources. For example, Stephen Clark complained that it 'smacks more of journalese' than of serious doctoral research.[102] Brencher's analysis rested heavily on interviews and correspondence conducted in the early 1990s with those who had known Lloyd-Jones personally, but there was little attempt to assess the value of these retrospective opinions, which were often unfavourable towards the Doctor. Milsom concluded, 'He writes with the zeal of an investigative journalist committed to discovering the truth against all the odds from people who are hesitant to speak to him for fear of reprisals. The book reveals a certain bitterness of spirit and overall is neither edifying nor helpful.'[103] Murray's critique was different. He acknowledged that this new biography was 'well-researched' and contained 'some helpful things and sympathetic observations', but criticized Brencher for succumbing to the demands of the secular academy by writing uncommitted history which left open the fundamental question of whether or not Lloyd-Jones's theology was 'true' according to Scripture.[104]

Meanwhile the *British Reformed Journal*, while sympathetic to Lloyd-Jones, welcomed Brencher's scrutiny. Its editor, Hugh Williams, reflected:

> As one matures toward old age, one can look back on one's parents. And one can, with the wisdom of hindsight and life-long experience, pick out the faults in one's own father and mother. One can see faults in them now, to which we were oblivious

---

100. Review by D. Densil Morgan, *Journal of Welsh Religious History*, vol. 3 (2003), pp. 98–99.

101. Brencher, *Lloyd-Jones*, back cover.

102. Stephen Clark, 'Prophet of the Lord or Troubler of Israel? D. M. Lloyd-Jones and British Evangelicalism', *Foundations*, no. 50 (Spring 2003), p. 45.

103. Review by Peter Milsom, p. 30.

104. Murray, *Lloyd-Jones: Messenger of Grace*, pp. 169, 190, 196. This chapter was originally published as Iain H. Murray, 'Dr Lloyd-Jones: A Review of Criticism', *The Banner of Truth*, no. 518 (November 2006), pp. 1–23.

when we were young, and clung to them in childlike affection. And what? When we see those faults, sins, errors, in those whom we loved, those who, under God, gave us life and breath and the gift of existence, do we learn therefrom to despise our own parents? Nay, but rather, on beholding their faults and sins, do we not feel the tremor in the lip, and the moistening in the eye, when we see and recognise their sheer humanity, stumbling through the odds of life, miscalculating, misapprehending, sinning, yet somehow striving for heaven? Does not this very humanity endear them all the more to us?

Thus then, Dr Lloyd-Jones, warts and all. Whatever his faults, his errors, his sins, he preached the Gospel, and preached it with all his might. Under God, hundreds, maybe thousands, gained their first saving touch with Christ under his ministry. And when we behold his faults, shall we not all feel that same moistening eye, and love this dear brother in Christ all the more. And then the glory too, is all to God, who, in His majestic course, works such mighty wonders by such poor human servants.[105]

Williams argued that for the best-balanced perspective of Lloyd-Jones, it was foolish to choose between the hagiography of Murray and the criticism of Brencher. In fact, both were needed and should be read alongside each other, because, 'Both together will provide a comprehensive and intelligent insight into the great preacher's life and work.'[106]

Engaging with Lloyd-Jones

In different ways Iain Murray, Christopher Catherwood, Gaius Davies and John Brencher have each made a significant contribution to Lloyd-Jones studies in the decades immediately following his death. The supporting cast has included Donald Macleod, Alister McGrath and Carl Trueman, amidst numerous other commentators, offering diverse and often contradictory perspectives. Lloyd-Jones's theology, character and legacy remain hotly contested and few have succeeded in contributing to the field without provoking some degree of controversy.

This volume of essays seeks to advance our understanding of Lloyd-Jones in a number of fresh directions by building on and engaging with the work of these earlier biographers and theologians. In an important first scene-setting essay David Bebbington shows that far from going into terminal decline after

---

105. Williams, 'Martyn Lloyd-Jones Warts and All', p. 40.
106. Ibid., p. 35.

the death of Charles Haddon Spurgeon in 1892, Calvinism remained a force on the British evangelical scene. Although the Reformed resurgence of the 1950s, led largely by Lloyd-Jones himself, was on a much larger scale, Bebbington shows that Lloyd-Jones both participated in and benefited from a more gradual revival of interest in Calvinism that reached well back into the interwar years.

Wales and Welshness were dominant in many aspects of Lloyd-Jones's thinking and ministry, a theme dealt with by David Ceri Jones. He focuses on the Doctor's influence within Wales, concentrating both on his early ministry in Sandfields and his later close identification with the Evangelical Movement of Wales. Nowhere was Lloyd-Jones's teaching less contested than in Wales, and the Evangelical Movement of Wales reflected both his theological and cultural preferences. From the late 1960s it became increasingly associated with his separatist stance and, as Jones argues, can be seen as the model of the kind of loose evangelical unity he envisaged. The concept of revival has long been a key element in the Welsh Christian tradition, exemplified by the widespread revival of 1904–5, and it played a major role in Lloyd-Jones's outlook. Ian Randall explores Lloyd-Jones's understanding of revival in a chapter which draws extensively on the Doctor's fullest treatment of the subject, a series of twenty-four sermons preached to mark the centenary of the 1859 revivals.

For many, including some of Lloyd-Jones's most enthusiastic followers, his views on the Holy Spirit have been among the most contentious aspects of his thought. In a substantial chapter drawing on new evidence, Andrew Atherstone, David Ceri Jones and William Kay investigate Lloyd-Jones's relationship with the charismatic and neo-Pentecostal movements. They analyse his teaching on the baptism, sealing and witness of the Spirit, and the reception of these sermons following their publication in the late 1970s and early 1980s. For others, Lloyd-Jones is best known as a preacher and throughout his life he devoted considerable energy to explaining what he thought preaching ought to be. Two chapters explore aspects of his thought in this area. Based on a close reading of *Preaching and Preachers* (1971), Ben Bailie looks at Lloyd-Jones's views on the decline of preaching during the course of the twentieth century. Philip Eveson examines his attitude to theological education and the dangers of the secular academy, paying particular attention to Lloyd-Jones's contribution to the founding of London Theological Seminary in 1977.

More overtly theological themes are dealt with in two chapters, the first of which asks to what extent Lloyd-Jones should be regarded as a fundamentalist. Robert Pope assesses Lloyd-Jones's doctrinal framework, arguing that in some areas he displayed fundamentalist-like ways of thinking, though he should best be labelled a 'conservative evangelical'. In a focused case study, Robert Strivens examines Lloyd-Jones's reading of the Swiss Reformed theologian

Karl Barth, especially his engagement with Barth's exposition of Romans 5. Here Strivens presents evidence for Lloyd-Jones's sustained interaction with some aspects of contemporary theological debate, as well as his reservations about many of the central features of neo-orthodoxy.

Anti-Catholicism has traditionally been seen as one of the core characteristics of the evangelical movement. Surveying a wide range of Lloyd-Jones's printed sermons, John Maiden teases out the full extent of his anti-Catholicism and argues that fear of a single united world church encompassing Rome lay behind much of Lloyd-Jones's rhetoric in his controversial address to the National Assembly of Evangelicals in 1966. The impact of that address, especially amongst evangelicals in the Church of England, is explored further by Andrew Atherstone. He argues that far from being the preserve of Lloyd-Jones and his Free Church friends, secession was a live issue among Anglican clergymen struggling to come to terms with the very different ecclesiastical landscape in which they found themselves after the 1967 Keele Congress and the publication of *Growing into Union* in 1970.

Throughout his life Lloyd-Jones remained an avid reader of history and at the Puritan and Westminster Conferences he helped to stimulate interest in the historical development of evangelical theology since the Reformation. John Coffey examines Lloyd-Jones's reading of the Protestant past and the ways in which he harnessed that heritage to address some of the problems confronting contemporary evangelicalism. Coffey argues that Lloyd-Jones and Packer adopted divergent interpretations of the Puritans in particular, which may help to explain their ecclesiological dispute in the late 1960s and early 1970s. The volume concludes with a substantial bibliography of Lloyd-Jones's English-language writings.

The team of historians brought together in this book represents a generational shift in Lloyd-Jones studies. His biographers to date have principally been those who knew him personally as far back as the 1950s. While some of the authors in this volume remember the Doctor vividly, or heard him preach at first hand, half the contributors were still young children when he died and have encountered his teaching in more recent years through his numerous publications. Martyn Lloyd-Jones remains deeply influential, even on a younger generation, more than three decades after his death. This study, in an appreciative yet also critical and judicious way, seeks to reassess his impact on twentieth-century British evangelicalism and his ongoing legacy in the twenty-first century.

© Andrew Atherstone and David Ceri Jones, 2011

1. LLOYD-JONES AND THE INTERWAR CALVINIST RESURGENCE

David W. Bebbington

'Calvinism in England', declared Charles Breed in 1932, 'appears to the casual observer to be declining.'[1] Breed, the pastor of Rehoboth Strict Baptist Chapel, Manor Park, was reporting to an international conference on the Reformed faith in London that was gathering information on the present position of Calvinism in the various countries of the world. He went on to paint a picture of steady decline in England since the Reformation, with Anglicans and Nonconformists sharing equally in the decay. But it is noteworthy that he qualified his depiction of a downgrade in his own day with the words 'to the casual observer'. He believed that, in the providence of God, there was hope of a resurgence of Calvinism. Historians have commonly supposed, like Breed's casual observer, that Reformed teaching was evaporating in interwar Britain. In *Evangelicalism in Modern Britain* (1989), for example, there is a comment that the first Puritan Conference organized under Martyn Lloyd-Jones in 1950 was 'the beginning of a revival of interest in the Reformed theological tradition'.[2] Lloyd-Jones's ministry, *The Banner of Truth* magazine and

---

1. Charles Breed, 'England', in *The Reformed Faith Commonly Called Calvinism: Report of the International Conference Held in May, 1932* (London: Sovereign Grace Union, 1932), p. 135.

2. D. W. Bebbington, *Evangelicalism in Modern Britain: A History from the 1730s to the 1980s*

its associated publishing house, the Evangelical Movement of Wales and the Crieff Brotherhood in Scotland follow in that book as symptoms of a recovery of Calvinism, but all arose in the postwar years. The interwar period is tacitly held to have been a time when Reformed beliefs languished. It is generally accepted that there was a Calvin revival on the continent in the 1930s, loosely associated with the rise of neo-orthodoxy but spearheaded by the Calvinist Society of France, founded by Auguste Lecerf in 1927.[3] What this chapter will show is that something similar was happening at the same juncture in Britain. The international conference of 1932 in which Breed participated was one of the leading symptoms of the phenomenon. There are grounds for seeing the interwar period as a time of Calvinist resurgence in Britain.

There is nevertheless a great deal of evidence in the years between the First and Second World Wars that Calvinism was unprecedentedly weak in Britain. The leaders of opinion were strikingly hostile. Thus in the last year of the First World War Maurice Bowra, later the celebrated Warden of Wadham College, Oxford, but then only nineteen, found himself in command of an artillery battery on a hill above the French town of Noyon. He received an order to flush out a party of Germans who were using the cathedral as an observation point, but Bowra was loath to open fire on an historic building. 'Then', he recounts in his autobiography, 'I remembered that Noyon was the original home of John Calvin, and my qualms vanished. I felt that nothing could be too bad, even after some four centuries, for this enemy of the human race, and I set to work with care. I fired a plus and minus, and my third shot fell neatly into the middle of the church.'[4] It may well be that Bowra was also responsible on this occasion for the destruction of the birthplace of John Calvin, which had to be reconstructed in the aftermath of the war.[5] In Scotland, where the sense of indebtedness to the Reformed faith was bound up with national identity, there was less corporate aversion to Calvinism. At the quatercentenary of the Reformer's birth in 1909, for example, there had been a celebration in St Giles' Cathedral, Edinburgh, attended by the Lord Provost and the councillors

(London: Unwin Hyman, 1989), p. 261. Cf. John J. Murray, *Catch the Vision: Roots of the Reformed Recovery* (Darlington: Evangelical Press, 2007), ch. 1.

3. Patrick Cabanel, 'French Protestants and the Legacy of John Calvin: Reformer and Legislator', in Johan de Niet, Herman Paul and Bart Wallet (eds.), *Sober, Strict and Scriptural: Collective Memories of John Calvin, 1800–2000* (Leiden: Brill, 2009), p. 63.

4. Maurice Bowra, *Memories, 1898–1939* (London: Weidenfeld and Nicolson, 1966), p. 83.

5. M. G. C[ampbell]., 'John Calvin's House', *Journal of the Presbyterian Historical Society of England*, vol. 3 (1925), pp. 86–89.

in their civic robes.[6] Nevertheless, even in Scotland there was a shifting of attitudes between the wars. The 'Scottish literary renaissance' led by Hugh MacDiarmid deplored what it saw as the restrictions on creativity forged by the cultural legacy of the Reformation. In 1933, for example, Eric Linklater, a prominent member of the group surrounding MacDiarmid, delivered a radio broadcast announcing that Scotland was 'still crippled by Calvinism'.[7] The teaching of Calvin was out of favour with those who set the tone of public debate.

Reformed belief, furthermore, was not strong in the churches. The Church of England was drifting in a higher and broader direction during the earlier twentieth century and so Calvinism, along with all other forms of evangelical belief, found itself pushed to the margins. Comments by representative men illustrate the point. In 1916 Bishop Winnington-Ingram of London declared that Calvinists worshipped an 'arbitrary tyrant'.[8] Percy Dearmer, the editor of two of the most widely used Anglican hymn books of the period, echoed the bishop eight years later by calling the God of the Calvinists 'cruel beyond words'.[9] In 1937 C. A. Alington, Dean of Durham, wrote in a daily newspaper about 'Calvin's Travesty of Christianity'.[10] Despite the Reformed roots of Congregationalists and most Baptists, English Free Churchmen often voiced similar criticisms of Calvinism. Congregationalists had gone furthest in repudiating their past. Already at the International Congregational Council held in London in 1891, when a visiting American preacher delivered a distinctively Reformed sermon in the pulpit of the City Temple, the minister, Joseph Parker, declared that he must have his pulpit fumigated. 'By this time Calvinism stinketh,' he said, 'for it hath been dead these two centuries.'[11] The mainstream Baptists, thanks largely to the legacy of C. H. Spurgeon, were generally less militantly anti-Calvinist, but it was probably at the South Wales Baptist College in Cardiff that a student who was upholding Calvin's teaching felt in 1929 that he was suffering persecution. The student was taunted with the nickname 'Calvin'. 'Here', he reported, 'Calvin is acknowledged as a man of God, but [it is thought] that he was too extreme, and that he was altogether wrong when he proclaimed the absolute sovereign power of

---

6. *British Weekly*, 27 May 1909, p. 188.
7. Quoted in *Peace and Truth* (January 1934), p. 13.
8. Quoted in *Peace and Truth* (July 1918), p. 43.
9. Quoted in *Peace and Truth* (April 1925), p. 37.
10. Quoted in *Peace and Truth* (July 1937), p. 74.
11. Quoted in *Peace and Truth* (January 1937), p. 3.

God.'[12] Even the English Presbyterians, who still formally respected the Reformation statements of faith and embraced the Westminster Confession, in practice disregarded their contents. 'The dogmatism of the sixteenth century', explained a council member of the Presbyterian Historical Society in 1922, 'has been largely modified.'[13] The Welsh Calvinistic Methodists, calling themselves Presbyterians from 1927, held similar opinions.[14] In England and Wales the doctrines of grace seemed to be utterly *passé*.

The situation in Scotland was rather different. The United Free Church was inching towards the Church of Scotland during the 1910s and 1920s and so there was much discussion about articles of faith. The predominant voices in the United Free Church sounded similar to those south of the border. The Westminster Confession, according to Alexander Martin, secretary of the United Free committee that drafted the articles for the reunited church, was unsuited to contemporary needs. Although Martin acknowledged that the Calvinism of the confession was moderate, he held that evangelical thought had moved on. Divine immanence had come to the fore so that there was less of a gap between nature and supernature than the confession assumed. The chief opposition to the draft of the articles came not from convinced Calvinists but from the inheritors of the United Presbyterian tradition led by James Barr who wanted the church to be allowed to alter its beliefs without any shackles forged by the state. The conservative case against the articles came mainly from the liturgically minded section of the Church of Scotland who desired less liberty to alter doctrine than the draft permitted.[15] So none of the main organized tendencies of opinion was professedly Reformed. Nevertheless, as a report on the position of Calvinism in Scotland to the international conference of 1932 asserted, there were many 'convinced and earnest Calvinists' in the now reunited Church of Scotland.[16] One J. Nicol of Stirling, for instance, belonged to a campaigning Calvinist organization at his death in 1933.[17] In

---

12. Quoted in *Peace and Truth* (January 1929), p. 14.

13. Mrs W. W. D. Campbell, 'Early English Presbyterianism and the Reformed Church of France', *Journal of the Presbyterian Historical Society of England*, vol. 2 (1922), p. 133.

14. D. Densil Morgan, *The Span of the Cross: Christian Religion and Society in Wales, 1914–2000* (Cardiff: University of Wales Press, 1999), pp. 107–122.

15. Douglas Murray, *Freedom to Reform: The 'Articles Declaratory' of the Church of Scotland, 1921* (Edinburgh: T. & T. Clark, 1993), pp. 96, 98, 105–106.

16. Donald Maclean, 'Scotland', in *Reformed Faith*, p. 141.

17. *Peace and Truth* (April 1933), p. 18.

the following year Murdo Campbell wrote to the *British Weekly* predicting that there would soon be a return to Geneva 'to drink anew life and wisdom at the works of John Calvin'.[18] In 1936 Daniel Lamont, Professor of Practical Theology at New College, Edinburgh, and a definite Calvinist, was chosen as moderator of the General Assembly of the Church of Scotland.[19] There was more of a Reformed presence in the established Presbyterian Church than in either the established Anglican Church or the Free Churches south of the border.

The most convinced Calvinists of the interwar period were a diverse set of people. Arthur W. Pink, whose *Studies in the Scriptures* (1922–53) were to prove influential in the postwar advance of the Reformed faith, was an isolated figure who found nowhere to preach regularly in Britain despite sustained quests in 1928–9 and 1934–6.[20] In the Church of England a handful of clergy, some of them swayed by the example of Bishop J. C. Ryle, continued to teach Reformed doctrine in their parishes. Several seemed a throwback to a previous age. William Lusk, for example, the rector of Stretton-en-le-Field, Leicestershire, who died in 1918, was an octogenarian who had spent nearly sixty years in the ministry. His sense of isolation was palpable. 'It is painful', he wrote, 'to feel that outside my own family I have not a single parishioner that thoroughly appreciates free-grace teaching.'[21] There were occasional new recruits to the cause. Thus H. A. Lewty, ordained in 1898 as an Anglo-Catholic, went to South Africa, where he experienced conversion. He returned to act as a curate in Brighton, where he embraced Keswick teaching but remained hostile to the doctrine of election. A visit to a Strict Baptist chapel in London while serving another curacy there, followed by a reading of Thomas Scott's *The Force of Truth*, an account of an earlier clergyman's pilgrimage towards Calvinism, eventually led Lewty, who became rector of Somersham in Cambridgeshire, to accept the doctrines of grace.[22] Alongside the Anglican Calvinists were the Strict Baptists, whose chapels were usually small but very tenacious of Reformed doctrine. Parts of England, especially the south-east and Lancashire, were studded with places of worship of this type. They retained some capable

---

18. Quoted in *Peace and Truth* (January 1934), p. 13.

19. *Proceedings of the Fourth Calvinistic Congress* (Edinburgh: Congress Executive, 1938), p. 10.

20. Iain H. Murray, *The Life of Arthur W. Pink* (Edinburgh: Banner of Truth, 2004), pp. 126–131, 150–165.

21. Quoted in *Peace and Truth* (April 1918), p. 27.

22. *Peace and Truth* (October 1936), pp. 113–117.

preachers such as J. K. Popham, editor of the *Gospel Standard* magazine that bound together the sternest exponents of a high Calvinism. Again, however, there was a sense that such men belonged to the past: Popham was in 1937 still preaching at Galeed Chapel, Brighton, at the age of eighty-nine.[23] The best-known Strict Baptist to a wider public was H. Tydeman Chilvers, pastor of Spurgeon's Tabernacle from 1919 to 1937.[24] Chilvers published in 1929 a collection of addresses at his church called *Is There a Future for Calvinism?* The very title suggests how he expected the Reformed faith to be regarded by the bulk of the Christian public.

Outside the Anglican and Strict Baptist contingents, a number of ministers and places of worship maintained a Reformed position in England and Wales. There were very conservative Independent chapels, the paedobaptist equivalent of the Strict Baptists, such as Zion in Morley, Yorkshire, and Rehoboth in Pemberton, Lancashire.[25] The Reformed Episcopal Church and the Free Church of England, two small episcopal bodies which merged in 1927, included ministers of firm Calvinist opinion such as H. W. Thornley of St Jude's, Walsall.[26] But the Scottish reinforcements of the Reformed host were more substantial. The Free Presbyterian Church of Scotland, a body limited to the Highlands that owed its existence to a refusal to abate its subscription to the Wesminster Confession, contained men of ability. J. S. Sinclair, its minister in Inverness, promoted Reformed doctrine through the *Free Presbyterian Magazine* that he edited down to his death in 1921.[27] But the richest resources for the Reformed cause were to be found in the Free Church of Scotland. Again this denomination originated in a refusal to compromise with looser views, in its case when the former Free Church merged with the United Presbyterian Church in 1900. When the negotiations for further Presbyterian union were proceeding in the 1920s, the Free Church sent a memorandum to the government pointing out that it alone was loyal to the Westminster Confession.[28] Some of its ministers were men of significant theological standing. J. R. Mackay, previously theological tutor for the Free Presbyterians, for example, became Professor of

---

23. J. H. Gosden, *Memoir and Letters of James Kidwell Popham* (London: C. J. Farncombe & Sons, 1938), p. 304.

24. Eric W. Hayden, *A Centennial History of Spurgeon's Tabernacle* (London: Clifford Frost, 1962), pp. 43–45.

25. *Peace and Truth* (January 1927), p. 7.

26. *Peace and Truth* (July 1925), p. 69.

27. *Peace and Truth* (July 1921), p. 45.

28. Murray, *Freedom to Reform*, pp. 93–95.

New Testament Exegesis at the Free Church College in Edinburgh in 1919 and published a translation of the important work *The Higher Criticism in Relation to the Pentateuch* (1923) by the Swiss scholar Edouard Naville. In 1929, the year he served as moderator of the General Assembly of his church, he launched the *Evangelical Quarterly* to defend the Reformed faith.[29] It was from this quarter that there was greatest potential for the future revival of Calvinism.

In the period down to about 1930, however, the weakness of the Reformed section of evangelical opinion was evident in a variety of ways. The Calvinist case often went by default because conservative evangelicals were taking up other causes. Keswick teaching, for instance, was flourishing. The annual convention in the Lake District proclaimed its distinctive message of holiness by faith to a wide audience, especially among Anglican evangelicals. Its approach to sanctification had been formulated, particularly by Evan Hopkins, so as to make it acceptable to Calvinists. There was no question of sinless perfection finding a place on its platform.[30] Yet there was a gulf between its idea that holiness comes by surrender to the Almighty and the traditional Reformed view that it is attained only by sustained effort. In 1930 a zealous adherent of the older position, Ralph Woodfield, visited the convention in order to distribute copies of J. K. Popham's book *Keswick Teaching – Weighed in the Balance and Found Wanting*.[31] Keswick functioned as an alternative to Calvinist doctrine rather than as its auxiliary. In a similar way the 1920s, the decade of the fundamentalist/modernist split in the United States, were marked in Britain by a sharpening cleavage between conservative and liberal evangelicals. Conservatives, some of whom were broadly sympathetic to Reformed views, spent their efforts on the fight against the inroads of higher criticism and broad-minded theology. Thus Isaac Siviter, vicar of St John's, Harborne in Birmingham, was prepared in 1920 to chair a public meeting advocating Reformed principles, but threw himself in subsequent years into promoting the Fellowship of Evangelical Churchmen, a conservative pressure group.[32] Although, conversely, the confessional Calvinists sympathized with the efforts of the conservatives, the stance of bodies such as the Fellowship of Evangelical Churchmen was too doctrinally imprecise for them. Even fundamentalism lacked backbone. 'Many

---

29. *Peace and Truth* (July 1939), p. 77.

30. J. C. Pollock, *The Keswick Story* (London: Hodder and Stoughton, 1964), p. 76.

31. *Peace and Truth* (October 1930), p. 74.

32. *Peace and Truth* (April 1920), p. 9. Isaac Siviter, 'The Incarnation', in J. R. Howden, *Evangelicalism: By Members of the Fellowship of Evangelical Churchmen* (London: Thynne and Co., 1925), pp. 1–41.

organisations call themselves "Fundamental,"' declared *Peace and Truth*, the leading Reformed magazine of the period, 'yet they omit the most fundamental doctrines of the Word of God.'[33] The actual defenders of Calvinism were at the margin of discussion even within the evangelical camp.

Nevertheless, there did exist in the 1920s a society whose *raison d'être* was the promotion of Calvinism. Its name was the Sovereign Grace Union (SGU); *Peace and Truth* was its journal. Founded as the Sovereign Grace Mission by Thomas Lawson, minister of Providence Independent Chapel, Brighton, in 1875, it was languishing by the early years of the twentieth century. In 1914, however, it was reconstituted as a Union with Henry Atherton, minister of Grove Chapel, Camberwell, as its general secretary.[34] In the 1920s it concentrated on organizing lectures. Atherton delivered a typical one on 'What are the Spiritual Principles of the Reformation?' at Shaw Street Particular Baptist Chapel, Liverpool, in 1923:

> Mr Atherton showed clearly what those truths were which, under the power of the Holy Spirit, produced the real vitality in the great movement known as the Reformation, which truths we also designate the 'Doctrines of Sovereign Grace'. He also showed the lamentable condition into which the Church, to which a number of the Reformers belonged, had fallen, and he ably exposed some of the grosser religious errors of the present day.[35]

In the following year, 1924, the Union possessed four branches with subscribers, each the result of effort by local individuals.[36] Bristol had as secretary a churchwarden of the parish church of St Mary-le-Port in the city centre, the rector of which, A. J. Day, denounced the teaching of liberal evangelicals as 'rotten'.[37] The Hastings branch was kept up partly by D. A. Thompson, a minister of the Free Church of England who was to become one of its bishops.[38] At Manchester the secretary was A. Lythgoe, an energetic layman who monitored newspaper controversy and republished Henry Cole's *Calvin's Calvinism* (1856), translations of two treatises by the Reformer.[39] And the Sheffield

---

33. *Peace and Truth* (April 1929), p. 43.

34. *Peace and Truth* (July 1926), p. 72.

35. *Peace and Truth* (January 1924), p. 9.

36. *Peace and Truth* (July 1924), p. 58.

37. *Peace and Truth* (July 1920), pp. 28–29.

38. *Peace and Truth* (April 1937), p. x.

39. *Peace and Truth* (July 1923), pp. 27, 31; (April 1927), p. 38.

branch was no doubt run by Henry Platt of the Sovereign Grace Mission (Calvinistic Independent) who named his home 'Grace Villa'.[40] These enthusiasts ploughed a lonely furrow, and it is suggestive that membership figures were never published. The SGU was not a popular cause.

Yet there were other organizations that maintained a similar standpoint. Although the SGU was always at pains to disclaim any connection, there was a body called Sovereign Grace Advent Testimony that acted as a vehicle for those in the Reformed camp who wished to profess a premillennial faith, then near the height of its popularity.[41] Several other bodies had links with Grove Chapel, Atherton or his circle. The Pure Truth Mission, run by George Stephenson of the Chapel until his death in 1924, distributed tracts of guaranteed Calvinist orthodoxy.[42] The Society for the Relief of Necessitous Protestant Ministers, serving Reformed men, had Atherton as its chairman.[43] Its secretary up to his death in 1929 was a deacon of Regent Street Chapel, where William Sinden was pastor until he died in 1926.[44] Sinden was himself secretary of a Calvinistic Protestant Union, which fulfilled a similar role to the SGU.[45] He was also associated with the Aged Pilgrim's Friend Society, which announced itself as 'Founded upon the vital and distinctive truths of the Everlasting Gospel' and assisted 'God's aged poor'.[46] For over thirty years Sinden was on the committee and then chairman of the Trinitarian Bible Society, which refused to circulate any text except the Authorized Version and which, though tolerating people of other evangelical views, was overwhelmingly Reformed in orientation.[47] Sinden also sat on the United Protestant Council, an umbrella body for the myriad minor anti-Catholic organizations of the era that in 1927–8 were to win an unexpected victory by persuading parliament to reject the revised Prayer Book.[48] Most of the participants in this

---

40. *Peace and Truth* (January 1937), p. vii.

41. *Peace and Truth* (January 1926), p. 8.

42. *Peace and Truth* (October 1924), p. 69.

43. *Peace and Truth* (January 1928), p. 9.

44. *Peace and Truth* (January 1929), p. 9.

45. *Peace and Truth* (April 1926), p. 26.

46. *Peace and Truth* (January 1937), p. ii.

47. *Peace and Truth* (April 1926), p. 26. Andrew J. Brown, *The Word of God among All Nations: A Brief History of the Trinitarian Bible Society, 1831–1931* (London: Trinitarian Bible Society, 1981), pp. 101–102.

48. John Maiden, *National Religion and the Prayer Book Controversy, 1927–1928* (Woodbridge: Boydell Press, 2009), pp. 63, 98.

world saw themselves as upholders of the Protestant constitution and adapted their politics accordingly. Both Atherton and the president of the SGU until his death in 1930, the clergyman William Sykes, belonged to the militantly Protestant Orange Order.[49] Here was an interlocking set of organizations, mostly small, some tiny, but all reinforcing loyalty to Calvinism, often with a political edge.

There was a considerable literary output from this network. *Peace and Truth* had originally begun in 1886 as a private venture by William Sinden and was passed to the SGU in 1918.[50] Published quarterly, its articles were chiefly sermons and addresses by its leading lights. The Union also issued tracts and booklets such as Atherton's *Calvinism* (1927), a sixteen-page pamphlet selling at twopence.[51] Many of the Union's titles were published by C. J. Farncombe and Sons, a firm specializing in Strict Baptist literature. It was Farncombe and Sons, for example, that was eventually responsible for the biography of F. K. Popham. A member of the family, Frederick John Farncombe, sat on the SGU committee from its reconstitution in 1914.[52] These circles managed to support a weekly newspaper, the *English Churchman*, which came into its own in the Prayer Book controversy.[53] But their oldest voice was *The Gospel Magazine*, founded in 1761 and once edited by Augustus Toplady. In the 1920s its editor was Thomas Houghton, who spoke from the SGU platform.[54] Its content at this period was presented in a dated typeface with Gothic script for titles. That was the public image of the Reformed world in the 1920s: backward looking, sternly resisting change and having no vision for the future. It was a symptom of a cause that seemed to be in decay.

The 1930s, however, witnessed a transformation in the Calvinist cause. There was no dropping of the old connections: the SGU still advertised the Aged Pilgrim's Friend Society and the publications of Farncombe and Sons in the late 1930s.[55] Yet the Sovereign Grace Union itself changed. The process began with a visit to England in 1928 by Dr Jan van Lonkhuyzen, a Dutch minister from Zieriksee who seven years before had published an article in the *Princeton Review* on Abraham Kuyper, the dynamic former leader

---

49. *Peace and Truth* (January 1928), p. 9; (October 1930), p. 67.

50. *Peace and Truth* (April 1926), p. 26.

51. *Peace and Truth* (October 1927), p. 79.

52. *Peace and Truth* (April 1945), p. 22.

53. Maiden, *National Religion and the Prayer Book Controversy*, p. 98.

54. *Peace and Truth* (July 1920), p. 29.

55. *Peace and Truth* (January 1937), pp. ii, iv.

of the ReReformed Churches and prime minister of the Netherlands. Van
Lonkhuyzen was eager to foster contacts with Calvinists in the English-
speaking world.[56] He invited Atherton to visit the Netherlands, where in April
1929 the Englishman was bowled over by admiration for the pillar of Dutch
society constituted by Kuyper's neo-Calvinists. Religion, Atherton enthused,
'enters into their everyday life'. 'Even a meal', he went on, 'is never taken
except a portion of Scripture is read, besides a blessing being sought before,
and thanks to God being offered afterwards.' On a Sunday the people flocked
to services where three quarters of the time might be occupied by the sermon.
The Calvinist political party founded by Kuyper was a potent force; it published a daily newspaper *De Standaard* and there were Calvinist burgomasters
who 'even on a crowded railway station would not hesitate to speak quite
openly of the doctrine of free grace'. Atherton dreamed that one day something similar could be realized in his own country. 'What a sight it would be
in England', he wrote, 'for the Calvinistic places of worship to be filled every
Sunday!'[57] He organized a further trip to the Netherlands later in the year,
visiting Kuyper's two daughters, and became a devotee of the Dutchman.[58]
Atherton praised Kuyper's Stone Lectures on Calvinism, previously virtually
unknown in Britain, as 'masterpieces of erudition'.[59] From that point on he set
about promoting a Reformed revival.

Its most obvious characteristic was that it was to be international. Apart
from the Dutch connection, Atherton forged links with Calvinists in Ireland
north and south, France, Germany, Hungary, South Africa and the United
States. He set about planning an international conference in London in May
1932. Each of the nations except southern Ireland, Hungary and the United
States was represented, but unfortunately Atherton's presidential address had
to be delivered on his behalf because he was already suffering from the ill
health that was to dog him until his death in the following year.[60] Atherton,
however, had sparked off a vigorous enterprise. Some of the attenders at the
conference were men of weight. One in particular, Auguste Lecerf, Professor
of Theology at the Protestant Faculty of the University of Paris and the leader
of the French Calvinist revival of the 1930s, was a remarkable catch. He called
for 'the restoration in all domains of the spirit of Calvinism', which in France

---

56. *Reformed Faith*, p. 4.
57. *Peace and Truth* (October 1929), pp. 83–84 (quoted at p. 84).
58. Ibid., pp. 73–75, 78.
59. *Peace and Truth* (April 1929), p. 39.
60. *Peace and Truth* (July 1932), p. 9; (July 1933), p. 3.

he interpreted as entailing endorsement of the right-wing politics of Charles Maurras's L'Action Française.[61] Lecerf remained identified with the global network as it developed into an International Federation of Calvinists, which set about organizing a further conference in Amsterdam two years later. That gathering attracted the Dutch prime minister, Hendrik Colijn, and confirmed the basis for continuing international cooperation based on the London offices of the SGU.[62] It was Lecerf who, with Jean de Saussure of Geneva, organized a third international conference in that city in 1936 marking the quatercentenary of the first publication of Calvin's *Institutes*. The SGU had representatives speaking there.[63] During the whole of the decade the Union's magazine registered activities abroad such as the work of the Federation of Calvinist Student Societies of South Africa and the foundation of a John Calvin Society in Budapest Theological Seminary.[64] It reviewed, discussed and used the writings of American Reformed writers such as B. B. Warfield ('the greatest English-speaking Calvinist theologian of modern times') and Cornelius Van Til.[65] The SGU had ceased to be an introverted and shrinking network and had become part of an international movement that was self-consciously aiming to reconquer lost ground.

The SGU also consolidated its role within the United Kingdom. Crucially it forged new links with Scotland. In 1930 it secured J. R. Mackay to preach its annual conference sermon and four years later obtained the services of Principal John Macleod for the same purpose, both from the Free Church College.[66] The most significant recruit to the SGU from Scotland, however, was Donald Maclean, Professor of Church History at the Free Church College since 1920. Maclean was co-editor with Mackay of the *Evangelical Quarterly*, but had other strings to his bow. He had frequently represented the Free Church at the General Synods of the Rereformed Churches of the Netherlands, and so had developed an appreciation of the legacy of Kuyper similar to Atherton's.[67] He gained the respect of his Dutch colleagues,

---

61. *Reformed Faith*, p. 54. Cabanel, 'French Protestants and the Legacy of John Calvin', p. 63.

62. *Peace and Truth* (January 1935), pp. 8, 11.

63. *Peace and Truth* (July 1936), p. 62.

64. *Peace and Truth* (October 1934), p. 25; (April 1936), p. 70.

65. *Peace and Truth* (April 1936), p. 40 (quoted); (October 1937), pp. 150–159.

66. *Peace and Truth* (July 1939), p. 77; (July 1934), p. 14.

67. G. N. M. Collins, *Donald Maclean, D.D.* (Edinburgh: Lindsay & Co., 1944), p. 73; *Monthly Record of the Free Church of Scotland* (November 1928), p. 270.

receiving an invitation to deliver in 1927 the first series of Calvin Lectures at
the Free University of Amsterdam on aspects of Scottish church history.[68] As
a corollary, Maclean elaborated a modern version of Calvinist political theory
at the Free Church College the same year. He credited Calvin with helping
to create 'almost all the progressive states of the modern world'.[69] Three
of the great revolutions, he claimed, the Dutch (against Spain), the British
(the Glorious Revolution of 1688) and the American (against Britain), were
essentially inspired by a Calvinist belief in divine sovereignty. In each case,
the tyrants were the true revolutionaries, rebelling against divine principles
of government, so that the people were trying to restore a just order. The
French Revolution, by contrast, asserted the sovereignty of reason and so, as
Kuyper's Anti-Revolutionary Party in the Netherlands insisted, its principles
were to be totally rejected as dishonouring to God.[70] The members of the
SGU recognized that Maclean, with his international contacts and systematic
worldview on the Dutch model, possessed something that they required and
so in 1935 successfully invited him to become their president.[71] With Maclean
at its head, the SGU had an appeal it had previously lacked. Maclean was the
Lecerf of Britain.

A further feature of the SGU in the 1930s was its more scholarly approach.
Maclean contributed much of the more academic tone to the Union, but there
were others who did something similar. E. C. Unmack, rector of West Horsley,
Guildford, from 1895 to 1933, gave his final years to the Calvinist cause, acting
as vice-president of the SGU for over two decades down to his death in 1939.
Unmack helped coordinate the international linkages when Atherton fell ill in
1932, but he also fostered intellectual interests. An able scholar of the biblical
languages, he could also preach in French, German and Spanish.[72] His paper
at the 1932 conference in London on 'The Philosophy of Calvinism' quoted
Plato and Augustine, which perhaps might be expected, but also Rabelais
(with the reference) and Renan, which might not.[73] Even more significant a
figure was Stephen Leigh Hunt, the editor of *Peace and Truth* from 1935 and

---

68. Donald Maclean, *Aspects of Scottish Church History* (Edinburgh: T. & T. Clark, 1927).

69. Donald Maclean, 'Influence of Calvinism on Scottish Politics', *Monthly Record of the
    Free Church of Scotland* (November 1928), p. 273.

70. Donald Maclean, 'Influence of Calvinism', *Monthly Record of the Free Church of
    Scotland* (April 1929), p. 87.

71. *Peace and Truth* (January 1935), p. 3.

72. *Peace and Truth* (July 1939), p. 77.

73. *The Reformed Faith Commonly Called Calvinism*, pp. 54–55.

contributor of many of its reviews.[74] Leigh Hunt was thought to have been an Irish Catholic, but in reality seems to have been born into a Brethren family in Hackney. He reached Ireland only in 1916, but did enter the Franciscan Order as a Catholic before returning to Protestantism through Irish Church Missions. He accepted the doctrines of free grace and was ordained into the ministry of the Free Church of England, becoming incumbent of Nathaniel Church, Brighton, where he served until the Second World War.[75] Leigh Hunt's questing religious spirit and capacity to devour primary texts made his contributions to the SGU distinctive. He criticized Keswick teaching, but in a nuanced way that allowed for differences between its exponents.[76] He was to show during the war that Lancelot Andrewes, though enshrined in the Anglo-Catholic Library, was definitely Reformed in his theology, so anticipating historical scholarship by forty or so years.[77] After the war he translated Lecerf's *Introduction to Reformed Dogmatics* for Lutterworth Press.[78] Although he was a retiring character, Leigh Hunt was a major proponent of Calvin's theology in the years leading up to and just after the Second World War.

The culmination of the three tendencies – to become more international, more Scottish and more scholarly – was the Calvinistic Congress held in Edinburgh in July 1938 to discuss 'The Reformed Faith and its Ethical Consequences'. It was fourth in the series of conferences begun in London six years before. The main speakers were drawn from many parts of the Reformed world. This time two, W. Childs Robinson of Columbia Theological Seminary and R. J. G. McKnight of Philadelphia, were from the United States. Two were identified as from France, Léon Wencelius of Strasbourg (though he served as a minister in Philadelphia) and Paul Musculus, a minister in the Vendée, and two from Switzerland, Jean de Saussure, pastor of the cathedral church of Geneva, and Wilhelm Vischer, a minister in Basel but originally from Germany. One, Victor Rutgers, was from the Netherlands, though then serving as Dutch delegate to the League of Nations, and one, E. Sebestyén, came from Hungary, where he taught in the Reformed Theological Seminary at Budapest. There was no-one from the

---

74. He is first mentioned as editor in *Peace and Truth* (January 1935), cover.
75. *Peace and Truth* (July 1938), p. 127; (March 1951), pp. 114–115, partly corrected by (August 1951), p. 137.
76. *Peace and Truth* (July 1936), pp. 92–93.
77. *Peace and Truth* (April 1944), pp. 36–44.
78. Auguste Lecerf, *Introduction to Reformed Dogmatics* (London: Lutterworth Press, 1949); *Peace and Truth* (July 1950), p. 116.

southern hemisphere. Of the one hundred and fifty or so delegates, nearly a third were from outside Britain, giving the gathering a fully international tone. Nevertheless, partly because the congress assembled in Edinburgh, well over half were Scottish. The Free Church, with twenty members, was overrepresented in relation to its size, but as many as fifty belonged to the Church of Scotland, a sign of the gathering strength of confessional Calvinism in the national church. England, however, had only fifteen and, within that small group, the Church of England had only four. Neither English Congregationalism nor Wales had any at all. The scholarly approach was stamped on the occasion by its meeting at New College, Edinburgh, but many of its contributors were able thinkers. De Saussure of Geneva was the co-leader of the continental Calvin revival with Lecerf, who was present to speak at a public meeting. J. H. S. Burleigh, Professor of Ecclesiastical History at New College, as one of the British main speakers, argued cogently against the Weber-Tawney thesis, absolving Calvinism of responsibility for capitalism, which in the 1930s was out of favour; and the attenders included the young Thomas Torrance, passing through from Basel to New York, who, remarkably, said nothing in discussion.[79] A growing body of academic talent was arrayed behind the cause of Calvinism.

There were several other agencies, more or less connected with the SGU, which also promoted the Reformed faith during the 1930s. One already mentioned was the *Evangelical Quarterly*, the periodical founded in 1929 by J. R. Mackay and Donald Maclean. Mackay became ill after a short while and so the editing fell largely to Maclean for most of the 1930s. Burleigh became assistant editor from 1938, eventually succeeding Maclean as editor five years later. The journal, like the SGU, was international, but with a Scottish emphasis, and scholarly. It was designed partly as a replacement for *The Princeton Theological Review*, which B. B. Warfield had edited until his death in 1921, but which ceased publication in the year the *Evangelical Quarterly* began.[80] In 1932 local assistant editors were appointed in the various lands where the periodical circulated so that it could fulfil its global ambitions.[81] In January 1937 they represented England, France, Germany, the Netherlands, Ireland, South Africa, Switzerland and the United States.[82] In the issue for January 1936 marking the quatercentenary of Calvin's *Institutes* there were contributions from Budapest,

---

79. *Proceedings of the Fourth Calvinistic Congress.*
80. Collins, *Maclean*, pp. 90–92.
81. *Peace and Truth* (January 1933), p. 6.
82. *Peace and Truth* (January 1937), p. vii.

Pittsburgh and Strasbourg.[83] Yet there was a decided preponderance of Scots. In the January 1937 issue, for instance, six out of ten were from Scotland, including Burleigh, already a New College professor, but also younger men of promise such as Torrance, who contributed a piece on 'The Giving of Sight to the Man Born Blind'.[84] The scholarship naturally varied in quality, but the aim was to sustain the standards of *The Princeton Review*. The journal was not, as the title might be understood, a pan-evangelical magazine, but emphatically committed to 'the Reformed Faith, regarded as the historic Christian Faith in its purest form'.[85] Subsequently, under the editorship of F. F. Bruce and I. Howard Marshall, it was to broaden its horizons, but in the 1930s it was an eloquent assertor of Calvinism.

Two more new agencies created to advance the Reformed faith during the interwar years deserve mention. One was the Beddington Free Grace Library under Geoffrey Williams, a dedicated bibliophile converted under F. K. Popham. Williams originally assembled the collection in his house and garage in Beddington, a suburb west of Croydon. By 1938, however, it had grown to 20,000 volumes and was well on its way to becoming the Evangelical Library.[86] Like the promoters of the *Evangelical Quarterly*, the librarian saw the interests of evangelicalism and those of Calvinism as identical. The other significant new body was the Inter-Varsity Fellowship (IVF), founded in 1927 by Douglas Johnson as an umbrella organization for the conservative evangelical Christian Unions run by students in British universities. Remarkably, though no-one would guess from the history written by Johnson,[87] the IVF aligned itself firmly with Calvinism in the later 1930s. Johnson, a versatile man of Brethren background, refused to avow a denominational allegiance but attended Cheam Presbyterian Church of England. Just after the First World War he had read History and English at University College, London. He probably reached a Calvinist position while reading Reformation history under A. F. Pollard, Professor of Constitutional History, who hoped the student would pursue a history doctorate. Johnson, however, wanted to hold a medical qualification ready for missionary service and so trained as a doctor, becoming secretary of the London Inter-Faculty Christian Union and then of the IVF, whose

---

83. *Peace and Truth* (January 1936), p. 36.

84. *Peace and Truth* (January 1937), p. 35.

85. Collins, *Maclean*, p. 90.

86. *Peace and Truth* (October 1938), p. xv. Cf. Murray, *Catch the Vision*, ch. 5.

87. Douglas Johnson, *Contending for the Faith: A History of the Evangelical Movement in the Universities and Colleges* (Leicester: Inter-Varsity Press, 1979).

organizer he remained until 1964.[88] Johnson's Reformed credentials are illustrated by the fact that he was one of the handful of Englishmen to attend the Calvinistic Congress in Edinburgh in 1938.[89] *In Understanding Be Men* (1936), the doctrinal handbook of the movement, tried to be even handed between the Calvinist and Arminian positions, but, since it was written by the fervently Reformed T. C. Hammond of Dublin and Sydney, in the last resort it leaned to the Calvinist side.[90] Always looking for eminent men to advance the cause, Johnson recruited Donald Maclean as IVF president for 1938. Maclean's presidential address, published under the title *The Revival of the Reformed Faith*, was a magisterial survey of the European scene, political and intellectual as well as religious, depicting the Reformed faith as the true philosophy that could confront the absolutism of the dictators. Maclean firmly located the IVF as one of a range of kindred Reformed societies.[91] Although the IVF was to retreat from an exclusive commitment to a Reformed position, for a while it stood as much in that world as the Free Grace Library.

The relationship of those who considered themselves orthodox Calvinists to Karl Barth was ambiguous. On the one hand, they were well aware that they should call no man master on earth and so frequently repudiated any exclusive allegiance to Calvin. In England, though not in Scotland, they used the word 'Reformed' relatively sparingly, but they preferred the phrase 'doctrines of grace' or even 'doctrines of the Word of God' to 'Calvinism'.[92] Hence it was open to them to recognize Barthianism as a twentieth-century variation on the theme. On the other hand, they felt uneasy with Barth's treatment of Scripture. At times, observed Leigh Hunt in the first full appraisal of Barth in *Peace and Truth* which appeared in July 1932, 'he will let fall remarks that are strangely reminiscent of Luther's *obiter dicta* concerning the Epistle of James'.[93] The ambiguity emerges in Donald Maclean's comment at the 1932 international conference that there was 'an influential and rapidly increasing group of young Barthian theologians in the Church of Scotland, who,

---

88. Information kindly provided by Professor Gordon Johnson, son of Douglas.

89. *Proceedings of the Fourth Calvinistic Congress*, p. 10.

90. T. C. Hammond, *In Understanding Be Men* (London: Inter-Varsity Fellowship, 1936), pp. 16, 112, 117–119.

91. Donald Maclean, *The Revival of the Reformed Faith* (London: Inter-Varsity Fellowship, 1938), especially p. 22.

92. *Peace and Truth* (October 1927), p. 75; (April 1933), p. 13. A rare English instance of 'the Reformed faith' is found in *Peace and Truth* (January 1929), p. 20 (Atherton).

93. *Peace and Truth* (July 1932), p. 17.

while they repudiate "liberal" theology, do not subscribe wholly to historical Calvinism'. He was willing to give them the benefit of the doubt because 'they have introduced into the pulpits a lost note of seriousness and awe found in Reformed theology'.[94] There was an official veering away from acknowledging Barthians as fellow combatants in later years. The SGU journal printed a stern condemnation of Barth by Cornelius Van Til in October 1937. It was good, declared the author, that the theologian had burned down the house of modern theology. 'But', added Van Til, 'Barth is also seeking to burn down the house of orthodox theology.'[95] At that point the reaction against Barth went so far that the SGU repudiated the third international Reformed Conference, which it had helped to organize, for tolerating the presence of Barthians.[96] Yet in the next year Maclean still included Barthians without offering any censure in his *tour d'horizon* of the Reformed world.[97] The truth is that most of the orthodox Calvinists were ill equipped to grasp the force of Barth's teaching on many points. They sometimes welcomed Barthians as allies, but they were not among those who took part in the reception of Barth during the 1930s.[98]

A further movement of that decade stood closer to the British Calvinist tradition than the Barthians. These were the so-called 'Genevans' who arose in English Congregationalism. The denomination had moved further away from Calvinism than any other body in Britain with a Reformed inheritance. Thomas Wigley, minister of Blackheath Congregational Church, led a group who in 1934 published a manifesto of provocative liberalism. 'In Jesus', it announced, 'we . . . see neither "interference" nor "miracle", but the highest expression of the law of our evolution.'[99] If this defection from orthodoxy was to be rebutted, Congregationalists needed to rediscover their roots. Nathaniel Micklem, Principal of Mansfield College, Oxford, led the way in denouncing the group of 'Black Heathens'. As the author of *What Is the Faith?* (1936) and as the commentator 'Ilico' in the *British Weekly*, Micklem trained some withering fire on liberal positions. His remedy was set out in an article of 1937 on 'The Genevan Inheritance of Orthodox Dissent'. Micklem celebrated 'the

---

94. Maclean, 'Scotland', in *Reformed Faith*, p. 142.

95. *Peace and Truth* (October 1937), p. 150.

96. Ibid., p. 182.

97. Maclean, *Revival of the Reformed Faith*, pp. 9–10.

98. D. Densil Morgan, *Barth Reception in Britain* (London: T. & T. Clark, 2010).

99. *A Re-Statement of Christian Thought*, by the Blackheath Group (1934), quoted by John W. Grant, *Free Churchmanship in England, 1870–1940* (London: Independent Press, n.d.), p. 303.

great name of John Calvin', Puritan piety, Puritan theology and the doctrine
of election. Yet there was more than a dash of speculative Romanticism
about this version of Reformed teaching, for Micklem argued that Rome,
Canterbury, Wittenberg and Geneva had together championed the historic
faith of the church and that Aquinas was a better exponent of election than
Calvin.[100] J. S. Whale, President of Cheshunt College, Cambridge, echoed
Micklem's praise of Calvin, but he too saw him in the context of Catholic tradition in a way that broke with traditional Protestant estimates.[101] The members
of the SGU were predictably in two minds about the Genevans, considering
them, like the Barthians, as no Calvinists but seeing them as moving in the right
direction.[102] The Genevan they most approved was Bernard Lord Manning,
Senior Tutor of Jesus College, Cambridge, and the author of *Essays in Orthodox
Dissent* (1939), who, as an historian, was the least theological of the group.[103]
This circle, which did much to revitalize postwar Congregationalism, was definitely Reformed in its thinking, but in the last resort it was more concerned
with churchmanship than with doctrine.

The Reformed resurgence of the interwar years is the necessary background to understanding Martyn Lloyd-Jones. The preacher appreciated its
significance, as he showed in a Welsh-language broadcast talk of 1944 that
referred to the recent rise of Calvinistic societies in Britain and abroad and the
Edinburgh conference of 1938.[104] Although Lloyd-Jones came to Calvinism
independently, through reading the Welsh fathers of the Methodist Revival
together with Jonathan Edwards and B. B. Warfield, he subsequently forged
connections with the organizations that orbited round the SGU in the 1930s.
The linking agency was the IVF. When Lloyd-Jones first attended an IVF
conference in 1935, the experience confirmed his impression of the shallow-
ness of English evangelicalism. But three years later, when he had arrived at
Westminster Chapel, he agreed once more to speak for the IVF. A primary
reason was the persistence of Douglas Johnson, but Lloyd-Jones was finally

---

100. Nathaniel Micklem, 'The Genevan Inheritance of Orthodox Dissent – The Present
     Need to Affirm It', *Hibbert Journal*, vol. 25 (1937), pp. 193–204, esp. pp. 195, 202,
     and quoted at p. 196.

101. J. S. Whale, *Christian Doctrine* (Cambridge: Cambridge University Press, 1941), pp.
     18–19, 146–149.

102. E.g. *Peace and Truth* (January 1937), p. 3; (October 1940), p. 123.

103. *Peace and Truth* (January 1940), p. 28.

104. Martyn Lloyd-Jones, 'John Calfin', in *Crefydd Heddiw ac Yfory* (Llandybie: Llyfrau'r
     Dryw, 1947), p. 43. I am grateful to E. Wyn James for this reference.

induced to accept Johnson's invitation by the recognition that the IVF possessed three qualities that he prized. It had international contacts, especially with the Netherlands, it valued theologians from Scotland, and it was scholarly.[105] By 1938 Johnson had steered the IVF into acquiring all three of these attributes. The embodiment of the combination was Donald Maclean. Having come to appreciate Maclean's worth through the *Evangelical Quarterly*, Lloyd-Jones greatly admired 'his special zeal for the propagating of the Reformed Faith'.[106] The Welshman was drawn into the IVF net, speaking at its international conference in Cambridge in 1939.[107] From that year until 1942, and again twice afterwards, he served as president of the IVF.[108] Lloyd-Jones visited Edinburgh to lecture at the Free Church College in 1941 and joined the committee of the *Evangelical Quarterly* in the following year.[109] Maclean realized the potential of Lloyd-Jones. 'You go on with your great work,' Maclean encouraged him in 1941. 'As an old campaigner in the battle for Truth, I give you my blessing.'[110] The mantle fell from Elijah onto Elisha, together with a double portion of his spirit.

Maclean died in 1943. During the war the SGU offices, the church of St Mary-le-Port, Bristol, and Grove Chapel were all destroyed by enemy action.[111] The next International Calvinistic Congress had been planned to be held in the Rhineland in 1940, an unfortunate choice. The alternative location of Montpellier was equally inaccessible to foreign delegates and so the event never took place.[112] International links were severed. The Americans, secure from the blasts of European war, held their own Calvinistic conferences, the second, in 1942, including Harold Ockenga, the leader of the resurgence of neo-evangelicalism in postwar America.[113] After the war there was an attempt to revive the international congresses in Europe. One took place in Amsterdam in 1948 on the theme of 'Calvinism and the Modern Mind',

---

105. Iain H. Murray, *D. Martyn Lloyd-Jones: The First Forty Years 1899–1939* (Edinburgh: Banner of Truth, 1982), pp. 253, 285–286, 297, 367.

106. D. Martyn Lloyd-Jones, 'Foreword', in Collins, *Maclean*, p. x.

107. Murray, *Lloyd-Jones: First Forty Years*, pp. 374–375.

108. Johnson, *Contending for the Faith*, p. 351.

109. Iain H. Murray, *D. Martyn Lloyd-Jones: The Fight of Faith 1939–1981* (Edinburgh: Banner of Truth, 1990), pp. 63, 238n.

110. Murray, *Lloyd-Jones: Fight of Faith*, p. 65.

111. *Peace and Truth* (January 1941), p. 1; (October 1944), p. 66.

112. *Peace and Truth* (July 1938), p. 102.

113. *Peace and Truth* (July 1942), p. 46.

attended by representatives of the SGU and the Free Church of Scotland and by Lloyd-Jones.[114] But no international movement such as that of the 1930s emerged and Lloyd-Jones's subsequent efforts for the revival of the Reformed faith, though encompassing international students, were chiefly on the British scene. The twin foci were the themes of the Puritans and revival, the special concerns of J. I. Packer and Lloyd-Jones. Neither of these characteristics had loomed large in the 1930s Reformed movement. There was continuity in the scholarly approach, as the rise of *The Banner of Truth* and the titles published by its Trust revealed. Along with the international dimension, however, the strong Scottish input of the 1930s was lost, being replaced through Lloyd-Jones by a Welsh orientation. The changes of emphasis help explain why the Reformed revival of the twentieth century is normally dated from the postwar years. The preceding period, when a languishing cause was transformed into a significant movement, has been forgotten. But the work of the SGU and its associates in the 1930s, crowned by the Edinburgh conference of 1938, deserves to be remembered. There was a Calvinist resurgence in interwar Britain.

© David W. Bebbington, 2011

---

114. *Peace and Truth* (July 1948), p. 76; (November 1948), p. 114.

2. LLOYD-JONES AND WALES

David Ceri Jones

In February 1925, Martyn Lloyd-Jones wrote to his friend, and soon to be brother-in-law, Ieuan Phillips, 'I have visions of a great Wales in the future, Ieuan, and, God-willing I think that you and I will play a part in its coming.'[1] Lloyd-Jones's letter was written in the midst of the furore that had blown up in the Welsh press following his lecture on 'The Tragedy of Modern Wales' which he had given to the Literary and Debating Society at the Welsh Chapel in Charing Cross just a few days earlier. While much of the lecture was a protest against those aspects of 1920s Wales that Lloyd-Jones found most disagreeable, it concluded with a discussion of the state of Christianity in Wales; both his diagnosis of the problem and the cure he prescribed were to change little over the succeeding fifty and more years of his public ministry. Preaching, he argued, had become professionalized; the chapels were half empty because 'it is almost impossible to determine what some of our preachers believe'.[2] The dilution of the gospel was singled out for particular criticism: 'we get

---

1. Martyn Lloyd-Jones to Ieuan Phillips, 10 February 1925, in Iain H. Murray (ed.), *D. Martyn Lloyd-Jones: Letters 1919–1981* (Edinburgh: Banner of Truth, 1994), p. 5.

2. Quoted in Iain H. Murray, *D. Martyn Lloyd-Jones: The First Forty Years 1899–1939* (Edinburgh: Banner of Truth, 1982), p. 71.

endless sermons on psychology, but amazingly few on Christianity'.[3] What was needed, Lloyd-Jones passionately argued, was preaching that gives men and women 'a new prejudice, in fact the only prejudice that counts – the Christian prejudice'.[4] The kind of preachers who were needed were 'men, men, men; not educated snobs, not bloated plutocrats, not conceited agnostics, but men, real men, men [quoting Wordsworth] "with vision and the faculty divine"'.[5] The men he had in mind were, of course, the Welsh Methodist fathers, Howel Harris, Daniel Rowland, William Williams. 'I am optimistic', he said, 'that a day is coming when Wales will once more be in the van of the Christian crusade. I feel that our past is a guarantee of our future.'[6]

Struggling to come to terms with a growing conviction that he should quit his blossoming medical career and offer himself for the full-time Christian ministry, one of the factors that weighed most heavily on Lloyd-Jones as he made this decision was his love for his native Wales and his concern for its spiritual condition. 'My working hours', he said, 'are filled with thoughts about her [Wales], and in my dreams I cannot escape from her; indeed everything else seems to be relative and subsidiary.'[7] Specifically Welsh expressions of Christianity remained foundational for him, and he was not averse on occasion to styling himself as 'a missioner' for the finer points of the Welsh Christian tradition.[8]

Lloyd-Jones's sense of calling to Wales remained a constant throughout his life. However, the Wales of Lloyd-Jones's formative years was undergoing profound and rapid change. While his native Cardiganshire was insulated from the most severe of these changes, rural depopulation aside, the old Welsh-speaking Liberal Nonconformist hegemony was beginning to unravel.[9] Large-scale migration from Welsh-speaking rural Wales to the more linguistically diverse industrial communities of South Wales was radically changing the face of the country, and the gradual emergence of the Labour Party, especially after the 1906 General Election, merely presaged still greater

------

3. Ibid.
4. Ibid., p. 67.
5. Ibid.
6. Ibid., p. 72.
7. Ibid., p. 67.
8. 'Nationalism, Tradition and Language', *Evangelical Magazine of Wales*, vol. 8, no. 4 (August – September 1969), p. 9.
9. Kenneth O. Morgan, *Wales: Rebirth of a Nation, 1880–1980* (Oxford: Clarendon Press, 1981), Pt 1.

and more fundamental change.[10] An ardent admirer of David Lloyd George in his youth,[11] Lloyd-Jones retained many of the features of the older Welsh Liberalism. Despite often claiming that he preferred the eighteenth century, at least in terms of its theological and spiritual climate,[12] in cultural and national-istic terms it was a Wales that had existed in the second half of the nineteenth century that Lloyd-Jones seems to have hankered after. Yet both Liberalism and the Nonconformist chapel upon which its political hegemony had been built were under significant strain in Wales by the end of the Great War. The high-water mark of chapel attendance had already passed,[13] and while the 1904 revival had temporarily stemmed the tide, theological liberalism and the social gospel were gradually challenging traditional modes of religious belief. Yet, while Lloyd-Jones's father Henry had been influenced by the 'new' theology of R. J. Campbell,[14] it was to hold few attractions for Lloyd-Jones himself. Relocated in London after his father's bankruptcy, Lloyd-Jones entered into many aspects of the still thriving social and religious culture of the London-Welsh scene. Welsh remained the language of his home and his life revolved around study, eventually at St Bartholomew's Hospital and the local Welsh Calvinistic Methodist Chapel at Charing Cross, with its varied diet of *eistedd-fodau*, literary and debating societies, as well as more overtly religious activities.[15] A rural Welsh upbringing and formative teenage years among the London Welsh, who tended to view the homeland which they had left behind with a certain misty-eyed nostalgia, reinforced in Lloyd-Jones a romantic longing for a Wales that was already rapidly fading from memory.

John Brencher has written extensively about the way that Lloyd-Jones's Welshness informed his ministry in a number of fundamental ways;[16] another

---

10. Duncan Tanner, Chris Williams and Deian Hopkin (eds.), *The Labour Party in Wales, 1900–2000* (Cardiff: University of Wales Press, 2000), chs. 3 and 4.

11. Murray, *Lloyd-Jones: First Forty Years*, p. 38.

12. Martyn Lloyd-Jones, *Preaching and Preachers* (London: Hodder and Stoughton, 1971), p. 120.

13. R. Tudur Jones, *Faith and the Crisis of a Nation: Wales 1890–1914*, ed. Robert Pope (Cardiff: University of Wales Press, 2004), p. 413.

14. Murray, *Lloyd-Jones: First Forty Years*, p. 4.

15. Emrys Jones (ed.), *The Welsh in London, 1500–2000* (Cardiff: University of Wales Press, 2001), pp. 167–177.

16. John F. Brencher, '"A Welshman Through and Through": David Martyn Lloyd-Jones (1899–1981)', *Journal of the United Reformed Church Historical Society*, vol. 6, no. 3 (December 1998), pp. 204–225.

chapter in this book explores Lloyd-Jones's appropriation of various elements of the Welsh Calvinistic Methodist tradition.[17] By contrast, this chapter tries to assess the nature and extent of Lloyd-Jones's influence within Wales itself. Despite the fact that he left Wales for the first time at the age of thirteen, and only lived there for a further twelve years as the minister of a church in Port Talbot between 1927 and 1939, Wales remained of primary importance and concern to him throughout his life. However, his presence usually polarized opinions and his influence in Wales consequently ebbed and flowed. While many in Wales came to regard him as their spiritual father, and some were to remain fiercely loyal to him, his tangible influence can be difficult to establish. For a time in the 1930s he was newsworthy, chiefly on account of the romantic nature of his quitting a high-flying career in medicine for the pulpit of a church in one of the most depressed areas of South Wales. This fact alone guaranteed him large congregations for a while. But when he moved to London in 1939 opportunities for further influence in Wales appeared to be limited, and it was not until the decades immediately following the Second World War that Lloyd-Jones came to exert a more telling influence on a generation of young evangelicals who had begun to cluster around the newly established Evangelical Movement of Wales. During the 1950s his influence was wholly positive, but by the 1960s his activities became more narrowly focused on the constituency represented by the Evangelical Movement of Wales, especially as it became the prototype of his ideal of an association of doctrinally pure churches, untainted by ecumenical attachment. His increasingly strident separatist stance inevitably made him a more marginal sectional figure in Wales during the latter years of his life. While he remains a powerful influence within some parts of Welsh evangelicalism, in wider contemporary Welsh Christian circles he appears to have been largely forgotten. The revival of Welsh Christianity to which he hoped to contribute, and which he so optimistically prophesied in 1925, never actually materialized.

The Sandfields years

Lloyd-Jones's arrival in Port Talbot in February 1927 as the new minister of the Bethlehem Forward Movement Church certainly captured the attention of the Welsh press, and for a brief period he enjoyed something approaching celebrity status. The main source for understanding this early phase of

_____

17. See in this volume, John Coffey, 'Lloyd-Jones and the Protestant past', pp. 293–325.

Lloyd-Jones's ministry remains the first volume of Iain Murray's authorized biography. Despite arriving in Port Talbot with little experience of Christian ministry and still less formal training, Lloyd-Jones had a clear sense of what he wanted to do. His sermon on his first Sunday as the new minister of the chapel set the tone of his entire ministry:

> My one great attempt here at Aberavon, as long as God gives me strength to do so, will be to try to prove to you not merely that Christianity is reasonable, but that ultimately, faced as we all are at some time or other with the stupendous fact of life and death, nothing else is reasonable. That is, as I see it, the challenge of the gospel of Christ to the modern world.[18]

Port Talbot, like most of South Wales, had suffered particularly badly during the General Strike of 1926; in its immediate aftermath poverty and hardship were endemic.[19] Reflecting back on his days in Port Talbot, Lloyd-Jones claimed that it had been his father's sense of social justice that lay behind the decision to become a minister in a deprived community in his native Wales.[20] Despite the dire poverty and chronic unemployment confronting him on a daily basis, Lloyd-Jones's early ministry lacked any obvious sense of social commitment; indeed, he very quickly persuaded E. T. Rees, the church secretary, to abandon his socialist political activities altogether.[21] He was driven by an overriding conviction that the gospel of Christ was the real answer to the needs of the unchurched and those whose lives were blighted by poverty and despair; what was required, he tirelessly maintained, was bold confidence in the power of that gospel and preaching designed to effect spiritual transformation. In Lloyd-Jones's thinking, this spiritual transformation was the essential prerequisite to social change. Port Talbot was the perfect place to put that thesis to the test.[22]

---

18. Quoted in Murray, *Lloyd-Jones: First Forty Years*, pp. 135–136.

19. For an insight into the impact of the General Strike and Depression in South Wales, see Steven Thompson, *Unemployment, Poverty and Health in Inter-War South Wales* (Cardiff: University of Wales Press, 2006).

20. Christopher Catherwood, *Martyn Lloyd-Jones: A Family Portrait* (Eastbourne: Kingsway, 1995), p. 48.

21. Robert Pope, *Building Jerusalem: Nonconformity, Labour and the Social Question in Wales, 1906–1939* (Cardiff: University of Wales Press, 1998), pp. 235–236.

22. Martyn Lloyd-Jones to E. T. Rees, 13 November 1926, in Murray (ed.), *Lloyd-Jones: Letters 1919–1981*, p. 12.

In practical terms this meant that the church was quickly stripped back to the bare bones. Out went all the extraneous activities, the temperance society and the amateur dramatics society, all thought necessary to connect with the unchurched, and in came prayer meetings, Bible classes and the *seiat* meetings (see below). In too came lengthy expositional sermons, energized by Lloyd-Jones's passionate belief in the power of preaching and the effectiveness of the evangelical gospel message. Indeed, printed sermons from these years pay eloquent tribute to his conviction that the power of the gospel alone was enough to transform the lives of men and women.[23] While Lloyd-Jones's approach initially raised eyebrows even within his own congregation, it soon began to pay dividends as the chapel began to fill, people began to be converted and the membership figures increased. While Iain Murray may be exaggerating slightly in describing Lloyd-Jones's ministry during these early years in Port Talbot as amounting to a revival,[24] the growth in the membership of the church was certainly significant. On his arrival it had stood at less than 150, but growth started almost immediately. In 1930, 84 new members had been added to the church, individuals converted largely 'from the world' rather than poached from other churches in the town.[25] The peak year was 1931 when 135 new members joined the church. By the beginning of 1932 the membership stood at 424.[26] While growth was never as rapid during the rest of his ministry, steady gains were made in each successive year, ensuring that the membership of the church remained around the 500 mark.[27] Equally remarkable were the kinds of people drawn into the orbit of the church. Bethan Lloyd-Jones's reminiscences from these years provide ample evidence that Lloyd-Jones's desire to reach those traditionally beyond the scope of the organized church could yield some remarkable results.[28]

Lloyd-Jones has been heavily criticized for the apparent disinterest he

---

23. D. M. Lloyd-Jones, *Evangelistic Sermons at Aberavon* (Edinburgh: Banner of Truth, 1983).

24. Murray, *Lloyd-Jones: First Forty Years*, ch. 10.

25. Port Talbot, Bethlehem Forward Movement Mission Archives, Church Minute Book, 14 January 1931, p. 167.

26. Port Talbot, Bethlehem Forward Movement Mission Archives, Church Minute Book, 13 January 1932, p. 177.

27. Port Talbot, Bethlehem Forward Movement Mission Archives, Church Minute Book, 17 January 1934, p. 189.

28. Bethan Lloyd-Jones, *Memories of Sandfields* (Edinburgh: Banner of Truth, 1983).

showed in the daily spiritual life of Westminster Chapel later in his ministry.[29]
While there may be some truth in these criticisms, during his first pastoral
charge Lloyd-Jones devoted himself to the building up and pastoral support
of a congregation experiencing significant growth. While baptisms may have
been rare at Westminster Chapel, they were a much more common occurrence
in Port Talbot; on one evening in November 1930, for example, Lloyd-Jones
baptized 43 adults by sprinkling.[30] While he increasingly left the week-night
activities of Westminster Chapel to an assistant, in Port Talbot he shouldered
the burden of the pulpit ministry, the Sunday afternoon Bible class, the weekly
prayer meeting, the Wednesday night fellowship meeting (a Lloyd-Jones
innovation modelled on the eighteenth-century Welsh Methodist *seiat*) and
the Saturday evening men's brotherhood meeting. In addition, he maintained
a demanding round of pastoral visitation, his medical skills being frequently
called upon. His commitment to preaching in various parts of South Wales
in the mid-week steadily increased too, especially once he had settled into
a regular ministerial routine. Lloyd-Jones was, in essence, the model pastor
and Bethlehem Forward Movement Mission was transformed into a growing
church with a vibrant spiritual fellowship. Lloyd-Jones's vision of church
where the evangelical gospel was preached in its simplicity was bearing fruit.

   The years in Port Talbot were also ones of spiritual formation for Lloyd-
Jones, particularly in theological terms. It is difficult to tell exactly when he
came to settled Reformed convictions, and it may well be that the basics of
the Calvinist system were in place almost from the beginning of Lloyd-Jones's
ministry, a combination of his long-standing interest in the Welsh Methodist
fathers and perhaps the set of the works of John Owen he received as a
wedding present![31] There seems to have been a hint of hyper-Calvinism in
Lloyd-Jones's early ministry, enough for one listener in Bridgend to challenge him over it in the late 1920s.[32] He was apparently falling into the trap
of preaching regeneration, rather than the atonement and justification by
faith, and the incident seems to have forced Lloyd-Jones into more serious
theological study. He turned for guidance to Vernon Lewis, Principal of the
Welsh Congregational College at Brecon, who pointed him in the direction

29. John Brencher, *Martyn Lloyd-Jones (1899–1981) and Twentieth-Century Evangelicalism*
      (Milton Keynes: Paternoster, 2002), pp. 68–82.
30. Port Talbot, Bethlehem Forward Movement Archives, Church Minute Book, 2
      November 1930, additional unnumbered page.
31. Murray, *Lloyd-Jones: First Forty Years*, pp. 155–156.
32. Ibid., p. 190.

of P. T. Forsyth, R. W. Dale and James Denney, each of whom had written extensively on the atonement.[33] Lloyd-Jones's influences during these years seem to have been surprisingly eclectic. While the discovery of the works of Jonathan Edwards in a second-hand bookshop in Cardiff in 1929 'helped me more than anything else',[34] and his discovery of B. B. Warfield while in Toronto in 1932 finally settled his Reformed convictions,[35] he also gained a degree of familiarity with the continental theologians Karl Barth and Emil Brunner.[36]

Yet, while he broadened out a little, the Welsh Calvinistic Methodist fathers remained the standard against which Lloyd-Jones measured each new theological discovery. Writing later, he confessed that 'my reading of the Calvinistic Methodist revival of the eighteenth-century . . . governed me and when anything presented itself to me, if it did not fit into that framework, I had no difficulty over my duty'.[37] The hagiographical *Y Tadau Methodistaidd* ('The Methodist Fathers') remained a constant companion during these years,[38] something that might account for the overly romantic way in which he often tended to talk about the early evangelical revivals. One of the more influential books he read during these years was Kenneth E. Kirk's *The Vision of God: The Christian Doctrine of the Summum Bonum* (1931), the Bampton Lectures from 1928. Drawing on ascetic, mystical and pietistic spiritualities, Kirk's lectures traced the development of the contemplative tradition within Western Christianity. Calling the book 'one of the greatest books which I ever read',[39] Lloyd-Jones was later to draw on a wide range of historical examples, both Catholic and Protestant, in support of his views on revival and the baptism with the Spirit; Kirk undoubtedly opened his eyes to the long-standing Christian emphasis on the pursuit of God. The theological and experiential, both emphases which were to become hallmarks of Lloyd-Jones's later ministry, were certainly there

---

33. The three books that proved crucial were R. W. Dale, *The Atonement* (London: Hodder and Stoughton, 1875); James Denney, *The Death of Christ* (London: Hodder and Stoughton, 1902); and P. T. Forsyth, *The Cruciality of the Cross* (London: Independent Press, 1909).

34. Murray, *Lloyd-Jones: First Forty Years*, pp. 253–254.

35. Ibid., p. 287.

36. Ibid., pp. 254, 291.

37. Ibid., p. 195.

38. John Morgan Jones and William Morgan, *Y Tadau Methodistaidd* (Swansea: Lewis Evans, 1895); Murray, *Lloyd-Jones: First Forty Years*, p. 156.

39. Murray, *Lloyd-Jones: First Forty Years*, p. 254.

in embryo during the Port Talbot years, but it was to be some time before he had worked out how to hold both in creative tension.

While Lloyd-Jones's influence in his own congregation and its immediate surroundings was obviously significant, his impact further afield and within the wider Welsh Christian community is much more difficult to quantify. From an early stage he began travelling to different parts of Wales to preach on mid-week evenings, usually to packed chapels.[40] While there were undoubtedly some who came to faith, many ministers booked Lloyd-Jones to speak because of his ability to draw a large crowd. His preaching on these occasions took place largely within the main Nonconformist denominations, particularly his own Calvinistic Methodists, and a visit from Lloyd-Jones, preaching twice, once in the afternoon and once in the evening, was for many a throwback to the kind of gatherings that had characterized Calvinistic Methodism in its prime. During these years, Lloyd-Jones seems to have been thoroughly committed to his own denomination and determined to work primarily within its boundaries. He was prepared to share the pulpit with those who held diametrically opposed views, his preaching alongside the notorious Tom 'Nefyn' Williams on a number of occasions during the late 1920s and 1930s being merely the starkest example of the mixed messages that such occasions could produce.[41] Lloyd-Jones started exercising a more strategic ministry during these years as well. He began speaking increasingly to gatherings of ministers and students, once more mainly within his own denomination; they were two groups with whom he would continue to invest considerable energy during the course of his ministry. However, his presence among these groups gradually alienated Lloyd-Jones from some within his own denomination. His passionate biblicism and his often starkly drawn warnings about the dangers of theological liberalism, Barthianism, or the 'Oxford Group Movement'[42] meant that there were at least some within his denomination who regarded him as a reactionary influence.

During these years Lloyd-Jones's attitude to the wider Welsh evangelical scene was often ambivalent. The interwar years had not been kind to evangelicals in Wales. An otherworldly piety, a consequence of the 1904–5 revival and

---

40. For an evocative description of these mid-week preaching events, see Rhys Davies, *My Wales* (London: Jarrolds, 1937), pp. 117–120. See also M. Wynn Thomas, *In the Shadow of the Pulpit: Literature and Nonconformist Wales* (Cardiff: University of Wales Press, 2010), pp. 126–127.

41. Murray, *Lloyd-Jones: First Forty Years*, pp. 164, 184–188.

42. Ibid., pp. 288–291.

Keswick teaching on victorious Christian living, together with a judgmental fundamentalism that encouraged a withdrawal from the world rather than creative engagement with society and culture, had brought about the largely self-imposed relegation of evangelicals not only to the margins of society, but also to the fringes of many of the mainline Welsh Nonconformist denominations.[43] Lloyd-Jones had little time for the annual 'Keswick in Wales' convention. While he spoke frequently about the need for revival and paid tribute to the influence and support of some of the *plant y diwygiad* ('children of the revival'), he had relatively little to do with the Pentecostal churches which had proliferated in Wales after the 1904 revival.[44] Similarly, while he did not altogether cut himself off from R. B. Jones and his more abrasive fundamentalist style of evangelicalism, he managed to keep him at arm's length.[45] He was also initially sceptical about much that went on in the student world under the auspices of the Inter-Varsity Fellowship; it was not until he got to know and warm personally to Douglas Johnson, another fan of Reformed theology, that some of his fears about the superficiality of English evangelicals began to be broken down and he agreed to speak at his first Inter-Varsity conference in 1935.[46] It was to prove the beginning of a long and fruitful relationship. The reality was that despite a successful growing church and a popular itinerant ministry, the Calvinistic and independent-minded Lloyd-Jones was struggling to negotiate his way around the wider evangelical community. There is a sense in which he never felt truly at home within the Welsh evangelical milieu during these years.

By 1938, after eleven years at Port Talbot, exhaustion, a sense that his ministry there had come to its natural end and perhaps a desire for a better platform from which he could exercise a wider ministry led Lloyd-Jones to begin looking for other ministerial openings, and even seriously to consider leaving Wales altogether. The impending next step in Lloyd-Jones's ministerial career provoked a flurry of interest and comment in the Welsh press: the *Western Mail,* in particular, took it upon itself to champion Lloyd-Jones's case and ensure that he got a role commensurate with his gifts. It has been

43. D. Densil Morgan, *The Span of the Cross: Christian Religion and Society in Wales, 1914–2000* (Cardiff: University of Wales Press, 1999), pp. 137–144.

44. James Robinson, *Pentecostal Origins: Early Pentecostalism in Ireland in the Context of the British Isles* (Milton Keynes: Paternoster, 2005), p. 105.

45. Noel Gibbard, *R. B. Jones: Gospel Ministry in Turbulent Times* (Bridgend: Bryntirion Press, 2009), pp. 134–135.

46. Murray, *Lloyd-Jones: First Forty Years,* pp. 295–297.

assumed that Lloyd-Jones's move to London was the result of his growing disillusionment with the liberal theological ethos of his denomination. This certainly seems to have lain behind Elwyn Davies' comment that many within the Calvinistic Methodist denomination would have been mightily relieved to see the back of Lloyd-Jones in 1939.[47] However, the reality seems to have been a little more complex. Lloyd-Jones had entered the ministry fully committed to Wales and its people, and also the denomination in which he had been raised and converted. This does not seem to have abated during the course of his first pastorate. So as he began considering the benefits of a London pastorate, and the extra influence which that might afford him, it was to one of his own denomination's London congregations, Marylebone Presbyterian Church, that he first preached with a view to a call.[48] He had already come to the attention of G. Campbell Morgan of Westminster Chapel,[49] and after increased media attention following preaching at the annual meetings of the Free Church Council Assembly at Bournemouth in March 1938, Morgan began trying to secure him as his assistant at Westminster,[50] efforts that were redoubled once he learned that Lloyd-Jones had turned down the call to Marylebone.[51]

Lloyd-Jones accepted Campbell Morgan's invitation in May 1938, but only as an interim arrangement in the first instance. His heart was still set on a bigger role within his own denomination in Wales. Initially the idea of him being made Connexional Missioner of the Forward Movement of his denomination, a role that would have seen him function as an evangelist-at-large, was mooted. The *Western Mail* was sure that this would be an inspired appointment: 'not a single Forward Movement hall in Wales . . . would not feel his galvanic influence'.[52] But the reluctance of the existing incumbent of the post to consider early

---

47. Quoted in Brencher, *Lloyd-Jones*, p. 208. It is a view reflected in Murray, *Lloyd-Jones: First Forty Years*, pp. 351–352.

48. Murray, *Lloyd-Jones: First Forty Years*, pp. 331–333.

49. J. E. Wynne Davies, 'Dr Martyn Lloyd-Jones and Dr G. Campbell Morgan', *Cylchgrawn Hanes: Historical Society of the Presbyterian Church of Wales*, rhif 7 (1983), pp. 53–54.

50. G. Campbell Morgan to Martyn Lloyd-Jones, 28 April 1938, in Murray, *Lloyd-Jones: First Forty Years*, p. 336.

51. Martyn Lloyd-Jones to Secretary of the South Wales Association of the Presbyterian Church of Wales, 16 May 1938, in Murray (ed.), *Lloyd-Jones: Letters 1919–1981*, pp. 17–19.

52. 'Man who may stop backward trend of Forward Movement', *Western Mail* (14 May 1938), p. 9.

retirement quickly put paid to that idea. The southern Association of the Presbyterian Church of Wales seem to have been determined to keep Lloyd-Jones in Wales, and it was at this point that they turned their attention to the vacancy at their college at Bala in North Wales. The *Western Mail* thought this a still more inspired idea:

> The suggestion may well be hailed as a brainwave, for it serves to provide Dr Martin [sic] Lloyd-Jones with a sphere in which he could render unique service not only to his own connexion, but also to the Principality at large. He would be in a strategic position for moulding the Welsh pulpit, as regards both its message and its power of appeal, in such a way as to leave the impress of his labours on the life and thought of our churches for a whole generation. One can conceive no finer sphere wherein his special gifts could find ampler scope or more striking results.[53]

It was this role that seems to have appealed most to Lloyd-Jones himself also. His eventual failure to secure the position has been laid at the door of liberal influences within the Presbyterian denomination, but the evidence tends not to bear out that interpretation. In reality, Lloyd-Jones's name seems to have become embroiled in a political dispute between the northern and southern Associations of the Presbyterian Church, each accusing the other of high-handed tactics in the securing of various appointments within the denomination.[54] It was this, rather than any liberal backroom manoeuvring, that seems to have scuppered Lloyd-Jones's chances. Lloyd-Jones simply got caught in the denominational crossfire. Indeed, even after Lloyd-Jones had accepted a permanent role at Westminster Chapel, the southern Association were still hoping that he could be confirmed in the post at Bala, still convinced that 'a great benefit to our church would be derived from it'.[55] The extent to which Lloyd-Jones himself held out for this appointment can be seen by the length of time it took him to accept Campbell Morgan's suggestion that he become co-pastor at Westminster. It was first suggested in October 1938 and accepted by the church itself in December, but it was to be a further four months before Lloyd-Jones finally accepted the position, and only after the chances of him becoming principal at Bala had evaporated.

The press speculated on the reasons why Lloyd-Jones was not appointed.

---

53. 'Dr Martin [sic] Lloyd-Jones and the Bala College Principalship', *Western Mail* (5 November 1938), p. 9.

54. Murray, *Lloyd-Jones: First Forty Years*, pp. 346–349.

55. Quoted in ibid., p. 350.

Again the *Western Mail* tried to speak up on Lloyd-Jones's behalf, pinpointing his lack of formal theological training as the likely reason why some within the denominational hierarchy 'looked askance at him because he has not entered the ministry in the orthodox way'. According to this feature writer, Lloyd-Jones had 'upset their professional equilibrium and made them jealous of his phenomenal success'.[56] They reacted by blocking his appointment to Bala. While the *Western Mail*'s rhetoric might have been a little overblown, and there would certainly have been some inconsistency had the non-theologically trained Lloyd-Jones been appointed to one of the chief theological colleges of a denomination which had prided itself on its provision of an educated ministry, the newspaper surely captured the sense of many that a real opportunity to affect the fortunes of their denomination for the good had been lost. While evidently disappointed, Lloyd-Jones himself still retained hopes that a possible sphere of telling denominational service could be found for him. In a letter written in September 1939, shortly after the outbreak of the Second World War, he confessed that he was still moved by the 'love, as well as the confidence of the denomination of which I am still proud to call myself a member'.[57]

In a sense Lloyd-Jones left Wales in 1938 under something of a cloud. While exhausted from his decade in Port Talbot, he initially seems to have regarded his role at Westminster as merely a short interlude before taking up a more prominent and influential role in Wales. This was certainly the opinion of the press who, ever since his arrival in Wales in 1927, had treated him as something of a religious celebrity. Even in 1938, on the eve of his leaving Wales, they were still speaking of him as the last best hope for the revitalization of the Nonconformist cause in the country.[58] Yet a measure of realism needs to be introduced into the impact of Lloyd-Jones's ministry at this point. While his preaching had certainly been effective in Port Talbot, there was a palpable sense of frustration from Lloyd-Jones himself that he had not managed to wean people away from the liberalism that they heard from their pulpits.[59] Despite the claims of a journalist that Lloyd-Jones was 'one of the few prophets who

---

56. 'Secrets behind the loss of a Prophet to Welsh Presbyterianism', *Western Mail* (27 May 1939), p. 9.

57. Martyn Lloyd-Jones to the Moderator of the South Wales Association, 11 September 1939, in Murray (ed.), *Lloyd-Jones: Letters 1919–1981*, p. 21.

58. 'Secrets behind the loss of a Prophet to Welsh Presbyterianism', *Western Mail* (27 May 1939), p. 9.

59. J. Elwyn Davies, 'God's Gift to a Nation', *Evangelical Magazine of Wales*, vol. 20, no. 2 (April 1981), p. 24.

has ever found honour in his own country',[60] during his twelve years in Wales his ministry had done comparatively little to challenge the prevailing culture of Welsh Christianity. Unknown to him at the time, the door to further influence within his own denomination had closed decisively in 1939. His attitude to the old denominations was to undergo a revolution in the years following the establishment of the World Council of Churches in 1948, to such an extent that his voice was to be heard only grudgingly within them in subsequent decades. The high-water mark of his influence within the denomination of his upbringing, therefore, had already passed. Relocated in London, it was to be some time before a number of altogether new spheres of influence, outside the main Welsh denominations, slowly began to open up for him.

Creating a Welsh evangelical movement

In many respects the late 1940s and 1950s were to see Lloyd-Jones at the height of his powers. The Westminster Chapel pulpit ensured that his preaching reached new audiences, new evangelical associations came into being – the rejuvenated Inter-Varsity Fellowship, of which he became the theologian-in-chief, the Puritan Conference, the Evangelical Library and the Banner of Truth Trust all bore his unmistakable imprint. While these were not years of revival by any means, they were certainly years in which evangelicals regained much of their theological vigour and evangelistic confidence.[61] They were also years in which Lloyd-Jones came to exert a profound influence on a new generation of young evangelicals in Wales, years when his influence was overwhelmingly positive, even constructive, largely free from the more divisive separatism that precipitated his marginalization from the late 1960s onwards.

The first signs of a more confident outlook among evangelicals in Wales can be detected among the small pockets of university students who had begun holding successful evangelistic missions in various towns in South Wales since 1946.[62] Some of these students had already benefited from Lloyd-

---

60. '"Prophet" Who is Honoured in his Own Land', *Herald of Wales* (24 October 1936), p. 8.

61. David W. Bebbington, *Evangelicalism in Modern Britain* (London: Unwin Hyman, 1989), pp. 259–263; Oliver Barclay, *Evangelicalism in Britain, 1935–1995: A Personal Sketch* (Leicester: Inter-Varsity Press, 1997), ch. 4.

62. Geraint D. Fielder, *'Excuse me, Mr Davies – Hallelujah!' Evangelical Student Witness in Wales 1923–83* (Leicester and Bridgend: Evangelical Press of Wales, 1983), ch. 6.

Jones's ministry at English Inter-Varsity conferences, reflecting his growing influence in student circles at this time.[63] But it was in North Wales during the late 1940s that the most important new alignments occurred. Here a group of Bangor university students, led by a candidate for the Independent ministry, Elwyn Davies,[64] had been meeting in a series of retreats in the months and years immediately following their often dramatic evangelical conversions. These periods of semi-seclusion bound the group together and became the context in which their burden for the spiritual future of Wales was intensified. Their activities were initially channelled into a highly successful evangelistic mission at Bala during Easter 1948, which alerted Lloyd-Jones and led him to speculate that 'something new was about to happen in the history of religion in Wales'.[65] It was at this stage that he became still more closely involved: he was persuaded to contribute the leading article to a new Welsh-language magazine, *Y Cylchgrawn Efengylaidd* ('The Evangelical Magazine'), a publication designed to serve the needs of scattered Welsh-speaking evangelicals.

Lloyd-Jones's article, 'Y Fydd Efengylaidd' ('The Evangelical Faith'),[66] bears close examination because of its foundational importance to what was eventually to become the Evangelical Movement of Wales. The spectre of ecumenism loomed large, and Lloyd-Jones urged the new group to stand resolutely for 'evangelical principles . . . when we are told so often that the business of everybody who proposes to be a Christian of any kind is to agree and

63. For a sense of the extent of Lloyd-Jones's influence in student circles in the late 1940s and early 1950s, see T. A. Noble, *Tyndale House and Fellowship: The First Sixty Years* (Leicester: Inter-Varsity Press, 2006), ch. 3; David Goodhew, 'Understanding Schism: The 1950 Peace Summit between the Student Christian Movement and the Inter-Varsity Fellowship', in Mark Smith (ed.), *British Evangelical Identities: Past and Present*, vol. 1 (Milton Keynes: Paternoster, 2009), pp. 35–45.

64. Very little work has been done on Elwyn Davies and his influence on Welsh evangelicalism. For some of his own reflections on this period, though again in Welsh, see J. Elwyn Davies, *O! Ryfedd Ras* (Pen-y-bont: Gwasg Bryntirion, 1998), Introduction.

65. Words of I. D. E. Thomas, quoted in Noel Gibbard, *The First Forty Years: The History of the Evangelical Movement of Wales, 1948–98* (Bridgend: Bryntirion Press, 2002), p. 27.

66. The article was first published in Welsh: Martyn Lloyd-Jones, 'Y Fydd Efengylaidd', *Y Cylchgrawn Efengylaidd*, cyf. 1, rhif. 1 (Tachwedd – Rhagfyr 1948), pp. 2–8. For an English translation, see Martyn Lloyd-Jones, 'This Evangelical Faith', *Evangelical Magazine of Wales*, vol. 40, no. 2 (April 2001), pp. 18–20.

to forget differences, and to unite against the common enemies threatening Christendom'.[67] Evangelicals, he argued, despite being scattered among the denominations, possessed an intrinsic unity. 'They are closer', he asserted, 'to those who are evangelical within other denominations than with those who are not evangelical within their own denomination; indeed, they always testify to the fact that the only real fellowship they have is with each other.'[68] He defined evangelicals historically in the first instance: they were those who stood in a long line from the Waldensians, John Wycliffe, the Reformers, the Puritans, the Pietists, Methodists and the Clapham Sect. He then singled out three defining characteristics of evangelicals. The first concerned attitudes to authority: evangelicals submitted only to Scripture, but also fiercely guarded their right to interpret it for themselves. 'This is the reason', he argued, 'why he is accused so often of being self-sufficient, individualistic and unco-operative.'[69] The other two features were dealt with more briefly: evangelicals trusted to the message of the gospel, defined in terms of personal regeneration, and they were those who lived lives devoted 'completely to following sanctity and godliness'.[70] From a very early point, almost immediately following the first meeting of the World Council of Churches in Amsterdam in 1948, Lloyd-Jones seems to have been finely attuned to the challenges of the ecumenical agenda. Ecumenism was to overshadow most aspects of Lloyd-Jones's relations with evangelicals in Wales. His answer to it, an evangelical unity predicated on doctrinal purity and energized by religious revival, remained largely unchanged throughout his life. The Evangelical Movement of Wales came to reflect these priorities almost exactly.

The link between Lloyd-Jones and this new group was cemented the following January 1949 when he accepted their invitation to be the main speaker at a mission hosted by the Evangelical Union at Bangor. Here in preaching and informal private discussions he was able to teach and counsel these young students still further, channelling their enthusiasm into seeing a thriving evangelical witness in Wales. The following August these same students went public at Wales's premier Welsh-language cultural gathering, the annual Eisteddfod, held that year at Dolgellau: under a banner bearing the title 'Y Cylchgrawn Efengylaidd', they spent the week preaching and witnessing to fellow Eisteddfod-goers and selling copies of their new magazine. In the

67. Lloyd-Jones, 'This Evangelical Faith', p. 18.
68. Ibid.
69. Ibid., p. 19.
70. Ibid., p. 20.

evening they held their own meetings, one of their speakers being Lloyd-Jones himself. For the first time, during this week, the activities of this new group began to attract the interest and comment of the Welsh-language press and radio.[71] Lloyd-Jones had already confided in Elwyn Davies that he thought that 'the work will continue to progress and deepen' and 'that something very definite was happening'.[72]

Further evidence of Lloyd-Jones's feeling that important new developments were afoot in Wales can be seen in the fact that little more than a month later he was back in Wales, this time as the main speaker at the inaugural Inter-Varsity Welsh Conference held at Borth outside Aberystwyth. This was the first of three such conferences at which Lloyd-Jones was the principal speaker and they became, in effect, mini-theological conferences at which he spoke on some of the key theological concerns of evangelicalism. At Borth his subject was the biblical doctrine of man, while in subsequent years at Cilgwyn, near Newcastle Emlyn, in 1950 and at Borth once again in 1951, he took as his themes the doctrine of the Holy Spirit and the sovereignty of God.[73] The importance of these occasions for the subsequent development of evangelicalism in Wales cannot be overemphasized. Lloyd-Jones taught a whole generation of Welsh evangelical students, many of whom were candidates for the ministry struggling against the prevailing theological liberalism in their denominations, basic evangelical and Reformed doctrine. During these years he ensured, almost single-handedly, that much of Welsh evangelicalism would be both theologically literate and guided in a thoroughly Calvinistic direction.[74] Having been moulded largely in Lloyd-Jones's image, this generation of Welsh evangelicals continued to look to him for inspiration and guidance; his emphases became theirs and his reading of the contemporary church situation was accepted almost entirely by them.

The activities of the friends of the *Cylchgrawn* mushroomed during the early 1950s. They continued to meet regularly in informal local *seiadau*, in various evangelistic campaigns around the country, at the annual Eisteddfod and, for those who were still students, at the various Inter-Varsity conferences. The first steps towards a more formalized presence occurred with the holding

---

71. Gibbard, *The First Forty Years*, pp. 33–35.

72. Martyn Lloyd-Jones to J. Elwyn Davies, 8 March 1949, in Murray (ed.), *Lloyd-Jones: Letters 1919–1981*, p. 127.

73. Iain H. Murray, *D. Martyn Lloyd-Jones: The Fight of Faith 1939–1981* (Edinburgh: Banner of Truth, 1990), p. 238.

74. Fielder, *'Excuse me, Mr Davies – Hallelujah!'*, pp. 157–158.

of their first conference at Bala in August 1952. It quickly became an annual event, the main speaker at the second conference at Caernafon in 1953 being Lloyd-Jones himself. Other activities then followed apace. The first camp for young people was held in August 1954, and in March 1955 an English-language magazine, *The Evangelical Magazine of Wales*, was printed for the first time, in recognition that there was now a genuine evangelical movement in Wales, with a significant presence among speakers of both languages. It was in this year too that a formal title was adopted, the Evangelical Movement of Wales, and Elwyn Davies was appointed to the role of General Secretary, a position he shared with the role of Travelling Secretary for the Inter-Varsity Fellowship.[75] Under the General Secretary a committee structure that operated at both a local and national level was put in place to manage and regulate the activities of the new Movement. While Lloyd-Jones was not closely involved in the nuts and bolts of the day-to-day running of the Movement, the title that had been adopted bore all the hallmarks of his influence,[76] appearing as it did to suggest an alternative, even a rival, to the ecumenical movement. Even at this stage, Lloyd-Jones appears to have anticipated the likely trajectory of the Evangelical Movement of Wales.

Lloyd-Jones remained committed to the Movement in the years that followed. Not least of the reasons for this commitment was the close affinity that had developed between him and Elwyn Davies. Although temperamentally quite different, theologically they were of one mind, especially in the priority that they gave to the concept of revival,[77] and crucially they shared the same reading of the contemporary church situation. Davies and Lloyd-Jones were in close and regular contact from the late 1940s onwards, and few new initiatives were undertaken in Wales without Lloyd-Jones's advice being first sought. Indeed, the minutes of the General Committee of the Movement, its main decision-making body, reveal the extent to which this was the case.[78] Lloyd-Jones's help could sometimes be practical also: when Davies was trying to raise funds to purchase a conference centre at Bala in 1958, Lloyd-Jones, hardly

---

75. Ibid., pp. 147–148.

76. 'Cynhadledd Y Cylchgrawn', *Y Cylchgrawn Efengylaidd*, cyf. III, rhif. VI (Hydref – Gaeaf 1955–6), pp. 43–45.

77. D. Eryl Davies, 'Rhagymadrodd', in John Emyr (gol.), *Porth yr Aur: Cofio J. Elwyn Davies* (Pen-y-bont ar Ogwr: Gwasg Bryntirion, 2011), pp. 11–46.

78. Bryntirion, Evangelical Movement of Wales Archives, Minutes of the General Committee (22–23 November 1968), p. 95; (13 January 1971), p. 145; (14–15 March 1975), p. 236.

known for his abilities as a fundraiser either, was able to use his influence with some well-heeled evangelicals, including the engineer John Laing, to secure a measure of financial support.[79]

Following the establishment of the Movement on a firm footing by the mid-1950s, Lloyd-Jones's influence in Wales came to be felt most keenly in a number of contexts. It was for his gifts as a preacher and pastor for which he remained in most demand. When the first English-language Evangelical Movement of Wales conference was held, at his old church in Port Talbot during 1957, Lloyd-Jones was the obvious choice as the main speaker. However, perhaps the most important development, quickly becoming the area in which Lloyd-Jones's influence among Welsh evangelicals was at its strongest and most unassailable, was the holding of the first ministers' conference under the auspices of the Movement in 1956, at Cilgwyn, near Newcastle Emlyn, rather than at Bala as later became customary. From 1962 until 1979, shortly before his death, the conference became an immovable fixture in Lloyd-Jones's calendar. Initially, membership was open to evangelical ministers of any denominational affiliation and the typical programme consisted of a varied mixture of sermons, prayer meetings and historical lectures.[80] Crucially, discussions were chaired by Lloyd-Jones and he always gave the final address, using it to discuss areas of contemporary concern and to interpret what was happening on the wider evangelical scene. It was an approach Lloyd-Jones had already honed at the Westminster Fellowship, founded in 1941.[81] Although the Welsh ministers' conference met only annually, compared with the monthly frequency of the Westminster Fellowship, alongside the annual ministerial gathering were a whole series of locally based fraternals in which Welsh ministers met to discuss the issues of the day on a regular basis. The titles of the addresses he gave on these occasions suggests that Lloyd-Jones chose a wide range of topics on which to speak, but in reality many of these addresses soon came around to some of his favourite topics. From the late 1950s and throughout the 1960s it was the need for evangelical unity that predominated, and most addresses ended with a call for more urgent prayer for revival.[82]

Others have drawn attention to Lloyd-Jones's tendency to dominate in his leadership of discussions in these contexts, and it would probably not be

79. Martyn Lloyd-Jones to J. Elwyn Davies, 28 April 1958, in Murray (ed.), *Lloyd-Jones: Letters 1919–1981*, pp. 134–135.

80. Martyn Lloyd-Jones to J. Elwyn Davies, 8 March 1949, in ibid., p. 127.

81. Murray, *Lloyd-Jones: Fight of Faith*, pp. 86–87.

82. Gibbard, *The First Forty Years*, pp. 54–55.

claiming too much to state that few had the temerity to challenge his conclusions on whatever the subject under discussion happened to be.[83] Yet if Lloyd-Jones could sometimes be domineering and unbending, there was always a more magnanimous and accommodating side as well. When some of those in attendance at the Welsh minsters' conference wanted to restrict the gathering solely to those of Calvinistic opinions, Lloyd-Jones insisted that the terms of membership be as generous as possible, within the ambit of the evangelical faith.[84] The bond between Lloyd-Jones and the Welsh ministers who attended the conference was undoubtedly close. He frequently referred to them with genuine affection as his 'boys', and many of them looked up to him as a father-type figure. Lloyd-Jones evidently felt at ease at Bala; he was often more candid in the way he expressed his opinions, confident that they would be welcomed with little criticism. The Movement inevitably came to mirror his concerns and priorities closely.

By the late 1950s, the Evangelical Movement of Wales was drawing together a wide cross-section of evangelicals in both languages from across the denominational spectrum. For the first time for decades evangelicals in Wales seemed to have regained a little confidence. Lloyd-Jones exerted a powerful influence. He maintained his gruelling mid-week preaching commitments and was frequently in Wales in these years, preaching to large congregations in all parts of the country. And he had enormous influence among those associated with the Movement. Through preaching, conferences and one-to-one counselling, Lloyd-Jones commended an evangelical faith that was both Reformed in theology and profoundly experimental. However, the 1960s were to usher in a change in the ethos and stance of the Evangelical Movement of Wales, one that mirrored Lloyd-Jones's own increasingly separatist language and gradual retreat, not only from the wider Christian community but from those evangelicals who did not share the same reading of the contemporary ecclesiastical scene as he. While the Movement had always been conscious of

83. Donald Macleod, 'The Lloyd-Jones Legacy', *The Monthly Record of the Free Church of Scotland* (October 1983), p. 209; Gaius Davies, 'Physician, Preacher and Politician: Dr D. Martyn Lloyd-Jones (1899–1981)', in Gaius Davies, *Genius, Grief and Grace: A Doctor Looks at Suffering and Success* (Fearn: Christian Focus, 2001), pp. 370–371.

84. J. Elwyn Davies, 'God's Gift to a Nation', *Evangelical Magazine of Wales*, vol. 20, no. 2 (April 1981), p. 26. Lloyd-Jones had taken the same line at the Banner of Truth conference in 1965, provoking considerable tension and disagreement. Iain H. Murray, 'Forty Years On: 1962–2002', *The Banner of Truth*, nos. 467–468 (August – September 2002), pp. 13–14.

the challenge of ecumenism, it had managed to remain comparatively eirenic, a para-church movement that gave evangelicals an opportunity to express their shared identity in spite of denominational differences. In the 1960s it was gradually transformed, under Elwyn Davies' sure-footed leadership, into an association or fellowship of evangelical churches. It was a transition in which Lloyd-Jones's guidance proved critical.

Until the early 1960s the standpoint of the Evangelical Movement of Wales had been relatively straightforward. As evangelicals, they were the ones who were most faithful to their denominations and so it was their responsibility to work from within to win them back to more orthodox positions.[85] However, from the late 1960s evangelicals, who had once cooperated harmoniously under the umbrella of the Evangelical Movement of Wales, were faced with the stark decision of whether to remain in those denominations or secede from them. Yet the close relationship between Nonconformity, the Welsh language and certain expressions of Welsh identity meant that this became a much more painful process for some than for others. Both the chapel and the Welsh language remained significant cultural markers in parts of rural Wales, in a way that did not pertain to the same extent in those more anglicized and secularized parts of South Wales.[86] These cultural and linguistic factors often played an important role in the decision-making process, and while some placed a premium on these age-old loyalties, others cut loose from them. Further division, even recrimination, was the inevitable outcome.

It was the Movement's wish to see the Welsh denominations won back to a more orthodox position that led it to issue an appeal in 1961, a challenge that called on the denominations to repent of their unbelief and return to the theological positions that had been held by their founders and forefathers.[87] The lukewarm reception which greeted the appeal appears to have come as a genuine surprise to the leadership of the Movement. Whether this was the event which ended their hopes of winning over the denominations is hard to tell, but when the four leading Welsh denominations, the Presbyterians, Independents, Wesleyan Methodists and Baptists (initially as observer members), formed a

---

85. J. Elwyn Davies, *Striving Together: A Statement of the Principles that have Governed the Aim and Policy of the Evangelical Movement of Wales* (Bridgend: Evangelical Press of Wales, 1984), p. 7.

86. D. Densil Morgan, *Wales and the Word: Historical Perspectives on Welsh Identity and Religion* (Cardiff: University of Wales Press, 2008), pp. 211–232.

87. Gibbard, *The First Forty Years*, pp. 59–60.

Committee of the Four Denominations the following year,[88] specifically to explore the possibility of union, the Movement's stance was altered from occasional protest against ecumenism to more concerted action. For almost six years there was heady talk of denominational reunification in Wales. Initially, a delegation from the Movement held a number of meetings with the committee, but they resolutely insisted that doctrinal agreement be a precondition to any plans for reunion.[89] The engagement was short lived.

These developments led the Movement to engage in a protracted internal consultation process, and a committee was formed and charged with the task of examining closely the New Testament teaching on the church. A series of short pamphlets engaging with the contemporary church situation were produced,[90] culminating in the publication in both Welsh and English of *The Christian Church – A Biblical Study* (1966), a short booklet which argued for a slightly modified form of independency.[91] It presented the efforts towards union among the four main Welsh Nonconformist denominations as a 'smokescreen of ecclesiastical verbiage and ecumenical equivocation that . . . clouds the present issues',[92] and reiterated the Movement's familiar baseline position that 'fellowship and unity must be founded upon a clear statement of and adherence to the truth as it is in Christ Jesus'.[93] The pamphlet then went on to argue, along precisely the same lines as Lloyd-Jones had been doing, that evangelicals should put their secondary differences entirely to one side and come together around their shared commitment to the gospel. The pamphlet presented independency, albeit with a nod towards occasional expressions of wider union, as the pattern of church order that the New Testament preferred and that 'under the guidance of the Holy Spirit must be vigorously maintained'.[94] This publication was a key moment of transition in the development of the Evangelical Movement of Wales.

---

88. Noel A. Davies, *A History of Ecumenism in Wales, 1956–1990* (Cardiff: University of Wales Press, 2008), p. 11.

89. Bryntirion, Evangelical Movement of Wales Archives, Minutes of the General Committee (27–28 September 1961).

90. The first of these was J. Elwyn Davies, *Eglwys Unedig Cymru* ('The United Church of Wales') (Port Talbot: Mudiad Efengylaidd Cymru, 1963).

91. *The Christian Church – A Biblical Study* (Port Talbot: Evangelical Movement of Wales, 1966), p. 2.

92. Ibid., p. 6.

93. Ibid., p. 7.

94. Ibid., p. 17.

It was a position identical to that outlined by Lloyd-Jones in his address to the National Assembly of Evangelicals in 1966. Lloyd-Jones had been privy to the writing of *The Christian Church* and thought the final version was 'excellent . . . and I believe puts the main issues before us'.[95] Lloyd-Jones and the Movement had been on a similar trajectory since the early 1960s, if not earlier. When he made his call for evangelicals in mixed denominations to come together 'not occasionally, but always' and 'as a fellowship, or an association, of evangelical churches'[96] it was among Welsh evangelicals, some of his closest friends and most loyal disciples, that his call was acted upon most decisively. The situation was thrown into sharp relief almost immediately when seven students at the Presbyterian Church of Wales's college in Aberystwyth quit their course citing their denomination's weak position on the doctrine of Scripture and its refusal to make the 1823 Calvinistic Methodist Confession of Faith binding on all ministerial candidates. 'Is it right', they asked, 'to work together in the same denomination when there is disagreement on fundamental doctrines?'[97] The issues at stake by this point were clear, as was a possible alternative.

Soon afterwards the Movement rewrote its constitution to allow churches to formally affiliate to it. The General Committee recorded its determination not to found a new denomination; churches that had withdrawn from their denominations were invited to affiliate if they agreed with the Movement's doctrinal basis and if they repudiated any involvement in ecumenical activities.[98] The newly formulated position was explained at length to the wider Movement constituency in a special double issue of the *Evangelical Magazine of Wales* in February and March 1968. Using the latest statistical evidence, the first article in the magazine spelled out the inevitability of further numerical decline among the mainline denominations.[99] Into the vacuum they left behind, so the magazine argued, would step a rejuvenated Roman Catholicism which 'has

---

95. Martyn Lloyd-Jones to Graham S. Harrison, 5 February 1965, in Murray (ed.), *Lloyd-Jones: Letters 1919–1981*, p. 163.

96. D. M. Lloyd-Jones, 'Evangelical Unity: An Appeal', in D. M. Lloyd-Jones, *Knowing the Times: Addresses Delivered on Various Occasions, 1942–1977* (Edinburgh: Banner of Truth, 1989), pp. 255, 257.

97. 'Aberystwyth Student Resignations', *Evangelical Magazine of Wales*, vol. 6, no. 2 (April – May 1967), p. 2.

98. Bryntirion, Evangelical Movement of Wales Archive, Minutes of General Committee (1 May 1967), pp. 59–60.

99. 'A Statistical Survey', *Evangelical Magazine of Wales*, vol. 7, no. 1 (February – March 1968), pp. 3–5.

adapted itself remarkably well to the Welsh situation' and towards which 'there has been a swing in popular sentiment'.[100] The solution was a new alignment of evangelical fellowships: 'we believe that in the interests of Christian fellowship, and of mutually encouraging each other in the work of the kingdom, all evangelical churches in Wales whose doctrinal beliefs coincide . . . should be encouraged to form a link of fellowship with each other by affiliating with the Movement.'[101] In summing up, the editors of the issue chose to identify themselves with the Methodist fathers: 'when God wrought the greatest spiritual work Wales has ever known, namely the Methodist Revival, He largely bypassed the existing churches and eventually brought new ones into existence.'[102] The implication was simple: doctrinally pure churches, protected by ecclesiastical separation and therefore free from both theological liberalism and ecumenical compromise, were a vital precursor to religious revival.

The process of separation began in earnest. In 1967 the Movement formally affiliated with the British Evangelical Council, a conservative association of churches that had been founded in 1952, behind which Lloyd-Jones also threw his weight as the fallout from his 1966 address became apparent.[103] The first Welsh church to affiliate to the Evangelical Movement of Wales on these terms was a small mission on the outskirts of Merthyr Tydfil,[104] and in the years that followed the number of churches that took the secession option slowly increased.[105] When Elwyn Davies became president of the British Evangelical Council in 1969, after initial hesitancy on Lloyd-Jones's part,[106] separatism and the Movement were inextricably wedded together.

Nevertheless, there was no overnight mass evangelical defection from the mainline Welsh denominations in the wake of these developments. Many ministers faced a difficult task persuading their churches of the necessity of

---

100. 'Roman Catholic Advance', ibid., p. 8.

101. 'The Evangelical Approach', ibid., p. 12.

102. 'Revival', ibid., p. 17.

103. Hywel Rees Jones, 'The Doctor and the British Evangelical Council', in Hywel Rees Jones (ed.), *Unity in Truth: Addresses Given by Dr D. Martyn Lloyd-Jones at Meetings Held under the Auspices of the British Evangelical Council* (Darlington: Evangelical Press, 1991), pp. 8, 13–19.

104. Bryntirion, Evangelical Movement of Wales Archives, Minutes of General Committee (15–16 September 1967), p. 62.

105. Gibbard, *The First Forty Years*, ch. 5.

106. Martyn Lloyd-Jones to J. Elwyn Davies, 11 October 1968, in Murray (ed.), *Lloyd-Jones: Letters 1919–1981*, p. 179.

secession, and many who had been active supporters of the Movement in its earlier days were deeply reluctant to cut denominational ties which often went back many generations. Lloyd-Jones, while seemingly disappointed by the response to his appeal,[107] also sometimes counselled caution. Sometimes he even positively encouraged people to stay where they were until the circumstances for secession were more propitious,[108] and he seems also to have harboured hopes that at some point enough people would become convinced of the secessionist case to enable a mass withdrawal to take place, thereby creating the maximum impact.[109] That situation was never to materialize.

Lloyd-Jones has been repeatedly criticized for calling evangelicals to come together in 1966 when he had little idea of what form that new alignment was to take.[110] While his appeal did certainly cause confusion among some, what he had in mind seems clear enough. His own case is instructive: Westminster Chapel refused to join the new Congregational Church in England and Wales when it came into being in 1966, and joined the Fellowship of Independent Evangelical Churches, itself a member of the British Evangelical Council, in 1967.[111] This was exactly what happened in Wales: churches that seceded affiliated to the Evangelical Movement of Wales, which in turn became a constituent member of the British Evangelical Council. Did Lloyd-Jones regard the Evangelical Movement of Wales as a kind of test case, or prototype? Covering a small enough geographical area to make unity a tangible reality, Lloyd-Jones perhaps thought that the alignments the Movement had fostered since the late 1940s had the best chance of evolving into a more coherent body of like-minded congregations. After 1967 it certainly reflected his preference for a loose confederation of independent evangelical churches, which occasionally came together to give expression to their corporate identity. For Lloyd-Jones, setting aside long-cherished denominational and confessional ties in the quest for evangelical unity was unproblematic and there were plenty in Wales who were prepared to follow him into evangelical

---

107. Brencher, *Lloyd-Jones*, pp. 132, 224.

108. Eryl Davies, '18th October 1966: What some papers and books have said', *Foundations*, no. 37 (Autumn 1996), p. 24.

109. Martyn Lloyd-Jones to Graham S. Harrison, 10 November 1967, in Murray (ed.), *Lloyd-Jones: Letters 1919–1981*, p. 175.

110. See, e.g., Alister McGrath, *To Know and Serve God: A Biography of James I. Packer* (London: Hodder and Stoughton, 1997), pp. 125–126.

111. London, Westminster Chapel Archives, Church Meeting Minute Book (January 1959 – May 1977), 20 January 1966, 16 March and 13 April 1967.

independency. Yet for others that transition did not become the panacea that it first seemed and created a nagging sense that something important had been jettisoned in the process.

The years after 1967 became difficult sifting years for evangelicals in Wales. Some, including a number who had been closely involved in the work of the Movement since its inception, chose not to resign from their denominations. Old friends therefore found themselves on opposite sides of the debate. As the number of churches that seceded gradually increased throughout the 1970s, secession had the unfortunate result of not only isolating many Welsh evangelicals, but also in many instances cutting one evangelical off from another. The division was not always complete. In smaller Welsh-speaking evangelical circles, denominational ministers continued to attend Movement events, but in English-speaking evangelical circles feelings often ran high and the demarcation lines were more firmly drawn. An anonymous letter in the *Evangelical Magazine of Wales* in 1969 berated those evangelicals who were prepared to remain in non-evangelical churches and listen to non-evangelical preaching and warned them in no uncertain terms that they shared 'the responsibility of its blinding effects on the many unbelieving hearers in these churches'.[112] Overwrought rhetoric of this nature was far from unusual.

Having resigned from Westminster Chapel in 1968, Lloyd-Jones devoted much of his energy in the 1970s to supporting and encouraging those newly independent evangelical congregations that had heeded his secessionist call. He was frequently in Wales during this final decade of his life, often preaching in small congregations in remote, out-of-the-way places. He remained committed to attending the annual Bala ministers' conference and made himself available to advise ministers who were struggling with whether or not to secede, or with the challenge of creating sustainable congregations within the often lonely ranks of evangelical independency. In many respects Lloyd-Jones adopted a bishop-like role among evangelicals in Wales. He became a pastor to pastors, was frequently called upon to advise on pastoral issues when many of these ministers felt simply out of their depth,[113] and was turned to when there were new men to be inducted into the pastorates of these infant

---

112. 'Attachment to non-evangelical churches', *Evangelical Magazine of Wales*, vol. 8, no. 1 (February – March 1969), p. 15.

113. See, e.g., *Holding Forth the Word of Life: The History of Heath Evangelical Church, Cardiff, 1900–2000* (Cardiff: Heath Christian Trust, 2000), p. 59; Peter Jeffrey, *Chains of Grace: Peter Jeffrey's Story* (Leominster: Day One, 2008), pp. 39–40.

congregations.[114] He regarded this kind of activity as absolutely indispensable. One of the consequences of the debates about ecumenism in the late 1960s was that it made the local autonomous congregation even more central to Lloyd-Jones's thinking. When an evangelistic mission called *Tell Wales*, led by the Argentinean evangelist Luis Palau, was planned for 1978, Lloyd-Jones in discussions with Welsh ministers counselled caution. Rather than turn to mass evangelism and import famous names to do their job for them, Lloyd-Jones urged the ministers to have confidence in their own ministerial calling and to depend entirely on the Holy Spirit to use their gifts and congregations in the task of reaching the unchurched. 'Do we need to import anyone?' he queried. 'Ask the Holy Spirit to do the work, to come in. Don't let anything come in that will distract people and prevent them having absolute dependence on the Holy Spirit.'[115] By the late 1970s, faithful, ecumenically unencumbered local churches in the hands of the Holy Spirit were Lloyd-Jones's preferred means for the evangelization of Wales.

Yet despite being so closely identified with the Evangelical Movement of Wales and its secessionist stance, Lloyd-Jones did not entirely cut himself off from the mainline Welsh denominational churches. He never formally resigned from the Presbyterian Church of Wales and maintained his practice of preaching regularly in denominational churches all over the country, still attracting very large congregations wherever he went. For many in Wales who agreed with neither Lloyd-Jones's theology nor his ecclesiology, he remained a powerful draw. Yet for others he seemed a slightly incongruous throwback to the glory days of a Welsh Nonconformist tradition that was in the twilight of its life.

Lloyd-Jones's Welsh legacy

Lloyd-Jones's death in March 1981 passed with relatively little comment in the secular Welsh press,[116] but fulsome tributes appeared thick and fast in the pages of Welsh evangelical periodicals. In the month following his death the Evangelical Movement of Wales issued a special glossy commemorative number of the *Evangelical Magazine of Wales*, in which contributors did not stint

---

114. Murray, *Lloyd-Jones: Fight of Faith*, pp. 677–680.

115. 'What is our need?', *Evangelical Times* (October 1988), p. 13.

116. One of the few English language obituaries appeared in the *Western Mail*. 'A king of orators', *Western Mail* (6 April 1981), p. 8.

in their praise. Elwyn Davies spoke of Lloyd-Jones in terms of 'God's gift to a nation',[117] while Vernon Higham assured readers, 'I do not believe I am exaggerating when I say that he was the prophet of this century for the world.'[118] Far from diminishing in subsequent years, Lloyd-Jones's influence within the constituency associated with the Evangelical Movement of Wales has been maintained and perhaps even strengthened in some quarters. The appearance of the majority of his sermons in print over the past forty years has helped keep his voice alive, but it has been the influence of a whole generation of Welsh ministers regarding themselves as the 'sons' of Lloyd-Jones[119] who have done most to perpetuate his memory. They have tended to regard Lloyd-Jones as their role model[120] and some have been among the most passionate defenders of his various theological emphases.[121] They have ensured that much of Welsh evangelicalism very closely mirrors his theological and ecclesiastical preferences, and sometimes even some of his personal tastes. According to one prominent Reformed Baptist pastor, Lloyd-Jones has been:

> influential in the formation of the basic Calvinistic ethos of Welsh evangelicalism. It is a millenial, serious minded, dignified, emphasising holiness of life, separation from the world, rejecting Keswick's traditional doctrine of sanctification and also the invitation system of modern evangelism. It is committed to expound systematically the Scriptures, especially the Pauline books in the canon, and from the Doctor it has learned a longing for a true revival of religion. Dr Lloyd-Jones has grasped the nettle of church discipline and reformation and thus the Evangelical Movement of Wales supports separation from Modernism and Romanism and is thus anti-ecumenical.[122]

---

117. J. Elwyn Davies, 'God's Gift to a Nation', *Evangelical Magazine of Wales*, vol. 20, no. 2 (April 1981), p. 23.

118. W. Vernon Higham, 'An Abundant Entrance', *Evangelical Magazine of Wales*, vol. 20, no. 2 (April 1981), p. 2.

119. 'An interview with Geoff Thomas', www.banneroftruth.co.uk (accessed 6 April 2011).

120. Geoff Thomas, 'Dr Lloyd-Jones and his "Minions"', www.banneroftruth.co.uk (accessed 7 April 2011).

121. See Graham S. Harrison, 'Joy Unspeakable: A review article on the recently published volume of sermons by Dr Martyn Lloyd-Jones on the Baptism with the Holy Spirit', *Evangelical Magazine of Wales*, vol. 24, no. 3 (June – July 1985), pp. 10–13.

122. Geoffrey Thomas, 'Wales greets Scotland', *Monthly Record of the Free Church of Scotland* (November 1979), p. 217.

However, beyond this there has also been a tendency among some to imitate Lloyd-Jones, especially perhaps in his homiletic style. The practice of preaching in the style of Lloyd-Jones on Sunday mornings, when congregations might be made up predominantly of professing Christians, and like Charles Haddon Spurgeon on Sunday evenings, presumably in a more evangelistic fashion, has been held up as the ideal.[123] For some, though, this approach has not been entirely without its pitfalls. Young ministers in their first pastorates launching into extended verse-by-verse expository series on Paul's letters to the Romans or the Ephesians, attempting to preach forensically detailed forty-five- or fifty-minute sermons, has not been unheard of. There has also been a tendency to imitate elements of Lloyd-Jones's style of church leadership. Recent work has shown that Westminster Chapel operated as Lloyd-Jones's personal fiefdom, in which largely quiescent church officers were rarely encouraged, or given the opportunity, to challenge his opinions.[124] Lloyd-Jones went to such pains to stress the importance of preaching and the role of the preacher that he had a tendency, at least in practice if not always in theory, to attach much less significance to some of the other offices and ministries of the vibrant local church. His was the classic one-man ministry and his church resembled an impersonal preaching centre a little too closely. Many evangelical ministers in Wales have regarded Westminster Chapel as a model to be copied and have therefore tended to replicate some of its strengths and weaknesses.[125]

The birth of many of these Welsh evangelical churches in separation from other denominational structures has also left a problematic legacy. Some have not just separated from churches they deem apostate, but have practised second-degree separation as well, dividing from fellow evangelicals who chose to remain within the older denominations. Yet this has never been without its difficulties and in 1984 Elwyn Davies seemed to recognize as much when, at a critical juncture, he argued that the Evangelical Movement of Wales should appeal to the broadest evangelical constituency, not just those churches that were formally affiliated to it.[126] Separatism has always been easier in theory than in practice. Where the separatist mindset has been more damaging perhaps has been the way in which it has encouraged a contentious spirit within many of these supposedly doctrinally pure congregations. It became all

---

123. Geoffrey Thomas, *Preaching: The Man, the Message and the Method* (Jackson, MS: Reformed Academic Press, 2009).

124. Brencher, *Lloyd-Jones*, pp. 77–78.

125. Thomas, 'Wales greets Scotland', p. 217.

126. Davies, *Striving Together*, pp. 23–24.

too easy for some to suspect other churches of slipping from the purity of the faith if they deviated from the accepted party line, wherever that happened to be drawn. The result has been a litany of further divisions and church splits with smaller churches being established by minority groups wishing to have the freedom to do things their own way. Sometimes these splits have been personality driven, but changes in the culture of worship, with a move away from the traditional Nonconformist hymn sandwich to less structured and more spontaneous forms of worship, or the introduction of modern Bible translations, have often caused significant damage, with some groups claiming to be more in touch with the contemporary *Zeitgeist* while others laud their faithfulness to the old paths. Born in the trauma of separation, many of these churches have found it comparatively easy to separate over and over again.[127]

By the late 1970s and early 1980s the Evangelical Movement of Wales had become a somewhat inward-looking community of churches. Many of those associated with it at times seemed blissfully unaware of the existence of much Welsh evangelical life beyond its boundaries.[128] Yet the post-1966 years were ones which saw the redrawing of the British evangelical landscape. Rob Warner has recently argued that by the end of the twentieth century evangelicalism in the British Isles possessed both fundamentalist and progressive wings, which were kept apart by a moderate majority of more neutral evangelicals who occupied the middle ground between these two extremes.[129] While that pattern was not replicated exactly in Wales, a renegotiation of the old evangelical alignments did take place. In some respects those who suffered most in this period were those evangelicals who remained within the older Welsh Nonconformist denominations: often they found themselves cut off from old evangelical friends who had taken the secessionist option, and an isolated and ever smaller minority in the denominations to which they endeavoured to remain loyal. This contrasted markedly with the position in the Church in Wales where there were signs of renewed confidence within its

---

127. For some reflection on this process, informed by knowledge of the Welsh scene, see Peter Jeffery, *Evangelicals: Then and Now* (Darlington: Evangelical Press, 2004). For the more general tendency to divisiveness among conservative evangelical groups, see John M. Frame, 'Machen's Warrior Children', in Sung Wook Chung (ed.), *Alister McGrath and Evangelical Theology: A Dynamic Engagement* (Grand Rapids, MI: Baker, 2003), pp. 113–146.

128. Thomas, 'Wales greets Scotland', p. 216.

129. Rob Warner, *Reinventing English Evangelicalism, 1966–2001: A Theological and Sociological Study* (Milton Keynes: Paternoster, 2007).

small evangelical wing. One of the consequences of the abolition of private patronage in the Welsh Church in the wake of disestablishment was that it had become difficult to guarantee successive generations of evangelical ministry in Welsh parishes.[130] However, the founding of the Evangelical Fellowship in the Church in Wales in 1967 under the watchful eye of John Stott[131] brought evangelical Anglicans in Wales together and indicated their determination to re-engage with the structures of their Church.[132] The evangelical presence in the Church in Wales has grown substantially as a consequence.

In Wales, as elsewhere, it was charismatic renewal that perhaps did most to change the evangelical landscape, with old divisions broken down and new alignments and networks created.[133] A revitalized Evangelical Alliance, which embraced organizational devolution following the formation of Evangelical Alliance Wales in 1986, has benefited most from this process, rapidly becoming the mainstream evangelical voice.[134] But even within the Evangelical Movement of Wales there was some recognition that the post-1960s solution had not been entirely satisfactory. The establishment of the Associating Evangelical Churches of Wales in 1988, and the affiliation of over sixty congregations that had previously come under the umbrella of the Movement,[135] was a tacit admission that the loose bonds of fellowship which Lloyd-Jones had championed often did not meet the needs of many of these churches. There now exists the anomalous situation in which some of the churches that seceded after 1968, particularly some of the more independent-minded Welsh language congregations, have remained affiliated to the Evangelical Movement of Wales, while the majority have transferred their loyalties to the Associating Evangelical Churches of Wales. The relationship between the two bodies remains ambiguous, but there has been a willingness among some, particularly those who did not live through the divisions of the 1960s and did not know Lloyd-Jones in person, to build bridges with non-separatist evangelicals.

---

130. P. M. H. Bell, *Disestablishment in Ireland and Wales* (London: SPCK, 1969), pp. 9, 257.

131. Timothy Dudley-Smith, *John Stott: The Making of a Leader* (Leicester: Inter-Varsity Press, 1999), pp. 444–447.

132. Roger L. Brown, *Evangelicals in the Church in Wales* (Welshpool: Tair Eglwys Press, 2007), p. 272.

133. Bebbington, *Evangelicalism in Modern Britain*, ch. 7.

134. Ian Randall and David Hilborn, *One Body in Christ: The History and Significance of the Evangelical Alliance* (Carlisle: Evangelical Alliance and Paternoster, 2001), p. 292.

135. www.aecw.org.uk/aecw/churches.php.

Evangelicalism in contemporary Wales remains fragmented. Lloyd-Jones's vision of a broad and inclusive evangelical unity has remained tantalizingly out of reach. While Lloyd-Jones's influence remains deeply persuasive for many within the ranks of the Evangelical Movement of Wales, the tendency of some to lionize him, accord his views special reverence and even to keep a weather eye open for his successor,[136] has occasionally made it difficult for others to move out of his shadow. Among a younger generation of minsters, many of whom entered the ministry after Lloyd-Jones's death, there is more willingness to question some of his views and actions and deal with his sometimes contentious legacy. Yet in many ways the wider evangelical constituency in Wales pays him little attention, such has been his identification with a narrow and sectarian expression of the evangelical faith since his death. This has to be seen as a shame. Lloyd-Jones was the last in a long tradition of Welsh Nonconformist pulpit giants, and he embodied a type of Calvinistic Methodism that was deeply rooted in the Welsh Christian past.

© David Ceri Jones, 2011

---

136. Geoff Thomas, 'Then and Now: 1966–1996', *Foundations*, no. 37 (Autumn 1996), p. 32.

3. LLOYD-JONES AND REVIVAL

Ian M. Randall

In 1947, in a foreword to a book by his friend Philip Edgcumbe Hughes which brought together studies on revival, Martyn Lloyd-Jones wrote, 'There is no subject which is of greater importance to the Christian church at the present time than that of revival. It should be the theme of our constant meditation, preaching and prayers.'[1] Although Lloyd-Jones's preaching covered many topics and was marked by painstaking biblical exposition, his conviction about the crucial importance of revival – and of preaching about it – never wavered. In an essay in 1986 (five years after Lloyd-Jones's death) on 'The Doctor as Preacher', Peter Lewis wrote about Lloyd-Jones as one of those preachers in a long tradition since the Protestant Reformation 'who have stood for the reformation and renewal of the church', 'the evangelization and awakening of the world around it' and 'pastoral counsel'. Lewis noted that while some ministers had seen revival, others had undertaken such work during hard times for the church. The calling that Lloyd-Jones had been given, Lewis suggested, was to minister 'outside' the experience of revival. But as someone who 'longed to see revival', Lloyd-Jones was determined to 'remind the church of its necessity and perhaps prepare a new generation for God's best and greatest work in

---

1. Philip E. Hughes, *Revive Us Again* (London: Marshall Morgan and Scott, 1947), p. 5.

the world'.[2] This chapter examines Lloyd-Jones's views on revival, looking at
his commitment to the reality of revival, his view of the need for revival, his
warnings about hindrances and mistaken approaches to revival, his analysis of
motives and desires in respect of revival and the vision of revival that he offered.

The reality of revival: a 'signal manifestation of God's power'

Writing to Philip Hughes in 1946, Lloyd-Jones spoke of his daily prayer for
revival, which he described as 'an unusual and signal manifestation of God's
power through the Holy Spirit'. This was the reality he sought. Without such
spiritual power he saw no hope, and he commented unenthusiastically to Hughes
on the recent Church of England report *Towards the Conversion of England*, which
he assumed Hughes (as an Anglican clergyman) had seen. The report contained
what Lloyd-Jones termed, rather wearily, 'the old story' of Christians who, in
their concern to see the Christian message advancing, were hoping – with what
Lloyd-Jones believed was a false expectation – that 'they can organise these
things'.[3] For Lloyd-Jones, that view was untrue to the Bible. He saw the true
source of hope in the reality of revival, which for him was rooted in the experience of the church in the New Testament. In one sermon, part of an extended
series of sermons on revival which he preached at Westminster Chapel in 1959,
he suggested (as he often did) that revivals were 'in a sense a repetition of the
day of Pentecost'. He continued, 'The essence of a revival is that the Holy Spirit
comes down upon a number of people together, upon a whole church, upon a
number of churches, districts, or perhaps a whole country. That is what is meant
by revival. It is, if you like, a visitation of the Holy Spirit, or another term that
has often been used is this – an outpouring of the Holy Spirit.'[4]

---

2. Peter Lewis, 'The Doctor as Preacher', in Christopher Catherwood (ed.),
    Martyn Lloyd-Jones: Chosen by God (Crowborough: Highland Books, 1986), pp.
    92–93. Although Lloyd-Jones did not see the revival for which he hoped, there was
    significant awakening in his earlier pastorate in South Wales. See Bethan Lloyd-
    Jones, *Memories of Sandfields* (Edinburgh: Banner of Truth, 1983). For this, and for
    Lloyd-Jones's early preaching on revival, see Iain H. Murray, *D. Martyn Lloyd-Jones:
    The First Forty Years 1899–1939* (Edinburgh: Banner of Truth, 1982), ch. 10.
3. D. M. Lloyd-Jones to Philip E. Hughes, 17 April 1946, in Iain H. Murray (ed.), *D.
    Martyn Lloyd-Jones: Letters 1919–1981* (Edinburgh: Banner of Truth, 1994), pp. 70–71.
4. D. M. Lloyd-Jones, *Revival: Can We Make It Happen?* (London: Marshall Pickering,
    1992), p. 100.

Although Lloyd-Jones referred back to the New Testament in his thinking about the experience of revival and also frequently expounded Old Testament passages, an address he gave to the Puritan Conference in London in 1959 was typical of his concern to highlight the occurrences of revivals throughout the story of the church. He defined revival as 'an experience in the life of the church when the Holy Spirit does an unusual work' in the 'reviving of the believers', and he then moved on to what he termed the 'best approach' to the subject, which was 'to start with the actual historical survey'.[5] The surveys that Lloyd-Jones gave of revival often had a special focus on the eighteenth century. Christopher Catherwood has noted that although Lloyd-Jones was one of those 'most responsible for the renewed interest in Reformed, and in particular Puritan, theology', his 'special affection' was for the leaders of the eighteenth-century revival.[6] Indeed, in 1945 Lloyd-Jones, in the course of arguing that 'the chief need is the revival and awakening of the church', suggested that 'what is needed today is for us to forget the nineteenth century completely and make a detailed study of the beginning of the eighteenth century'.[7] In similar vein, in his 1959 Puritan Conference address he argued that, whereas there had never been revival in the Roman Catholic Church, and while after 1860 or 1870 revivals in Protestantism 'become rather exceptional phenomena', much of the eighteenth century, by contrast, could be described as 'an age of revival'.[8] On other occasions, however, Lloyd-Jones could paint on a larger canvas. Even the pre-Reformation Catholic movement, the Brethren of the Common Life, was identified by Lloyd-Jones as a revival movement, in a sermon entitled 'The Way to Revival', and in this same sermon he also included twentieth-century revivals in Wales, Korea, the Congo and the Isle of Lewis.[9]

The fascination that Lloyd-Jones had with the eighteenth-century Evangelical Revival or (in North America) Great Awakening is illustrated by the many occasions on which he referred to the lives and ministries of

---

5. D. M. Lloyd-Jones, 'Revival: An Historical and Theological Survey', in D. M. Lloyd-Jones, *The Puritans: Their Origins and Successors: Addresses Delivered at the Puritan and Westminster Conferences 1959–1978* (Edinburgh: Banner of Truth, 1987), p. 2.

6. Christopher Catherwood, 'Afterword', in Catherwood (ed.), *Chosen by God*, p. 273.

7. D. M. Lloyd-Jones, 'Religion Today and Tomorrow', in D. M. Lloyd-Jones, *Knowing the Times: Addresses Delivered on Various Occasions, 1942–1977* (Edinburgh: Banner of Truth, 1989), p. 30.

8. Lloyd-Jones, 'Revival: An Historical and Theological Survey', pp. 2–4.

9. D. M. Lloyd-Jones, *Joy Unspeakable: The Baptism with the Holy Spirit* (Eastbourne: Kingsway, 1984), pp. 276–278.

Jonathan Edwards in New England, of Howel Harris in Wales, and of George Whitefield. Lloyd-Jones's discovery of Edwards dated back to the late 1920s. His interest was aroused in 1927 and two years later, 'quite by accident' (as he put it in 1976), he found two volumes of the works of Edwards. 'I was', he said, 'like the man in our Lord's parable who found a pearl of great price. The influence upon me I cannot put into words.'[10] Lloyd-Jones's admiration for Edwards – described by Michael Eaton as Lloyd-Jones's 'great hero' – was evident in a 1942 address he gave to a meeting of the Crusaders' Union. He told his audience, 'I would commend to you a very thorough study of that great American divine, Jonathan Edwards. It was a great revelation to me to discover that a man who preached in the way he did could be honoured of God as he was, and could have such great results in his ministry.'[11] The phrase 'the way he did' is a reference to Edwards preaching from a full manuscript. Four decades later, Lloyd-Jones's enthusiasm for Edwards was undiminished. He invited those at the Westminster Conference in 1976 to 'look at this man who has had such a lasting influence, and who seems to be becoming again almost a dominating influence in religious thought in America'. Lloyd-Jones confessed that evaluating Edwards was 'one of the most difficult tasks I have ever attempted'. He found the theme almost impossible. 'I am afraid,' he told his audience, 'and I say it with much regret, that I have to put him ahead even of Daniel Rowland and George Whitefield.'[12]

Surprisingly, however, it was the transatlantic revival of the late 1850s that prompted Lloyd-Jones to deliver his fullest treatment of the subject of revival. At the beginning of this sermon series at Westminster Chapel, he spoke about 1959 as 'a year in which many will be calling to mind and celebrating the great revival, the great religious awakening, the unusual outpouring and manifestation of the Spirit of God, that took place one hundred years ago'. Lloyd-Jones referred to revival taking place at that time, 'first in the United States of America, and afterwards in Northern Ireland, in Wales and parts of Scotland, and even in certain parts of England'.[13] The 'even in . . . England' was

---

10. D. M. Lloyd-Jones, 'Jonathan Edwards and the Crucial Importance of Revival', in Lloyd-Jones, *The Puritans*, p. 352.

11. Michael A. Eaton, *Baptism with the Spirit: The Teaching of Martyn Lloyd-Jones* (Leicester: Inter-Varsity Press, 1989), p. 129, citing D. M. Lloyd-Jones, *The Presentation of the Gospel* (London: Inter-Varsity Press, 1949).

12. Lloyd-Jones, 'Jonathan Edwards and the Crucial Importance of Revival', p. 355.

13. Lloyd-Jones, *Revival*, p. 7.

in tune with Lloyd-Jones's remarks at the Puritan Conference of that year, in which he noted that 'revivals in the history of the church have generally been outside England', and he suggested tentatively that there might be a danger of the English temperament being more liable to 'the sin of quenching the Spirit' than other temperaments.[14] For Lloyd-Jones, this was all the more reason to emphasize revival in his London preaching. It was not surprising, therefore, that he took the opportunity in 1959 to preach on revival, and he repeated his much-loved phrase as he spoke about the subject: revival was a 'great and signal movement of the Spirit of God'. He was not, however, simply following the lead of others who were interested in revival – he was setting out to make the case on his own terms as to 'why the Church of God should be very concerned about it at this present juncture'.[15]

The understanding that Lloyd-Jones had of how revival operates within the story of the church was set out early in his 1959 sermon series. 'If you look back across the history of the Christian Church', he claimed, 'you immediately find that the story of the Church has not been a straight line, a level record of achievement. The history of the Church has been a history of ups and downs. It is there to be seen on the very surface.'[16] In the eighteenth century, in Wales, William Williams ('Pantycelyn') spoke about cycles of renewal and decline.[17] Jonathan Edwards also believed that 'cyclical revival' was God's way of extending his kingdom.[18] This view is examined by Kathryn Long in her study of the revival of 1857–8 in America. She shows how this 'cyclical' view, which was especially the product of the Calvinist theological tradition, was adopted and developed.[19] 'The Christian church', Lloyd-Jones maintained, 'would have been dead and finished centuries ago and many times over were it not for revivals.' History showed, he believed, that God revived his church from time to time. 'When the life has gone he has sent it again; when the power has vanished he sends it again. That has been the history of the Christian church

----

14. Lloyd-Jones, 'Revival: An Historical and Theological Survey', p. 11.

15. Lloyd-Jones, *Revival*, p. 7.

16. Ibid., p. 26.

17. Eryn White, 'Revival and Renewal amongst the Eighteenth-Century Welsh Methodists', in Dyfed Wyn Roberts (ed.), *Revival, Renewal and the Holy Spirit* (Milton Keynes: Paternoster, 2009), p. 4.

18. J. I. Packer, 'A Kind of Puritan', in Catherwood (ed.), *Chosen by God*, p. 55. Packer notes that this cyclical view was not found in the Puritans.

19. Kathryn T. Long, *The Revival of 1857–58: Interpreting an American Religious Awakening* (New York: Oxford University Press, 1998), p. 18. See also pp. 16–25.

from the first century until today.'[20] He took the view that the church had
'many times been as she is today, counting so little in the life of the world and
of society; so lacking in life, and vigour, and power, and witness', but he took
comfort from the way in which, after such weakness, an 'outpouring of the
Spirit of God' had often come. Revivals were also a 'going back to something
that was there before'.[21] Lloyd-Jones was not in favour of innovation: the
periods of power in the past constituted the pattern for the future.

The need for revival: 'urgent need of some manifestation'

Although the basic spiritual needs of humankind were unchanged over time,
Lloyd-Jones recognized that the world in which he lived and preached had
certain specific features. 'The very belief in God', he suggested, 'has virtually
gone.'[22] He spoke sombrely about being 'confronted by materialism, worldliness, indifference, hardness, and callousness', and also 'a recrudescence of
black magic and devil worship and the powers of darkness as well as drug
taking and some of the things it leads to'. Because of this, he saw the 'urgent
need of some manifestation, some demonstration, of the power of the *Holy
Spirit*'.[23] But Lloyd-Jones also resisted the idea that the twentieth century had
thrown up challenges that were completely new. He argued that the much-
vaunted entertainment culture had been present in the past – in cock fighting,
card playing and gambling. Scientific knowledge was nothing new: there had
been a scientific awakening in the seventeenth century. Lloyd-Jones urged,
'Read the story of the fight the Church had with rationalism.'[24] He hoped that
all who were listening to him were 'sick and tired' of hearing that the problems
facing the church had to do with new circumstances, although at the same time
he acknowledged that aspects of the church's situation had deteriorated. 'Is it
not obvious to all of us', he asked in 1959, 'that the Church is patently failing
. . . that she does not count even as much as she did in the memory of many of
us today?'[25] Here was the continuing need, and revival was the answer.

─────────────

20. Lloyd-Jones, *Joy Unspeakable*, p. 275.

21. Lloyd-Jones, *Revival*, p. 26.

22. Ibid., p. 13.

23. D. M. Lloyd-Jones, *Prove All Things: The Sovereign Work of the Holy Spirit* (Eastbourne:
    Kingsway, 1985), p. 25.

24. Lloyd-Jones, *Revival*, pp. 29–30.

25. Ibid., pp. 9, 29.

It followed logically that the need could not be met by the normal activities of the church, however biblically based these might be. Lloyd-Jones did not, in taking this approach, minimize the significance of the week-by-week ministries that took place in local churches, although the powerful stress on revival had that danger. In 1957, in his annual letter to the Westminster Chapel members, he spoke warmly of 'all who have been convicted and converted by the Truth in our midst during the past year'.[26] He was also thankful for the conversions that were taking place 'regularly in evangelical churches'; but the need of the day, he contended, was 'for an authentication of God, of the supernatural, of the spiritual, of the eternal, and this can only be answered by God graciously hearing our cry and shedding forth again his Spirit upon us and filling us as he kept filling the early church'.[27] In 1959, after noting that only 6% of the population attended church regularly, Lloyd-Jones made this point strongly: 'What is needed is some mighty demonstration of the power of God, some enactment of the Almighty, that will compel people to pay attention, and to look, and to listen. And the history of all the revivals of the past indicates so clearly that that is invariably the effect of revival, without any exception at all.' He added dramatically, 'When God acts, he can do more in a minute than man with his organising can do in fifty years.'[28] Yet Lloyd-Jones did accept that the fruit of revival might be seen over time. He linked revival with gradual social transformation when he argued that the Trade Union movement, the movement for the Abolition of Slavery, and even the 1832 Reform Act could be attributed to the fruits of revival.[29]

The dismissal of 'organizing' was typical. Lloyd-Jones was adamant that the pressing needs he outlined could not be met by the kind of organized evangelistic campaigns which were a feature of the postwar years. There was a mistaken notion, he believed, that human evangelistic enterprise could stem the tide of decline. He considered that a major reason for this erroneous way of thinking was the erosion of belief in the sovereignty of God. 'It is only since the decline of Calvinism', he stated in 1968 (speaking on William Williams and Welsh Calvinistic Methodism), 'that revivals have become less and less frequent. The more powerful Calvinism is the more likely you are to have a

---

26. D. M. Lloyd-Jones to the Members of Westminster Chapel, January 1957, in Murray (ed.), *Lloyd-Jones: Letters 1919–1981*, p. 95.

27. Lloyd-Jones, *Joy Unspeakable*, p. 278.

28. Lloyd-Jones, *Revival*, pp. 121–122.

29. D. M. Lloyd-Jones, 'John Calvin and George Whitefield', in Lloyd-Jones, *The Puritans*, p. 108.

spiritual revival and re-awakening. It follows of necessity from the doctrine . . .
You know that you are entirely dependent upon God. That is why you pray
to Him and you plead with Him and you argue, and you reason with Him.'[30]
In one of his 1959 sermons, Lloyd-Jones made this defiant pronouncement:
'A revival is . . . something that is *done to* the Church . . . You can have a great
evangelistic campaign, but it may leave your church exactly where it was, if
indeed it is not worse.' Lloyd-Jones was apparently constantly being told of
churches that were suffering from 'post evangelistic campaign exhaustion'.[31] It
is difficult to avoid the conclusion that the reference was to the Billy Graham
campaigns of 1954–5. Lloyd-Jones had declined to take part in ministers' gatherings held in conjunction with Graham's London meetings, and although he
mentioned in prayer at Westminster Chapel the 'brethren' who were 'ministering in another part of the city', he spoke of reports from the campaign as 'most
confusing'.[32] For him it was a profound mistake to suggest, as he alleged some
were doing, 'Well, things are very bad, everything is going down – what shall
we do? We had better have an evangelistic campaign.'[33]

Lloyd-Jones argued that among the evangelical groups undermining a focus
on the need for revival were the Plymouth Brethren. He told the Puritan
Conference audience in his 1959 address that he did not know exactly what
was believed by present-day Brethren, but that early Brethren 'taught, and
taught very strongly, that it was wrong to pray for revival because, they said,
the Holy Ghost had been given once for all on the day of Pentecost'.[34] Lloyd-
Jones was right to note what he called 'the pervasive effect' of Brethren thinking at that time. It was estimated that around 28% of the counsellors at Billy
Graham's London meetings at the Harringay Arena in 1954 were Brethren.[35]
It is unlikely that Lloyd-Jones did not know what contemporary Brethren were
teaching, since his knowledge of ecclesiastical developments was formidable.
Later in his Puritan Conference address he was even more forthright in his
criticism, stating that 'no more mischievous and misleading theory could be

---

30. D. M. Lloyd-Jones, 'William Williams and Welsh Calvinistic Methodism', in ibid., p.
    211.
31. Lloyd-Jones, *Revival*, pp. 99–100.
32. Iain H. Murray, *D. Martyn Lloyd-Jones: The Fight of Faith 1939–1981* (Edinburgh:
    Banner of Truth, 1990), p. 338.
33. Lloyd-Jones, 'William Williams and Welsh Calvinistic Methodism', p. 211.
34. Lloyd-Jones, 'Revival: An Historical and Theological Survey', p. 12.
35. Roger Shuff, *Searching for the True Church: Brethren and Evangelicals in Mid-Twentieth-
    Century England* (Carlisle: Paternoster, 2005), pp. 152–153.

propounded, nor any one more dishonouring to the Holy Spirit, than the principle adopted by the Plymouth Brethren, that because the Spirit was poured out at Pentecost, the church has no need, and no warrant, to pray any more for the effusion of the Spirit of God'.[36] Lloyd-Jones lamented that over the previous seventy or eighty years (his estimate), since the 1880s, 'this whole notion of a visitation, a baptism of God's Spirit upon the Church, has gone'.[37]

In Lloyd-Jones's mind revival was closely linked with the need for the baptism of the Holy Spirit. From the mid-1950s he became convinced that this baptism was a post-conversion experience.[38] In a paper in 1973 on Howel Harris and the eighteenth-century revival in Wales, Lloyd-Jones addressed this issue through the lens of Harris's experience. Lloyd-Jones opposed the view that 'every man at regeneration receives the baptism of the Spirit, and all he has to do after that is to surrender to what he has already'. What was needed, he argued, was for individuals to have the Spirit 'poured out' on them.[39] In the case of Harris, this 'crucial experience' took place, Lloyd-Jones said, on 18 June 1735, when Harris was in Llangasty church. Lloyd-Jones continued, 'To me, there is only one expression to use. It was the expression used by these men themselves and by their successors. It was a baptism "of fire" or a "baptism of power".'[40] On other occasions he argued that the baptism with the Holy Spirit was 'always something clear and unmistakable, something which can be recognized by the person to whom it happens and by others who look on at this person'.[41] He did not affirm the Pentecostal view that speaking in tongues was evidence of Spirit baptism, arguing that 'it is possible for one to be baptized with the Holy Spirit without having some of these special gifts'.[42] But while he rejected Pentecostal teaching, it seemed to him that other evangelicals, who held that Spirit baptism 'happens to everybody at regeneration', were denying the New Testament and 'definitely quenching the Spirit'.[43] The passion with which Lloyd-Jones expressed himself on this issue cannot be understood

---

36. Lloyd-Jones, 'Revival: An Historical and Theological Survey', p. 21.

37. Lloyd-Jones, *Revival*, p. 54.

38. Christopher Catherwood, 'Introduction', in Lloyd-Jones, *Joy Unspeakable*, pp. 12–13.

39. Lloyd-Jones, 'Howell Harris and the Revival', in Lloyd-Jones, *The Puritans*, p. 289.

40. Ibid., pp. 289–290.

41. Lloyd-Jones, *Joy Unspeakable*, p. 52.

42. Lloyd-Jones, *Prove All Things*, p. 121. In the introduction to these sermons, J. I. Packer expressed his agreement with Lloyd-Jones on this point, but queried Lloyd-Jones's 'analysis of Spirit-baptism as a particular experience of assurance' (p. 10).

43. Lloyd-Jones, *Joy Unspeakable*, p. 141.

without recognizing the close link he made with revival.[44] For Lloyd-Jones, a revival was 'a large number, a group of people, being baptized by the Holy Spirit at the same time'.[45] Those who denied that individuals needed this baptism were inevitably, for him, questioning the need for revival itself.

Hindrances to revival: things 'that are proving to be useless'

At the same time as he taught that God was sovereign in revival, Lloyd-Jones also suggested ways in which revival could be hindered. The church could do this, he argued in his 1959 sermon series, by relying on things 'that are proving to be useless'. He then offered an examination of the 'useless' things on which 'Christian people are still pinning their faith'. The first was apologetics, which he defined as 'the belief that what we really have to do is to make the Christian faith acceptable to and commendable to the men and women of today'. Lloyd-Jones spoke of books, lectures and sermons which attempted to present the Christian faith in philosophical terms. He highlighted in particular the interest in reconciling science with religion.[46] It is possible that Lloyd-Jones later concluded that his condemnation of apologetics had been too fierce. In his subsequent address that year to the Puritan Conference he said, 'God forbid that we should become a body of people who just denounce activism and do nothing! That is what is said about some of us.' He continued, with specific reference to apologetics, 'Let us do everything we can by every biblical and legitimate means to propagate and defend the faith. Let us use our apologetics in their right sphere.'[47] Lloyd-Jones expressed thankfulness that efforts being made by evangelicals were producing results and added that these were not to be despised, but he returned to his main theme, that 'nothing less than revival is needed' and that the church had to 'wait, expect, and pray' for this.[48] To focus on alternative solutions was a diversion, even a hindrance.

Lloyd-Jones also spoke in his 1959 sermon series on the hindrances caused by the use of what he called 'particular methods'. He found it 'tragic' that faith was being pinned on methods of evangelism and he outlined four areas about

---

44. Eaton states that for Lloyd-Jones revival and baptism with the Spirit were 'virtually the same thing'; Eaton, *Baptism with the Spirit*, p. 197.

45. Lloyd-Jones, *Joy Unspeakable*, p. 51.

46. Lloyd-Jones, *Revival*, pp. 15–16.

47. Lloyd-Jones, 'Revival: An Historical and Theological Survey', p. 20.

48. Ibid., pp. 20–21.

which he was concerned. The first was excitement about new translations of the Bible. For Lloyd-Jones, whatever their value, these translations were not going to solve the problem of the evil in the human heart. The second false hope was to think that radio and television could be used to communicate to people. Lloyd-Jones was dismissive of 'these short snappy messages' that characterized the media. A third mistake was to advertise what the church was doing. 'Big business succeeds because it advertises, so we must advertise the Church, and set up our publicity agencies in the Church.' Finally, Lloyd-Jones condemned, as he often did, 'popular evangelism, in which all this is put into practice'. His appraisal of such evangelism was uncompromisingly bleak: 'Everything that can appeal to the modern man, the last word in presentation is used, in the belief that when it is done, and you do it with a modern technique, then you will get hold of the modern man.' Lloyd-Jones accepted that some individual conversions were taking place, since 'almost any method you like to employ will do that', but his question, a telling one, was this: 'What of the situation, what of the bulk of men and women, what of the working classes of the country, are they being touched at all, are they being affected at all? Is anybody being affected, except those who are already in the Church or on the fringe of the Church?'[49]

A further area of hindrance, which was examined by Lloyd-Jones in some detail in his 1959 sermons, was doctrinal weakness. There was a tension here. In looking at Howel Harris, Lloyd-Jones acknowledged that 'revival does not always come after a preliminary reformation', and he continued, 'Revival sometimes follows reformation, but revival sometimes precedes reformation; and for us to lay it down that reformation must precede revival, and that doctrinal orthodoxy is essential to revival is simply to fly directly into the face of facts.'[50] But in his 1959 sermons his focus was on the way in which the church in 'periods of declension' denied or neglected truths 'which are essential to the whole Christian position', yet still revival came. Lloyd-Jones, typically, used the eighteenth century as an example. Before the Evangelical Revival the church was 'moribund, it was useless, the vast majority of people did not attend a place of worship'. He also referred to the 1859 revival in the north of Ireland and the way in which revival was opposed by those holding to false doctrine. The Roman Catholic Church, he noted, was selling holy water and urging people to sprinkle themselves with it to avoid being touched by the revival.[51] However, Catholic responses in 1859 were more complex than Lloyd-Jones indicated.

---

49. Lloyd-Jones, *Revival*, pp. 17–18.

50. Lloyd-Jones, 'Howell Harris and the Revival', p. 289.

51. Lloyd-Jones, *Revival*, pp. 33–35.

One Catholic, Chief Baron Pigott, sitting as a judge in County Down, was reliably reported to have said that 'the religious movement' in 1859 had 'extinguished all party animosities, and produced the most wholesome moral results upon the community at large'. He hoped 'that it would extend over the whole country'.[52] Nonetheless, the case being made by Lloyd-Jones was a compelling one: doctrinal heterodoxy tended to be a hindrance to revival.

It was not the case, however, that doctrinal orthodoxy guaranteed revival either. Lloyd-Jones was particularly critical of the holiness teaching promulgated at the large annual Keswick Convention, although the evangelical centralities which he preached were also evident there. One of his claims was that Keswick played down experience.[53] He spoke of many evangelical Christians 'who hold feeling and emotion at a discount . . . They are afraid of the power of the Holy Spirit.'[54] Yet formative Keswick teachers such as F. B. Meyer, while they urged people not to rely on feelings, could speak enthusiastically of occasions when – as Meyer put it – hearers received an 'overwhelming baptism of the Holy Spirit'.[55] In 1951 Duncan Campbell, who had recently experienced revival in the Isle of Lewis and was a preacher Lloyd-Jones appreciated, spoke at the Keswick Convention and his message led to a deep desire to pray for revival.[56] Two years after this, however, Lloyd-Jones queried whether Keswick teaching gave 'a true awareness of sin'.[57] This seems a sweeping statement, although Charles Inwood, a leading international Keswick representative, had expressed worries in the interwar years that Keswick was not pressing home as strongly as it should the demands of holiness.[58] The critique by Lloyd-Jones was paralleled by a scathing attack on Keswick by James Packer, who worked

52. William Gibson, *The Year of Grace: A History of the Ulster Revival of 1859* (Edinburgh: Andrew Elliott, 1860), pp. 163–164.

53. Lloyd-Jones to Mr and Mrs H. F. R. Catherwood, 5 April 1954, in Murray (ed.), *Lloyd-Jones: Letters 1919–1981*, p. 118.

54. D. M. Lloyd-Jones, *The Unsearchable Riches of Christ: An Exposition of Ephesians 3:1 to 21* (Edinburgh: Banner of Truth, 1979), p. 247.

55. Ian M. Randall, *Spirituality and Social Change: The Contribution of F. B. Meyer (1847–1929)* (Carlisle: Paternoster, 2003), p. 103.

56. *The Keswick Week*, 1952, cited in Charles Price and Ian M. Randall, *Transforming Keswick* (Carlisle: Paternoster, 2000), pp. 181–182.

57. Lloyd-Jones to Raymond Johnston, 17 January 1953, in Murray (ed.), *Lloyd-Jones: Letters 1919–1981*, p. 130.

58. Ian M. Randall, *Evangelical Experiences: A Study in the Spirituality of English Evangelicalism, 1918–1939* (Carlisle: Paternoster, 1999), p. 28.

closely with Lloyd-Jones in the Puritan Conference. In an article in 1955 in
the *Evangelical Quarterly*, Packer dismissed Keswick teaching as 'Pelagian'.[59]
However, aspects of the perspectives of Lloyd-Jones and Packer seem to
cancel each other out. Lloyd-Jones wanted Keswick to acknowledge the place
of feeling, while Packer's view was affected by his failure to experience the life
of spiritual power held out by Keswick speakers.[60]

Keswick was examined by Lloyd-Jones from a distance: he never attended
what he once called 'the Evangelical Ascot'.[61] By contrast, when it came to
analysing the relationship of Reformed teaching to revival, Lloyd-Jones was an
insider. Indeed few, if any, preachers knew this area better than Lloyd-Jones. It
might seem contradictory for him to consider Reformed teaching as a potential
hindrance to revival, since he argued that what he saw as the diminishing desire
to pray for revival from the 1860s onwards was due to a decline in commitment
to Reformed theology.[62] However, Lloyd-Jones was unflinching in addressing
the problems of Reformed orthodoxy. He found it 'surprising but tragic' when
books by leading Calvinists omitted all reference to revival. For example, when
Lloyd-Jones turned to the great American Reformed theologian Charles Hodge
for help with the subject of revival, he found none. 'Charles Hodge', he concluded, 'does not seem to have been interested in revival.'[63] Speaking to Baptist
Revival Fellowship ministers in 1956 and 1957, he urged the importance of
the central doctrines of the faith and then pronounced that in preaching it was
essential to have the baptism of the Spirit 'or we fail'.[64] He also spoke about an
excessive reaction in Reformed circles to Pentecostalism and its phenomena.[65]
He warned of the danger of being fearful of the supernatural, of the unusual,
of disorder. 'You can be so afraid of disorder,' Lloyd-Jones asserted, 'so concerned about discipline and decorum and control, that you become guilty of
what the Scripture calls "quenching the Spirit".'[66] The warning to the Reformed
constituency could not have been clearer.

---

59. J. I. Packer, '"Keswick" and the Reformed Doctrine of Sanctification', *Evangelical
    Quarterly*, vol. 27 (July 1955), pp. 153–167.

60. Price and Randall, *Transforming Keswick*, ch. 11.

61. Philip E. Hughes, 'The Theologian', in Catherwood (ed.), *Chosen by God*, p. 169.

62. Lloyd-Jones, 'Revival: An Historical and Theological Survey', p. 5.

63. Ibid., p. 7.

64. D. M. Lloyd-Jones, 'Evangelical Principles Essential to Revival', *Life of Faith* (7
    February 1957), pp. 89–90.

65. Lloyd-Jones, 'Revival: An Historical and Theological Survey', p. 9.

66. Lloyd-Jones, *Joy Unspeakable*, p. 18.

Desire for revival: 'a concern about the glory of God'

The reason why Lloyd-Jones gave such detailed attention on so many occasions to mistaken approaches that in his view could be, and were, hindrances to revival was because of his overwhelming desire for what he saw as the genuine article. As he sought to stimulate this desire in others, he applied his outstanding diagnostic skills rather than simply engaging in exhortation. In his 1959 sermons on revival, he addressed the question: why pray for revival? His first reason was: a concern for the glory of God.[67] He then asked: 'How often do you hear annual conferences and assemblies expressing a concern about the glory of God, and the honour of the name of God? No, our attitude seems rather to be that the Church is a human organization, and of course we are concerned about what is happening to it.'[68] The desire for the glory of God to be known was at the heart of all that Lloyd-Jones said and did.[69] A second important motivation for Lloyd-Jones was a deep concern for the state of the whole church. 'It seems to me', he observed, 'that there is no hope for revival until you and I, and all of us, have reached the stage in which we begin to forget ourselves a little, and to be concerned for the Church, for God's body, his people here on earth.'[70] A third motive behind the desire for and prayers made for revival was the situation of those outside the church. Lloyd-Jones saw himself, to the surprise of some, as primarily an evangelist.[71] As he probed the issue of reaching those outside, he declared, 'It is a terrible state for the Church to be in, when she merely consists of a collection of very nice and respectable people who have no concern for the world, people who pass it by, drawing in their skirts in their horror at the bestiality, and the foulness, and the ugliness of it all.'[72]

The desire for revival should also, Lloyd-Jones was convinced, be evident in the desire of preachers to know power in their preaching. In his book on the preaching of Lloyd-Jones, *The Sacred Anointing*, Tony Sargent says, 'More than anything else he wished to witness an outpouring of the Spirit which would lead the Church into revival,' and he connects this with Lloyd-Jones's

---

67. Lloyd-Jones, *Revival*, p. 188.
68. Ibid., p. 189.
69. I am indebted to Elizabeth Catherwood, Lloyd-Jones's eldest daughter, for this insight.
70. Lloyd-Jones, *Revival*, p. 192.
71. Lewis, 'The Doctor as Preacher', p. 82.
72. Lloyd-Jones, *Revival*, p. 194.

vision for preaching. Lloyd-Jones wanted preachers 'to be powerful in their proclamation with ministries set ablaze by the Spirit's anointing'. Lloyd-Jones, as Sargent notes, gave the last chapter of his book *Preaching and Preachers* (1971) to declaring and defending the conviction that a preacher's ministry could be 'impoverished by an inadequate pneumatology'.[73] In an early sermon on Romans, Lloyd-Jones contended that it was possible to 'have a highly educated, cultured ministry, but it will be useless without this power' and such preaching could end up as 'nothing better than entertainment'.[74] He was convinced of the need to return to the kind of preaching that characterized periods of revival, particularly that seen during the eighteenth century. But in one of his 1959 sermons he pictured some objections to this. He imagined listeners – probably especially in the later nineteenth century – saying, 'We are now becoming more educated and we have advanced. Of course we do not want the sort of thing they had in past centuries under Whitefield and Wesley and so on. We now want learned sermons.' The way in which preachers had become reliant on 'human learning and knowledge and wisdom' was, according to Lloyd-Jones, 'one of the main causes and explanations of the state of the Church'.[75]

Lloyd-Jones knew, however, that the history of preaching since the eighteenth century was not as simple as that. He used the example of Dafydd Morgan, who 'preached like a lion' in Wales during the 1859 revival. The secret of this preaching, Lloyd-Jones argued, was not Morgan's gifts (although he was a minister, he was apparently 'a man of no gifts whatsoever') but that 'power came upon him'. This lasted for two years and the power was quite as suddenly then withdrawn.[76] Lloyd-Jones stressed that the power that came on preachers in revival did not remain the same over subsequent post-revival years. He spoke of the revival in Wales in 1904–5, when 'large numbers of people were suddenly experiencing the baptism of the Spirit'. Some younger people were surprised that an old minister, who had been touched by the 1859 revival, did not seem to be having 'the ecstatic joy which they were experiencing', but the minister explained that there is a difference between first falling in love and the love of more stable married life. The latter is not lesser, and can be seen as

---

73. Tony Sargent, *The Sacred Anointing: The Preaching of Dr Martyn Lloyd-Jones* (London: Hodder and Stoughton, 1994), p. 67.

74. D. M. Lloyd-Jones, *Romans 1: The Gospel of God* (Edinburgh: Banner of Truth, 1985), pp. 223–224.

75. Lloyd-Jones, *Revival*, p. 125.

76. Ibid., pp. 110, 114.

deeper.[77] Yet for Lloyd-Jones what was of greatest interest was what happened at the height of revival periods. Thus in the 1904–5 Welsh revival, 'the man that God used' was Evan Roberts, a 'very ordinary man'.[78] Lloyd-Jones acknowledged that in telling these stories of preachers from the past he wanted to highlight what he called the 'romantic' element in the history of the church.[79]

As well as stressing that preaching 'under the Spirit's anointing' was vital, Lloyd-Jones also highlighted the desire to pray as a crucial element in revival. In his sermon 'The Way to Revival' he concluded by offering the encouragement of what happened in New York in 1857, when 'just one man began to pray at first, and then two or three joined him, and then more until they had to move to a bigger building'. The revival spread. Lloyd-Jones linked this with the story from the same period in Northern Ireland of 'a very simple labourer, James McQuilkin. He began to pray alone . . . then others began to pray and on and on they went.'[80] Revival ensued. To some extent, inevitably, these accounts by Lloyd-Jones were simplified. The 'one man' in New York was Jeremiah Lanphier, and as well as drawing businessmen into his prayer circle, he and others used the main daily newspapers to publicize what was happening in their 'mid-day' (lunchtime) meetings.[81] In the case of McQuilkin, described by Lloyd-Jones as 'the Moses in Northern Ireland',[82] the beginnings of the movement there were complex, with more than one source being identified.[83] However, Lloyd-Jones's purpose was not to evaluate the historiography, but rather to stimulate spiritual desire. 'Here is the vital question,' he proposed. 'Have you seen the desperate need of prayer, the prayer of the whole Church? I shall see no hope until individual members of the Church are praying for revival, perhaps meeting in one another's homes, meeting in groups amongst friends, meeting together in churches, meeting anywhere you like . . . There is no hope until we do. But the moment we do, hope enters.'[84]

In one of his 1959 sermons, Lloyd-Jones outlined the specific nature of the

---

77. Lloyd-Jones, *The Unsearchable Riches of Christ*, p. 158.

78. Lloyd-Jones, *Revival*, p. 114.

79. Ibid., p. 163.

80. Lloyd-Jones, *Joy Unspeakable*, p. 279.

81. Long, *The Revival of 1857–58*, p. 36.

82. Lloyd-Jones, *Revival*, p. 198.

83. Janice Holmes, *Religious Revivals in Britain and Ireland, 1859–1905* (Dublin: Irish Academic Press, 2000), p. 31. See also Ian M. Randall, *Rhythms of Revival: The Spiritual Awakening of 1857–1863* (Milton Keynes: Paternoster, 2010), pp. 12–13.

84. Lloyd-Jones, *Revival*, p. 20.

prayer which he felt could and should be offered. Drawing in his exposition from the example of Moses, Lloyd-Jones encouraged prayer for the personal assurance of God's presence and God's love.[85] In similar vein, in his address in 1968 on William Williams, Lloyd-Jones placed great weight (as he did on many occasions) on the way Calvinistic Methodists knew 'the direct witness of the Spirit himself to the fact that they were the children of God'.[86] Linking this on another occasion with the experience of the love of God, Lloyd-Jones described just such an overwhelming experience in the life of Evan Roberts. 'He stood up in a meeting in a chapel, and suddenly this love of God so came upon him that he literally fell to the ground. Many present thought he was actually dead. What had happened was that he had had a realization of this overwhelming love of God.' Lloyd-Jones saw this incident as 'a crucial moment' in the story of the 1904–5 revival.[87] He saw this kind of experience, as Christopher Catherwood puts it, not as something 'that could be induced, or produced either instantly or gradually by human means – it was something sent by God in His sovereign power and grace'.[88] Yet there was a pressing need to be open to such experiences.

A vision of revival: 'experiential religion'

Lloyd-Jones's vision was for a thoroughly revived church. His model of church life was largely shaped by his appreciation of eighteenth-century Methodism, especially Welsh Calvinistic Methodism. It did not have to do with types of church structures or even primarily with doctrine. He defined Methodism not as a theological position but as 'essentially experimental or experiential religion and a way of life'. Lloyd-Jones illustrated this by referring to the first meeting between George Whitefield and Howel Harris in Cardiff in 1739. The first question Whitefield asked Harris was this: 'Mr Harris, do you know that your sins are forgiven?' The key issue was about assurance. Harris was able to answer affirmatively. There was also a great concern among Methodists, Lloyd-Jones noted, about what Whitefield called a 'felt' Christ. Lloyd-Jones continued, 'They were not content with orthodoxy, correct belief;

---

85. Ibid., pp. 176–178.
86. Lloyd-Jones, 'William Williams and Welsh Calvinistic Methodism', pp. 198–199.
87. Lloyd-Jones, *The Unsearchable Riches of Christ*, p. 213.
88. Christopher Catherwood, *Five Evangelical Leaders* (London: Hodder and Stoughton, 1984), p. 93.

they wanted to "feel" Him. They laid tremendous emphasis upon the place of feelings in our Christian experience.'[89] Lloyd-Jones contrasted this with the common evangelical approach which said, 'Do not worry about your feelings, believe the bare word of God.' For Lloyd-Jones this was 'the lowest form of assurance'.[90] Lloyd-Jones found it significant that the eighteenth-century Methodists, in England and in Wales, as they met together in little groups or classes, had as their main aim 'to state their experiences to one another, and to examine one another's experiences, and to discuss them together'. He argued that 'the thing that characterized Methodism was this pneumatic element. Over and above what they believed, there was this desire to feel and to experience the power of the Spirit in their lives.'[91]

It was natural, as Lloyd-Jones set out this vision in the 1960s and 1970s, that some people would ask how what he was describing related to Pentecostal or new charismatic churches. There were elements in the spirituality of the charismatic movement which Lloyd-Jones queried. Speaking to the Westminster Conference in 1976, he noted that Jonathan Edwards always spoke of 'an outpouring of the Spirit', whereas, Lloyd-Jones commented, 'we are hearing much about what is called "renewal"', a common term used by charismatic leaders.[92] Lloyd-Jones was not impressed. 'They dislike the term revival; they prefer "renewal". What they mean by that is that we have all been baptized with the Spirit at the moment of regeneration, and that all we have to do therefore is to realize what we already have and yield ourselves to it. That is not revival!'[93] However, Lloyd-Jones had no doubt that gifts of the Spirit such as speaking in tongues and miracles remained present in the church. From his study of revival, he had a framework which helped him to assess unusual phenomena. He noted in a 1959 sermon that, in revival, phenomena begin to be manifest: 'Sometimes people are so convicted and feel the power of the Spirit to such an extent that they faint and fall to the ground . . . And sometimes people seem to fall into a state of unconsciousness, into a kind of trance, and may remain like that for hours.' In a later sermon, Lloyd-Jones suggested that 'these phenomena are not essential to revival . . . yet it is true to say, that, on the whole,

---

89. Lloyd-Jones, 'William Williams and Welsh Calvinistic Methodism', pp. 195–196.

90. Lloyd-Jones, *Joy Unspeakable*, pp. 91–92. See also Lloyd-Jones, 'William Williams and Welsh Calvinistic Methodism', pp. 198–199.

91. Lloyd-Jones, 'William Williams and Welsh Calvinistic Methodism', p. 200.

92. See Peter Hocken, *Streams of Renewal: The Origins and Early Development of the Charismatic Movement in Great Britain* (2nd ed., Carlisle: Paternoster Press, 1997).

93. Lloyd-Jones, 'Jonathan Edwards and the Crucial Importance of Revival', p. 368.

they do tend to be present when there is a revival'. He also referred to 'certain mental phenomena . . . You will find this phenomenon of prophecy, this ability to foretell the future, frequently present.'[94] All of this, for Lloyd-Jones, had to do with a revived church. 'The Spirit', he affirmed, 'is sovereign and in revival manifests his sovereignty.'[95]

The revived church, for Lloyd-Jones, was not necessarily a united church. Indeed, he sometimes suggested that revival would lead to separation. Speaking to the British Evangelical Council's annual conference in Westminster Chapel in October 1973, he drew lessons from Elijah's clash with the prophets of Baal (1 Kgs 18): 'If your revival is not to be ephemeral and end in nothing, you must follow this right through and destroy the false. You must rid yourself of the heretics. The tragedy of the present hour is that the church has tolerated the heretics.' If the false prophets could not be excommunicated, because evangelicals were in a small minority within their denomination, the only option was separation:

> The only occasion that you will find in the history of revivals when a revival has not led to a separation has been when the church has held to orthodox doctrine and the fire has come upon that. There is no need to separate then. But when the church has gone wrong, secession follows . . . The Spirit will not come down when the prophets of Baal are in control and mainly in evidence.[96]

Lloyd-Jones vehemently opposed the view that Christian unity was needed before revival was experienced. The answer to that error was 'all in Church history'. Those who made unity a priority were 'so blinded by their prejudice, that they deny blatant facts. The first of these is that in the past, even when the Church has been acutely divided, more so than she is today, God has sent revival.' Lloyd-Jones considered that the Spirit did bring people together in unity, but he also argued that 'revival creates a new division, such as had happened between the Church of England and Methodism'.[97] It was relatively uncontroversial to propose that revival caused division between those who opposed it and those who accepted it, but there was

---

94. Lloyd-Jones, *Revival*, pp. 110–111, 134–135.

95. Lloyd-Jones, *Prove All Things*, p. 121.

96. D. M. Lloyd-Jones, 'True and False Religion', in Hywel Rees Jones (ed.), *Unity in Truth: Addresses Given by Dr D. Martyn Lloyd-Jones at Meetings Held under the Auspices of the British Evangelical Council* (Darlington: Evangelical Press, 1991), p. 164.

97. Lloyd-Jones, *Revival*, p. 31.

the deeper problem of the historical divisions between those who were equally committed to revival – most notably the Arminian and Calvinistic divide. Lloyd-Jones acknowledged that he found it 'very difficult' to account for the bifurcation. One suggestion he made was 'national characteristics'. John Wesley, the Arminian Methodist, was described by Lloyd-Jones as 'the most typical Englishman of whom I have ever read'.[98] It was significant, for Lloyd-Jones, that in Wales the Methodists 'remained purely Calvinistic' until the end of the nineteenth century.[99] Lloyd-Jones was Welsh, 'not just nationally but spiritually'.[100] From the mid-1960s, Lloyd-Jones focused on evangelicals coming together outside mixed denominations and it is surely no coincidence that among Baptists it was largely leaders of the Baptist Revival Fellowship who left the Baptist Union.[101] In this context, Packer questioned how Lloyd-Jones's belief in the sovereignty of God in revival related to 'the certainty he seemed to have that an alliance of separated churches would have unique spiritual vitality'.[102] However, this is to over-play Lloyd-Jones's interest in any alliance of churches. The vision of revival dwarfed questions of church unity.

Although spiritual experience was at the heart of Lloyd-Jones's vision, he also believed that a revival should be accompanied by careful theological thinking. It was here that Jonathan Edwards was so important to him. Edwards was, for Lloyd-Jones, 'pre-eminently the theologian of revival, the theologian of experience, or as some have put it "the theologian of the heart"'.[103] Lloyd-Jones, as Hughes commented, 'had little patience with the type of Christianity that is thoughtless or irrational or easy-going, that is to say, untheological Christianity'.[104] What inspired Lloyd-Jones about Edwards was that here was someone with a 'mighty intellect' who was at the same time unparalleled in his knowledge of 'the workings of the human heart, regenerate and unregenerate'. To turn from Edwards's writings to a well-known book like William James's *Varieties of Religious Experience* (1902) was like 'turning from a solid book to

---

98. Lloyd-Jones, 'William Williams and Welsh Calvinistic Methodism', p. 201.

99. Ibid., p. 202.

100. Christopher Catherwood, 'Afterword', in Catherwood (ed.), *Chosen by God*, p. 275.

101. See Ian M. Randall, 'Baptist Revival and Renewal in the 1960s', in Kate Cooper and Jeremy Gregory (eds.), *Revival and Resurgence in Christian History* (Woodbridge: Boydell Press), pp. 341–353, esp. pp. 350–351.

102. Packer, 'A Kind of Puritan', p. 55.

103. Lloyd-Jones, 'Jonathan Edwards and the Crucial Importance of Revival', p. 361.

104. Hughes, 'The Theologian', p. 166.

a paper-back'.[105] Edwards was 'unique', 'superlative' and 'pre-eminently the expert' in his analysis of individual and communal spiritual experience. 'If you want to know anything about true revival,' Lloyd-Jones insisted, 'Edwards is the man to consult. His knowledge of the human heart, and the psychology of human nature, is quite incomparable.'[106]

Inevitably, Lloyd-Jones paralleled the Edwardsian balance of thought and experience with Welsh Calvinistic Methodism. In Wales a new hymn book by William Williams came out in 1763 and 'as the people began to sing these great expressions of theology a revival broke out'.[107] Singing on its own was not an exercise usually commended by Lloyd-Jones as having spiritual value. He believed, for example, that the time given to singing in charismatic meetings was 'inordinately long'.[108] What for Lloyd-Jones was significant about Williams, as a hymn-writer who stimulated revival, was that he combined the great theological themes taken up and versified by Isaac Watts with the experience to be found in Charles Wesley's hymns. This combination was part of the genius of Calvinistic Methodism. Lloyd-Jones argued that although Calvinistic Methodists read the Puritans a great deal, Calvinistic Methodism was not a mere continuation of Puritanism. The new element was 'the revival aspect'. In the light of this, Lloyd-Jones suggested that 'Jonathan Edwards must be called a Calvinistic Methodist'.[109] Whether Edwards, the New England Congregationalist, would have recognized this description is not the point: what mattered was that for Edwards, who for Lloyd-Jones was the doyen of theological thinkers, religion was that which 'belongs essentially to the heart'.[110]

The vision of a revival that would change society was implicit in much of what Lloyd-Jones said as he examined revivals from the past, but he rarely spelled out how contemporary societal change might happen. In 1959 all-night prayer meetings for revival were organized and it was hoped that Lloyd-Jones would lend his support. That did not happen.[111] Perhaps one reason for this was that he had a vision for the radical redirection of the church which he realized was not widely shared. Indeed, he argued in 1959 that it was no use saying 'Let's pray for revival', since there were ways in which the church's thinking

---

105. Lloyd-Jones, 'Jonathan Edwards and the Crucial Importance of Revival', p. 361.

106. Ibid., p. 362.

107. Lloyd-Jones, 'William Williams and Welsh Calvinistic Methodism', pp. 202–203.

108. Henry Tyler, 'The Encourager', in Catherwood (ed.), *Chosen by God*, p. 247.

109. Lloyd-Jones, 'William Williams and Welsh Calvinistic Methodism', p. 205.

110. Lloyd-Jones, 'Jonathan Edwards and the Crucial Importance of Revival', p. 357.

111. Murray, *Lloyd-Jones: Fight of Faith*, p. 384.

and acting had to change before such prayer was made.[112] There was no future, according to Lloyd-Jones, for churches that stressed 'mass meetings' or 'entertainment'. Those outside the church were 'attracted finally by power'.[113] Preaching on Ephesians 4:4–6, Lloyd-Jones spoke about the effects of revival: Christians becoming aware of 'a presence, of a power, or a glory', a 'clarity of understanding of truths', a 'sense of unity' (although this was perhaps slightly at odds with some of his other statements about unity), and powerful effects on unbelievers, 'fools who came to scoff remained to pray'.[114] Revival stimulates life in the church and then affects those outside.[115] Lloyd-Jones offered statistical evidence of the lasting effects of the revivals of the eighteenth century and the mid-nineteenth century.[116] However, he seems to have struggled to envision a new revival. In an interview in 1980 he stated, 'All my life I've opposed setting "times and seasons", but I feel increasingly that we may be in the last times.' He saw no prospect for evangelical renewal in England. 'Nothing but a great outpouring of the Spirit – which is what I mean by revival – can possibly retrieve the situation.' But that seemed unlikely. 'I am afraid', he admitted, 'I see nothing but collapse.'[117] 'Then', he said in a 1959 sermon, 'the Church was filled with life, and she had great power, the gospel was preached with authority, large numbers of people were converted regularly.'[118] Lloyd-Jones found it easier to talk about such power 'then' – at times in the past – than 'now'.

Conclusion

Revival, for Lloyd-Jones, was real and powerful. The two main characteristics of revivals in the history of the church, he told the 1959 Puritan Conference, were an 'extraordinary enlivening of the members of the church' and 'the conversion of masses of people'.[119] There was, he argued consistently, a tremendous need for such a revival. Only through the experience of revival would the

---

112. Lloyd-Jones, *Revival*, p. 37.

113. Ibid., pp. 62–63.

114. D. M. Lloyd-Jones, *Christian Unity: An Exposition of Ephesians 4:1 to 16* (Edinburgh: Banner of Truth, 1980), pp. 78–80.

115. Lloyd-Jones, *Revival*, p. 99.

116. Ibid., pp. 105–107.

117. Carl Henry, 'An Interview', in Catherwood (ed.), *Chosen by God*, pp. 104–105, 108.

118. Lloyd-Jones, *Revival*, p. 26.

119. Lloyd-Jones, 'Revival: An Historical and Theological Survey', p. 2.

church become – as had happened in the past – 'alive and full of power, and of vigour, and of might'.[120] All other solutions to the needs of the time were hopelessly inadequate. He was adamant that a revival is a 'miracle', something that can only be explained as 'the direct action and intervention of God'. While human efforts could produce evangelistic campaigns, 'they cannot and never have produced a revival'.[121] Queries might be raised about this. Did this teaching divert people away from the normal work of seeking to build up strong Christian communities that were effective in evangelism even when they did not see revival? Leith Samuel noted with approval that in 1979 Lloyd-Jones said that he was now persuaded that godliness was more important than revival.[122]

Lloyd-Jones was also well aware of the queries raised about the way he linked revival with the baptism of the Spirit. The arguments for a post-conversion Spirit baptism seemed to many to be biblically insecure. Yet Lloyd-Jones strongly opposed the idea that the baptism of the Spirit was received at regeneration, suggesting that when this kind of theology was promoted people stopped praying for revival and the church was weakened.[123] As he outlined the hindrances to revival, he expressed his fear that some of the Reformed teaching which opposed the understanding of the baptism of the Holy Spirit that he espoused could mean a 'quenching of the Spirit'. He saw this as a tragedy which would 'tend to delay revival'.[124] Alongside such forthright warnings, Lloyd-Jones's positive aim was to stimulate a desire for a more powerful awareness of spiritual things, and in particular he was determined to focus attention on the awareness of 'the glory and the holiness of God' and a 'clear view of the love of God'.[125] Lloyd-Jones held out a grand and inspirational vision of revival to his hearers, painting a picture of the story of revivals with sweeping brush strokes. He was convinced that what was once more required was 'something that is so striking and so signal that it will arrest the attention of the whole world. That is revival.'[126]

© Ian M. Randall, 2011

---

120. Lloyd-Jones, *Revival*, p. 26.
121. Ibid., pp. 111–112.
122. Leith Samuel, 'A Man under the Word', in Catherwood (ed.), *Chosen by God*, p. 202.
123. Murray, *Lloyd-Jones: Fight of Faith*, pp. 386–387.
124. Lloyd-Jones to J. A. Shep, 28 February 1969; Lloyd-Jones to Klaas Runia, 28 February 1969, in Murray (ed.), *Lloyd-Jones: Letters 1919–1981*, pp. 196–201.
125. Lloyd-Jones, *Revival*, pp. 100–102.
126. Ibid., p. 183.

4. LLOYD-JONES AND THE CHARISMATIC CONTROVERSY

Andrew Atherstone, David Ceri Jones and William K. Kay

Martyn Lloyd-Jones's relationship with the Pentecostal and charismatic movements has long been a source of intense controversy, both during his lifetime and in subsequent decades. His posthumously published sermons, *Joy Unspeakable: The Baptism with the Holy Spirit* (1984) and *Prove All Things: The Sovereign Work of the Holy Spirit* (1985), originally preached in 1964–5, have provoked fiercer debate than any of his other writings. John Piper, addressing the Bethlehem Conference for Pastors in Minneapolis in 1991, claimed that the sermons reveal that Lloyd-Jones discovered 'power evangelism' long before John Wimber.[1] Others have argued that *Joy Unspeakable* and *Prove All Things* are inconsistent with Lloyd-Jones's Reformed principles, evidence of 'a great man in decline, possibly suffering from a sort of theological Alzheimer's disease'.[2] Yet similar doctrine underpins earlier expositions, delivered in the

---

1. John Piper, 'A Passion for Christ-Exalting Power: Martyn Lloyd-Jones on the Need for Revival and Baptism with the Holy Spirit' (1991), www.desiringgod.org (accessed 5 April 2011). For Wimber's debt to Lloyd-Jones, see 'God's Wonder Worker', *Christianity Today* (14 July 1997), p. 47; J. I. Packer, 'The Intellectual', in David Pytches (ed.), *John Wimber: His Influence and Legacy* (Guildford: Eagle, 1998), p. 259.

2. Reported in Graham Harrison, 'Dr D. M. Lloyd-Jones', in *God Is Faithful: Papers Read at the 1999 Westminster Conference* (London: Westminster Conference, 2000), p. 106.

mid- and later 1950s and edited by the Doctor's own hand for the Banner of Truth Trust.

Lloyd-Jones's teaching on baptism with the Holy Spirit has already been examined in detail by Michael Eaton and, especially as it applies to preaching, by Tony Sargent.[3] This chapter sheds new light on the subject by analysis of two interwoven themes. It considers his relationship with emerging charismatic leaders during the 1960s and 1970s, principally Michael Harper, Terry Virgo and R. T. Kendall, as well as one senior Pentecostal pastor, Billy Richards. It also examines the reception of his published sermons on Spirit baptism, brought forth during his retirement and immediately after his death, and the growing crescendo of controversy which engulfed them.

'Only half converted'?

In September 1962 one of Lloyd-Jones's friends and confidants, the Anglican evangelical scholar Professor Philip E. Hughes, published a remarkable editorial in the *Churchman*. He described his recent visit to California where glossolalia and other Pentecostal phenomena had broken out within the Protestant Episcopal Church, led by clergymen like Dennis Bennett of St Mark's Church, Van Nuys in Los Angeles and Frank Maguire of Holy Spirit Church, Monterey Park. At first sceptical, the professor was impressed by what he witnessed because it seemed to result in transformed lives and revitalized congregations, increased urgency in daily evangelism, heightened joy and love among Christian disciples and victorious prayer for physical healing. It reminded Hughes of the book of Acts and he concluded that it 'points only in one direction, namely, that the Breath of the Living God is stirring among the dry bones of the major, respectable, old-established denominations, and particularly within the Episcopalian Church'.[4] Meanwhile, on the other side of the Atlantic, within the Church of England, young evangelical clergymen began to testify to similar spiritual encounters. For example, David Watson (curate at the Round Church in Cambridge) prayed to be filled with the Spirit and discovered a new reality of the presence of God, joyful spontaneous praise (though not yet in 'tongues'),

---

3. Michael A. Eaton, *Baptism with the Spirit: The Teaching of Dr Martyn Lloyd-Jones* (Leicester: Inter-Varsity Press, 1989); Tony Sargent, *The Sacred Anointing: The Preaching of Dr Martyn Lloyd-Jones* (London: Hodder and Stoughton, 1994).

4. Philip E. Hughes, 'Editorial', *Churchman*, vol. 76 (September 1962), p. 131.

a heightened love for the Bible and remarkable fruitfulness in personal evangelism.[5] Michael Harper (curate of All Souls, Langham Place under John Stott) had a parallel experience in September 1962 which he described as 'earthshaking . . . everything leapt off the page of the scripture'.[6] He received deep conviction of sin, 'wonderfully fresh revelations of truth' from the Bible, a new love for people, intimacy in prayer and 'liberty and power in my ministry which I had never thought possible'.[7] Other Anglican friends were also eagerly caught up in this wave of charismatic renewal, such as John Collins (vicar of St Mark's, Gillingham) and David MacInnes (curate of St Helen's, Bishopsgate under Dick Lucas). As these young ministers struggled to interpret their spiritual experiences in the light of biblical theology, it was to Martyn Lloyd-Jones they turned for advice. Harper made the first approach and Lloyd-Jones pronounced himself 'delighted' with the news, urging that they must meet 'without delay',[8] so the men gathered together at Westminster Chapel on 9 April 1963.[9] As they shared their testimonies, the Doctor spoke of a similar experience in his own life, during a convalescence in Wales in 1949, which had given him a new authority in preaching.[10] Lloyd-Jones pronounced, 'Gentlemen, I believe that you have been baptized with the Holy Spirit,' though Watson thought this was a category mistake and continued to interpret his experience as filling with the Spirit.[11] This private encouragement of young charismatics was not an isolated instance. On another occasion, Lloyd-Jones was approached by a student who was troubled after receiving the gift of tongues. The preacher asked, 'Well what

---

5. David Watson, *You Are My God: An Autobiography* (London: Hodder and Stoughton, 1983), pp. 54–56.

6. Robbie Low, 'The Interview: Michael Harper', *New Directions*, vol. 1, no. 17 (October 1996), p. 18.

7. Michael Harper, 'An Anglican Priest and the Holy Spirit' (1964), quoted in Peter Hocken, *Streams of Renewal: The Origins and Early Development of the Charismatic Movement in Great Britain* (2nd ed., Carlisle: Paternoster, 1997), p. 75.

8. Martyn Lloyd-Jones to Michael Harper, 5 April 1963, London, Lambeth Palace Library [LPL]: Harper Papers.

9. Hocken, *Streams of Renewal*, p. 77; Teddy Saunders and Hugh Sansom, *David Watson: A Biography* (London: Hodder and Stoughton, 1992), p. 71.

10. For this 'foretaste of glory' amidst spiritual anguish, see Iain H. Murray, *D. Martyn Lloyd-Jones: The Fight of Faith 1939–1981* (Edinburgh: Banner of Truth, 1990), pp. 207–221.

11. Watson, *You Are My God*, p. 57.

are you worried about? Bring along some of your friends who have been blessed, & we'll have fellowship.'[12]

In May 1963 Harper hosted a confidential meeting at All Souls for evangelical ministers to hear Frank Maguire. Lloyd-Jones recommended a number of men from the Westminster Fellowship who should be invited,[13] and he went himself, sitting alongside Stott.[14] Several other Pentecostal and charismatic pioneers from the United States of America began to tour through Britain, hosted by Harper, such as Larry Christenson (a Lutheran pastor from California), David du Plessis of the Assemblies of God (known as 'Mr Pentecost'), and Jean Stone (editor of *Trinity* magazine).[15] There were, however, some disasters, like the visit in the autumn of 1963 by Samuel Doctorian, an Armenian revivalist and faith healer nicknamed 'the Billy Graham of the East'.[16] Lloyd-Jones initially offered his support and was said to be '*right* behind Doctorian', unlike Stott or Lucas.[17] Yet when Lloyd-Jones spoke with Doctorian in person he was immediately suspicious, partly because the prophet was 'too nicely dressed'. He concluded that the visitor was a counterfeit, a verdict confirmed in his mind by reports which Lloyd-Jones received from friends in the United States.[18]

Among the staff team at All Souls, divisions were deepening over Spirit baptism and speaking in tongues. Stott tackled the topic at the Islington Clerical Conference in January 1964, in a lecture soon published as *The Baptism and Fullness of the Holy Spirit*. He exhorted his listeners and readers, especially those who had had the privilege of receiving 'some unusual visitation of the Spirit', not to urge upon others a baptism with the Spirit 'as a second and subsequent experience entirely distinct from conversion, for this cannot be proved from Scripture'.[19] Indeed, he argued that Spirit baptism was 'the

---

12. Reported in Jeanne Harper to David Lillie, 26 August 1964, LPL: Harper Papers.

13. Martyn Lloyd-Jones to Michael Harper, 11 April 1963, LPL: Harper Papers.

14. Michael Harper, *None Can Guess* (London: Hodder and Stoughton, 1971), p. 57; Michael Harper, 'Divided Opinions', *Renewal*, no. 187 (December 1991), p. 19.

15. Hocken, *Streams of Renewal*, pp. 113–118. On Du Plessis see further, Brinton Rutherford, 'From Prosecutor to Defender: An Intellectual History of David J. Du Plessis' (unpublished PhD thesis, Fuller Theological Seminary, 2000).

16. See further, Samuel Doctorian, *God Will Not Fail You: A Life of Miracles in the Middle East and Beyond* (Washington, DC: Believe Books, 2006).

17. Jeanne Harper to David Lillie, nd (c. 26 July 1963), LPL: Harper Papers.

18. Michael Harper to David Lillie, 28 December 1963, LPL: Harper Papers.

19. John R. W. Stott, *The Baptism and Fullness of the Holy Spirit* (London: Inter-Varsity Fellowship, 1964), pp. 38–39.

initiatory Christian experience'.[20] Despite never referring to Stott directly, Lloyd-Jones publicly opposed his doctrine from the pulpit at Westminster Chapel, a dispute described by one observer as a 'clash of the Titans'.[21] It was perhaps even more significant than the famous confrontation between the two men over church unity at the National Assembly of Evangelicals in Westminster Central Hall two years later.

By March 1964 Harper had announced his resignation from All Souls and soon established the Fountain Trust, to stimulate charismatic renewal among the old mainline denominations and to pray for worldwide revival. He was heartened that Lloyd-Jones seemed much more sympathetic to the aims of the emerging charismatic leadership than did Stott. Nonetheless, the fragility of this alliance was starkly exposed by the Doctor's address to the annual meeting of the Evangelical Library in December 1963. Speaking unguardedly to what Iain Murray calls his 'inner circle', Lloyd-Jones surveyed the contemporary scene.[22] He spoke pejoratively of the 'recrudescence' of interest in the gifts of the Holy Spirit, especially tongues-speaking, among Episcopalians, Lutherans, Methodists and other doctrinally mixed denominations in the United States. In particular he assailed Du Plessis for flirting with the World Council of Churches, Lloyd-Jones's *bête noire*. Du Plessis had defended this involvement in *The Spirit Bade Me Go: The Astounding Move of God in the Denominational Churches* (1963), but Lloyd-Jones spoke out against him:

> They are obviously very ready to listen to his message. Unfortunately, in that message he says that doctrine does not matter, that what matters is a living experience. That is what they are ready to believe in their bankruptcy, because they are not Reformed in their doctrine. They are ready to listen to a man who can speak in an authoritative manner on the basis of personal experience. Doctrine is being discounted and experience is being exalted at its expense.[23]

Nevertheless, at the same time, Lloyd-Jones celebrated that many within the old Pentecostal denominations on both sides of the Atlantic were awakening to their need of Reformed theology as propagated by the Evangelical Library, the Banner of Truth Trust and the Puritan Conference.

When the address was published, George Canty (a pastor in the Elim

---

20. Ibid., p. 19.
21. Watson, *You Are My God*, p. 59.
22. Murray, *Lloyd-Jones: Fight of Faith*, p. 482.
23. D. M. Lloyd-Jones, 'Address', *Annual Meeting of the Evangelical Library* (1963), p. 13.

Pentecostal Church) wrote on behalf of the British Pentecostal Fellowship to explain that in their view there was 'no basic clash' between Reformed and Pentecostal doctrine. He also observed that Lloyd-Jones had a significant following among the older Pentecostal denominations because of his abilities as a Bible expositor.[24] However, among Harper's circle there was consternation behind the scenes. David Lillie, a former Plymouth Brother and leading charismatic, complained to Harper that the Evangelical Library address was

> a very painful revelation of the Doctor's real position in relation to the things of the Holy Spirit, and it is quite different from what I had been led to think . . . Frankly the article is in a most divisive and partisan spirit, and reveals what I had always rather feared concerning this new 'puritan' movement; viz: a dangerous tendency to boost the old puritans as infallible interpreters of 'the truth' and to discourage all independent thinking on matters theological. I find it hard to reconcile what the Doctor said in this address with all that I had previously heard as to his views. I begin to wonder what his motive was in cultivating your fellowship. Did he want to lead you gently into the sure paths of the Puritans and away from these American enthusiasts?[25]

Lillie believed that pitting Reformed against Pentecostal theology in the way Lloyd-Jones had done was 'really pernicious, and hardly the way to advance the cause of Christian unity'.[26] He continued:

> I find it hard to understand how such an intelligent and spiritual man can be so unbalanced. In view of his unique position among evangelicals this bald advocacy of 'reformed doctrine' as the 'open sesame' to all that is blessed, is quite dangerous. Better to expose it now than later when indoctrination has done its deadly worst with the usual camp followers.[27]

Harper chastised Lillie for his harsh tone,[28] but concurred with his general diagnosis:

> I'm afraid that I do agree with you. It seems that PURITANISM is another of those props which the Lord would have us get rid of. It saddens me greatly to see the

---

24. Letter from George Canty, *English Churchman* (22 May 1964), p. 9.
25. David Lillie to Michael Harper, 23 August 1964, LPL: Harper Papers.
26. David Lillie to Michael Harper, 28 August 1964, LPL: Harper Papers.
27. David Lillie to Michael Harper, 31 August 1964, LPL: Harper Papers.
28. Michael Harper to David Lillie, 7 September 1964, LPL: Harper Papers.

effect all this has on people. It makes them narrow, controversial and blind to new insights. I wish people would see that these phrases REFORMED THEOLOGY, CALVINISM, PENTECOSTALISM, are meaningless to the Lord. He wants us to be Bible Christians – not leaning on past teachers . . . I still think Dr L-J is sincere and sees partially the things we do – but he is only half-converted and the other half seems to blind him to seeing the whole.[29]

In a strike against the ministry of the Evangelical Library and the Banner of Truth Trust in disseminating old literature, Harper declared that the Lord's blessing would rest on those who were 'not looking to past history, but waiting upon God to make new glorious church history'. Despite Lloyd-Jones's private encouragements, the Harpers began to sense (in the words of Jeanne Harper) that 'his Calvinist Puritan views have come to the fore-front again. Many years of study & the intellectual approach must be hard to break for anyone.'[30] In the autumn of 1964 Michael Harper concluded that Lloyd-Jones's stance had 'considerably hardened' and that he was 'strongly opposed to the present movement of the Spirit'.[31] Ironically this verdict coincided with the launch of Lloyd-Jones's longest treatment of the subject of the baptism and gifts of the Holy Spirit. The sermons, which focused on the account of Jesus' baptism in the River Jordan and his subsequent anointing by the Spirit, arose naturally as part of Lloyd-Jones's exposition of the early chapters of John's Gospel. Later published as *Joy Unspeakable* and *Prove All Things*, they gained a posthumous reputation (as will be seen below) for being highly sympathetic to charismatic theology.

Despite their obvious disagreements, Harper continued to meet with Lloyd-Jones approximately twice a year throughout the 1960s, even after the Doctor's retirement from Westminster Chapel.[32] He recalled, 'I received regular invitations to have tea privately with him. He always called me "my boy", and ended by encouraging me just before I left. "Keep it up, boy", he would say, in contrast to the rather icy conversations I had on this subject with John Stott.'[33] Nevertheless, these encouragements remained firmly behind

---

29. Michael Harper to David Lillie, 26 August 1964, LPL: Harper Papers.

30. Jeanne Harper to David Lillie, 26 August 1964, LPL: Harper Papers. Jeanne Harper had herself been converted through the preaching of Lloyd-Jones in the early 1950s, while she was a student at the Royal Academy of Music and attended Westminster Chapel; Jeanne Harper to Andrew Atherstone, 23 February 2011.

31. Michael Harper to David Lillie, 4 October 1964, LPL: Harper Papers.

32. Michael Harper to Iain Murray, 3 January 1989, LPL: Harper Papers.

33. Harper, 'Divided Opinions', pp. 19–20.

closed doors. Harper tried to persuade Lloyd-Jones to speak on behalf of the Fountain Trust, but without success: 'I always found him evasive about it and I think on the whole he was not too keen to be publicly seen to be supporting our approach to the ministry of the Holy Spirit.'[34] Although some in the 1960s may have wished to make Lloyd-Jones the figurehead of charismatic renewal in Britain, Harper was under no such illusion: 'He would have none of that. He remained a sympathetic spectator, nothing more.'[35]

Lloyd-Jones did, however, enjoy closer friendship with some Pentecostal ministers during the 1960s, notably with W. T. H. (Billy) Richards, a fellow Welshman.[36] Richards was part of a Pentecostal and coal-mining family from Crosskeys, in the valleys of South Wales near Cardiff, and at the age of fourteen he joined his father down the local pit. A few years later he felt called to be a preacher, after a vivid dream in which he saw himself on a platform with the leading Pentecostal pastors of the day. In 1937, aged twenty-one, Richards left home for the Assemblies of God Bible College in London and pastored two small congregations in the capital at the height of the Blitz. In June 1943 he founded the Slough Gospel Tabernacle (since renamed King's Church International), which began with five people in a dilapidated Scout hut but rapidly grew so that within fifteen years it had three hundred members and six Sunday schools in the district catering for five hundred children.[37] Richards pioneered Christian Witness youth camps, 'doorbell evangelism', a popular correspondence course on soul-winning and a bi-monthly magazine, *Dedication*, which built up a circulation of six thousand. His publications included *Pentecost Is Dynamite* (1972) and a series of 'charismatic booklets' on themes such as *Power Over Demons, Spirit-Filled Christians* and *Speaking in Tongues in the Local Church*.[38]

When Lloyd-Jones first met Richards at Windsor in the early 1940s, he was 'greatly impressed' with the young Pentecostal evangelist.[39] The two men stayed in touch over the years, but were drawn into deeper friendship during the 1960s by their common concern for biblical truth in defiance of ecumenism.

---

34. Michael Harper to Iain Murray, 3 January 1989, LPL: Harper Papers.

35. Harper, 'Divided Opinions', p. 20.

36. On Richards, see especially William K. Kay, *Inside Story: A History of British Assemblies of God* (Mattersey: Mattersey Hall, 1990), pp. 209–212.

37. *To God Be The Glory: The Story of the Birth and Growth of the Gospel Tabernacle, Slough, Buckinghamshire: A Record of Fifteen Years of Revival, 1943–1958* (Slough, 1958).

38. *Dedication*, vol. 5 (September – October 1973), p. 20.

39. D. M. Lloyd-Jones, 'This Man Was a Spiritual Statesman', *Dedication*, vol. 6 (November – December 1974), p. 21.

Richards joined the Westminster Fellowship and Lloyd-Jones occasionally preached for him at the Slough Gospel Tabernacle.[40] The Doctor came to view Richards as a 'spiritual statesman'.[41] Likewise Omri Jenkins (secretary of the European Missionary Fellowship and a close colleague of Lloyd-Jones) celebrated Richards's big-hearted embrace for all who loved the Scriptures and his fearless exposure of anything which undermined basic evangelical truth.[42] For example, when the Fountain Trust invited charismatics from across the theological spectrum to address its ground-breaking Guildford Conference in 1971, including Roman Catholics, Richards wrote strongly against it.[43]

When Richards died suddenly in September 1974, aged fifty-eight, Lloyd-Jones delivered a tribute at his funeral in Slough and later hosted a memorial service in Westminster Chapel. His memorial sermon was a clarion call to uncompromising evangelical conviction in the face of the ecumenical threat. He contrasted the new charismatic movement, or 'neo-Pentecostalism', unfavourably with classic Pentecostalism as represented by Richards and the Assemblies of God. Lloyd-Jones declared, 'I never like the prefix "neo". Whether it is neo-Calvinist, neo-Pentecostal, neo-anything. It generally means that it isn't the original thing at all, but that it wants to appear as if it were.'[44] He warned that modern charismatics were seeking to foster Christian unity, even with Roman Catholics and Modernists, on the basis of a common spiritual experience rather than shared doctrine. Yet he praised Richards's witness for weighty biblical truth:

> This was our friend's emphasis and this, if I may say so, was the emphasis of early Pentecostalism. It was sound in the faith. It called itself fundamentalist and it was fundamentalist and I don't think we would be here tonight and we wouldn't have the story of Pentecostal Churches in this country were it not for their adherence to the Scriptures. They 'stood fast in the faith'.[45]

---

40. See, e.g., *Dedication*, vol. 6 (March – April 1974), p. 15.

41. Lloyd-Jones, 'This Man Was a Spiritual Statesman', p. 21.

42. T. Omri Jenkins, 'A Man of Exceptional Calibre', *Dedication*, vol. 6 (November – December 1974), p. 13.

43. Michael Harper, 'Renewal – The First Twenty Years', *Renewal*, no. 121 (February – March 1986), p. 4. See further, Ho Yan Au, 'Grassroots Unity and the Fountain Trust International Conferences: A Study of Ecumenism in the Charismatic Renewal' (unpublished PhD thesis, University of Birmingham, 2008).

44. D. M. Lloyd-Jones, 'Fight for Survival', *Dedication*, vol. 7 (January – February 1975), p. 12.

45. Ibid., p. 13.

Lloyd-Jones exhorted the congregation, 'The greatest need of this country tonight is a spiritual revival, an outpouring of the Spirit of God . . . that was what our friend, Mr Richards, stood for. That's what I stand for and it was a privilege to stand with him in this.'[46] Seven years later, after Lloyd-Jones's own death, Billy Richards's son Wesley Richards (the new pastor of Slough Gospel Tabernacle) wrote of the high esteem for Lloyd-Jones in the older Pentecostal denominations:

> The breadth of vision and immense spiritual stature of Dr Martyn Lloyd-Jones have long been appreciated by many of us in 'classical Pentecostal' circles. In this specially-sent servant of God we recognised a memorable ministry, confirming the possibility (and not mere desirability) of combining a gifted exposition of objective truth with a fresh up-to-date anointing of the Holy Spirit. Whatever the differences of view about spiritual gifts and callings, who could dissent from the Doctor's increasingly insistent theme that the great need of the church today is of a baptism with the Holy Spirit quite distinct from regeneration or sanctification – a baptism of fire?[47]

Wesley Richards observed that Lloyd-Jones 'would not be smeared with an anti-charismatic brush . . . Quite simply the Doctor could not and, more to the point, would not be pigeon-holed, no matter who tried to caricature him, as either a compromising charismatic or a cold-eyed Calvinist.'[48]

Reformed Pentecostalism?

Martyn Lloyd-Jones preached frequently during the 1950s and 1960s on the doctrine of the Holy Spirit, but it was only during the last decade of his life, as he prepared these sermons for publication during his retirement, that they began to attract wider attention and controversy.

One of Lloyd-Jones's first new books after leaving Westminster Chapel was *Preaching and Preachers* (1971), a set of lectures originally delivered at Westminster Theological Seminary in Philadelphia. In the final lecture, the climax to the series, he expounded what he called 'the greatest essential in connection with preaching', the 'unction and the anointing of the Holy Spirit'.[49] In

---

46. Ibid., p. 16.

47. A. Wesley Richards, 'And the Pentecostals', *Evangelical Times* (April 1981), p. 16.

48. Ibid.

49. D. M. Lloyd-Jones, *Preaching and Preachers* (London: Hodder and Stoughton, 1971), p. 304.

his customary way he turned to the historical books of the New Testament and argued that the repeated outpourings of the Holy Spirit on the early Christians should be regarded as normative. He dismissed those who 'confine all this to the Apostolic era' as 'leaving very little for us at the present time' and accused them of an act of 'prejudice'.[50] Drawing on a variety of historical examples that included Hugh Latimer and John Bradford, the seventeenth-century Scot John Livingstone, John Wesley and George Whitefield, and Dafydd Morgan, one of the leaders of the 1859 revival in Wales, Lloyd-Jones in a rousing *tour de force* urged that 'nothing but a return of this power of the Spirit on our preaching is going to avail us anything'.[51] From a charismatic perspective, Michael Harper in *Renewal* magazine was celebrating: 'The passages on the work of the Holy Spirit will thrill all those who have already discovered the secret of anointed power in preaching, and will encourage others to seek for this blessing.'[52] Yet for Donald Macleod (minister of a Free Church of Scotland congregation in Glasgow, and Professor of Systematic Theology from 1978 at the Free Church College, Edinburgh), *Preaching and Preachers* was the first hint that something was awry with Lloyd-Jones's pneumatology.

This initial 'misgiving' had grown to 'distress' by the time Macleod read *The Sons of God* (1974), Lloyd-Jones's exposition of Romans 8:5–17, originally preached at Westminster Chapel on Friday nights between March 1960 and April 1961.[53] Of the thirty-three sermons in the published volume, eighteen dealt with just verses 15–17, and eight, amounting to well over a hundred pages and a quarter of the whole book, focused on Paul's teaching about the witness of the Spirit in verse 16. For Lloyd-Jones this was entirely justified because verse 16 contained 'one of the most glorious statements concerning Christian experience found anywhere in the Bible from beginning to end' and was a verse that 'constitutes the hallmark of the evangelical Christian'.[54] In his painstaking exposition of these verses Lloyd-Jones tied the witness of the Spirit to the Christian's assurance of salvation, seeing the witness as largely synonymous with the baptism of the Spirit. The witness, he argued, was a 'direct operation' of the Holy Spirit 'on our minds and hearts and spirits', the

---

50. Ibid., pp. 314–315.

51. Ibid., p. 325.

52. Michael Harper, 'Raising Standards', *Renewal*, no. 37 (February – March 1972), p. 35.

53. Donald Macleod, 'The Sealing of the Spirit', *Monthly Record of the Free Church of Scotland* (January 1979), p. 3.

54. D. M. Lloyd-Jones, *Romans: An Exposition of Chapter 8:5–17: The Sons of God* (Edinburgh: Banner of Truth, 1974), p. 285.

'acme, the zenith of assurance and certainty of salvation!'[55] More controversial perhaps were his comments on how this experience was to be accessed. While he freely admitted that it could sometimes come through reading the Bible, the Spirit could also work directly, without the intermediary of the written Scriptures. 'It has happened to many without any words at all,' Lloyd-Jones asserted, 'it is just an inner consciousness in the spirit given by the Spirit of God Himself, apart from Scripture.'[56] To support his case he peppered his sermons with wide-ranging examples from evangelical history. The Puritans John Owen, Thomas Goodwin and John Flavel were prominently quoted, as were Jonathan Edwards, Whitefield, Wesley, Howel Harris and William Williams, Pantycelyn, from the eighteenth century and C. H. Spurgeon, Charles Finney and D. L. Moody from the nineteenth.

Lloyd-Jones was aware that his opinions on the witness of the Spirit ran contrary to 'the common evangelical teaching',[57] but he was unrelenting in his criticism of those who argued that Spirit baptism was synonymous with conversion. It was a view, he asserted, that 'does great violence' to the book of Acts and that quenches the Spirit.[58] A similar emphasis is apparent in Lloyd-Jones's more extensive treatment of quenching the Spirit in May 1961, part of his series on Ephesians 6:10–13, published as *The Christian Warfare* (1976). He reiterated:

> There is nothing, I am convinced, that so 'quenches' the Spirit as the teaching which identifies the baptism of the Holy Ghost with regeneration. But it is a very commonly held teaching today, indeed it has been the popular view for many years. It is said that the baptism of the Holy Spirit is 'non-experimental', that it happens to every one at regeneration. So we say, 'Ah well, I am already baptized with the Spirit; it happened when I was born again, at my conversion; there is nothing for me to seek, I have got it all.' Got it all? Well, if you have 'got it all', I simply ask in the Name of God, why are you as you are? If you have 'got it all', why are you so unlike the Apostles, why are you so unlike the New Testament Christians?[59]

The *Evangelical Magazine of Wales* celebrated the expositions in *The Sons of God* as 'excellent', proclaiming that Lloyd-Jones's teaching on Spirit baptism

---

55. Ibid., pp. 301–302.
56. Ibid., p. 307.
57. Ibid., p. 327.
58. Ibid., p. 310.
59. D. M. Lloyd-Jones, *The Christian Warfare: An Exposition of Ephesians 6:10 to 13* (Edinburgh: Banner of Truth, 1976), p. 280.

was 'most convincing' and beyond refutation.[60] Billy Richards's magazine, *Dedication*, was equally enthusiastic:

> In many ways the crisis of the ecumenical challenge to the evangelical position
> has been overtaken by the greater crisis of the present charismatic movements.
> Confusion abounds world-wide as to what is genuine and what is spurious. Sadly,
> some evangelicals have retreated to the shaky ground of prejudice and tradition,
> but here in this volume is a clarion call to men of God everywhere to examine the
> scriptural position, to pursue the Divine experience and so live it and teach it that
> assurance and enlargement are the inevitable blessings.[61]

However, some readers discerned a 'leaning towards (neo-) Pentecostalism'.[62] Professor Robert Strong of Reformed Theological Seminary, Jackson, Mississippi, believed that Lloyd-Jones lacked his 'customary cogency' when discussing Spirit baptism.[63] Likewise the *Monthly Record of the Free Church of Scotland* warned that his doctrine of post-conversion experience 'makes too many second-class citizens in the kingdom of God'.[64]

Concerns were further heightened in some Reformed circles by the publication of *God's Ultimate Purpose* (1978), Lloyd-Jones's exposition of Ephesians 1, originally preached between October 1954 and July 1955. Most controversial were the five sermons devoted to Ephesians 1:13 and the 'sealing with the Spirit'. As with his exposition of the witness of the Spirit, Lloyd-Jones conflated the sealing of the Spirit with the baptism of the Spirit, seeing them as interchangeable terms for basically the same experience.[65] He therefore maintained that the sealing with the Spirit was an experience distinct from conversion, 'something subsequent to believing, something additional to believing',[66] a position that differed markedly from what he had argued in an

---

60. Review by Brian Harris, *Evangelical Magazine of Wales*, vol. 14 (August – September 1975), p. 20.

61. Review by Eric Lavender, *Dedication*, vol. 7 (January – February 1975), p. 19.

62. Review by Leslie C. Allen, *Harvester*, vol. 54 (November 1975), p. 317.

63. Review by Robert Strong, *Westminster Theological Journal*, vol. 38 (Spring 1976), p. 412.

64. Review by R. A. Finlayson, *Monthly Record of the Free Church of Scotland* (October 1975), p. 162.

65. D. M. Lloyd-Jones, *God's Ultimate Purpose: An Exposition of Ephesians One* (Edinburgh: Banner of Truth, 1978), pp. 263–264.

66. Ibid., p. 250.

earlier printed lecture[67] and left him open to the charge of teaching a second blessing or at least a two-stage Christian experience. Lloyd-Jones hung his exegesis on the translation of the Authorized Version ('*after* that ye believed, ye were sealed with that Holy Spirit of promise')[68] whereas the recently published New International Version (1978) offered a significant alternative ('*when* you believed, you were marked with a seal, the promised Holy Spirit'). In these sermons the sealing with the Spirit was also linked closely with the issue of revival. With characteristic hyperbole, he asserted that 'it is one of the most vital of all the New Testament doctrines with respect to revival and reawakening in the Christian Church'.[69] As with his sermons on Romans 8:16, Lloyd-Jones used extensive historical evidence to support his case, though it sometimes had the unfortunate effect of appearing to carry more weight than the scriptural exposition. In these sermons he drew on Richard Sibbes, Flavel, Goodwin, Wesley, Edwards, the Welsh Baptist Christmas Evans, Moody and Finney, quoting personal testimonies that could be interpreted as examples of the sealing with the Spirit. The experiences of each of these men seemed to fit Lloyd-Jones's central contention that the sealing, baptism or witness of the Spirit was something 'God tends to do . . . for us at certain special times'. Few occasions were more significant in Lloyd-Jones's reckoning than times of heightened spiritual emotion and religious revival.[70]

Reviewers of *God's Ultimate Purpose* were especially critical of these five sermons on Ephesians 1:13, challenging Lloyd-Jones's exegesis and argumentation at several points.[71] From Sydney in Australia, John Chapman (a leading evangelist) warned his fellow Anglican evangelicals that Lloyd-Jones's views on Spirit baptism were 'exactly the same as present day charismatics'.[72] From Scotland, Macleod went further, assailing the whole tenor of the volume:

---

67. D. M. Lloyd-Jones, 'Christ our Sanctification', in *Christ our Freedom: The Message of the Fourth International Conference of Evangelical Students, Cambridge, 1939* (London: Inter-Varsity Fellowship, 1940), pp. 60–68.

68. Lloyd-Jones, *God's Ultimate Purpose*, pp. 248–250.

69. Ibid., p. 244.

70. Ibid., p. 299.

71. E.g, review by Andrew T. Lincoln, *Journal of the Evangelical Theological Society*, vol. 23 (June 1979), pp. 172–173; review by 'F. M.', *Free Presbyterian Magazine*, vol. 84 (June 1979), pp. 185–186; review by Keith Weston, *Churchman*, vol. 93 (1979), p. 264; review by F. F. Bruce, *Evangelical Quarterly*, vol. 51 (October – December 1979), pp. 245–246.

72. Review by John C. Chapman, *Australian Church Record* (2 July 1979), p. 6.

Its whole orientation fills us with foreboding. How, for example, does all this differ from Pentecostalism? We find the same doctrine of Holy Spirit baptism and the same appeal to certain passages in the Book of Acts, and although Dr Lloyd-Jones does not teach that Spirit baptism is always attested by tongue-speaking he nowhere criticises modern pretensions to that gift. This is all the more remarkable when one considers his sustained and vigorous condemnation of non-experiential Calvinism or dead orthodoxy. The threat posed by the latter is not nearly as serious as that represented by the charismatic movement, which seems set to swamp English evangelicalism in a wave of mindless hedonism. The need of the hour is to confront the new Finneyism. Instead, the most highly respected figure within Reformed theology speaks in such a way that the new charismatics claim him as one of themselves – and with some plausibility.[73]

Macleod continued:

The views now being put forward by the Doctor imply a serious disparagement of the ordinary Christian, who is portrayed as lacking the baptism of the Spirit, the sealing of the Spirit and even the earnest of the Spirit. By any standards these are serious defects and yet, allegedly, they characterise most Christians. It is impossible to harmonise this point of view with the New Testament . . . But the most disconcerting thing of all is that in Dr Lloyd-Jones' new emphasis we have a reversion to the theology of *plus*, which in its various forms has bedevilled the Christian church. For the Galatians, it was Christ plus circumcision. For mediaeval Catholicism, it was Christ plus the sacraments. For Wesley, Christ plus sinless perfection. For Dispensationalism, Christ plus an earthly millennium. For Pentecostalism, Christ plus Holy Spirit baptism. Now from within the very bosom of Reformed theology there comes the same plea for *more*, not merely for growth or progress but for a new definitive experience which will put us in a special category. We reject the whole concept of *plus*.[74]

Reformation Today joined the cry of alarm. Its editor, Erroll Hulse (pastor of Cuckfield Baptist Church in Sussex), likened Lloyd-Jones to Tertullian, the great theologian of the early church who had joined the quasi-charismatic Montanist sect in his latter years.[75] Hulse had attended Westminster Chapel during his time as a student at London Bible College in the mid-1950s and

---

73. Macleod, 'Sealing of the Spirit', p. 4.
74. Ibid., pp. 4–5.
75. Erroll Hulse, 'Tertullian – A Present Day Parallel?', *Reformation Today*, no. 48 (March – April 1979), p. 1.

greatly admired Lloyd-Jones's preaching which he thirstily imbibed.[76] He was a close friend of Iain Murray and was business manager of the Banner of Truth Trust for its first decade, from 1957.[77] Nevertheless, Hulse now suggested that Lloyd-Jones had got away with publishing his unexpurgated sermons on Romans 8 and Ephesians 1, without major revision, because there was no-one at the Banner of Truth Trust strong enough to challenge him:

> Such was the Doctor's reputation that there was no question of correcting his doctrine. It was difficult enough to urge abridgement to reduce the inevitable repetition that comes from any worthy preacher, but to have said that his doctrine on Ephesians 1:13 was wrong, or to have said that the section on Romans 8:15ff was erroneous, and in some places is story-telling rather than exposition, would have been preposterous. Whereas most literary contributions are severely scrutinised, there was nobody who could correct the Doctor.[78]

Meanwhile, Geoffrey Thomas (minister of Alfred Place Baptist Church, Aberystwyth) portrayed Lloyd-Jones and his followers within the Evangelical Movement of Wales as 'theoretically Pentecostal', because they held to a Pentecostal doctrine of Spirit baptism but never allowed opportunity for miracles, prophecy or glossolalia in their tightly controlled conduct of public worship.[79] Indeed, this was a charge brought by Donald Macleod as well. Recalling Lloyd-Jones's style in the 1960s, Macleod wryly observed, 'Nothing could have been further removed from Pentecostal worship than the service in Westminster Chapel – the most inflexible in which we have ever participated.'[80] According to Iain Murray, Lloyd-Jones (now almost an octogenarian) was 'indignant' at Thomas's suggestion that his practice and teaching were contradictory. In private the Doctor complained to Murray, 'I was against Pentecostalism and still am. My doctrine of the baptism of the Spirit is that it

---

76. Erroll Hulse, 'The Life and Legacies of Martyn Lloyd-Jones', *Reformation Today*, no. 211 (May – June 2006), pp. 3–17.

77. John J. Murray, *Catch the Vision: Roots of the Reformed Recovery* (Darlington: Evangelical Press, 2007), pp. 113, 121.

78. Erroll Hulse, 'Will You Attend the Wedding?', *Reformation Today*, no. 84 (March – April 1985), p. 13.

79. Geoffrey Thomas, 'Wales Greets Scotland', *Monthly Record of the Free Church of Scotland* (November 1979), p. 217.

80. Donald Macleod, 'The Lloyd-Jones Legacy', *Monthly Record of the Free Church of Scotland* (October 1983), p. 209.

gives full assurance. I have never been satisfied with any speaking in tongues that I have heard . . . It is very unfair to put the label pentecostal on me.'[81]

Just months before Lloyd-Jones's death, controversy was renewed at the annual conference of the British Evangelical Council, held in Carlisle in November 1980.[82] Amongst the keynote speakers was Peter Lewis, whom Christopher Catherwood called 'one of the Doctor's more brilliant young followers . . . very much in tune with the Doctor's thinking on the baptism with the Holy Spirit'.[83] In 1969, at the age of twenty-three, Lewis had been appointed pastor of Hyson Green Baptist Church in Nottingham, later renamed Cornerstone Evangelical Church.[84] He enjoyed a close association with Lloyd-Jones throughout the 1970s and described him as 'the greatest single earthly factor in my ministry . . . my spiritual father'.[85] Influenced by Lloyd-Jones's calls to evangelical unity, Lewis led his congregation in 1976 out of the doctrinally mixed Baptist Union and into the Fellowship of Independent Evangelical Churches. He was a popular speaker and author with a monthly column in the *Evangelical Times*.[86]

At the British Evangelical Council conference Lewis urged the need for rapprochement between Reformed and charismatic Christians as one of the keys to evangelical unity in the 1980s, especially in the face of the secularist advance.[87] He argued that increasing fragmentation between these two constituencies was threatening to ruin evangelical witness. Lewis declared:

> Being evangelical is not simply having the right creed: it is word *and* spirit, it
> is revelation *and* inspiration, it is holding fast to the form of sound words *and*
> demonstrating their timeless truth by their present power. It is only such true and
> full-orbed evangelicalism that can reverse the advances of liberalism in the Christian
> church today.

---

81. Murray, *Lloyd-Jones: Fight of Faith*, p. 695.
82. 'On the Brink of Advance', *Evangelical Times* (December 1980), pp. 1, 20.
83. Christopher Catherwood, *Martyn Lloyd-Jones: A Family Portrait* (Eastbourne: Kingsway, 1995), p. 175.
84. Colin Wolfe, 'Cornerstone: Rising Above "The Square Mile of Crime"', *Evangelical Times* (October 1984), pp. 2–3.
85. Peter Lewis, 'As a Young Man's Man', *Evangelical Times* (April 1981), p. 17.
86. Lewis's column in the *Evangelical Times*, 'Come to think of it', ran from October 1980 to May 1983.
87. Peter Lewis, 'And Now For . . . The Evangelical Advance', *Evangelical Times* (February 1981), pp. 12–13.

He appealed for an end to party names like 'Calvinist' and 'Charismatic', and urged both sides to come together under one united banner to constitute

> an evangelical force of quite astounding potential. We all recall how Spurgeon longed to unite the theology of the old Calvinists with the fire of the old Methodists – and we know how well he exemplified the mingling of both elements in his bright and beautiful life. A solidly Reformed leader among us today professes with relish to be more than half a Calvinist-Methodist [a thinly-veiled reference to Martyn Lloyd-Jones] and that carefully-cherished balance has kept him miles in front of most of us.

Lewis suggested that many Reformed evangelicals 'reasoned like liberals' by, *de facto*, cutting two entire chapters out of an apostolic epistle (1 Cor. 12; 14) and that they 'argued like Catholics' by interpreting Scripture through the lens of Reformed tradition. Since the purpose of the British Evangelical Council was to promote evangelical unity, he urged the organization to shed its 'overwhelmingly traditionalist and reformed image' by making a concerted effort to attract the Pentecostal and house church movements: 'It is time now to accept (at long last) the traditional Pentecostal churches as our equals and fellow-travellers.' As a practical sign of mutual appreciation, Lewis recommended that Reformed pastors should exchange pulpits with ministers from the Assemblies of God and the Elim Pentecostal Church.

These controversial exhortations to the British Evangelical Council were delivered, according to Lewis, with the blessing and imprimatur of Lloyd-Jones himself. He recalled how Lloyd-Jones had urged him to fresh study of the Reformed/charismatic question and how he went to the Doctor with a draft of his BEC address, 'full of excitement but also full of trepidation':

> I had more than encouragement from him – he positively glowed! 'But', I said, 'is there nothing that you disagree with or disapprove of?' 'Nothing at all', he replied emphatically, 'I am with you one hundred percent without reservation.' Thereafter, for no less than three months leading up to the Conference, he followed up his encouragement with constant and fervent prayer: 'I am praying for this every single day – and it is a burden from the Holy Spirit.' That sentence was repeated in almost every telephone conversation. He felt that the call to the churches on that occasion might be the beginning of a breakthrough which he clearly wanted to see.[88]

---

88. Lewis, 'As a Young Man's Man', p. 17.

It was no surprise, therefore, that the chief critics of Lloyd-Jones on Spirit baptism were also critics of Lewis. Hulse acknowledged that these views derived directly from the Doctor, but warned, 'In his plea for us to attend the wedding of Mr Reformed and Miss Charismatic, Peter Lewis is still unable to see that the two systems are incompatible.'[89] Likewise Macleod rejected the suggestion that Pentecostals and charismatics knew more of spiritual experience than those in the Reformed tradition, pointing to the flood of experimental theology which had flowed from 'the Calvinistic fountain-head' through Puritan authors like Richard Sibbes, John Howe, Thomas Manton, Thomas Brooks and John Owen. Macleod complained:

> We are used enough to tirades against Calvinistic aridity. But to get them,
> even in small bulk, from intelligent Calvinists such as Mr Lewis is too much
> . . . Pentecostalism cannot simply become Calvinism plus tongue-speaking.
> It has a radically different order of priorities and a totally divergent view of the
> work of Christ, of conversion, of faith and of holiness. We fear it as we do
> Romanism or Dispensationalism and not even the charming, impulsive volubility
> of Mr Lewis can placate us. In short, he must choose between us and the
> charismatics.[90]

Elsewhere Macleod wrote:

> The idea of fusing Calvinism with Pentecostalism is absurd. They belong to different
> theological universes. To seek a form of worship with more spontaneity, openness
> and participation is one thing. To seek to merge a theology which says we are
> complete in Christ with one which denies it is quite another. By the standards of
> historic orthodoxy, Pentecostalism is not simply an error. It is a heresy, fundamentally
> anti-trinitarian and legalistic.[91]

Nevertheless, at Lloyd-Jones's death in March 1981, it was Lewis not Macleod who was given the honour of preaching at his packed memorial service in Westminster Chapel. In the *Evangelical Times* he continued to emphasize the priorities of his mentor: 'He was a man of the Spirit; a man of experience and vision; a charismatic long before the popular movement which is called by

---

89. Hulse, 'Will You Attend the Wedding?', p. 14.

90. Donald Macleod, 'Can we become Calvinistic Pentecostals?', *Monthly Record of the Free Church of Scotland* (February 1981), p. 37.

91. Macleod, 'The Lloyd-Jones Legacy', p. 209.

that name.'[92] In *Renewal* magazine Lewis argued that Lloyd-Jones had refused to write off the Pentecostal and charismatic movements as so many other Reformed theologians had done because of 'his loyalty to Scripture, his sense of history, his breadth of reading and his profound humility before the things of God'.[93]

One of the leading proponents of a marriage between Reformed and charismatic theology was Terry Virgo, who had been a contemporary of Peter Lewis at London Bible College from 1965 to 1968. As a young student Virgo was a member of a charismatic church near Charing Cross, but the congregation only met on Sunday mornings so he was free to spend each Sunday evening at Westminster Chapel during Lloyd-Jones's last three years in charge. Virgo recalled, 'One could hardly imagine a greater contrast in church life, but the magnificent preaching of the Doctor made up for the formality and impersonal nature of the meetings.'[94] He was impressed by the similarities in theological emphasis between Lloyd-Jones and Arthur Wallis (a prominent neo-Pentecostal), and thrilled by the Doctor's 'breadth and depth of vision. He was no narrow-minded, safe, evangelical but a man with a big God who was to be sought for all his many blessings.' Troubled by raging student arguments over the validity of charismatic gifts, Virgo sought out Lloyd-Jones for advice in the vestry of Westminster Chapel after one evening service. In this memorable private interview Lloyd-Jones informed Virgo that 'the great sin of the evangelical world was to put God in a box and tell him what he could and could not do'. He urged the young student to pray continually for revival through the outpouring of the Holy Spirit.[95]

For eleven years Virgo pastored an Evangelical Free Church in Seaford, near Brighton, gradually moving it in a charismatic direction. From 1979 his widening sphere of influence throughout Sussex and beyond led to oversight of a growing family of churches, first styled 'Coastlands' and later 'New Frontiers'. He became an 'apostle' in the 'restoration' movement which aimed to restore the church to its primitive glory, more radical ecclesiologically than charismatic 'renewal',[96] and established the Downs Bible Week, an annual restorationist

---

92. Lewis, 'As a Young Man's Man', p. 17.

93. Peter Lewis, 'Lessons for a Weak Church', *Renewal*, no. 115 (February – March 1985), p. 43.

94. Terry Virgo, *No Well-Worn Paths* (Eastbourne: Kingsway, 2001), p. 60.

95. Ibid., p. 71.

96. See especially, Andrew Walker, *Restoring the Kingdom: The Radical Christianity of the House Church Movement* (4th ed., Guildford: Eagle, 1998); William K. Kay, *Apostolic*

convention modelled on Bryn Jones's Dales Bible Week at Harrogate. Virgo's home church from 1979 was Brighton and Hove Christian Fellowship (since renamed Church of Christ the King), whose pastor, Henry Tyler, had been a member of the Westminster Fellowship and was drawn into charismatic renewal through the Baptist Revival Fellowship in the mid-1960s.[97] Tyler and Virgo visited Lloyd-Jones to share their vision for the restoration of the church and the Doctor encouraged them with the need for Spirit-led revival. He starkly told his guests, 'Evangelicalism is dead. God must do a new thing.'[98] This encounter reveals that Lloyd-Jones's private encouragement of charismatic leaders, far from being limited to men like Michael Harper in the mid-1960s, continued unabated up to the end of his life. He also agreed to speak publicly at one of Virgo's large meetings in Hove Town Hall, but reluctantly withdrew under pressure from some members of the Westminster Fellowship who sent a delegation to his home begging him not to go.[99]

Virgo was happy to describe himself as 'a charismatic Calvinist . . . I have always been extremely comfortable with the combination of reformed doctrine and charismatic experience, feeling deeply convinced that they are both rooted in biblical revelation.'[100] In December 1983 he was invited to address the Westminster Fellowship on the principles of the restoration movement, but faced a barrage of antagonistic questions from a packed auditorium. In the words of *Restoration* magazine, it was 'nearly the scene of his imminent martyrdom'.[101] Lewis, who was chairing the meeting, was 'outraged' at this rude treatment of the visiting speaker and accused his colleagues of 'coming from their backstreet Bethels with their deep-frozen Berkhofs and thinking that they spoke for all of Christendom'. Virgo felt that the majority of the Westminster Fellowship had 'written me off as an upstart heretic who needed to be put soundly in his place', and contrasted this hostile reception with the warm encouragement he had personally received from Lloyd-Jones in the same chapel some years earlier.[102]

Networks in Britain: New Ways of Being Church (Milton Keynes: Paternoster, 2007); Terry Virgo, *Restoration in the Church* (Eastbourne: Kingsway, 1985).

97. Hocken, *Streams of Renewal*, p. 135.

98. Henry Tyler, 'The Encourager', in Christopher Catherwood (ed.), *Martyn Lloyd-Jones: Chosen By God* (Crowborough: Highland Books, 1986), p. 248.

99. Peter Lewis to Andrew Atherstone, 26 May 2011.

100. Virgo, *No Well-Worn Paths*, p. 62.

101. 'People Profile', *Restoration* (May – June 1987), p. 13.

102. Virgo, *No Well-Worn Paths*, pp. 135–136.

Another charismatic leader who received early encouragement from Lloyd-Jones was R. T. Kendall, his successor as minister of Westminster Chapel from 1977. Kendall was brought up in Kentucky in the American Deep South within the Church of the Nazarene, an evangelical denomination which sprang from the Wesleyan holiness movement. In 1973, aged thirty-eight, he arrived in England with his wife and children to undertake doctoral research in Puritan history at Oxford University.[103] He was soon invited to lecture on the Puritans at the Westminster Conference and the Evangelical Library, and came to Lloyd-Jones's attention.[104] Meanwhile, Westminster Chapel was struggling to find a new minister after the shock departure in May 1974 of Glyn Owen, who resigned after only four and a half years and moved to Toronto.[105] At first the pastorate committee recommended Eric Alexander from the Church of Scotland, but because he did not share Lloyd-Jones's separatist convictions he did not win sufficient backing from the chapel membership.[106] Next they called John Blanchard of the Movement for World Evangelization, but he declined the invitation in September 1976 despite the urging of Lloyd-Jones and endorsement by 91% of the members.[107] During these years of hiatus, more than sixty different visiting preachers occupied the Westminster Chapel pulpit

----

103. R. T. Kendall, 'The Nature of Saving Faith from William Perkins (d. 1602) to the Westminster Assembly (1643–1649)' (unpublished DPhil thesis, University of Oxford, 1976); later published as R. T. Kendall, *Calvin and English Calvinism to 1649* (Oxford: Oxford University Press, 1979).

104. R. T. Kendall, 'In the Teaching of William Perkins and his Followers', in *Living the Christian Life* (London: Westminster Conference, 1975), pp. 45–60; R. T. Kendall, 'John Cotton: First English Calvinist?', in *The Puritan Experiment in the New World* (London: Westminster Conference, 1977), pp. 38–50; R. T. Kendall, *The Influence of Calvin and Calvinism upon the American Heritage* (London: Evangelical Library, 1976).

105. London, Westminster Chapel Archives [WCA]: Church Meeting Minute Book (January 1959 – May 1977), 27 February 1974.

106. WCA: Church Meeting Minute Book, 26 November 1974 and 22 January 1976. Alexander had also been considered as minister in immediate succession to Lloyd-Jones, before Glyn Owen; see WCA: Church Meeting Minute Book, 24 April and 12 June 1969; D. M. Lloyd-Jones to Eric Alexander, 29 March 1969, in Iain H. Murray (ed.), *D. Martyn Lloyd-Jones: Letters 1919–1981* (Edinburgh: Banner of Truth, 1994), pp. 216–217.

107. WCA: Church Meeting Minute Book, 9 June and 15 September 1976; Brian H. Edwards, *John Blanchard: Guernsey's Evangelist, Author and Christian Apologist* (Leominster: Day One, 2009), pp. 72–74.

and the congregation dwindled to approximately one hundred and fifty.[108] In some desperation, the pastorate committee turned to Kendall. He happened to be preaching at Westminster Chapel on the Sunday after Blanchard's rejection letter arrived, and was asked to serve as visiting minister for six months to provide some continuity while they searched for a permanent replacement.[109] Martyn and Bethan Lloyd-Jones went personally to visit the Kendalls at their home in Northamptonshire to persuade them, and Lloyd-Jones told Kendall, 'You have nothing to lose. It will be good for Westminster Chapel and it will be good for you.'[110]

Kendall's early ministry was warmly approved and in May 1977 he was invited to stay permanently, endorsed by 92% of the membership.[111] Lloyd-Jones encouraged him that it was a higher proportion of the vote than Campbell Morgan or he would have received.[112] The Kendalls settled in Ealing in West London, deliberately so as to be near the Lloyd-Joneses, and the two men developed a mentor relationship. Each Thursday morning Kendall met with the Doctor for two hours, to seek advice on chapel ministry and to talk through what he planned to preach the following Sunday. He also called on Lloyd-Jones each Sunday evening to report on the day's activities.[113] Lloyd-Jones's warm acceptance of the American opened doors for him within the Reformed community across Britain. Kendall was elected as national president of the Fellowship of Independent Evangelical Churches in 1981 and was invited to speak for the Evangelical Movement of Wales, the Free Church of Scotland and the British Evangelical Council. Nevertheless, in these circles he still felt 'like a fish out of water. Some of the dear brothers seemed so narrow.'[114]

Kendall regularly chauffered Lloyd-Jones to Charing Cross Hospital for medical tests during his final illness and wept at his bedside on the morning he died, on St David's Day 1981.[115] However, after Lloyd-Jones's death the

---

108. WCA: Church Meeting Minute Book, 31 March 1976; R. T. Kendall, *In Pursuit of His Glory: My 25 Years at Westminster Chapel* (London: Hodder and Stoughton, 2002), pp. 18, 244.

109. WCA: Church Meeting Minute Book, 13 October 1976; Kendall *In Pursuit of His Glory*, p. 7.

110. Kendall, *In Pursuit of His Glory*, p. 8.

111. WCA: Church Meeting Minute Book, 25 May 1977.

112. Kendall, *In Pursuit of His Glory*, p. 12.

113. Ibid., pp. 25, 49.

114. Ibid., pp. 41–42.

115. Ibid., pp. 35, 37.

atmosphere at Westminster Chapel quickly changed. During April and May 1982, Kendall persuaded the American evangelist Arthur Blessitt to preach for six Sunday evenings in a row. Blessitt's visit was, in Kendall's words, the start of 'a new era' for the chapel and the 'greatest turning point for the whole of my twenty-five years in London'.[116] It was 'like the earthquake that rolled the stone away on Easter morning . . . It set us free, broke us loose from doing things as they had always been done.'[117] Blessitt introduced three significant innovations – charismatic choruses sung with a guitar, street evangelism and an altar call at the end of each sermon. Soon afterwards Kendall ceased to preach in the traditional Geneva gown. The chapel entered a volatile period and several members resigned. Kendall's invitations to speak on Reformed platforms dried up. When Billy Graham preached at Westminster Chapel in May 1984, prior to 'Mission England', Kendall told him that instituting the changes they had begun was 'like turning a battleship around in the middle of a river'.[118] During the resulting turmoil the minister was even accused of heresy by six of his twelve deacons, for allegedly teaching antinomianism in *Once Saved, Always Saved* (1983) and other published writings.[119] Kendall rode out the storm and continued to move the chapel in a charismatic direction. He was happy to be labelled 'a clandestine Pentecostal' and during the 1990s he worked in close collaboration with North American neo-Pentecostals like Paul Cain and Rodney Howard-Browne. Through their ministry Westminster Chapel witnessed dramatic healings, prophetic utterances and the manifestations of the

---

116. Ibid., pp. 66–67.

117. Ibid., p. 71.

118. Ibid., p. 87.

119. For the dismissal of the dissenting deacons in January 1985, see R. T. Kendall. *The Anointing: Yesterday, Today, Tomorrow* (London: Hodder and Stoughton, 1998), p. 149; Iain H. Murray, '"Openness to the Holy Spirit": How Westminster Chapel was Turned Round', *The Banner of Truth*, no. 486 (March 2004), pp. 29–31. For Kendall's perspective on this antinomian controversy, see R. T. Kendall, *Once Saved, Always Saved: Biblical Reassurance for Every True Believer* (London: Hodder and Stoughton, 1983); R. T. Kendall, 'Speaking Theologically: Antinomianism and the Law', *Westminster Record*, vol. 60 (March 1985), pp. 14–18; Kendall, *In Pursuit of His Glory*, pp. 94–98. For a critique by one of the sacked deacons, see Richard Alderson, *No Holiness, No Heaven! Antinomianism Today* (Edinburgh: Banner of Truth, 1986); Richard Alderson, 'The Theology of R. T. Kendall', *CRN Journal* (Christian Research Network), no. 1 (Autumn 1997), pp. 23–25; no. 2 (Spring 1998), pp. 23–25; no. 8 (Spring 2000), pp. 13, 30–32.

Toronto Blessing. Kendall celebrated that Lloyd-Jones's former domain had at last become 'a Spirit Church, not just a Word Church'.[120]

In his memoir of his quarter-century at Westminster Chapel, *In Pursuit of His Glory* (2002), Kendall emphasized his close relationship with Lloyd-Jones in order to legitimate the changes he had ushered in. A dominant theme of the book is Lloyd-Jones's fondness and respect for Kendall and his encouragement and endorsement of Kendall's ministry. He described himself as 'utterly devoted' to the Doctor, whom he called 'a friend, confidant and teacher', likening their relationship to that between Paul and Timothy. Kendall wrote, 'For nearly four years the Doctor and I were very like father and son. There was a time when I may have been closer to him than anybody outside his family.'[121] He claimed that Lloyd-Jones 'warmly supported' his historical thesis on the divergence between Calvin and English Calvinism,[122] and also his controversial teaching on the role of the Law in the life of the Christian.[123] Indeed, he asserted that between 1977 and 1981 'virtually every word' he spoke from the Westminster Chapel pulpit had first been 'vetted' by Lloyd-Jones.[124] In an earlier interview for *Renewal* magazine, to mark Kendall's first decade at the chapel, he exclaimed:

> He knew in advance what I would utter from the pulpit because I went over my sermons with him. That was a priceless privilege. I've missed him, and every week something comes up which makes me wish I could get his advice. I knew how his mind worked and believe that almost everything I have done is in consequence of what he taught me.[125]

Likewise, in *The Anointing* (1998) Kendall reiterated:

> Next to my father, Dr Lloyd-Jones has had more influence on me than anyone else. He put me where I am and taught me how to think . . . Surely no minister this century

---

120. Kendall, *In Pursuit of His Glory*, pp. 167, 169.

121. Ibid., p. 40.

122. Ibid., pp. 15–16, 26–27.

123. Ibid., pp. 43–44, 51–52, 198. Iain Murray contrasts the views of Kendall and Lloyd-Jones in Iain H. Murray, 'Will the Unholy be Saved?', *The Banner of Truth*, no. 246 (March 1984), pp. 1–15; and Murray, *Lloyd-Jones: Fight of Faith*, pp. 721–726.

124. Kendall, *In Pursuit of His Glory*, pp. 247–248.

125. Edward England, 'American Preacher Londoners Love', *Renewal*, no. 131 (April 1987), p. 9.

had such a privilege as I. I could see how his mind worked. I asked him hundreds of questions. I shared with him my secrets and fears. He was like a father to me. I felt so much love from him.[126]

On one occasion Kendall asked the Doctor if he would allow his mantle to fall on him, to which Lloyd-Jones replied, 'It already has if I had any . . . My ministry in Westminster was a wilderness ministry. But I think you are going to take the people over into the Promised Land.'[127]

When it came to pneumatology, Kendall was at particular pains to show that he and Lloyd-Jones were in harmony. He thought that Lloyd-Jones was attracted to him mainly because of his Nazarene background and he understood Lloyd-Jones's exhortation to 'preach like a Nazarene' as a reference to openness to the Holy Spirit.[128] He recounted to the Doctor his intense experience of 'baptism in the Spirit' in Tennessee as a student in 1955 and believed, 'If I am honest, it is what he loved most about me . . . My old experience, combined with the way Dr Lloyd-Jones taught me to think, kept me open to *anybody* in whom I saw an unusual anointing.'[129] The two men were in agreement that sealing with the Spirit was a post-conversion experience, and Kendall wrote:

> Had it not been for Dr Lloyd-Jones's teaching on the 'immediate and direct' witness of the Holy Spirit – he insisted on those very words – I would never have survived at the Chapel. All in the Chapel who were present in the Doctor's day not only knew his views (even if some didn't agree) but also knew how important such was to him. Therefore when I have stressed an openness to the Spirit it was apparent to them that it was not novel teaching. But for Dr Lloyd-Jones, then, I would not have made it through.[130]

And again:

> This made it easier for me. By openness to the Spirit I therefore mean the 'immediate and direct' witness of the Spirit, a phrase Dr Lloyd-Jones would use again and again. It means that we want to know the Holy Spirit directly – not simply through the Word . . . I have taught that we must be open to any way God would choose

---

126. Kendall, *The Anointing*, pp. 1–2.
127. Kendall, *In Pursuit of His Glory*, pp. 34–35.
128. Ibid., pp. 31, 214.
129. Kendall, *The Anointing*, p. 4.
130. Kendall, *In Pursuit of His Glory*, p. 31.

to turn up, whether it has to do with the gifts of the Spirit or signs, wonders and miracles. This is why I have been open to people like Paul Cain and Rodney Howard-Browne.[131]

Kendall reported that Lloyd-Jones was 'very taken' with Blessitt, though he admitted his illustrious predecessor would never have invited Blessitt into the Westminster Chapel pulpit. He was also convinced that Lloyd-Jones would have 'fully accepted' Paul Cain had he lived to meet him.[132] Although Kendall acknowledged that Lloyd-Jones and Cain were 'poles apart theologically', they had a common bond of openness to the Spirit's direct witness.[133]

Kendall's memoir admits almost no disparity between himself and his mentor, though there are hints. For example, he was disappointed when Lloyd-Jones refused in 1978 to write a foreword for his published sermons on Jonah because the young preacher had not yet 'earned my spurs'.[134] He also acknowledged that their relationship was sometimes under strain and that they had 'serious quarrels', though he does not elucidate further.[135] Iain Murray warned readers not to take Kendall's memoir 'at face value'. He suggested that despite the glowing impression given by *In Pursuit of His Glory*, the relationship between Kendall and Lloyd-Jones in fact 'broke down so seriously' that Lloyd-Jones indicated prior to his death that Kendall should have no part in his memorial service. Murray asserted that Kendall knew he had 'given grave theological offence to the Doctor' and did not enjoy his confidence, though again the nature of the offence is not specified.[136] Murray professed his thankfulness that Lloyd-Jones did not live long enough to witness the introduction of neo-Pentecostalism and 'full-blown charismatic confusion' into his former pulpit.[137] Likewise *Reformation*

---

131. Ibid., p. 231.

132. Ibid., pp. 63, 165.

133. Kendall, *The Anointing*, p. 1.

134. Kendall, *In Pursuit of His Glory*, p. 49. See R. T. Kendall, *Jonah: Sermons Preached at Westminster Chapel, London* (London: Hodder and Stoughton, 1978).

135. Kendall, *In Pursuit of His Glory*, p. 36.

136. Murray, 'Openness to the Holy Spirit', pp. 27–28. Kendall did, however, conduct the memorial service for Bethan Lloyd-Jones at Westminster Chapel in February 1991; see Kendall, *In Pursuit of His Glory*, p. 165.

137. Iain H. Murray, *Lloyd-Jones: Messenger of Grace* (Edinburgh: Banner of Truth, 2008), p. 159.

Today saw Kendall's memoir as a revelation of 'what really went wrong at Westminster Chapel'.[138] Nevertheless, Kendall reflected that the true reason he was shunned in Reformed circles was not because of what he taught, but because of where he taught it. The Reformed wing of evangelicalism had for many decades viewed Westminster Chapel and Lloyd-Jones's pulpit as 'sacrosanct and in a very real sense *theirs*', but Kendall transgressed by taking it away from them.[139]

Joy unspeakable

Lloyd-Jones's longest treatment of the baptism and gifts of the Holy Spirit, originally delivered at Westminster Chapel on Sunday mornings between November 1964 and June 1965 as part of his exposition of the early chapters of John's Gospel, was never published in his lifetime. Soon after his death the cassette tapes of these twenty-four sermons were in wide circulation, supplied to eager listeners by the Martyn Lloyd-Jones Recordings Trust in Sussex and heartily endorsed by both *Renewal* magazine and the *Evangelical Times*.[140] Lloyd-Jones had begun to edit the transcripts for publication during his latter years, but he left the task unfinished until it was picked up by his grandson, Christopher Catherwood. The sermons were posthumously published as *Joy Unspeakable: The Baptism with the Holy Spirit* (1984) and *Prove All Things: The Sovereign Work of the Holy Spirit* (1985), not with the Banner of Truth Trust but with Kingsway, a prominent publisher of charismatic literature. It was an unfortunate decision to divide the series into two separate volumes, a year apart, with the order muddled – Graham Harrison called it 'a blunder'.[141] The eight sermons in *Prove All Things*, generally more cautious than those in *Joy Unspeakable*, were actually the central sermons in the original series. They were separated not for any theological reason, but simply because on economic grounds Kingsway were initially unwilling to publish such a long book.[142] Not

---

138. Conrad Mbewe, 'Westminster Chapel – What Happened?', *Reformation Today*, no. 193 (May – June 2003), p. 21.

139. Kendall, *In Pursuit of His Glory*, pp. 150–151.

140. 'Lloyd-Jones Tapes', *Renewal*, no. 113 (October – November 1984), pp. 31–32; full-page advertisement, *Renewal*, no. 114 (December 1984 – January 1985), p. 42; 'The Spirit', *Evangelical Times* (December 1984), p. 21.

141. Harrison, 'Dr D. M. Lloyd-Jones', p. 106.

142. Christopher Catherwood to Andrew Atherstone, 25 April 2011.

until 1995 were the sermons restored to their proper position in a combined volume.[143]

Seasoned readers of Lloyd-Jones encountered little that was new in these two volumes. Anyone familiar with his sermons on Romans 8 or Ephesians 1, or the emphases of his later ministry, was already accustomed to his constant stress on the ministry of the Holy Spirit and the overriding need for revival. Nonetheless, these sermons were his most exhaustive treatment of Spirit baptism, which he again interpreted as the highest form of assurance. He used the terms baptism, sealing and witness of the Spirit interchangeably and bolstered his case with the by now familiar historical examples. Early Protestant Reformers, a select band of English and colonial Puritans and some of the leading evangelicals from the eighteenth and nineteenth centuries all featured once more, but so did some more unexpected names. Tertullian and the Montanists, as well as the North African Donatists and the Waldensians were held up as examples of vital over formal institutional religion. In this volume Lloyd-Jones also drew on Roman Catholic case studies: Thomas Aquinas, the Brethren of the Common Life, some of the late medieval mystics, Savonarola, the German John Tauler and the French Jansenist Blaise Pascal were all pressed into active service.[144]

One of the ways in which this sermon series departed significantly from others on the same subject was in the length to which Lloyd-Jones went to outline the tests that should be applied to distinguish genuine spiritual experience from the counterfeit. These eight sermons at the heart of the larger series formed the separate volume *Prove All Things*. His comments were directed towards two groups in particular. He was, first, determined to warn those who might be susceptible to various forms of charismatic excess. Yet he was equally, if not more, outspoken in his criticisms of those who dismissed Spirit baptism out of hand and were wedded to a cessationist hermeneutic. He argued that in the early church 'the gospel was authenticated . . . by signs, wonders and miracles of various characters and descriptions', and castigated those who believed that this was only a temporary arrangement until the canon of Scripture had been closed, as if they knew 'much more than the apostle Paul of God's truth'.[145] However, he also issued stern warnings against founding

---

143. D. M. Lloyd-Jones, *Joy Unspeakable: The Baptism and Gifts of the Holy Spirit, incorporating Prove All Things* (Eastbourne: Kingsway, 1995).

144. D. M. Lloyd-Jones, *Joy Unspeakable: The Baptism with the Holy Spirit* (Eastbourne: Kingsway, 1984), pp. 105–107, 112–113, 125.

145. Martyn Lloyd-Jones, *Prove All Things: The Sovereign Work of the Holy Spirit* (Eastbourne: Kingsway, 1985), pp. 28, 32.

a movement on the gifts alone, insisting that 'the teaching of Scripture itself, plus the evidence of church history, establishes the fact that the baptism with the Spirit is not always accompanied by particular gifts'.[146] While on the one hand he indicated his willingness to accept the operations of the gifts in the contemporary church,[147] on the other he counselled caution and urged the necessity of testing the spirits.[148] Graham Harrison humorously observed that if Reformed commentators had 'lost their cool' when reviewing Lloyd-Jones on Ephesians 1 and Romans 8, then *Joy Unspeakable* and *Prove All Things* would almost certainly send them over the edge:

> What seems to 'bug' them is that here is not some simplistic Pentecostal from the backwoods . . . but without doubt the greatest preacher of the century, a man mighty in logic and argument, to whom we all owe so much . . . Well, if those earlier volumes sent their blood pressure soaring this one may be guaranteed to give them apoplexy – and signs are not wanting in some quarters that such in fact is the case.[149]

The foreword to *Joy Unspeakable* was contributed by Peter Lewis, who took the opportunity to plead again for a rapprochement between Reformed and charismatic evangelicalism. He insisted, 'For many reasons – biblical, historical and experiential – it is becoming increasingly untenable and even absurd to see these two movements as fundamentally alien to one another.'[150] Lewis claimed that *Joy Unspeakable* was proof that Lloyd-Jones believed charismatic theology to be compatible with the historic Reformed tradition. Likewise, Catherwood maintained that the sermons showed his grandfather to be 'both reformed and charismatic, in the biblical senses of the terms'.[151] He argued that Lloyd-Jones was 'a Bible Calvinist not a System Calvinist. If the Scripture taught something, he had to proclaim it!'[152] At the same period, Catherwood made a point of emphasizing in *Five Evangelical Leaders* (1984) that Lloyd-Jones had

---

146. Ibid., p. 53.

147. Ibid., p. 135.

148. Ibid., ch. 3.

149. Graham Harrison, 'Joy Unspeakable', *Evangelical Magazine of Wales*, vol. 24 (June – July 1985), pp. 11–12.

150. Peter Lewis, 'Foreword', in Lloyd-Jones, *Joy Unspeakable* (1984), p. 8.

151. Christopher Catherwood, 'Introduction', in Lloyd-Jones, *Joy Unspeakable* (1984), p. 13.

152. Christopher Catherwood, *Five Evangelical Leaders* (new ed., Fearn: Christian Focus, 1994), p. 101.

encouraged charismatic and neo-Pentecostal spokesmen like Michael Harper and Terry Virgo and was generally sympathetic to their aims – an interpretation of history strongly resisted by several Reformed reviewers.[153] *Reformation Today* questioned the motives behind the publication of *Joy Unspeakable*, to which the Lloyd-Jones family replied that their intention was simply that 'the Doctor should be allowed to speak for himself', rather than be the posthumous subject of ignorant claims about his true position.[154]

Iain Murray was unconvinced by the arguments in *Joy Unspeakable*. Nevertheless, he did his best to defend his mentor by interpreting the sermons in the most favourable light. He maintained that Lloyd-Jones's views on the baptism with the Spirit could be harmonized with the teaching of the Westminster Confession on assurance, and emphasized that the series had been preached to a biblically literate congregation in the mid-1960s where evangelical foundations could be taken for granted, a very different context from the charismatic crisis of the mid-1980s.[155] Other authors in *The Banner of Truth* likewise insisted that Lloyd-Jones was by no means a 'closet Charismatic' and that any apparent connection with Pentecostalism was merely 'a coincidence of terminology . . . Though we are upset by the very mention of baptism with the Spirit, there is nothing in the Doctor's teaching or experience which would have appeared heretical or even unusual to any Reformed preacher from Calvin to Kuyper.'[156] Harrison, writing in the *Evangelical Magazine of Wales*, was more enthusiastic, celebrating the sermons as Lloyd-Jones at his

---

153. Christopher Catherwood, *Five Evangelical Leaders* (London: Hodder and Stoughton, 1984), pp. 92–94, 104. For responses see, e.g., review by John Marshall, *The Banner of Truth*, no. 257 (February 1985), pp. 27–29; Graham Harrison, 'Five Aces', *Evangelical Magazine of Wales*, vol. 25 (April – May 1986), pp. 10–15.

154. Erroll Hulse, 'Holding Church History in Perspective', *Reformation Today*, no. 92 (July – August 1986), p. 1; 'A Letter from Family Lloyd-Jones', *Reformation Today*, no. 94 (November – December 1986), p. ii.

155. Iain H. Murray, 'Martyn Lloyd-Jones on the Baptism with the Holy Spirit', *The Banner of Truth*, no. 257 (February 1985), pp. 8–15. See further, Murray, *Lloyd-Jones: Messenger of Grace*, pp. 127–163.

156. R. B. Lanning, 'Dr Lloyd-Jones and the Baptism with the Holy Spirit', *The Banner of Truth*, no. 271 (April 1986), pp. 4–5. See also John Marshall, 'Martyn Lloyd-Jones: Prove All Things', *The Banner of Truth*, no. 270 (March 1986), pp. 24–28; R. B. Lanning, 'Prove All Things: Some Further Observations', *The Banner of Truth*, no. 278 (November 1986), pp. 26–29.

'devastating best'.[157] He applauded their theology, but still continued to resist the identification of Lloyd-Jones as a 'reformed charismatic': 'The trouble with being such a great man, as Dr Martyn Lloyd-Jones undoubtedly was, is that when you are removed from the scene the merest pygmies try to claim you as one of them. No one has suffered more in this respect than the beloved Doctor.' Therefore, Harrison insisted, charismatic attempts to 'corner' Lloyd-Jones and posthumously claim his blessing must be resisted.[158]

Not all commentators were convinced by attempts at the Banner of Truth Trust and the Evangelical Movement of Wales to exonerate Lloyd-Jones from the charge of charismatic excess. For example, Hulse believed that the Doctor built his case 'in typical Pentecostal fashion'.[159] Murray was willing to admit that there was a 'degree of looseness' about Lloyd-Jones's teaching on the work and gifts of the Spirit, but Hulse thought this a 'gross understatement'.[160] He wrote:

> My chief difference with my close and longstanding friend Iain Murray, of the Banner of Truth, is that he has always believed that the Doctor's spiritual stature would be adequate to cover the fact that on paper he was always an old time Pentecostalist. As my colleagues in the ministry will testify I always predicted that as soon as the Doctor left this world the Charismatics would capitalise on his Pentecostal views, and all restraints set up by Iain Murray or anybody else, would be about as effective as inflatable children's toys left on a beach. That is precisely what is happening. All the Doctor's sermons on tape are in the hands of the Charismatics who have wasted no time in bringing out their own book to add to the Banner of Truth's Pentecostal material in the volume on Romans 8. To say that the Doctor did not really mean to be Pentecostal, or that he really means something else, is to think sentimentally not realistically.[161]

From a different perspective, Peter Lewis later noted, 'If anyone could "pin down" MLJ's attitude to the Pentecostal/charismatic phenomenon, Mr Murray would do so. Happily, it's not possible! Choosing his quotations with

---

157. Harrison, 'Joy Unspeakable', p. 11.

158. Graham Harrison, in response to Christopher Catherwood, *Evangelical Magazine of Wales*, vol. 25 (April – May 1986), p. 19.

159. Hulse, 'Will You Attend the Wedding?', p. 14.

160. Murray, *Lloyd-Jones: Fight of Faith*, p. 491; Erroll Hulse, 'Dr Martyn Lloyd-Jones: A Prophet of the 20th Century', *Reformation Today*, no. 121 (May – June 1991), p. 23.

161. Hulse, 'Will You Attend the Wedding?', p. 13.

great care, taking deadly aim – he fires! However, many of MLJ's words remain
to jog his arm and spoil the fun.'[162]

Negative reviews of Lloyd-Jones's teaching poured forth from Reformed
commentators. For example, Victor Budgen (minister of Milnrow Evangelical
Church, Rochdale), despite acknowledging that there was much in *Joy
Unspeakable* and *Prove All Things* 'to challenge, to stimulate, to thrill and to
allure', nonetheless chose to focus on their 'grave deficiencies'.[163] From the
United States of America, *The Standard Bearer*, a Reformed magazine, warned
that *Joy Unspeakable* was 'a bad book' full of 'spiritual dangers', contrary to the
teaching of Scripture. The magazine was not surprised that R. T. Kendall had
been able to lead Westminster Chapel so quickly in a charismatic direction,
because Lloyd-Jones had laid 'explicitly charismatic' foundations.[164] The most
outspoken reaction came in *Sword and Trowel* from Peter Masters (minister of
the Metropolitan Tabernacle), a prominent cessationist.[165] He spoke of his
admiration for Lloyd-Jones's call in the 1960s to evangelical separation, but
warned that the Doctor's extensive influence misled many to accept his teaching on spiritual gifts 'without question or criticism . . . and the outcome has been
catastrophic'. Masters described the publication of *Joy Unspeakable* and *Prove
All Things* as 'major tragedies' likely to do 'incalculable harm' to the Reformed
churches. Although he acknowledged Lloyd-Jones was 'by no means a 100%
card-carrying charismatic', he felt it necessary to refute his teaching in order to
help evangelicals withstand 'the current charismatic onslaught':

> The views expressed in these books have led many reformed evangelicals in Britain
> to take an extremely open and tolerant attitude towards the burgeoning charismatic
> movement. Numerous ministers have meekly accepted charismatic infiltration of
> their churches, leading to the loss of a very substantial proportion of previously
> sound causes.[166]

---

162. Peter Lewis, 'For a Generation', *Evangelicals Now* (January 1991), p. 11.

163. Victor Budgen, 'Two Controversial Books Reviewed', *Reformation Today*, no. 92 (July
     – August 1986), pp. 27–28.

164. Herman C. Hanko, 'Charismatic?', *Standard Bearer*, vol. 62 (15 May 1986), p. 378.

165. For Masters's cessationist viewpoint, see especially 'Proving the Gifts Have
     Ceased', in Peter Masters, *The Healing Epidemic* (London: Wakeman Trust, 1988),
     pp. 112–135; Peter Masters and John C. Whitcomb, *The Charismatic Phenomenon*
     (London: Wakeman Trust, 1988).

166. Peter Masters, 'Opening the Door to Charismatic Teaching', *Sword and Trowel*
     (September 1988), p. 24.

Masters particularly assailed *Prove All Things* as 'probably the worst piece of exegesis and the most ill-informed book ever to appear under the Doctor's name'.
He thought it 'heavily laced with dogmatism and intimidation', because of the
'withering and intolerant' comments directed at cessationists. Lloyd-Jones had
rebuked them for acting on prejudice and putting 'a limit upon the power of
God, the Holy Spirit', and warned that 'the greatest opposition to a true revival
in the church, or to the work of individual men who have been baptized in the
Spirit, has almost invariably come from the church herself'.[167] In reply, Masters
accused Lloyd-Jones of 'a combination of misrepresentation and sheer pulpit
steamrollering' in his ridiculing of the cessationist position.[168] He complained:

> Naturally the Doctor's hearers (and readers) wilt under such strictures, and many
> a pastor scuttles into his bolt-hole terrified to utter a word against charismatic
> manifestations for a long time. When Dr Lloyd-Jones unleashes such severe
> denunciations upon people who are prepared to write off *all* the strange
> manifestations of our day, then the evangelical constituency trembles. But here lies
> the problem! This is precisely why so many reformed evangelicals in Britain have
> been timidly reluctant to face out the charismatic threat. This is why so few have been
> prepared to speak up for the old ways . . .
>
> From all the bombardments and sniping directed at them throughout this book,
> one would never guess that these cessationists are the very people from whom the
> Doctor learned all his theology, and to whom he owed all his ministerial influence.
> He, after all, lived and preached as the successor of the Puritans, the Matthew
> Henryites, the Warfieldites, and so on. It was because he learned from them, drew his
> scriptural views from them, and perpetuated and reproduced them (in the best sense)
> that so many people appreciate his work today. In the light of this it is rather jarring
> to note the ferocity with which Dr Lloyd-Jones demolishes his mentors and forebears
> on the matter of the doctrine of the Spirit.[169]

When it came to the spiritual tests offered in *Prove All Things*, Masters found
them 'stunningly puny and inadequate', sufficient for eliminating blatant
heretics but no help whatsoever 'on how to sift and discern the miracles and
prophecies of those who come (these days in their droves) wearing orthodox
evangelical garb'.[170] He concluded:

---

167. Lloyd-Jones, *Prove All Things*, pp. 45, 55–56.

168. Masters, 'Opening the Door', pp. 24–26, 28.

169. Ibid., pp. 24–25.

170. Ibid., p. 27.

It has been particularly sad to see the fawning and mealy-mouthed way in which certain reformed periodicals have reviewed these books. Tip-toeing between the charismatic opinions, and clutching desperately at the non-charismatic sentiments, they have sought to commend them as a noble and balanced contribution to this vexed subject. They have claimed that *Joy Unspeakable* (with its classical Pentecostal second-blessing teaching) is balanced by the fine spiritual tests of *Prove All Things*. The truth is that both books most forcefully reject the biblical principles of cessationism held by the entire reformed (and dispensational) traditions, and put totally inadequate 'tests' of spiritual phenomena in their place. Both books fog and misrepresent the arguments constantly, and both are characterised by a heavily intimidating seam of ridicule and dogmatism.[171]

There was similar alarm north of the border, particularly within the Free Presbyterian Church of Scotland (the so-called 'Wee Wee Frees', a Victorian breakaway from the Free Church of Scotland). Its annual synod in Glasgow in May 1986 passed a formal censure on Lloyd-Jones, fearful that his books were allowing Pentecostal and charismatic theology to take root in Reformed circles.[172] Iain Murray was 'incredulous' and brushed aside this 'sensational' criticism as unworthy of response.[173] Nevertheless, one of the promoters of the synodical resolution, Roy Middleton, answered:

Dr Lloyd-Jones was a highly intelligent and articulate man and he does not need Mr Murray as his expositor. During his lifetime Dr Lloyd-Jones knew quite well that his name was being linked with Charismatic Theology, and if he wished, he could have easily distinguished his position from that of the Charismatic Movement with its pretensions to tongue speaking. The plain fact is, that whilst he vigorously condemned non-experiential Calvinism as dead orthodoxy, there is no condemnation of the central tenets of the Charismatic position.[174]

Middleton suggested that while magazines like *Reformation Today* and *Sword and Trowel* were willing to speak out in protest, *The Banner of Truth* was so in awe of

---

171. Ibid., p. 29.
172. 'Meeting of Synod 1986', *Free Presbyterian Magazine*, vol. 91 (July 1986), pp. 201–202.
173. Iain H. Murray, 'A "Warning" about Dr Lloyd-Jones', *The Banner of Truth*, no. 281 (February 1987), p. 12.
174. Roy Middleton, 'The Synod Resolution on the Pentecostal-Charismatic Movement and the Teaching of Dr D. M. Lloyd-Jones', *Free Presbyterian Magazine*, vol. 92 (May 1987), p. 155.

Lloyd-Jones that its trumpet gave 'a less than certain sound' on the dangers of the charismatic movement. He concluded:

> How many more Reformed Churches are to be divided on the Charismatic issue? How many more of the rising generation are to leave us? How many more magazines are to be divided before the whole Reformed community lifts up a united voice against this most potent error that has grown so dramatically in our day – even if this does involve a warning about an aspect of Dr Lloyd-Jones' teaching?[175]

The division at the *Evangelical Times* was especially acute. The monthly newspaper, originally founded by Peter Masters in 1967, had been edited since March 1973 by Robert Horn who doubled the circulation to 16,500 during his thirteen years in charge. During the early 1980s Horn's editorial policy attracted increasing scrutiny from some Reformed readers because of his apparent reluctance to dismiss the charismatic movement. Indeed, some went so far as to allege that the *Evangelical Times* had adopted a 'pro-charismatic policy'.[176] For example, when David Watson died in February 1984, Herbert Carson (chairman of the *Evangelical Times* board of directors) penned a sympathetic tribute, published alongside Horn's enthusiastic review of Watson's autobiography.[177] In contrast, volumes such as Arnold Dallimore's *The Life of Edward Irving: Forerunner of the Charismatic Movement* (1983) attracted negative comment. Dallimore asserted that the teaching of Irving in the 1830s and charismatics in the 1980s was 'very much alike',[178] but Horn rejected the link as unfair and divisive.[179] Similarly Victor Budgen's *The Charismatics and the Word of God* (1985) was slated in a review by Roy Clements (pastor of Eden Baptist Church, Cambridge). Budgen denounced the movement in no uncertain terms as a 'contemporary delusion' for its spurious claims concerning

---

175. Ibid., p. 157.

176. Erroll Hulse, 'The Evangelical Times', *Reformation Today*, no. 89 (January – February 1986), p. 2.

177. Robert M. Horn, 'David Watson: From Humanism to Evangelism', and Herbert M. Carson, 'David Watson: A Personal Tribute', *Evangelical Times* (April 1984), pp. 12–13.

178. Arnold Dallimore, *The Life of Edward Irving: Forerunner of the Charismatic Movement* (Edinburgh: Banner of Truth, 1983), p. 175.

179. Robert M. Horn, 'Who Follows Irving?', *Evangelical Times* (August 1983), p. 19. For letters in response see *Evangelical Times* (September 1983), p. 17; (October 1983), p. 11.

prophecy, tongues, healing and apostleship.[180] He freely criticized numerous contemporary authors, including Lloyd-Jones, and alleged there had been a doctrinal shift at the *Evangelical Times*, especially lamenting Peter Lewis's monthly column.[181] In reply, Clements derided Budgen's book as 'marred by dubious exegetical arguments and disparaging personal comments', likely only to deepen the rift between pro-charismatic and anti-charismatic protagonists: 'For all the copious footnotes, this is a book of polemic rather than scholarship. And in that respect I believe the author has misjudged the need of the hour. It is not a time for Luther-like diatribes but for Aquila- and Priscilla-like diplomacy.'[182] In the furore which followed, several Reformed authors jumped to Budgen's defence, including Macleod who rebuked Clements for being 'surly and dismissive':

> Behind the emotive language lies the idea that it is bad taste to criticise Charismatics. We need diplomacy, not polemics. Yet what is the Charismatic movement itself but a sustained attack on traditional Christianity? Its very *raison d'être* is that the main-line churches are dead.[183]

Erroll Hulse at *Reformation Today* led the attacks on Horn's editorial policy at the *Evangelical Times*, mourning, 'Many pastors in the UK regret that a paper that they have supported in good faith should be used to promote errors which are the most divisive faced in our generation.' He provocatively suggested it would be more honest if Horn went to work for a charismatic magazine and allowed the *Evangelical Times* to appoint a new editor in keeping with its original cessationist ethos under Peter Masters.[184] Horn strongly refuted these claims that he was operating under a pro-charismatic bias, pointing to recent articles critical of John Wimber, as well as to his own cautious review of *Joy Unspeakable* and *Prove All Things*.[185] He insisted that the *Evangelical Times* was the ally of

---

180. Victor Budgen, *The Charismatics and the Word of God* (Welwyn: Evangelical Press, 1985), ch. 12.

181. Ibid., pp. 202–204.

182. Review by Roy Clements, *Evangelical Times* (December 1985), p. 19.

183. Review by Donald Macleod, *Monthly Record of the Free Church of Scotland* (January 1986), p. 10.

184. Erroll Hulse, 'Kingdom, Cult or New Denomination?', *Reformation Today*, no. 89 (January – February 1986), p. 30.

185. Robert M. Horn, 'Direct Experience: The Doctor on the Baptism with the Holy Spirit', *Evangelical Times* (October 1985), pp. 14–15.

no party and was determined to scrutinize both charismatic and cessationist theology, to give both a fair hearing in the light of Scripture. He said it was Hulse himself who was guilty of fomenting 'this sad internecine strife'.[186] Horn pleaded for evangelical unity between 'the reformed, the renewed and the restored', observing, 'Some evangelicals and churches seem constitutionally unable or sinfully unwilling to get on with other evangelicals. The reason is not important doctrine – that is just the cover for a divisive spirit.' He maintained that it should be possible to disagree with aspects of David Watson's teaching, for example, and yet still acknowledge him as 'a mighty man of God'.[187] Yet it did not escape the attention of *Reformation Today* that Horn was a member of Barcombe Baptist Chapel near Lewes, a congregation whose pastors were increasingly attracted to the charismatic theology of New Frontiers.[188] It was here that Lloyd-Jones had preached his last sermon in June 1980,[189] and it was also the home of the Martyn Lloyd-Jones Recordings Trust.[190]

The crisis came to a head in May 1986 when Willis Metcalfe, a wealthy Yorkshire farmer and the majority shareholder in the *Evangelical Times*, used his financial muscle to place his own nominees on the company's board.[191] In protest, Carson resigned as chairman and Horn soon departed as editor, along with his assistant John Benton and the rest of the newspaper's staff.[192] They saw Metcalfe's interference as an assault on editorial freedom and a threat to evangelical unity,[193] and quickly launched a rival newspaper, *Evangelicals Now*, to continue the work as before. Their declared aim was evangelical unity in

---

186. Robert M. Horn, '"ET" Under Fire: Let the Reader Judge', *Evangelical Times* (March 1986), p. 21. For responses, see John Marshall, 'A Question of Temperature or Truth?', *Reformation Today*, no. 90 (March – April 1986), pp. 30–32; Iain Murray, 'Editors in Collision', *The Banner of Truth*, no. 273 (June 1986), pp. 1–2.

187. Robert M. Horn, 'The Great Divide', *Evangelical Times* (March 1986), p. 19.

188. Hulse, 'Kingdom, Cult or New Denomination?', p. 30; Marshall, 'A Question of Temperature or Truth?', p. 31. The charismatic trajectory of Barcombe Baptist Chapel soon led to the departure of the Horn family in 1987; Joy Horn to Andrew Atherstone, 27 April 2011.

189. Murray, *Lloyd-Jones: Fight of Faith*, p. 737.

190. 'Lloyd-Jones Building Opens', *Evangelical Times* (September 1983), p. 9.

191. On Metcalfe, see Roger Fay, 'A Tribute to Willis Metcalfe', *Reformation Today*, no. 230 (July – August 2009), p. 10.

192. Letter from Sir Fred Catherwood, *Evangelicals Now* (July 1986), p. 3.

193. Robert M. Horn, 'The Future of the "Evangelical Times"', *Evangelical Times* (May 1986), pp. 12–13.

submission to Scripture, with a preference for 'persuasion rather than confrontation' and a refusal 'to push any party line'.[194] Sir Fred Catherwood (Member of the European Parliament and Lloyd-Jones's son-in-law) galvanized the efforts behind this initiative and served as the first chairman of the new board, alongside Herbert Carson, Roy Clements and others.[195] This close connection with the Catherwood family gave *Evangelicals Now* privileged access to Lloyd-Jones material, which helped it both to attract readers and to stake its claim for theological legitimacy. Its very first issue, in July 1986, contained a double-page spread with extracts from one of Lloyd-Jones's sermons on Romans 2, trumpeted as 'published here for the first time'.[196] Later Bethan Lloyd-Jones contributed her memories of the 1904–5 Welsh Revival, another *Evangelicals Now* exclusive.[197] Meanwhile, in October 1986 Horn marked the twentieth anniversary of Lloyd-Jones's famous appeal to the National Assembly of Evangelicals in Westminster Central Hall by arguing that his newspaper's priorities coincided with those of the Doctor. He declared, 'The inner logic of the October 1966 message was that the gospel is supreme for the expression of unity . . . We have to be exceedingly sure that the conditions we lay down to admit others to fellowship with us will stand the gaze of the crucified Lord.' He warned that evangelicals were guilty of 'majoring on minors' and that, just as they had allowed denominationalism to divide them in the 1960s, so now in the 1980s they were in danger of succumbing to 'factionalism' by splitting into charismatic and Reformed parties. Horn concluded:

> Big leaders, like the Doctor, see beyond. They don't operate under flags or labels or groups. They try to embrace all who are embraced by the cross. They trust God's truth to march on and believe it will do so more speedily if it is not cornered by one group as theirs . . . There seems to be something of a groundswell for this gospel unity today. Many are tired of self-justifying reactions, of in-fighting, or impeccable arguments that end in division, or 'faithfulness to truth' that drives Christians away. Maybe it is time to stand up and be counted, to put aside fear of others and make

---

194. 'Why a New Paper?', *Evangelicals Now* (July 1986), p. 2.
195. 'New Board', *Evangelicals Now* (December 1986), p. 3.
196. D. M. Lloyd-Jones, 'Don't Go By the Label', *Evangelicals Now* (July 1986), pp. 10–11. This sermon was eventually published in book form as D. M. Lloyd-Jones, *Romans: An Exposition of Chapter 2:1 to 3:20: The Righteous Judgment of God* (Edinburgh: Banner of Truth, 1989), pp. 1–15.
197. Bethan Lloyd-Jones, 'My Memories of the 1904–05 Revival in Wales', *Evangelicals Now* (September 1987), pp. 9–11; (October 1987), pp. 9–11.

voices heard for *acceptance* of those Christ has accepted, who equally accept the Bible's gospel.[198]

Evangelicals Now was energetically promoted at the 'Life in the Spirit' leaders' conference at High Leigh Conference Centre in Hertfordshire in February 1987, an annual gathering of Reformed pastors seeking renewal (first established in 1979). Peter Lewis was among the keynote speakers and charismatic worship and prayer ministry featured prominently, alongside teaching on prophecy, healing, deliverance, contemporary music and church growth. *Reformation Today* published a detailed exposé from a correspondent who had attended the conference in some trepidation. He recounted the gossip amongst delegates:

> Dr Lloyd-Jones's name came up in several conversations. 'How he would have loved this conference', one man said. (Somehow, I doubt that.) Another man said he thought the Banner of Truth Trust had been embarrassed to publish certain of the Doctor's volumes on Ephesians and Romans which have seemingly given impetus and even (so he claimed) respectability to the fledgling Reformed and Renewed movement. Another man criticised the Banner's Leicester conference for its 'long faces and miserable worm theology' . . . I told one man I thought the Banner was the best thing since sliced bread. He agreed but added that even sliced bread could be improved by a bit of butter.[199]

More fuel was added to the fire with the publication by Kingsway of Lloyd-Jones's *Healing and Medicine* (1987), a collection of ten addresses on medical subjects, originally delivered between 1953 and 1974, the majority to the Christian Medical Fellowship. In a lecture from 1971 entitled 'The Supernatural in Medicine', Lloyd-Jones gave his most extended treatment of the subject of faith healing, urging his listeners to keep an open mind. He quoted instances of healings at the Roman Catholic shrine at Lourdes and insisted that evangelicals must not 'refuse to recognise facts because our theory regards them as impossible'. Yet at the same time he counselled caution, with the need 'to maintain our healthy sceptical and critical attitude to everything that is reported to us'.[200] This was exemplified in his assessment of

198. Robert M. Horn, 'October Revolution?', *Evangelicals Now* (October 1986), p. 2.

199. Anthony Coppin, 'Life in the Spirit', *Reformation Today*, no. 97 (May – June 1987), p. 26.

200. D. M. Lloyd-Jones, *Healing and Medicine* (Eastbourne: Kingsway, 1987), pp. 102–103.

Kathryn Kuhlman (1907–76), the controversial American faith healer who was a major influence on televangelist Benny Hinn.[201] Lloyd-Jones was prepared to take her seriously because she 'preaches the Lord Jesus Christ and she seems to be correct in her doctrine', but at the same time he expressed reservations about the psychological element in her ministry, the laughter and joking in her meetings and, of course, her gender.[202] As in his sermons on the baptism with the Spirit, Lloyd-Jones showed once more his openness to the gifts of the Spirit in general, but tempered by his cautious attitude towards individual reports of their manifestation.

The newly reconstituted *Evangelical Times* admitted that much in the collection was 'superb', but also warned readers that 'the master has clay feet'.[203] It was particularly perturbed by Lloyd-Jones's unwillingness to denounce Kuhlman, as was Peter Masters in his fiery critique.[204] In contrast, *Renewal* magazine hailed the publication of *Healing and Medicine* by adorning its front cover with a full-page photograph of Lloyd-Jones, much in the style of *The Banner of Truth*, and printing extended extracts from his chapter on demon possession.[205] It welcomed the teaching in this latest volume with the comment, 'Once again we find that he had a more open mind than many of his followers . . .'[206]

A contested legacy

As this chapter has demonstrated, Martyn Lloyd-Jones had the ability to provoke fierce controversy in death as in life. His published sermons on Spirit baptism caused a furore which began to gather momentum during his retirement but exploded in the mid-1980s. Such was his significance for British evangelicalism that even after his decease, his views could not be ignored. It is clear that his personal sympathy for charismatic and Pentecostal pioneers

201. See further, Benny Hinn, *Kathryn Kuhlman: Her Spiritual Legacy and Its Impact on My Life* (Nashville: Thomas Nelson, 1999).
202. Lloyd-Jones, *Healing and Medicine*, p. 104.
203. Review by Verna Wright, *Evangelical Times* (October 1987), p. 19.
204. Masters, 'Opening the Door', pp. 29–31.
205. D. M. Lloyd-Jones, 'How to Distinguish Between Spiritual and Physical Problems', *Renewal*, no. 132 (May 1987), pp. 9–13.
206. Ann England, 'Through the Eyes of the Doctor', *Renewal*, no. 122 (April – May 1986), p. 44.

extended far beyond Michael Harper and Billy Richards in the 1960s to men such as Henry Tyler and Terry Virgo in his final years. Yet as feelings ran high, Lloyd-Jones became a posthumous battleground for rival interpreters. Although a few within the Reformed community, like Peter Masters, distanced themselves entirely from the Doctor, the majority aimed to show that they were his true inheritors, whether Peter Lewis, Iain Murray, R. T. Kendall, *Renewal* magazine or *Evangelicals Now*. Lloyd-Jones's unimpeachable status as the doyen of the evangelical movement led many to claim his legacy in order to legitimate their own viewpoint concerning the ministry and gifts of the Holy Spirit. He had become a totemic, and yet contested, icon in the struggle for theological dominance in the contemporary church.

© Andrew Atherstone, David Ceri Jones and William K. Kay, 2011

5. LLOYD-JONES AND THE DEMISE OF PREACHING

Ben Bailie

British church historian Michael Watts entitled his 1995 Friends of Dr Williams' Library Lecture 'Why Did the English Stop Going to Church?'[1] There has been no shortage of answers to that question.[2] Historians, sociologists and theologians have all offered explanations. This chapter offers another, that of Martyn Lloyd-Jones. Lloyd-Jones would probably not agree with Callum Brown that 'Christian Britain' came to a sudden and violent end in the tumultuous days of the 1960s. For he would likely say, '*Christian* Britain? There never was any such thing as *Christian* Britain!' He would, however, agree that a cataclysmic transformation had occurred in British churches in the twentieth century. In fact, one could say that answering the question 'Why did the English (or Welsh) stop going to church?' dominated Lloyd-Jones's adult life.

On 6 February 1925, speaking to the Literary and Debating Society at the Welsh chapel in Charing Cross Road, the twenty-five-year-old Lloyd-Jones, a

---

1. Michael Watts, 'Why Did the English Stop Going to Church?', Friends of Dr Williams' Library, 49th Lecture (London: Dr Williams' Library, 1995).

2. For an excellent survey of the range of answers, see Hugh McLeod, 'Introduction', in Hugh McLeod and Werner Ustorf (eds.), *The Decline of Christendom in Western Europe, 1750–2000* (Cambridge: Cambridge University Press, 2003), pp. 1–26.

new Member of the Royal College of Physicians, electrified (or scandalized) the audience with a prophetic jeremiad entitled 'The Tragedy of Modern Wales'.[3] Fundamentally, this 'tragedy' was the increasing ineptitude and decreasing vitality of the Welsh churches. Bankers, educators and the 'great abomination' of preacher-politicians all came under censure, as did silk stockings, the wireless and daily bathers. Yet the heart of his critique was levelled against preachers. They were the root cause of the tragedy. Two months later Lloyd-Jones was invited to 'reiterate and re-emphasize' his message at the Union of Welsh Societies in Pontypridd. There he starkly stated:

> Preaching has very largely become a profession. Instead of real Christian sermons we are given second-hand expositions of psychology. The preachers say that they give the congregations what they ask for! What a terrible condemnation both of the preachers themselves and their congregations! Daniel Rowland, Llangeitho used to preach Hell. Has there been preaching which has had anything like the effect of his preaching since those days? We know quite well that there has not been. I am one of those who believe that until such men rise again in our midst, our condition – far from improving – will continue to deteriorate. Our pulpit today is effete and ineffective. It is the final touch in the tragedy of Modern Wales![4]

Even though the 'tragedy' permeated much of Welsh society, its cause and climax was to be found primarily in the pulpit.

The two lectures caused a storm of controversy. Lloyd-Jones's position was quickly critiqued both in person and in print. In Pontypridd, the pastor in whose church Lloyd-Jones delivered his address instantly rose and vigorously defended the Welsh pulpit. The *British Weekly*, *Western Mail* and the *South Wales News* all offered skewed summaries and stark critiques of Lloyd-Jones's address, seeking to exonerate the bankers, educators and other offended members of Welsh society. The most adamant and annoyed response came from the editor of the *South Wales News* who concluded his thoughts with the words, 'If Dr Martin [sic] Lloyd-Jones talks like this at twenty-five, we tremble to think what he will say about us when he is fifty.'[5] Yet the anxious editor need not have worried. In many ways, time mollified his critique. Bankers,

---

3. For a full account of this dramatic episode as well as significant extracts from the lectures, see Iain H. Murray, *D. Martyn Lloyd-Jones: The First Forty Years 1899–1939* (Edinburgh: Banner of Truth, 1982), pp. 66–92.

4. Ibid., pp. 88–89.

5. Ibid., p. 76.

bathers, silk stockings and the wireless were all exonerated. Yet Lloyd-Jones's critique of the pulpit, as both the cause and the climax of the tragedy, would remain largely the same throughout his life. Speaking forty-four years later at Westminster Theological Seminary in Philadelphia in 1969, he stated, 'If the people are not attending places of worship I hold the pulpit to be primarily responsible.'[6]

In what ways could the pulpit be blamed for the church's increasing ineptitude and decreasing vitality in the twentieth century? Lloyd-Jones believed the answer to that question lay in an understanding of the nineteenth century. He would tell the seminary students, 'Nothing is needed more urgently than an analysis of the innovations in the realm of religious worship in the nineteenth century – to me in this respect [it was] a devastating century.'[7] This chapter is not such an analysis. Its aim is more modest. It seeks to examine what Lloyd-Jones thought were the devastating nineteenth-century innovations in the realm of religious worship as they related to the preaching and the preachers of the age. The thesis of this chapter is that for Lloyd-Jones the crisis in British Christianity was the fruit of the uncritical implementation and adaptation, by the church in general and preachers in particular, of certain methods and mentalities from the late Victorian era.[8] It will examine the influence of those methods and mentalities – first and primarily on the preaching of the age, then second and briefly on two other realms of religious worship: church architecture and worship music.

Preaching

The primary source material for this chapter is *Preaching and Preachers* (1971), a series of lectures originally delivered at Westminster Theological Seminary in the spring of 1969. They represent the fruit of a lifetime of thought on the subject. In these lectures Lloyd-Jones expresses himself very forcefully.

---

6. D. M. Lloyd-Jones, *Preaching and Preachers* (London: Hodder and Stoughton, 1971), p. 52.

7. Ibid., p. 265.

8. Throughout *Preaching and Preachers*, Lloyd-Jones uses the term 'Victorianism' and references to the nineteenth century in a synonymous and elastic manner. The terms are also not limited to a British context, as he sees the mentalities and methods that he labels 'Victorian' as being influential in the United States as well as in Britain. This chapter uses those terms in a similar manner.

The *leitmotif* that will drive this chapter is 'abomination'.[9] For those familiar with Lloyd-Jones's methodology, this chapter offers the 'negative', or what preaching is not. He saw this as an essential preliminary to any discussion on the true nature of biblical preaching. Although a more positive exposition of Lloyd-Jones's theology of preaching is beyond the scope of this chapter, a few vital presuppositions are essential for understanding and interacting with Lloyd-Jones's critique of the preaching and preachers of his age and of the Victorian influences that shaped them.[10] The fundamental thesis of *Preaching and Preachers*, and indeed one of the core convictions of Lloyd-Jones's life, was that 'preaching is the primary task of the Church, and of the minister of the Church'.[11] While all sixteen lectures are an elaboration and expansion of that proposition, the first two are foundational. Here Lloyd-Jones outlined his biblical and theological rationale in order to substantiate his thesis. These biblical and theological convictions are easily overlooked due to the short amount of space they received in the lectures. Yet to overlook them would significantly skew one's understanding of Lloyd-Jones's preaching in general and his argument in *Preaching and Preachers* in particular. They were the fundamental convictional infrastructure on which the entire argument of the lectures were built.[12] In what might well be the most important paragraph in *Preaching and Preachers*, he states:

> The ultimate justification for asserting the primacy of preaching is theological. In other words I argue that the whole message of the Bible asserts this and drives us to this conclusion. What do I mean by that? Essentially I mean that the moment you consider man's real need, and also the nature of the salvation announced and

---

9. The methodology for this study has been to first isolate the 'abominations', then synthesize them, and then to seek the underlying principle that gave rise to the objection.

10. For a fuller account of his preaching, see Iain H. Murray, *Lloyd-Jones: Messenger of Grace* (Edinburgh: Banner of Truth, 2008); and Tony Sargent, *The Sacred Anointing: The Preaching of Dr Martyn Lloyd-Jones* (London: Hodder and Stoughton, 1994).

11. Lloyd-Jones, *Preaching and Preachers*, p. 45. See also pp. 19, 23, 25, 26, 28, 30.

12. The scriptural justification can be found on pp. 20–24. Lloyd-Jones cites as his primary evidence the example of both Jesus and the apostles. He argues that Jesus' primary object was to preach and teach, citing or alluding to Matthew 6:33; 22:21; Luke 4; 12:14; John 6:15; 8:12. Likewise he argues that the apostles' primary task was to be a witness of the Lord Jesus Christ, showing how this conviction is central in Acts and in 1 and 2 Timothy.

proclaimed in the Scriptures, you are driven to the conclusion that the primary task of
the Church is to preach and to proclaim this, to show man's real need, and to show
the only remedy, the only cure for it.[13]

Here were the two theological convictions that Lloyd-Jones believed should
inform both the rationale for why one should preach as well as the criterion
for what one should preach.

First, anthropologically, he believed that it was essential to begin with an
accurate diagnosis of humanity's ultimate need ('accurate' here meaning biblical). It is not that human beings are sick, unhappy, poor or uneducated, for
those are too superficial a diagnosis. Man's 'real trouble is that he is a rebel
against God and consequently under the wrath of God'.[14] The essential trouble
is that people are dead in trespasses and sins, spiritually blind and in darkness.
Their 'ultimate disease' can be summed up in the word 'ignorance'.[15] Second,
soteriologically, Lloyd-Jones believed that the Bible is God's announcement of
how to deal with this ignorance. Salvation is the result of 'bringing men to this
"knowledge" which they lack, it is dealing with this ignorance'.[16] Preaching is
the primary act of the church because:

> If this is the greatest need of man, if his ultimate need is something that arises out of
> this ignorance of his which, in turn, is the result of rebellion against God, well then,
> what he needs first and foremost is to be told about this, to be told the truth about
> himself, and to be told of the only way in which this can be dealt with. So I assert that
> it is the peculiar task of the Church, and of the preacher, to make all this known.[17]

These twin theological convictions served, for Lloyd-Jones, as the ecclesiastical evaluative standard by which all preaching and ministerial activity must be
relentlessly assessed and examined.

For Lloyd-Jones, the church is a 'specialist institution' which alone is called
of God to deal with humanity's deepest and most fundamental problem. This
particular task is performed through preaching. Preaching is at the centre of
the church's activity. Yet he believed that the modern church was awash in
confusion over the true nature of its task. This confusion was due to the subtle,

---

13. Lloyd-Jones, *Preaching and Preachers*, p. 26.

14. Ibid., p. 27.

15. Ibid., p. 28.

16. Ibid.

17. Ibid., pp. 28–29.

yet pernicious permeation of certain Victorian mentalities. The desire for respectability, the exaltation of entertainment and a 'pseudo-intellectualism', Lloyd-Jones believed, had been incubated within the church and were spawning ecclesiastical destruction. The two most significant of these poisonous fruits were professionalism and moralism.

The first and most insidious Victorian influence on preaching and preachers is what Lloyd-Jones called 'professionalism'. He saw this as 'the greatest of all dangers in the ministry. It is something preachers have to fight as long as they live. Professionalism is, to me, hateful anywhere, everywhere. I abominated it as much when I was practicing medicine as I do now.'[18] He believed there was nothing that would neuter a preacher of spiritual power quite like professionalism. Furthermore, it was antithetical to the true nature of biblical preaching. He believed that professionalism generally took two forms, the first being academic professionalism. This is the peculiar temptation of the more educated man, driven by a desire to be thought of as respectable and enlightened by the congregation. The second form is a more popular manifestation of professionalism and is generally motivated by a desire to draw people by means of entertainment. The academic professional's great fear is to be thought ignorant. The popular professional's great fear is to be thought boring. For Lloyd-Jones, both fears were equally reprehensible.

The academic professional can most easily be discerned by the type of sermon he preaches. Lloyd-Jones believed that it was here, more than in any other sphere of preaching, that the Victorian desire for respectability bore its most poisonous fruit. As Michael Watts notes, 'Respectability had become, by the mid-nineteenth century, the great idol of the middle and upper working classes.'[19] For Lloyd-Jones, the academic professional was the chief false prophet serving the idol of respectability. What type of sermonic offering would the false prophet offer to the god of respectability? He would offer up either a well-crafted literary essay or a very learned lecture, both of which Lloyd-Jones felt were good in their proper sphere. Yet when they masqueraded as true biblical preaching, they were an abomination.

Hughes Oliphant Old, in his seven-volume *The Reading and Preaching of the Scriptures in the Worship of the Christian Church* (2007), labels the Victorian era as a

---

18. Ibid., p. 252.
19. Michael R. Watts, *The Dissenters: Volume II: The Expansion of Evangelical Nonconformity* (Oxford: Clarendon Press, 1995), p. 595.

'golden age of preaching'.[20] By this he means that preaching in the Victorian age had become a popular art.[21] He states that the 'reading of sermons was very much in vogue on the quiet Sunday afternoons of nineteenth-century England'.[22] Thus the sermons were often not constructed as an oral transaction between the preacher and the congregation; rather they were written to be read by the fireside in fashionable London homes. Lloyd-Jones, however, believed that the rise of this literary emphasis in the Victorian era was actually an old foe to true preaching in new dress. He thought that this type of preaching was a resurrection of that exemplified by the Caroline Divines. He believed that the Victorian pulpit was mimicking the preaching of Bishop Andrewes, Jeremy Taylor and John Donne.[23] Their preaching was literary. The style was wonderful. The prose was marvellous. The congregation would gather as spectators and listen to the masterful performance. Yet Lloyd-Jones believed such preaching produced no spiritual life.[24] The congregation may be mesmerized by a literary masterpiece and remain ignorant of saving truth. For Lloyd-Jones, ornate sermons produced empty chapels.

Lloyd-Jones illustrated this obsession with the ornate by an anecdote he read in Bishop Hensley Henson's three-volume autobiography *Retrospect of an Unimportant Life* (1942), in which Henson spends three weeks producing and polishing what he considers the perfect sermon. Lloyd-Jones believed that this was utterly reprehensible. He asked the students at Westminster Theological Seminary, 'Can you conceive of the Apostle Paul spending three weeks in the preparation of one sermon, polishing phrases, changing a word here and there, putting in another adjective or adding another *bon mot*? The whole thing is utterly inconceivable.'[25] The inconceivable nature of this is due to what

---

20. Hughes Oliphant Old, *The Reading and Preaching of the Scriptures in the Worship of the Christian Church, Volume 6: The Modern Age* (Grand Rapids, MI: Eerdmans, 2007), pp. 347–348.

21. Ibid., p. 348.

22. Ibid., p. 350.

23. Lloyd-Jones, *Preaching and Preachers*, p. 217. For a fuller account of Lloyd-Jones's thoughts on the style of these three Anglican ministers, see D. M. Lloyd-Jones, 'Preaching', in *The Puritans: Their Origins and Successors: Addresses Delivered at the Puritan and Westminster Conferences 1959–1978* (Edinburgh: Banner of Truth, 1987), pp. 382–383.

24. See D. M. Lloyd-Jones, *The Unsearchable Riches of Christ: An Exposition of Ephesians 3:1 to 21* (Edinburgh: Banner of Truth, 1979), pp. 14–15.

25. Lloyd-Jones, *Preaching and Preachers*, p. 219. Lloyd-Jones wrote, 'As lighter reading I have read *Retrospect of an Unimportant Life* by Hensley Henson. It is a sheer delight

Lloyd-Jones believed was the apostolic method of true preaching. He held that for the apostles preaching was a living presentation and declaration of the truths of the gospel.[26] This living presentation often will commit egregious stylistic violations. In a fascinating sermon on Ephesians 3:1, Lloyd-Jones maintained that the apostle Paul interrupted the flow of his argument and was guilty of what the literary purists would call a horrific blemish of style: anacoluthia. This is bad style, but great preaching. It is preaching that is supremely concerned with impressing on the congregation the living realities of the truths proclaimed.[27] Or consider his comments on Romans 1:8–11:

> We are so set, and so formal today. We not only have our points, our numbers, but we will insist on having alliteration as well, as we almost have to force the truth into our little system of five p's and five s's, or whatever it is. The form is so marvellous, and we say, 'how clear, how beautiful, how wonderful it was, how neat!' And sometimes it seems to me almost the neatness of death. The lifelessness of mere form without a living substance with it! 'First' says this man Paul, and then he proceeds to forget he has said it, and never comes to the second or the third . . . the epistles of this man are not 'beautiful epistles'; they are massive; they are dynamite; they are volcanoes hurling out their great power. Thank God, I say, for a man who says 'First' and forgets to say second and third.[28]

Lloyd-Jones believed that the trouble with so many pulpits of his day was that they had forgotten this apostolic pattern and method. They were more Henson-like than Pauline. They had become too concerned with style and literary form. He argued that 'there must be form, but we must never give inordinate attention to it'.[29] This he saw as the plague of the academic professional.

Lloyd-Jones believed that the academic professional was driven by a

---

from the standpoint of style. Important also as a history of the C. E. during the past fifty and sixty years. Illuminating also as an illustration of the difference between a humanist and a Christian.' Lloyd-Jones to Leslie Land, 17 April 1943, in Iain H. Murray (ed.), *D. Martyn Lloyd-Jones: Letters 1919–1981* (Edinburgh: Banner of Truth, 1994), p. 67.

26. Lloyd-Jones, *Preaching and Preachers*, p. 218.
27. Lloyd-Jones, *The Unsearchable Riches of Christ*, pp. 12–14.
28. D. M. Lloyd-Jones, *Romans: Exposition of Chapter 1: The Gospel of God* (Edinburgh: Banner of Truth, 1985), p. 188.
29. Lloyd-Jones, *Preaching and Preachers*, p. 219.

dangerous Victorian mentality that he called 'pseudo-intellectualism',[30] which was a 'deadly menace'.[31] It poisoned the pulpit, in that ministers began to lace their sermons with quotations and footnotes. No longer were they concerned with their quality of mind or their capacity for original thought – the essential thing was how many quotations and footnotes one's sermon contained. They read books of quotations to give the appearance of intelligence and thought no sermon complete without the perfect quotation or poem. To this Lloyd-Jones responded characteristically, 'There is only one comment to make on that kind of thing – it is sheer prostitution.'[32]

This pseudo-intellectualism poisoned the pews as well. Lloyd-Jones strongly disapproved of the popular practice of announcing the subject of the sermon in advance, whether in the newspaper or in some other form of advertisement. His objection was that this practice originated in and helped perpetuate this pseudo-intellectualism in the pews. He stated, 'Towards the middle of the last century people began to regard themselves as educated and intellectual and felt that they must have "subjects".'[33] Prior to that, they were simply meeting together to worship God and hear an exposition of Scripture. But now they were educated. They were no longer simple sinners needing to hear the Word plainly spoken. They needed an 'address' or a lecture. Now that they were people of understanding, they wanted 'food for thought' or intellectual stimulus.[34] Any practice that pandered to this pseudo-intellectualism was inherently bad. 'Nothing can militate more against true preaching than this.'[35]

The second form in which professionalism had influenced the pulpit was in a more popular manifestation. This was driven by the Victorian obsession to entertain. The popular professional could most easily be discerned by looking at the type of man he was and the methods he chose to execute his ministry. He was likely to be a clone of one of the great pulpiteers of the Victorian age. These men could occupy a pulpit. They would dominate it and dominate the people. They were professionals. They were showmen who were experts at handling a congregation and playing on the emotions of people.[36] Lloyd-Jones told his American audience that the paradigmatic pulpiteer in their country had

---

30. Ibid., p. 244.
31. Ibid., p. 220.
32. Ibid., p. 221.
33. Ibid., p. 245.
34. Ibid.
35. Ibid., p. 220.
36. Ibid., p. 13.

been Henry Ward Beecher. Beecher believed that the role of the preacher, if he were to be effective, was to impress his personality on the congregation.[37] His personality makes the Word effective. By personality, Beecher meant the showmanship, the gregariousness, the theatrical ability and the charisma of the speaker or performer. Lloyd-Jones believed that the current popular aversion to and dismissal of preaching in the general culture was largely a reaction against this type of preaching. He stated, 'Now this, I am sure, has produced a reaction; and that is a very good thing. These pulpiteers were to me – with my view of preaching – an abomination; and it is they who are in many ways largely responsible for this present reaction.'[38] Lloyd-Jones believed that the fundamental driving impulse behind the pulpiteers was the desire to attract a crowd through entertainment, and that desire manifested itself in an exaltation of form over truth. He argued that in the late Victorian age, 'the truth was noticed, they paid a passing respect to it, but the great thing was the form'.[39] The tragedy of the preceding generations was that the truth had been lost and only the focus on the form remained. For Lloyd-Jones, a focus on form irrespective of the truth was sheer prostitution.

Lloyd-Jones would have agreed with Hughes Oliphant Old's assessment that preaching in the Victorian age had become a popular art, but in the hands of the popular professional, Lloyd-Jones believed, the art had become the artifice of the prostitute. The prostitute has one primary aim, to entice. All her efforts to adorn herself serve that one aim. The Victorian pulpiteers wanted to

---

37. Henry Ward Beecher, *Yale Lectures on Preaching* (New York: J. B. Ford and Co., 1872), pp. 2–5. In *The Making of American Liberal Theology: Imagining Progressive Religion, 1805–1900* (Louisville, KY: Westminster John Knox Press, 2001), Gary Dorrien argues that Beecher's understanding of preaching can best be seen in the architecture of Brooklyn Heights sanctuary, which was designed by Beecher. There was no platform, no pulpit, and the seating was in a large semicircle. It was appropriately called the 'Auditorium'. Dorrien states, 'The novel seating arrangement, which allowed Beecher to be heard without raising his voice, gave the impression of intimacy and informality and accentuated the role of the preacher as performer' (p. 194). He then quotes Beecher: 'It is perfect because it is built on a principle – the principle of social and personal magnetism, which emanates reciprocally from a speaker and from a close throng of hearers. I want them to surround me, so that they will come up on every side, and behind me, so that I shall be in the center of the crowd, and have the people surge all about me' (p. 194).

38. Lloyd-Jones, *Preaching and Preachers*, p. 14.

39. Ibid., p. 5.

draw and attract people to their message. Thus great emphasis was placed on
the trappings of communication – delivery styles, stories, illustrations, anecdotes and other communicative devices meant to adorn the proclamation. Yet
he believed that when these devices became central in a preacher's homiletical
preparation, then that preacher had prostituted the pulpit. Of this mentality he
would say, 'To me, that kind of thing is not only professionalism at its worst,
it is, as I say, the art of the harlot, because it pays too much attention to, and
is too much concerned about, enticing people.'[40]

Lloyd-Jones told the Westminster students that the difference between true
art and the art of the harlot can be seen in the distinction highlighted in an
article he once read in which the author distinguished between 'The Artifice
of Artistry' and the 'Inevitability of Art'.[41] True art and the type of literary and
rhetorical art, or adornment, that is acceptable and commendable in preaching
is art that has an inevitable quality to it. Thus, if a man has a well-stocked mind
and a classical illustration or quotation which comes to mind naturally, then
it is perfectly acceptable to use it in preaching. On the other hand, the man
who spends hours searching a book of illustrations for the perfect story is a
prostitute. That type of 'art' is artificial, as Lloyd-Jones said. 'It is an artifice, it
is always the characteristic of the prostitute out to produce an effect to serve
her own ends. We must never be guilty of that. We must always make sure that
there is this quality of "inevitability".'[42] This was the governing principle that
shaped his convictions on the use of humour, illustrations and eloquence in
preaching. They were acceptable in and of themselves, as long as there was this
inevitable quality about them. But the man who tried to be funny or eloquent
in the pulpit was seen as an abomination.

Lloyd-Jones believed that popular homiletical books illustrated the fatal
outworking of this mentality. In his opinion, homiletical instruction – which
was practically an abomination in and of itself – had denigrated into simply
instructing ministers in the art of the prostitute. In speaking of books like
W. E. Sangster's *The Craft of Sermon Illustration* (1946), Lloyd-Jones stated, 'That
kind of thing is to me an abomination. "The Craft" does not come in to this
realm at all. That is prostitution again.'[43] He advised the students, 'All your

40. Ibid., p. 232.

41. Ibid., p. 221.

42. Ibid.

43. Lloyd-Jones, *Preaching and Preachers*, pp. 231–232. Sangster was the minister
    from 1939 to 1955 at Westminster Central Hall, which was probably the largest
    Nonconformist congregation in London at the time and less than a mile from

books such as *The A.B.C. of Preaching* or *Preaching Made Easy* should be thrown into the fire as soon as possible.'[44] *Preaching Made Easy* or *The Craft of Sermon Illustration* were fit only for the flames because they were symptoms of the terminal disease of the popular professional. Their popularity bore testimony to the dominance of the Victorian mentality that preferred to entertain rather than proclaim.

The outworking of the art of the harlot, however, was not limited to the rhetorical devices with which ministers adorned their sermons. It was also a fundamental impulse that shaped the methods in which many ministers and churches sought to revitalize depleting congregations. The methods of the popular professional, when mixed with the congregation's carnal desire to be entertained, created a lethal toxin that, when consumed, devastated the body of Christ. This methodology can best be demonstrated by the rise of what Lloyd-Jones called the 'sporting parson'. In one of his first sermons in Wales in 1927, he contrasted the real minister with the 'sporting parson':

> Instead, however, we provide so called 'sporting parsons', men of whom the world can say that they are 'good sports' – whatever that may mean. And what it does so often mean is that they are men who believe that you can get men to come to chapel and church by playing football and other games with them. 'I'll fraternize with the men,' says such a minister. 'I'll get them to like me and to see that I'm not so different from them after all, and then they'll come to listen to my sermons.' And he tries it, but thank God, he almost invariably fails, as he richly deserves . . .[45]

Forty-two years later, Lloyd-Jones was still warning about the mentality of the 'sporting parson', of whom an Anglican minister, Geoffrey Studdert Kennedy, was supposed to be the paradigmatic exemplar. As an army chaplain in the First World War, Kennedy famously sought to minister to the soldiers by fraternizing with them, smoking and swearing as they did in the belief that they would be drawn to his ministry. He was affectionately dubbed 'Woodbine Willie', for freely distributing cheap cigarettes to the men. Lloyd-Jones

---

Westminster Chapel. Given the proximity and popularity of the two preachers, one wonders if there is more to this reference than what is stated explicitly.

44. Lloyd-Jones, *Preaching and Preachers*, p. 119. This is a reference to David Francis, *The ABC of Preaching* (London: Epworth Press, 1968) and an obscure, out-of-print book by Thomas Flynn, published in 1923.

45. Sermon preached on 20 March 1927, on Hebrews 13:14. Quoted in Murray, *Lloyd-Jones: First Forty Years*, p. 142.

believed that this ministerial method was destined to fail since it was based on a 'pathetic psychological ignorance' as well as dubious theology.[46] For Lloyd-Jones, this methodology could only be plausible in a milieu in which popular professionalism reigned supreme.

The methods of the popular professional were not only evident in the 'sporting parson', they were also apparent in sporting congregations. In an attempt to stem the tide of congregational depletion, many churches had resorted to offering recreations and entertainments to entice an audience. When Lloyd-Jones arrived at the small mission church in Port Talbot in 1927, the struggling congregation had been engaged in organizing football matches, musical evenings and a dramatic society. These efforts, however, found no sympathy with the new pastor. In the same sermon quoted above, Lloyd-Jones moved his critique from the 'sporting parson' to the congregation:

> The churches organize whist-drives, fetes, dramas, bazaars and things of that sort, so as to attract people. We are becoming almost as wily as the devil himself, but we are really bad at it; all our attempts are hopeless failures and the world laughs at us. Now, when the world persecutes the church, she is performing her real mission, but when the world laughs at her she [the church] has lost her soul. And the world today is laughing at the church, laughing at her attempts to be nice and to make people feel at home. My friends, if you feel at home in any church without believing in Christ as your personal Saviour, then that church is no church at all, but a place of entertainment or a social club.[47]

For Lloyd-Jones, these efforts to entice the world were another manifestation of the art of the harlot. When he arrived in Port Talbot, he terminated all activities that might misconstrue the church as a place of entertainment. This created several logistical dilemmas. For example, what was the church to do with the wooden stage that was built for the dramatic society? Lloyd-Jones's response was characteristic: 'You can heat the church with it.'[48] All the trappings of the art of the harlot, whether dramatic stages or *The Craft of Sermon Illustration*, were, in Lloyd-Jones's view, no better than fuel for the fire.

Another Victorian influence plaguing the church of Lloyd-Jones's day were the moralistic sermons which had replaced real evangelical preaching.

---

46. Lloyd-Jones, *Preaching and Preachers*, p. 139.

47. Murray, *Lloyd-Jones: First Forty Years*, p. 142.

48. Lloyd-Jones, *Preaching and Preachers*, p. 135. The stage was, in fact, donated to the local branch of the YMCA.

He viewed this, ironically enough, as one of the negative consequences of the great revivals of 1859. Following any great revival or movement of the Spirit, he argued, there was an increasing tendency 'to regard the baptised children of church members as Christians'.[49] When this happens on a large scale, the gospel becomes assumed and the emphasis of preaching moves from gospel proclamation to edification. This he saw as the great danger and temptation of the second generation following a religious awakening: preachers stop preaching evangelistically. He stated, 'The main danger confronting the pulpit in this matter is to assume that all who claim to be Christians, and who think they are Christians, and who are members of the Church, are therefore of necessity Christians. This, to me, is the most fatal blunder of all; and certainly the commonest.'[50]

For Lloyd-Jones, the blunder of the late Victorian age was the assumption that all who were members of the church were true believers. This was a 'very great and grievous fallacy' that he knew from his own experience. For many years, he assumed that he was a Christian when he was not, even though he regularly attended worship. He never remembered hearing preaching that addressed him as a sinner and pressed upon him his need for grace: 'The preaching we had was always based on the assumption that we were all Christians.'[51] He believed that this fatal assumption manifested itself in the life of the church in two key areas: the preaching of morality instead of the gospel and the overemphasis on social crusades, both of which became particularly pronounced in the late Victorian era and continued to have a detrimental impact on the churches. The first problem was the preaching of the Christian ethic, or morality, apart from the preaching of the gospel. To put it another way, it was the preaching of righteousness without first preaching godliness. For Lloyd-Jones, Thomas Arnold of Rugby was the quintessential exemplar of this fatal assumption. He commented, 'That is where, I suppose, the final enemy of the Christian faith is morality. And that is why I sometimes feel that Thomas Arnold, of Rugby fame, was perhaps of all men in the last century the one who did the greatest harm.'[52] Arnold's brand of public-school Christianity was so injurious because it was primarily 'concerned about producing a gentleman, not a saint, but a gentleman. You

---

49. Ibid., p. 152.
50. Ibid., p. 146.
51. Ibid.
52. D. M. Lloyd-Jones, *Darkness and Light: An Exposition of Ephesians 4:17 – 5:17* (Edinburgh: Banner of Truth, 1982), p. 82.

see the distinction! A man must behave properly. He has got to be orderly in his conduct. But they were not really interested in a vital knowledge of God.'[53] It was not that Lloyd-Jones was against morality or orderly conduct. Rather, what made this so fatal was that it presented Christian morality as an end in itself. Lloyd-Jones believed that you could not have morality apart from godliness. The chief blunder of the late Victorians and the social gospellers of his own day was that they had changed the focus and attempted to preserve the morality while discarding the godliness. When the fruit of morality is stripped from the root of a living piety, the result was what Lloyd-Jones called a 'false Puritanism'.[54]

False Puritanism was a perpetual plague on vital Christianity and a great hindrance to the growth and health of the church. In a sermon in April 1958 on Ephesians 4:22–23, Lloyd-Jones attacked this confusion between morality and real Christianity:

> In a sense, this was the curse of the closing years of the Victorian period and the
> early years of this present century. Christian churches were filled with people who
> had taken off the old and put on the new, but the spirits of their minds had not
> been changed. They did not know why they were doing it; it was the tradition; they
> had been brought up to go to places of worship; not to do this, but to do that.
> That, without a doubt, was the curse of Victorianism. Thank God we have come
> to the end of it! I would rather have the present position than that, because those
> Victorians who had this form of godliness thought of themselves as true Christians,
> and yet many of them had never been Christians and had no heart knowledge of the
> Faith.[55]

For Lloyd-Jones, the contemporary position with its appalling moral decline was preferable to the Victorian age, because the lines that demarcated the Christian from the non-Christian were much clearer.

Yet, ironically, Lloyd-Jones believed that it was the preaching of morality alone that had led to the appalling moral decline in England. Speaking in November 1959, he said, 'I am increasingly convinced that so much in the state of the Christian church today is to be explained chiefly by the fact that for nearly a hundred years the church has been preaching morality and ethics,

---

53. D. M. Lloyd-Jones, *Romans: Exposition of Chapter 1: The Gospel of God* (Edinburgh: Banner of Truth, 1985), p. 361.

54. Lloyd-Jones, *Darkness and Light*, p. 86.

55. Ibid., p. 164.

and not the Christian faith.'[56] For Lloyd-Jones, the Victorian confusion of morality with vital Christianity led many in his day simply to think of salvation as a little bit of morality or decency sprinkled onto one's life. At this common assumption he took great offence: 'What an insult to the Christian! as if the Christian were just a good and a nice and a harmless individual. Not at all! He is a man who has undergone this tremendous change . . . He has been raised, resurrected; he is in the heavenly places.'[57] For Lloyd-Jones this confusion radically undermined the doctrine of regeneration and the new birth, thus creating profound confusion over the nature of a true Christian.

Victorian moralism created confusion not only over the identity of a Christian, but also over the activity of a Christian. In addressing the current weakness of the church, he would say, 'I am one of those who hold the view that the real damage was done toward the end of last century when the Christian Church began to form organisations to deal with particular sins. She dropped unconsciously from the spiritual level to the moral level.'[58] This was Lloyd-Jones's primary criticism of movements such as the temperance movement. He felt they were attacking sin from the wrong end. They were not addressing humanity's chief need. For Lloyd-Jones, the doctrine of original sin meant that humanity's fundamental trouble was not moral, physical, political or social. The church must never forget her first principles: 'Man's real trouble is that he is a rebel against God and consequently under the wrath of God.'[59] It was the church alone, and preaching the gospel in particular, that was designed to meet this need. The church, as a specialist institution, alone

---

56. D. M. Lloyd-Jones, *Life in the Spirit in Marriage, Home and Work: An Exposition of Ephesians 5:18 to 6:9* (Edinburgh: Banner of Truth, 1974), p. 19. Horton Davies' analysis is similar to that of Lloyd-Jones. He places as the central change in the theological emphases of English preaching from 1900 to 1960 the 'New Theology', which was a 'socialistic version of the historic Christian faith' that replaced 'Christ the Saviour with Christ the philanthropist and social reformer'. Horton Davies, *Varieties of English Preaching, 1900–1960* (London: SCM, 1963), pp. 24–29. Likewise, O. C. Edwards maintains that by the turn of the twentieth century, Romanticism had triumphed and it dominated both American and British pulpits, characterized most fundamentally by its moral and social emphases. O. C. Edwards, *A History of Preaching* (Nashville, TN: Abingdon Press, 2004), pp. 591–658.

57. D. M. Lloyd-Jones, *God's Way of Reconciliation: An Exposition of Ephesians 2:1 to 22* (Edinburgh: Banner of Truth, 1972), p. 21.

58. Lloyd-Jones, *Darkness and Light*, p. 118.

59. Lloyd-Jones, *Preaching and Preachers*, p. 27.

was called and equipped to deal with humanity's most basic and fundamental need: one's relationship with God. The tragedy of the modern church was that it had abandoned this primary purpose for the sake of lesser causes. In a powerful sermon on the transformation brought about by regeneration as being the only hope for the world, Lloyd-Jones explained:

> That is Christianity. Not simply a political, moral programme, no, no – this living Jesus with all power . . . That is the message of Christianity. That is what has made the church what it is. Do men and women need to be told about some kind of programme that will give them better conditions? That is not our greatest need. Our greatest need is to know God. If we were all given a fortune, would that solve our problems? Would that solve our moral problem? Would that solve the problem of death? Would that solve the problem of eternity? Of course not. The message of Christianity is not about improving the world, but about changing people in spite of the world, preparing them for the glory that is yet to come. This Jesus is active and acting to that end, and he will go on until all the redeemed are gathered in, and then he will return and the final judgment will take place, and his kingdom will stretch from shore to shore.[60]

Music and architecture

Two secondary but significant Victorian innovations that Lloyd-Jones also believed had a detrimental impact relate to worship music and church architecture. Lloyd-Jones believed that in the middle of the nineteenth century, Nonconformist churches in Britain became inordinately obsessed with styles of music and architecture. For Lloyd-Jones, there was generally an inverse relationship between a church's focus on these external matters and the spirituality of that church. Thus the increased attention to the externals of worship in the late Victorian era demonstrated a profound spiritual declension. In his lectures on *Preaching and Preachers*, he stated his fundamental principle as follows: 'the greater the amount of attention that has been paid to this aspect of worship – namely the type of building, and the ceremonial, and the singing, and the music – the greater the emphasis on that, the less spirituality you are likely to have; and a lower spiritual temperature and spiritual understanding and desire can be expected.'[61] Just as Lloyd-Jones believed an inordinate desire for respectability

---

60. D. M. Lloyd-Jones, *Authentic Christianity: Sermons on the Acts of the Apostles*, vol. 1 (Edinburgh: Banner of Truth, 1999), pp. 13–16.

61. Lloyd-Jones, *Preaching and Preachers*, p. 267.

drove the Victorian innovations in preaching, so too he felt that this motivation drove these other changes in public worship.[62]

Lloyd-Jones's preferred term for a church building was a 'meeting house'.
The church was to be the place where believers gathered together in order to
meet with God through worship and especially the preaching of the Word.
He argued that until the middle of the nineteenth century, chapels had generally been very simple buildings. Yet a change came in and they began to 'erect
these great and ornate buildings in the mock-Gothic style'.[63] Nonconformists
began to view themselves as respectable, more educated and more cultured.
They therefore began to imitate the buildings of the Anglicans and Roman
Catholics. Lloyd-Jones believed the 'idea was to show how they had advanced
from illiteracy and the coarseness of evangelicalism, but what it actually proclaimed was a tragic decline in spirituality. As the buildings become more
ornate the spirituality invariably declines.'[64]

Why do ornate buildings lead to spiritual decline? Because, Lloyd-Jones
believed, they were counterproductive to the true purpose for which a church
meets. The architecture reflected the theology. For Lloyd-Jones, the fundamental purpose of the congregation in gathering was to meet the living God
through the means of the preached Word. The 'real presence' is experienced
as the Holy Spirit anoints and accompanies the Word as it is proclaimed. Thus
the buildings should be simple and the pulpit central. Furthermore, the ornate
curves and angular peculiarities of Gothic-style architecture hindered the
preaching of the Word from an acoustical standpoint. That is why Lloyd-Jones
told the students at Westminster Theological Seminary, 'Curves and angles
are an abomination. Flat ceilings should be compulsory.'[65] Before electronic
amplification, a flat ceiling was extremely advantageous for a preacher to be
heard comfortably. Thus the architectural style reveals the congregation's

---

62. Ibid., p. 162. David Bebbington also links worship music and architecture as
    illustrative of the evangelical impulse to seek respectability in the mid-1800s.
    See David Bebbington, *The Dominance of Evangelicalism: The Age of Spurgeon and
    Moody* (Leicester: Inter-Varsity Press, 2005), p. 68. Likewise, Michael Watts asserts
    that worship music and architecture were two of the primary means by which
    Dissenting churches sought respectability between 1840 and 1859. His chapter on
    these matters is tellingly entitled: '1840–1859: Intellectuality and Surface Culture:
    The Respectability of Dissent', Watts, *The Dissenters, Volume II*, pp. 593–670.

63. Lloyd-Jones, *Preaching and Preachers*, p. 161.

64. Ibid., p. 162.

65. Ibid.

understanding of the purpose of worship. It should be a physical demonstration of the priority of preaching.

The desire for respectability also had a detrimental impact on the church's notions of proper worship music. Lloyd-Jones stated that in the nineteenth century 'a fatal turn took place in so many respects . . . and very prominent among the changes introduced was the place given to music in various forms.'[66] He believed that those changes could be seen in the rise of choirs, best illustrated by the rise of the modern, American-style 'song-leader'. He described this song-leader as someone 'whose special function it is to conduct the singing and to do what they can to get the people into the right mood and condition for the reception of the message'.[67] Yet he felt that the approach of the song-leader often detracted from, rather than enhanced, the preaching that was to follow. Speaking at Westminster Chapel, he told of a time when he was at a tent revival meeting and the song-leader jumped into the pulpit, cracked a joke and then, looking at the band, said, 'Let it rip . . . and I didn't mean the tent of course!' This anecdote produced a considerable amount of laughter among the Westminster congregation, to which Lloyd-Jones responded, 'Yes, well all right, you laugh at this but this is something we should weep at – they were singing hymns of praise unto God, hymns of worship and adoration. That joking and jocularity, that is the type of thing that happens in the drunken orgies!'[68] It was the jocular manner that Lloyd-Jones was so against because it hindered the church's true task, to encounter God through worship and preaching. The easy familiarity and the entertainment ethos that was so characteristic of the modern song-leader could only be popular in a milieu that exalted entertainment over worship and revelry over reverence. For Lloyd-Jones, this perfectly exemplified the triumph of the Victorian obsession with entertainment.

Conclusion

To the ministerial students at Westminster Theological Seminary, Lloyd-Jones said, 'I commend, as being most important, a study of the subtle changes that

---

66. Ibid., p. 266.

67. Ibid., p. 265.

68. D. M. Lloyd-Jones, 'True Melody' (29 November 1959), Martyn Lloyd-Jones Recordings Trust, audio file MLJ 4157. The laughter can be very clearly heard on the audio recording. For the revised version, as published, see D. M. Lloyd-Jones, *Singing to the Lord* (Bridgend: Bryntirion Press, 2003), p. 37.

took place somewhere round about the middle of the last century.'[69] He went on to remind them that if they were going to engage in such a study, they would have to 'do so in terms of its total effect upon the life of the Church, remote as well as immediate'.[70] Lloyd-Jones believed the effect of those subtle Victorian changes was catastrophic. They lay at the heart of why the English had stopped going to church. He continued, 'The sooner we forget the nineteenth century and go back to the eighteenth, and even further to the seventeenth and sixteenth, the better. The nineteenth century and its mentality and outlook is responsible for most of our troubles and problems today.'[71] The Victorian desire for respectability, the desire to entertain, the pseudo-intellectualism and the confusion of the gospel with morality produced practices that Lloyd-Jones thought abominable. It was these abominations, he passionately argued, that had caused the late-twentieth-century desolation of the church.

© Ben Bailie, 2011

---

69. Lloyd-Jones, *Preaching and Preachers*, p. 245.
70. Ibid., p. 249.
71. Ibid., pp. 265–266.

6. LLOYD-JONES AND MINISTERIAL EDUCATION

Philip H. Eveson

At the opening of the London Bible College's new premises in May 1958, Martyn Lloyd-Jones was the guest preacher. During the course of his sermon he pointedly asked his congregation, 'Are the men more certain of the truth at the end of their studies than at the beginning? . . . Do they know God better and desire to serve God better than when they came in? . . . You may have more BDs than any College in the country but only if the result is that your people know God better!'[1] His address, based on the text of 2 Timothy 2:15–16, gave voice to long-held convictions and increasing unease concerning the usual preparation for Christian ministry that students were following and it proved an uncomfortable message to the college faculty who consequently refused to publish the sermon.

In John Brencher's evaluation of Lloyd-Jones's contribution to twentieth-century evangelicalism, his attitude towards education is listed as one of the 'unresolved points' omitted for lack of space.[2] While it may be true that his views on education were not an issue central to his life and ministry, they

---

1. Iain H. Murray, *D. Martyn Lloyd-Jones: The Fight of Faith 1939–1981* (Edinburgh: Banner of Truth, 1990), pp. 310–311.
2. John Brencher, *Martyn Lloyd-Jones (1899–1981) and Twentieth-Century Evangelicalism* (Carlisle: Paternoster, 2002), p. 5.

were far from being marginal. This chapter explores Lloyd-Jones's views on education in general, beginning with his seemingly contradictory attitudes towards scholarship and theological training and ending with some assessment of the vision that led him to support a wholly new venture in ministerial education.

Attitudes to education and scholarship

At the same time as Lloyd-Jones was passing through the educational system of his day, from which he would, by the age of twenty-five, obtain the highest qualifications in the medical profession, he was questioning attitudes towards education and scholarship. 'Modern education' was his chosen subject in a speech which he gave to the Literary and Debating Society at his local church in Charing Cross when he was only twenty-one. Though no record of what he said is available, his thinking can be gleaned from subsequent talks to the Society. In an address in March 1924, one of his illustrations for the moral chaos of his day was 'the rage for degrees and diplomas'.[3] He expanded on this the following year in a hard-hitting lecture that brought his name to prominence in the land of his birth. He argued that in the 'great struggle' between education and real Christianity, Wales had become 'intoxicated with the idea of education . . . We worship today any man who knows many facts and we despise the man who knows the only thing that is really worth knowing.' He concluded his speech by calling for 'real men' not 'educated snobs'.[4]

Later, in 1927, Lloyd-Jones was invited to speak at the annual prize-giving day at his old secondary school in Tregaron. On this occasion he returned to the theme of true education. He warned his audience of 'the tyranny of knowledge', arguing that there 'was no real value in education unless it helped to build character'.[5] No doubt he gleaned information on Wales and Welsh aspirations through family, friends, fellow chapel members and his reading of Welsh newspapers and periodicals. Some of his criticisms arose out of childhood impressions. From his own recollections he mentioned his village as being 'rich in characters'. He commented, 'There is nothing more interesting

---

3. Iain H. Murray, *D. Martyn Lloyd-Jones: The First Forty Years 1899–1939* (Edinburgh: Banner of Truth, 1982), p. 65.

4. Ibid., pp. 68–72.

5. Ibid., p. 174.

than natural, original characters; unfortunately education has almost wiped them out.'[6]

For Lloyd-Jones, the primary indication of his country's degeneration was the 'tendency to judge a man by his degrees and diplomas rather than by his character'. He continued, 'What has become of those discussions that used to take place in the workshops of the blacksmith and the shoe-maker?'[7] He is also reported to have said, 'The most truly cultured people he had met were not those to be found in universities, but the people he had met in Llangeitho and Tregaron, who had not received any special education . . . A cultured man was one who thought.'[8] Such views were reinforced when he was ministering among the working-class people of South Wales. In the Saturday night Brotherhood at Sandfields, Port Talbot, he found more 'original characters', men with little or no formal education, but men who thought deeply.[9] Lloyd-Jones admired people whose individuality was unspoilt by an educational system that tended to produce an artificial uniformity. In a tribute to Peter Hughes Griffiths, his minister at Charing Cross, he wrote of his independence of mind and of the concern he had 'that genius and originality were being throttled and strangled by the mechanical ideas governing church and state'.[10]

Was this critical attitude to purely academic training and his obvious primitivist enthusiasm for natural talent evidence of a deep mistrust of all formal education for the betterment of the individual? His own stellar educational achievements and the way in which he used his medical training to good effect both in the pulpit and pastoral situations suggest otherwise.[11] What remained a concern to him throughout his life, though, was intellectual pride and the 'snobbish element' attached to learning, as well as the acquiring of information that left little room for deep thought or, more importantly, the development of spiritual character.[12]

---

6. Ibid., pp. 10–14. Later he was to warn preachers against the temptation to be a 'character'; see D. M. Lloyd-Jones, *Preaching and Preachers* (London: Hodder and Stoughton, 1971), p. 97.

7. Murray, *Lloyd-Jones: First Forty Years*, p. 68.

8. Report in the *Welsh Gazette*, 29 December 1927, cited in Murray, ibid., p. 174.

9. Murray, ibid., p. 233.

10. Ibid., pp. 36–37.

11. See ibid., p. 147, where Lloyd-Jones admits that his preaching betrayed a 'medical approach'.

12. See D. M. Lloyd-Jones, *Romans: Exposition of Chapter 12: Christian Conduct* (Edinburgh: Banner of Truth, 2000), pp. 450, 453–454.

Lloyd-Jones was not averse to people achieving high academic attainments and he himself had engaged in advanced postgraduate medical research.[13] During the 1940s, in correspondence with his close friend Philip Edgcumbe Hughes, whose theological mind, writing style and scholarship he admired, Lloyd-Jones bemoaned the lack of evangelical scholars and writers. He wrote about how he had been constantly looking out for such men and urged Hughes to obtain higher degrees in theology for future usefulness.[14] To this end Lloyd-Jones was a major contributor in the early discussions that led to the research centre at Tyndale House, Cambridge and the formation of the Tyndale Fellowship. He understood the need for detailed, meticulous biblical research and chaired the Biblical Research Committee from 1951 to 1957. His concern to encourage scholarship at the highest level by evangelical postgraduates continued in subsequent years by his chairmanship of the awards subcommittee that managed the Tyndale research grants. He remained an active participant in the Tyndale Fellowship until his retirement from Westminster Chapel in 1968.

Nevertheless, from the beginning of his involvement Lloyd-Jones did not cease to warn of the hazards of overspecialization and to emphasize biblical scholarship's subsidiary role. He argued that scholarship should not become the master, determining doctrine and its practical application. He was at pains to stress that the research worker's task should not be isolated from wider biblical and systematic theology.[15] The wisdom of this viewpoint was appreciated by J. I. Packer who pleaded unsuccessfully that research facilities at Tyndale House should include theology. However, there were those on the Biblical

---

13. It has been assumed that Lloyd-Jones was awarded his doctor of medicine (MD) in 1923 for his research into bacterial endocarditis (infection of the heart), but this work did not begin until the following year when through Thomas Horder's influence he was the first to benefit from the newly founded St John Harmsworth Memorial Research Fund. Some of his experiments are recorded in notebooks held at the National Library of Wales, dated 1925 and 1926, and the results were published as 'An Experimental Study of Malignant Endocarditis', an appendix to Charles B. Perry, *Bacterial Endocarditis* (Bristol: J. Wright and Sons, 1936). It is possible that his doctoral research was investigating a type of Hodgkin's disease called Pell-Epstein disease for which he held the Baillie Research Scholarship.

14. Martyn Lloyd-Jones to Philip Edgcumbe Hughes, 3 February and 15 June 1942, 17 April 1946, 11 March 1949, in Iain H. Murray (ed.), *D. Martyn Lloyd-Jones: Letters 1919–1981* (Edinburgh: Banner of Truth, 1994), pp. 61, 64–65, 68–69, 73.

15. T. A. Noble, *Tyndale House and Fellowship: The First Sixty Years* (Leicester: Inter-Varsity Press, 2006), pp. 39–40.

Research Committee who feared that doctrine would bring unnecessary divisions, particularly over Calvinism. Lloyd-Jones, like Packer, was a Calvinist, but he tended to steer a careful course in his associations with the wider evangelical student movement, emphasizing the gospel essentials on which Calvinists and Arminians could agree. In the end, provision was made under the auspices of the wider Tyndale Fellowship for other scholarly interests such as church history and theology.[16]

While Lloyd-Jones appreciated the place of 'technicians', and if their work earned them recognition in the academic world that was not to be despised, his primary concern was for rigorous scholarship that would benefit the wider church. For him, Philip Edgcumbe Hughes was the ideal person to be the resident librarian at Tyndale House, one who possessed 'a theological mind' that was 'controlled' by an 'over-ruling devotion to our Lord' and a 'passion to serve him'.[17] In other words, he was anxious to see a leader with a holistic appreciation of the various branches of biblical and theological studies who sought to apply scholarship to the pressing spiritual concerns of the day.

The Calvinist-Arminian issue was but a smokescreen hiding the much more fundamental question of the Bible's authority. Lloyd-Jones was deeply aware of the dangers relating to an academic approach to the Bible and the desire for 'unfettered scholarship'. He has been criticized for not appreciating first hand the problems raised by biblical criticism and for his tendency to be suspicious of higher criticism.[18] The implication of such a comment is that only academics engaged in literary criticism of the Bible are in a position to judge the work of other scholars. But this was precisely the concern of Lloyd-Jones and it has since been vigorously endorsed by Carl Trueman who writes, 'Theological scholars should not make the technical nature of their work an excuse for unbridled freedom, but see their work in the context of the church as a whole.'[19]

Much of the blame for the undermining of the Bible's authority Lloyd-Jones laid firmly at the door of the so-called higher critical movement, as he explained at the National Bible Rally in 1961. Could one approach the Bible purely as a human production and hope to hold to an evangelical position?

---

16. Ibid., pp. 112–113.

17. Murray, *Lloyd-Jones: Fight of Faith*, p. 130.

18. Noble, *Tyndale House*, p. 70. See Iain Murray's comment in *Lloyd-Jones: Messenger of Grace* (Edinburgh: Banner of Truth, 2008), pp. 196–197.

19. Carl R. Trueman, 'The Impending Evangelical Crisis', *Evangelicals Now* (February 1998), p. 10.

Philosophy and human understanding had replaced divine revelation, where the Scriptures 'must be regarded as every other book, and examined in the same way as every other book is examined'.[20] This was a swipe as much at liberal-minded conservative scholars as it was at the modernistic community.[21] There was a failure to appreciate that academics did not approach the Scriptures with completely open minds. They too had preconceived ideas that influenced the outcome of their research. There was, as Lloyd-Jones frequently pointed out, no such thing as 'pure' scholarship when it came to the biblical text.[22]

He continually emphasized that a biblical perspective on most issues of life meant holding in tension opposing positions, keeping a balance between extreme views: between divine sovereignty and human responsibility, rigidity and laxity, legalism and antinomianism. The same applied when it came to scholarship and obscurantism, intellectualism and pietism.

Training preachers

Similar paradoxes are observable in assessing Lloyd-Jones's position on ministerial education, but again his overriding desire was to keep a biblical balance. His earlier outspoken criticisms of the prevailing attitudes towards education go some way towards explaining why he was in two minds about the education available at many of the leading theological colleges of his day. He found it 'pathetic' that a nation that had produced such men as Howel Harris and John Elias was now found 'worshipping at the altar of degrees. That it should have crept into our chapels is still worse.'[23] At the back of his mind he was probably thinking of the mixed blessings left by Lewis Edwards, the first

---

20. D. M. Lloyd-Jones, 'How can we see a return to the Bible?', in D. M. Lloyd-Jones, *Knowing the Times: Addresses Delivered on Various Occasions 1942–1977* (Edinburgh: Banner of Truth, 1989), p. 107.

21. Douglas Johnson writes, 'In the light of its past history . . . the biggest single danger to the Evangelical Movement at each stage comes not from its declared opponents, but from some of those who claim to be its friends.' Douglas Johnson, *Contending for the Faith* (Leicester: Inter-Varsity Press, 1979), p. 342. See also, Oliver Barclay, *Evangelicalism in Britain 1935–1995: A Personal Sketch* (Leicester: Inter-Varsity Press, 1997), pp. 128–129.

22. D. M. Lloyd-Jones, *An Exposition of Romans 8:17–39: The Final Perseverance of the Saints* (Edinburgh: Banner of Truth, 1975), p. 320.

23. Murray, *Lloyd-Jones: First Forty Years*, p. 68.

principal of the Welsh Calvinistic Methodist College at Bala, and by his son, Thomas Charles Edwards, the first principal of the Aberystwyth University College of Wales.[24] Constantly he warned of the danger of making a god out of education.[25]

By the end of the nineteenth century the main denominational theological colleges in England and Wales had all established links with the universities and encouraged their students to sit for examinations set by these academic institutions.[26] This coincided with the spread of secularism throughout British universities. Even before he entered the ministry, Lloyd-Jones considered it 'blasphemous' that Welsh people were quoting the Bible as they would Shakespeare and treating it merely 'as a text-book of history or literature'.[27] The education given in the University Colleges of Wales had led preachers to doubt the Bible's authority and the existence of hell, and he emphasized that degrees and diplomas were useless when faced with such stern realities as death.[28]

His early views on ministerial education are important when considering Lloyd-Jones's own rejection of formal theological training. After many months agonizing over his sense of call to full-time Christian ministry, in December 1926 he accepted a call to become the lay pastor of Sandfields Forward Movement Hall, Port Talbot. Like some of the outstanding preachers of eighteenth-century Calvinistic Methodism and the early evangelists of the denomination's Forward Movement, Lloyd-Jones was unordained and one wonders whether he would have preferred to have remained in that position.[29] Under pressure from his denomination he was eventually ordained without any theological training, much to the annoyance of those who stood for strict

---

24. W. P. Griffiths, 'Edward Matthews, Nonconformity and Welsh Identity', in Robert Pope (ed.), *Religion and National Identity* (Cardiff: University of Wales Press, 2001), pp. 72–73. For a more positive assessment of Lewis Edwards's contribution, see D. Densil Morgan, 'Lewis Edwards (1808–87)', *Welsh Journal of Religious History*, vol. 3 (2008), pp. 15–28.

25. E.g., see D. M. Lloyd-Jones, *Old Testament Evangelistic Sermons* (Edinburgh: Banner of Truth, 1995), p. 68.

26. Philip Eveson (ed.), *The Gospel Ministry Today: Practical Insights and Application* (Darlington: Evangelical Press, 2005), pp. 159, 162.

27. Murray, *Lloyd-Jones: First Forty Years*, p. 68.

28. Ibid., pp. 86–88.

29. D. M. Lloyd-Jones, *Inaugural Address* (London: London Theological Seminary, 1978), p. 4.

order. He had considered entering the denominational college at Aberystwyth and began studying Greek as one of the entrance requirements, but after his interview with the principal he was convinced that a two- or three-year training programme for a theological diploma or degree with a further pastoral year at the Bala College was not the way forward for him. The denomination had similarly waived its rules in 1893 to ordain Seth Joshua, one of the original leaders of the Forward Movement.[30]

It would seem that from the late 1950s Lloyd-Jones had become even more doubtful about the benefits of theological college training.[31] This can be detected from his preliminary remarks at the opening of the London Theological Seminary (LTS) in 1977.[32] He certainly believed that men called to the Christian ministry needed their minds stretched and trained through study, but this did not necessarily mean they needed 'formal teaching' in a theological college. The apostles were 'mighty preachers', as were many of the eighteenth-century exhorters and lay preachers, yet 'from the modern standpoint' they had no training.[33] Others who displayed those character traits he so much admired and were without college training included Charles Spurgeon, Joseph Parker and his predecessor at Westminster Chapel, Campbell Morgan. In Lloyd-Jones's tribute to Campbell Morgan following his death in 1945, he made this telling remark:

> The next point I want to make about him is that he was a great individualist. And, surely, we ought to thank God for that in a day like this when we are all becoming so regimented. Dr Morgan never went to a Theological College. No College could ever have produced such a man. I would go further, and say, no College could even have spoiled such a man! He never went to a Theological College, and he often delighted to repeat his list of men who had never been to a Theological College. It is a most interesting and significant list![34]

---

30. T. Mardy Rees, *Seth Joshua and Frank Joshua* (Wrexham: Hughes & Son, 1926), p. 59; Geraint Fielder, *Grace, Grit and Gumption* (Bridgend: Evangelical Movement of Wales, 2004), pp. 86–87.

31. Murray, *Lloyd-Jones: Fight of Faith*, p. 712.

32. Lloyd-Jones, *Inaugural Address*, p. 1.

33. Ibid., p. 3.

34. *Westminster Record*, vol. 19 (July 1945). In a letter to his father in 1853, Spurgeon wrote, 'I told the deacons that I was not a College man, and they said, "That is to us a special recommendation, for you would not have much savour or unction

It was not that he despised the need for ministers to be trained or felt beyond the need of help himself. As Donald Macleod makes clear, 'Whatever his attitude to theological colleges Dr Lloyd-Jones had had the advantage of a rigorous university education. He had also received a thorough professional training as a medical clinician. Beyond that, certainly, he taught himself.'[35] During the early days of his ministry in Port Talbot he received pastoral guidance from senior ministers and when his attention was drawn to genuine deficiencies he listened to his critics and sought to rectify the imbalance.[36] He immersed himself in the Puritans and absorbed the weighty tomes of Jonathan Edwards and Benjamin Warfield. He also read a wide selection of more contemporary theologians, including Karl Barth and Emil Brunner, and through perusing 'good book reviews' in a range of Christian periodicals, journals and newspaper supplements he was able to select the most significant books to study. In all of his reading he attempted to think through issues as thoroughly as he was able.[37] As for his approach to homiletics and pastoralia, his medical training remained 'a powerful influence'.[38]

Although Lloyd-Jones shunned formal theological training, the fact that he considered becoming principal of his denomination's theological college at Bala in 1938 indicated that he was not entirely averse to the idea of ministerial training in a formal college setting. It was at Bala that all of his denomination's ministerial students undertook a year's course in pastoral studies, its aim being to relate their academic study of theology 'to the practical needs and difficulties which they will meet as preachers and pastors of churches'.[39] Lloyd-Jones would undoubtedly have found this position appealing and he was familiar with the college, having been invited to address the students during the 1932–3

if you came from College".' C. H. Spurgeon, *Autobiography: The Early Years*, vol. 1 (Edinburgh: Banner of Truth, 1962), p. 249.

35. Donald Macleod, 'The Lloyd-Jones Legacy', *Monthly Record of the Free Church of Scotland* (October 1983), p. 208.

36. Murray, *Lloyd-Jones: First Forty Years*, pp. 190–191.

37. Frederick and Elizabeth Catherwood, *Martyn Lloyd-Jones: The Man and His Books* (Bridgend: Evangelical Library of Wales, 1982), pp. 26–27; J. I. Packer, 'A Kind of Puritan', in Christopher Catherwood (ed.), *Martyn Lloyd-Jones: Chosen by God* (Crowborough: Highland Books, 1986), pp. 41–42.

38. Brencher, *Lloyd-Jones*, p. 9. See also Murray, *Lloyd-Jones: Fight of Faith*, p. 184.

39. *Calendar of the United Theological College Aberystwyth and Bala for 1940–1941 and Records of Sessions 1932–40* (Caernarvon: Calvinistic Methodist or Presbyterian Church of Wales, n.d.), p. 43.

session.[40] No doubt, as a number of South Wales ministers were hoping, he saw it as an opportunity to influence for the better those whose faith might well have wilted from being subjected to the destructive biblical criticism required for degree and diploma courses. That he did not in the end take up the position was the decision of the denomination rather than the result of any doubts in Lloyd-Jones's mind concerning the need.[41]

How well informed was Lloyd-Jones about theological education outside his own denomination? In his early ministry at Sandfields he had associations with R. B. Jones and his Bible Institute at Porth in the Rhondda Valley,[42] and he was heavily involved in the establishment of the London Bible College (LBC). Declining the invitation to become principal of LBC, he was nevertheless committed to the whole enterprise and became vice-chairman of the College Council in 1943.[43] In the late 1950s Lloyd-Jones participated in discussions with the Strict Baptists over the future of their Bible Institute at Brockley, Lewisham, but declined an invitation to join their committee.[44] During the early 1970s he was made aware of student unrest over what some considered the overly harsh discipline at the South Wales Bible College (originally the Barry School of Evangelism).[45]

Lloyd-Jones's attitude and responses to these institutions and their leadership reveal the extremes he wished to avoid and the paradoxes that are so much a feature of his position on ministerial education. On the one hand, he was not sympathetic towards those who displayed an essentially negative, censorious spirit. He considered it counterproductive. This came to be true of R. B. Jones, who began increasingly to model himself on the pugnacious T. T. Shields of Jarvis Street Baptist Church, Toronto.[46] In addition, he was unhappy with the narrow position taken by the Strict Baptists who required

40. Ibid., p. 47.

41. Murray, *Lloyd-Jones: First Forty Years*, pp. 346–352.

42. Ibid., pp. 192–193; Noel Gibbard, *R. B. Jones: Gospel Ministry in Turbulent Times* (Bridgend: Bryntirion Press, 2009), pp. 134–135, 176.

43. H. H. Rowdon, *London Bible College: The First Twenty-Five Years* (Worthing: Henry Walter, 1968), p. 27.

44. Philip Grist, 'Strict Baptist Bible Institute', *Strict Baptist Historical Society*, no. 10 (Summer 2002), pp. 9–10. In 1958 the Institute was rebranded as 'The Calvinistic Training College'.

45. Noel Gibbard, *Taught to Serve: The History of Barry and Bryntirion Colleges* (Bridgend: Evangelical Press of Wales, 1996), p. 168.

46. Murray, *Lloyd-Jones: First Forty Years*, pp. 273–274; Gibbard, *R. B. Jones*, pp. 189–191.

all students to be of that denomination.[47] Lloyd-Jones was also opposed to the regimental type of training that characterized many Bible colleges of that period, where students were expected to engage in their private devotions, study or relaxation at set times each day and to regurgitate the lecture notes in order to pass examinations. Such legalism and lack of thought ran counter to the kind of intellectual and ministerial training that Lloyd-Jones had in mind.[48] However, on the other hand, he eventually 'lost interest' in London Bible College when Principal Ernest Kevan began preparing students for London University's Bachelor of Divinity degree in 1946.[49] This policy was introduced largely to gain recognition as a worthy educational establishment, acceptable to denominations such as the Baptist Union. Lloyd-Jones appreciated the problem that LBC students were experiencing in gaining accreditation from mainline denominations, but he was adamant that the university curriculum was spiritually unhelpful for the work of the Christian ministry. The aim of the college from the start was for academic standards recognized by the university. However, by encouraging Kevan's appointment, Lloyd-Jones may have hoped he would steer the college away from preparing its ministerial students for London qualifications, especially as Kevan originally came from within Strict Baptist circles where theological degrees were not encouraged.[50]

Lloyd-Jones's London Bible College address in May 1958 sparked renewed interest in the subject of ministerial training. At the Puritan Conference in December that year, following the first paper, there was, in J. I. Packer's words, 'a lively discussion of what is and is not needed in the way of theological training if ministers of the Puritan stamp are to be made today'.[51] It included a contribution by Principal Kevan in which he spoke of the usefulness of the BD (Bachelor of Divinity) course.[52] In the following spring, continued interest in the subject was fuelled by articles in *The Banner of Truth* magazine on well-known

---

47. Grist, 'Strict Baptist Bible Institute', p. 10.

48. Lloyd-Jones, *Inaugural Address*, pp. 9, 15.

49. Barclay, *Evangelicalism in Modern Britain*, p. 129.

50. Ian Randall suggests that Lloyd-Jones's views 'may have been crystallising', but as indicated above they were already well formed by this stage. Ian Randall, *Educating Evangelicalism: The Origins, Development and Impact of London Bible College* (Carlisle: Paternoster, 2000), p. 105. See further, Paul Brown, 'The Life and Legacy of E. F. Kevan', in *Old Paths New Shoes* (London: Westminster Conference, 2009), pp. 68–71.

51. J. I. Packer, 'Foreword', in *A Goodly Heritage* (London: Wickliffe Press, 1958), pp. 6–7.

52. Murray, *Lloyd-Jones: Fight of Faith*, p. 311.

nineteenth-century preachers. Iain Murray informed readers that John Angell James (1785–1859), minister of Carr's Lane Chapel and chairman of the Spring Hill Congregational College, Birmingham (later to become Mansfield College, Oxford), had become alarmed at what he saw as 'an excessive regard to talent, genius and eloquence in the ministry of the word. Ours is an age of man-worship, and idolatry of genius.'[53] Murray also referred to James's biographer, Dr John Campbell (1795–1867), the minister of Whitefield's Tabernacle, Tottenham Court Road, London, who questioned the wisdom of the Nonconformist colleges adopting the University of London degree courses. Campbell had maintained that such training only sent out 'companies of tutors, rather than Evangelists . . . The churches ask for *Preachers*, and they are offered BA's, MA's and LLB's! I submit that the entire system is wrong.'[54]

These concerns raised by respected Congregational preachers of the past indicated that the minister of Westminster Chapel was no Welsh maverick in alerting his generation to the dangers of looking to scholarship and knowledge as the key to power in the pulpit. Lloyd-Jones had admired the stand of J. Gresham Machen and the formation of Westminster Theological Seminary, Philadelphia, in the 1930s as a bulwark of orthodoxy. However, in the desire to defend the faith in an intelligent way with scholarship and learning, he believed 'a lack of balance' had occurred at Westminster Seminary, an inevitable 'lack of vitality and power in the propagation of the gospel'.[55]

In his 1969 lectures to the students at Westminster Seminary, later published as *Preaching and Preachers* (1971), Lloyd-Jones presented his mature thoughts on preaching. They include a statement that epitomized his position and what lay behind so many of his concerns: 'What is the chief end of preaching? I like to think it is this. It is to give men and women a sense of God and His presence.'[56] While not denying the value of scholarship, and emphasizing that 'the abler a man is the better preacher he should be', he opined that the preacher's authority was spiritual and should not be seen to rest on his status as a scholar. It was in this context that he raised the subject of academic attire in the pulpit. While he commended the black preaching gown which he viewed as a sign of a person's call to the gospel ministry, he vehemently disapproved of the wearing of degree gowns and hoods. His reasons were consistent with

53. Quoted in Iain Murray, 'A Hundred Years Ago – Part II', *The Banner of Truth*, no. 15 (April 1959), pp. 6–7.

54. Quoted in ibid., pp. 8–9.

55. Murray, *Lloyd-Jones: Fight of Faith*, pp. 619–620.

56. Lloyd-Jones, *Preaching and Preachers*, p. 97.

his belief. Academic dress drew attention to the man himself and his scholastic abilities, distracting attention from 'the spiritual authority of the preacher'.[57]

Lloyd-Jones's London Bible College message and subsequent comments also reveal some disquiet over the subject of apologetics. In closing the December 1958 Puritan Conference discussion on ministerial training, Lloyd-Jones wondered whether theological degrees taken in evangelical colleges were leading to 'an over-concern with the apologetic at the expense of the positive'.[58] Such courses inevitably meant that an inordinate amount of time was spent in first setting out the views of the biblical critics and then, for evangelicals, it meant seeking to counteract their arguments point by point. As he was to indicate with relish some twenty years later, the assured results of biblical criticism over the past century had more or less come to nothing. He concluded, 'So all the fuss and the bother, and all the weariness that has been caused to endless generations of poor students who have had to grapple with this nonsense, has all proved to be completely valueless and useless!'[59]

This fondness for hyperbole, which heightened his seemingly paradoxical positions, was also used against those evangelicals whom he believed were putting too much faith in the apologetics of Francis Schaeffer (1912–84), the founder of the L'Abri Fellowship. Lloyd-Jones was to tell the Welsh Ministers' Conference in 1971, 'Nothing has so caused us to forget God . . . as our concern for apologetics.'[60] He had used such pejorative language in 1957 at an International Fellowship of Evangelical Students conference in Canada, where he stated, 'I am not sure that apologetics has not been the curse of evangelical Christianity for the last twenty to thirty years.'[61] While recognizing the place of apologetics in refuting false teaching, he warned of the danger of becoming too worldly wise and concentrating on the negative at the expense of the positive.[62]

Another discernible element in Lloyd-Jones's position on ministerial education arising from his 1958 London Bible College address was his concern that

57. Ibid., pp. 159–160.

58. Murray, *Lloyd-Jones: Fight of Faith*, p. 311.

59. Lloyd-Jones, *Inaugural Address*, p. 5. Paul Brown suggests that students may well have expressed their concerns to Lloyd-Jones, as many of them attended Westminster Chapel; Brown, 'The Life and Legacy of E. F. Kevan', p. 70.

60. Robert Horn, 'His Place in Evangelicalism', in Catherwood (ed.), *Chosen by God*, p. 21.

61. D. M. Lloyd-Jones, *Authority* (London: Inter-Varsity Fellowship, 1958), p. 14.

62. Lloyd-Jones, *Inaugural Address*, p. 14.

theological students 'know God better'.[63] It was a theme to which he constantly returned.[64] At the 1960 Puritan Conference he warned of the dangers of a purely theoretical and academic interest in truth and urged the importance of 'knowing' over against 'knowing about' a subject. The 'whole end and object of theology is to know God'. He likened it to the difference between 'preaching about the Gospel and preaching the Gospel'. While Lloyd-Jones held that the intellect certainly had priority over feeling, it was not to be isolated from heart and will.[65] The same note had been struck as far back as 1947. Though prominence was being given to the Bible among those influenced by Barth, 'there is a difference', he argued, 'between preaching the Word and preaching about the Word'.[66]

This emphasis on the experiential was the reason why, in December 1952, Lloyd-Jones was somewhat cool in his reply to Philip Edgcumbe Hughes's suggestion of closer ties with the continental Calvinists. He was suspicious of 'the cold intellectualism' that characterized some of their number.[67] His Luther address in 1967 contained a similar concern for spiritual experience in place of dry, academic theology: 'You do not get reformations through an Erasmus; it is through a Luther . . . Your dry-as-dust theologians and your scholars never lead to reformations.'[68] Again, in saying this, he was not despising the work of scholars. Lloyd-Jones acknowledged in the same address that Luther was no mean scholar, but pointed out that, unlike Erasmus, he was a man 'with an intense personal experience of salvation' who was moved and led on by God to achieve what he did.[69] This was consistent with his previous concern over the policy pursued by Tyndale House. Lloyd-Jones also used his Luther address to criticize the ecumenical movement. He was not alone in viewing it as 'a movement of professors and ecclesiastics'.[70] Such theological professionals he considered lacked 'this volcanic element, this living element, this experimental

---

63. Murray, *Lloyd-Jones: Fight of Faith*, p. 311.

64. Lloyd-Jones, *Inaugural Address*, p. 15.

65. D. M. Lloyd-Jones, 'Knowledge – False and True', in *Increasing in the Knowledge of God* (London: Puritan Papers, 1961), pp. 52–53. See also D. M. Lloyd-Jones, *Evangelistic Sermons at Aberavon* (Edinburgh: Banner of Truth, 1983), p. 40.

66. D. M. Lloyd-Jones, *Crefydd Heddiw ac Yfory* ('Religion Today and Tomorrow') (Llandybie: Llyfrau'r Dryw, 1947), pp. 11–12.

67. Murray, *Lloyd-Jones: Fight of Faith*, p. 196.

68. D. M. Lloyd-Jones, *Luther and His Message for Today* (London: British Evangelical Council, 1968), p. 22.

69. Ibid., pp. 20, 22–23.

70. Ibid., p. 22. Ian Henderson, in *Power Without Glory: A Study in Ecumenical Politics*

element' to be found in Luther.[71] In emphasizing this, he may also have had in mind the way in which 'bright theological college staff or academics' and 'certain young activists' had influenced the National Evangelical Anglican Congress at Keele in April 1967, as they would the Nottingham Congress ten years later.[72]

The 'experiential element' preferred by Lloyd-Jones was thoroughly consistent with the warm, experimental Calvinism of his Welsh Methodist background.[73] He was concerned that many eminent theologians lacked this aspect to their faith and therefore did not usually recommend them as helps for ministers. While he was impressed with the first volume of Karl Niebuhr's work on *The Nature and Destiny of Man* (1941), he regarded this neo-orthodox theologian as having only undergone a 'philosophical conversion'.[74] He likewise considered Karl Barth and Emil Brunner to have fallen short of 'the real thing'.[75]

The founding of London Theological Seminary

Lloyd-Jones's reservations about theological colleges arose in part out of his strongly held belief that 'preachers are born not made', a belief that he felt might also apply to pastors,[76] as well as his opposition to the traditional methods of training ministers. However, in the 1970s 'solid arguments' had persuaded him of the need for a new institution for the training of preachers and pastors. The fact that some Free Church students were going to Anglican colleges was perhaps the argument that finally tipped the balance for

(London: Hutchinson, 1967), also argued that the British ecumenical movement was primarily concerned with academics and church officials looking for power.

71. Lloyd-Jones, *Luther*, p. 22.

72. Horn, 'His Place in Evangelicalism', p. 26; Roger Beckwith, 'Keele, Nottingham and the Future', in David Samuel (ed.), *The Evangelical Succession* (Cambridge: James Clarke, 1979), pp. 104–105. See also, Barclay, *Evangelicalism in Britain*, pp. 127–132.

73. There are striking parallels with the views of William Williams, Pantycelyn, the chief theologian of eighteenth-century Welsh Methodism. See Eifion Evans, *Pursued by God* (Bridgend: Evangelical Press of Wales, 1996), pp. 170–175.

74. Martyn Lloyd-Jones to Leslie Land, 17 April 1943, in Murray (ed.), *Lloyd-Jones: Letters, 1919–1981*, p. 66.

75. Martyn Lloyd-Jones to Bethan Lloyd-Jones, 21 September 1939, in ibid., p. 46.

76. Lloyd-Jones, *Inaugural Address*, p. 10.

immediate action. Against the background of the ecumenical movement with its moves to amalgamate colleges and his fear of 'empire builders' from within his own constituency, he also saw this new venture as an opportune moment to express something of the evangelical unity he had been calling for over the preceding decade.[77]

Beyond the immediate situation, it was a concern for the future of gospel ministry that ultimately persuaded him of the need for a training programme where the essential features of such ministry would be encouraged. Not that he was the instigator of this fresh approach. As with most, if not all, of the agencies and movements in which he was involved, the initiative came from others. As chairman of a sponsoring committee that consisted of men belonging to various denominational backgrounds, but all under the umbrella of the British Evangelical Council, Lloyd-Jones was able to see some of his own long-held views brought to fruition in the new institution, London Theological Seminary, launched in October 1977, sharing a site with Kensit Memorial College in Finchley.

His opposition to the kind of theological training then available went much deeper than the usual criticisms being voiced. Even those institutions like London Bible College that were established to safeguard evangelical truth he considered had made a 'fatal mistake'. He was not merely concerned that the secular universities were setting the agenda for ministerial students, but that they had allowed 'the curriculum to be determined by the liberal outlook'[78] and so-called 'academic objectivity' where students were encouraged to view the Bible, church history and theology like any other subject. This outlook and method he considered completely out of place in an establishment for the training of preachers and pastors. They were to appreciate the spiritual nature of all they were studying and seek to apply it to their ministerial work. In advocating the 'spiritual' over against the 'scientific' approach, Lloyd-Jones was not being pietistic or anti-intellectual. He was not reacting in a way that some evangelicals were doing by advocating a training that was 'spiritual as opposed to academic'.[79] Quoting Anselm, he emphasized that while belief must come before reason, an enlightened spiritual mind needed to be encouraged to reason out and understand as far as possible what was believed.[80] He

---

77. Ibid., pp. 2–3.
78. Ibid., p. 5.
79. See D. P. Kingdon, *Training for the Ministry: An Historical Survey* (London: Evangelical Library, 1969), p. 22.
80. Lloyd-Jones, *Inaugural Address*, p. 9.

therefore advocated rigorous study for ministerial students in the various branches of theology.[81]

Another facet of the training that demanded a different approach concerned the 'spiritual knowledge' that both pupil and teacher possessed. In the case of other subjects, he argued, the pupil begins by knowing virtually nothing. But in the case of theological training, every Christian 'in a sense has the same knowledge as the preacher and the pastor has'. The difference lay merely in extent. Every spiritually minded ministerial student is someone 'who has a certain minimum knowledge'. He will have been affected personally by the subject, whereas in the study of science or philosophy the personality is not involved in the same way.[82]

It was this concern with 'spiritual knowledge', the importance of which has already been highlighted, that, for Lloyd-Jones, put the training of preachers into a different realm, where degrees and diplomas 'do not belong' and where 'it is almost blasphemous' to think of examinations in connection with such knowledge.[83] Dissenting most strongly from the positions of both London Bible College and Westminster Theological Seminary, he stated that a ministerial training college should not in any way be compared with an institution of higher education.[84] In this the aims of Lloyd-Jones were similar to those of Spurgeon. In setting up his Pastors' College in the 1850s, Spurgeon's intention was 'to train preachers and pastors rather than scholars and masters of arts . . . The universities are the fit places for producing classical scholars, let them do it; our work is to open up the Scriptures, and help men to impress their fellows' hearts.'[85]

Lloyd-Jones's vision was for a 'method' of training where men would be encouraged to be preachers and pastors, 'not mere teachers still less lecturers'.[86] To that end he urged that the tutors must not be primarily 'academics', but themselves pastors and preachers. Again, he was not undervaluing the need for well-trained teachers, for in the next breath he drew special attention to the tutors' university degrees, ironic in view of his trenchant criticisms of academic attainment! Neither was he opposed to students going on to specialize in the

---

81. Ibid., pp. 11–15.

82. Ibid., p. 8.

83. Ibid., p. 9.

84. Ibid., p. 10.

85. C. H. Spurgeon, 'The ministry needed by the churches and measures for providing it', *The Sword and the Trowel* (May 1871), p. 226.

86. Lloyd-Jones, *Inaugural Address*, pp. 4, 6.

biblical languages or theology at university.[87] Yet Lloyd-Jones's vision for London Theological Seminary highlighted his view of preaching as not merely giving people information, but proclaiming a message that had first gripped them. It was consistent with his long-standing view that biblical scholarship was to be of practical service to the church.

Lloyd-Jones had a crucial role in determining the content of the initial syllabus for London Theological Seminary. The curriculum was to provide a thorough grounding in the Scriptures. This was to entail sufficient instruction in the original languages to enable the preacher to use the commentaries and various translations of the text intelligently. He dissented most strongly from the position of J. Gresham Machen, who insisted that 'you cannot read the Bible for yourself unless you know the languages in which it was written', arguing that some of the greatest preachers of the Christian church were ignorant of Hebrew, Aramaic and Greek.[88] The key to understanding the Bible was a spiritual matter.

Training was needed in exegesis and particularly hermeneutics and Lloyd-Jones himself gave a lecture on the latter subject in the seminary's first years. Grasping the message of the text and applying it was all-important. All the familiar emphases concerning the way theology was to be taught were reiterated in his inaugural address at the London Theological Seminary opening service. Biblical theology was essential, but not at the expense of systematics. The history of God's activity through the ages and the rise of denominations together with the development of Christian doctrine he regarded as extremely important, but no time was to be wasted on psychology and philosophy. Apologetics was to have a subordinate place in refuting arguments brought against Christianity, showing the futility of false teaching and exposing heretical views. For Lloyd-Jones the object of ministerial training

---

87. In 1999 the Board of London Theological Seminary established the John Owen Centre to help pastors continue with more advanced theological study. In October 2001 it linked with Westminster Theological Seminary to offer the ThM programme in historical theology.

88. Lloyd-Jones, *Inaugural Address*, pp. 11–12. Lloyd-Jones's copy of Machen's address at the opening of Westminster Theological Seminary includes exclamations and underlining where he makes these assertions. A few paragraphs later, when Machen speaks of the perspicuity of Scripture, Lloyd-Jones notes in the margin how this contradicts the previous statements. See J. Gresham Machen, 'Westminster Seminary: Its Purpose and Plan', in J. H. Skilton (ed.) *Studying the New Testament Today* (Grand Rapids, MI: Presbyterian and Reformed, 1974), pp. 161–169.

was 'to widen the knowledge' the student already possessed, 'to give him a deeper understanding, to make him a more profound thinker'.[89] The final word again echoed earlier concerns that the seminary should not be a 'dry-as-dust' academic institution producing men with first-class degrees, but should prepare them in such a way that they would be used by the Spirit to God's glory.

From the beginning the seminary faced considerable prejudice. Some in Wales were unhappy, seeing London Theological Seminary as a direct rival to the Bible College at Barry.[90] On the other hand, despite the representative nature of the Sponsoring Committee (later the London Theological Seminary Board), there were not a few who viewed the seminary as a Welsh enclave, too parochial and separatist in tone and character and far too much influenced by Lloyd-Jones's obsessive concern for Spirit-anointed preaching and revival. The committee members were certainly not all in the Lloyd-Jones mould and before the final faculty appointments were made, Herbert Carson had been approached to serve as principal and Donald Macleod as a full-time tutor. Both declined due to their ministerial commitments.

At first London Theological Seminary had no principal, each tutor taking it in turns to chair faculty meetings and present the annual report. John Caiger (secretary of the Keswick Convention and the Westminster Fellowship) acted as pastor to the students. Futhermore, well-known evangelicals were invited to give occasional lectures relating to ethical and contemporary issues, such as C. G. Scorer, Oliver Barclay, Herbert Carson, Leith Samuel and Fred Catherwood. From the United States visiting speakers included J. H. Gerstner and Carl Henry.

Notwithstanding the initial discouragements, during the first ten years of its life over one hundred men from various church backgrounds and cultures passed through the seminary. Not all became pastors, but the majority have proved themselves faithful gospel ministers. Far from having a separatist mentality, Lloyd-Jones's real concern was for evangelical unity and this the seminary sought to foster. London Theological Seminary took its stand over the ecumenical movement, but it did not bar anyone applying from the mainline denominations or from charismatic circles. The press release announcing the new seminary read, 'A concern for the primacy of the Gospel ensures that

---

89. Lloyd-Jones, *Inaugural Address*, p. 15.

90. The Barry college (South Wales Bible College) became the Evangelical Theological College of Wales, at Bryntirion, Bridgend in 1985. In 2007 it was rebranded as the Wales Evangelical School of Theology.

the Seminary will not be the preserve of a sectarian or partisan segment of Evangelicalism.'[91] Issues of baptism and church government were in the early years examined by John Nichols for the Presbyterians and Jack Hoad and Robert Sheehan for the Baptists. Men of divergent views learned to appreciate each other's positions better, which later resulted in closer fellowship between evangelical churches.

Focusing exclusively on preparing men for gospel ministry was not a short-sighted policy. Suitable training institutions already existed for those seeking to enter other areas of Christian service. As a medical school is devoted to train doctors, so London Theological Seminary was devoted to the task of training preachers. It enabled all the tutoring, even the language lessons, to be approached in the light of the gospel ministry. End-of-term examinations were outlawed, but a student's progress was monitored by continual assessment through class participation, leadership of the daily communal worship, essays, language tests and feedback from churches. Lloyd-Jones was not averse to preaching classes as such, and his own lectures at Westminster Theological Seminary in 1969 reveal his desire to help students with sermon preparation. What he regarded as 'an abomination' was the kind of professionalism represented by books such as W. E. Sangster's *The Craft of Sermon Illustration* (1946).[92]

For the seminary's first tutors, it was inevitable that they sometimes found it difficult to balance commitments to their churches and to the London Theological Seminary, but as one has written, 'the principle of having working ministers as lecturers did add pastoral reality to the college situation'.[93] Another lecturer testifies that the vision of Lloyd-Jones helped him to focus on the contemporary relevance of his subject and the importance of being 'passionate in proclaiming the truth and of maintaining a close walk with the Lord'.[94] Lloyd-Jones's vision gave decisive shape to London Theological Seminary's distinctive ethos. His high view of the ministry, his strong emphasis

---

91. London Theological Seminary, 'Press Release' (22 June 1977), p. 1.

92. Lloyd-Jones, *Preaching and Preachers*, pp. 231–232.

93. Graham Harrison to Philip Eveson, 14 January 2011. Harrison was minister of Emmanuel Evangelical Church (Baptist), Newport until 2010 and travelled to London every fortnight to teach Christian doctrine for over thirty years.

94. Andrew Davies to Philip Eveson, 14 January 2011. Davies combined lecturing at the seminary, first in church history (1977–89) and later in homiletics (1999–2006), with ministerial responsibilities at Chessington Evangelical Church (1976–82), Lonlas, Swansea (1982–5), Free School Court, Bridgend (1985–97) and Kensit Evangelical Church, Finchley (1999–2006).

on the primacy of preaching and the necessity for that preaching to be in the power of the Holy Spirit remain hallmarks of the seminary to this day.

© Philip H. Eveson, 2011

7. LLOYD-JONES AND FUNDAMENTALISM

Robert Pope

Writing at the end of the 1950s, J. I. Packer warned the (evangelical) world that the word 'fundamentalist' had become a 'theological swear word' and that 'the important thing about a swear word . . . is not what it means but the feelings it expresses'. Indeed, he opined, it 'is a word that combines the vaguest conceptual meaning with the strongest emotional flavour'.[1] Packer's advice reflected the fact that, while the term was first coined by – or about – North American Protestants who sought to designate certain Christian doctrines as essential (admittedly in opposition to the identification of certain *essences* by the theological liberals),[2] it soon came to be used in order to evoke a particular, and usually adverse, reaction by the public at large. A letter from John Stott, published in *The Times* in 1955, claimed that the word 'fundamentalism' described 'the bigoted rejection of all Biblical criticism, a

---

1. J. I. Packer, *'Fundamentalism' and the Word of God* (Leicester: Inter-Varsity Press, 1958), p. 30.
2. E.g., Adolf Harnack's lectures *Das Wesen des Christentums*, published in English as *What is Christianity* (London: Williams and Norgate, 1901), highlighted the kingdom of God and its coming, the fatherhood of God and the value of the human soul, and the so-called higher morality as the *essence* (*Wesen*) of the faith.

mechanical view of inspiration and an excessively literalist interpretation of scripture'.[3] Indeed, by the late twentieth century, the word had become a 'synonym for religious dogmatism or ideologically rooted authoritarianism'.[4] Words such as 'bigoted', 'mechanical' or 'literalist' are not used lightly and in popular use, especially in religious contexts, 'fundamentalism' possesses only negative connotations. Fundamentalism, then, is virtually synonymous with a menace, a threat, a peril, and *reasonable* people might do well either to oppose it, or to avoid it at all costs. The result is that, especially in British ecclesiastical circles, few (if any) people own it through self-designation. Instead, it is most commonly applied to individuals and to groups in order to label them and, in so doing, to warn others of the dangers that might result from getting too close.

Martyn Lloyd-Jones was, during his lifetime, tarred with this kind of brush. John Brencher has argued that Lloyd-Jones's influence 'lay almost entirely within the evangelical sector of the church and, after 1967, this shrank to a minority of like-minded people'. Those beyond that constituency 'branded him as a "fundamentalist" and fanatical'.[5] And there were other occasions when the standpoint of which Lloyd-Jones was a prominent spokesman – particularly the unwavering opposition to the ecumenical movement and the commitment to the authority of Scripture – was branded fundamentalist even if the term was not directly applied to him.[6] There can be little doubt that those who employed this criticism believed it properly to reflect Lloyd-Jones's religious outlook, or that they abhorred what he stood for, but in none of these instances did it emerge as the result of identifying the detail of what he believed or from offering an argument as to *why* this might be termed a funda-mentalist position. Instead the label was used to denigrate him as a pernicious

3. Letter from John R. W. Stott, *The Times* (25 August 1955), p. 14. The letter was part of a debate which lasted several weeks and was sparked by the invitation of the Cambridge Inter-Collegiate Christian Union to Billy Graham to lead a mission in the University Church. For a brief analysis of the debate, see Harriet Harris, *Fundamentalism and Evangelicals* (Oxford: Clarendon, 1998), p. 54.

4. James Davidson Hunter, 'Fundamentalism in its Global Contours', in Norman Cohen (ed.), *The Fundamentalist Phenomenon: A View from Within; A View from Without* (Grand Rapids, MI: Eerdmans, 1995), p. 56.

5. John Brencher, *Martyn Lloyd-Jones (1899–1981) and Twentieth-Century Evangelicalism* (Milton Keynes: Paternoster, 2002), p. 196.

6. See, e.g., Iain H. Murray, *D. Martyn Lloyd-Jones: The Fight of Faith 1939–1981* (Edinburgh: Banner of Truth, 1990), pp. 298, 314.

force, running contrary to the times and offering only a partial and retrograde understanding of Christian faith.

In what follows, the meaning and use of the word 'fundamentalism' will first be explored, drawing especially from its historical employment as well as from the academic study of the phenomena associated with it. Following this, Lloyd-Jones's attitude towards Scripture and doctrine will be considered. Much of the evidence for this analysis comes from Lloyd-Jones's lectures on biblical doctrines delivered in Westminster Chapel on Friday evenings between 1952 and 1955 and later published as *Great Doctrines of the Bible*. Some other significant aspects of his ministry will then be discussed before a conclusion is offered about Lloyd-Jones and fundamentalism.

Fundamental difficulties

Use of the word 'fundamentalism' to describe religious groups expanded over the course of the twentieth century. Initially it was associated with Christian groups who perceived themselves to be defending true doctrine. Although there is no generally accepted fundamentalist creed,[7] the early identification of fundamental doctrines tended to emphasize the same points. To take two examples of its earliest manifestation, namely *The Fundamentals: A Testimony to the Truth*, which was a series of ninety essays published in twelve volumes between 1910 and 1915, and the declaration by the Northern American Presbyterian Church Assembly in 1910 which identified the fundamentals of Christian faith, an element of consistency exists between them. Their 'fundamentals' included the inspiration and authority of Scripture (the Presbyterians used the term 'infallibility'), the virgin birth of Christ and the historical reality of miracles, the atoning and specifically penal death of Christ as well as his physical resurrection and personal, eschatological return.[8]

As the century unfolded, the word was applied to those who adopted a particular socio-political stance which understood society to be corrupt and who issued a prophetic call to action in order to conform the world to the divine

7. The point is made by Jaroslav Pelikan in '"Fundamentalism and/or Orthodoxy?" Toward an Understanding of the Fundamentalist Phenomenon', in Cohen (ed.), *The Fundamentalist Phenomenon*, pp. 3–21.

8. *The Fundamentals*, edited by A. C. Dixon, L. Meyer and R. A. Torrey (Chicago: Testimony Publishing Co., c. 1909–15). See also Harris, *Fundamentalism and Evangelicals*, pp. 26–28; Packer, *'Fundamentalism' and the Word of God*, p. 28.

plan.[9] This allowed use of the term to be extended to adherents of religions other than Christianity, especially to Islamist militants, political Buddhists and Hindus and territorially minded Jewish leaders. Such activism can also be found among Christians and, while a particular understanding of doctrine undoubtedly underlies their activity, the truth is that, in a media age, it is activism rather than motivation which makes the headlines. Fundamentalists in the United States of America are far more likely to be identified by their protests about abortion, evolution and Islamist extremism than they are for their belief in the infallibility and inerrancy of Scripture, even if, for them, there is a direct link between biblical interpretation and socio-political activism.

Martyn Lloyd-Jones did not belong to such a media age and, in any case, he eschewed involvement in political protest. He maintained that the individual Christian had the duty to fulfil his or her civic duty and public vocation, but the church's sole responsibility was the proclamation of the gospel and the salvation of souls.[10] Alongside this, it has to be remembered that relationships between church and state in Britain are very different from those in the United States. Accordingly, in Britain, the word 'fundamentalist' – when employed of Christians – tends not to concern political involvement at all, but to identify a doctrinal stance, especially in relation to inerrant Scriptures,[11] alongside a definite and authoritarian style of leadership, with both linked to claims of infallibility. There may, of course, be a conflation of interest between conservative Christians on both sides of the Atlantic: they tend to be politically conservative, pro-life in relationship to abortion and anti-evolutionist. But whereas this has led to high-profile public involve-

---

9. According to Bruce B. Lawrence, the advocacy of a 'pure minority viewpoint' within a 'corrupt' dominant group, and the oppositional stance which seeks to transform the status quo, are both characteristics of fundamentalism. See Bruce B. Lawrence, *Defenders of God: The Fundamentalist Revolt Against the Modern Age* (Columbia, SC: University of South Carolina Press, 1995), p. 236.

10. D. M. Lloyd-Jones, *The Assurance of Our Salvation: Exploring the Depth of Jesus' Prayer for His Own* (Wheaton, IL: Crossway Books, 2000), p. 359; Carl Henry, 'An Interview', in Christopher Catherwood (ed.), *Martyn Lloyd-Jones: Chosen By God* (Crowborough: Highland Books, 1986), p. 106; John Peters, *Martyn Lloyd-Jones: Preacher* (Exeter: Paternoster Press, 1986), p. 61.

11. In his insightful, if somewhat polemical, work *Fundamentalism* (London: SCM, 1977), James Barr made the point that fundamentalists tend not to be literalists in their approach to the Bible. Instead, they assert biblical inerrancy and the result is a particular interpretation of biblical material.

ment in North America, Britain has witnessed very few organized protests on such issues. Accordingly, 'fundamentalists' in Britain are more likely to be identified as a consequence of internal debate within ecclesiastical circles rather than as the result of their political protest or social activism. This difference in context is important and enables the discussion about Lloyd-Jones and fundamentalism to take place, beginning with an account of his view of Scripture and its authority.

Infallible Scriptures

Underlying Lloyd-Jones's doctrinal scheme was a specific understanding of the nature and role of Scripture. He made much of the need to believe *biblical* doctrine, but this required a particular attitude to the Bible itself. While this attitude appeared to be straightforward, in fact there was a subtlety, if not complexity, associated with it which might not have been obvious to his congregations. Lloyd-Jones asserted that the Bible was not primarily concerned with world history, but with the revelation (which admittedly occurred in history) of God's plan of human salvation. Scripture was not merely a record but a revelation, it did not simply recount events but explained them and showed exactly how they should be understood in the context of the metanarrative of salvation history. The Bible was therefore absolutely authoritative not in matters of world history, or of science and technology, for it had no interest in those things, but as far as salvation was concerned it was the exclusive, authoritative revelation. It was absolute truth.

> Thus in the Bible we have the record of God's greatest redemptive acts. But we have also God's comment upon those acts; God's exposition of them; God's explanation of the work of salvation as well as the unfolding of the way itself. And the Bible claims that it alone has this revelation – there is no other.[12]

Lloyd-Jones adhered to belief in the verbal, plenary inspiration of the Scriptures: 'It is not merely that the thoughts are inspired,' he said, 'not merely the ideas, but the actual record, down to the particular words. It is not merely that the statements are correct, but that every word is divinely inspired.'[13]

---

12. D. M. Lloyd-Jones, *Great Doctrines of the Bible, Volume I: God the Father, God the Son* (Wheaton, IL: Crossway Books, 2003), p. 21.

13. Ibid., p. 24.

However, knowledge of the original languages was not required, providing that the translation was 'plain and accurate'.[14] By this he meant that the Bible had been translated by godly and prayerful men who believed in the Word of God. It seems that his attitude to the King James Bible, for example, was in part dictated by his belief that it was the result of such a process of translation. In an address to the National Bible Rally at the Royal Albert Hall in October 1961, he made the point very clearly in reference to those who had translated the 'Authorized Version'.

> These translators were all men who were orthodox in the faith. They believed the Bible is the infallible Word of God and they submitted to it as the final authority . . . Here, I say, were fifty-four men, scholars and saintly, who were utterly submitted to the Book. You have never had that in any other version. Here and here alone you have a body of men, who were absolutely committed to it, who gave themselves to it, who did not want to correct or sit in judgment upon it, whose only concern and desire was to translate it and interpret it for the masses of the people.[15]

Other, more modern, translations were tainted by biblical criticism and the liberalization of theology which occurred during the nineteenth century, and therefore could not be trusted. He articulated this very criticism in regard to the Revised Standard Version. While willing to recognize its popularity, he was keen to warn its readers of the preconceptions of its translators: 'But let us never forget that the men responsible for that translation are all men who are liberal in their theology, and it is interesting how that comes out even in . . . their translation,' he said.[16] Lloyd-Jones believed that the gospel was most properly articulated through words such as justification, sanctification, propitiation and redemption.[17] When these words – and concepts – were missing, the translation was inevitably deficient, and such deficiency arose from the view that human minds are able to correct the biblical revelation. Such translations

---

14. Ibid., p. 42.
15. D. M. Lloyd-Jones, 'How can we see a return to the Bible?', in D. M. Lloyd-Jones, *Knowing the Times: Addresses Delivered on Various Occasions, 1942–1977* (Edinburgh: Banner of Truth, 1989), p. 114.
16. D. M. Lloyd-Jones, *Romans: The Gospel of God: An Exposition of Chapter 1* (Edinburgh: Banner of Truth, 1985), p. 196; also Tony Sargent, *Gems from Martyn Lloyd-Jones: An Anthology of Quotations from 'The Doctor'* (Milton Keynes: Paternoster, 2007), p. 38.
17. Lloyd-Jones, 'How can we see a return to the Bible?', pp. 110–112.

– and he reserved special criticism for the New English Bible[18] – were dependent on human ideology rather than on divine inspiration, and they involved the mind's judgment of the words rather than the Word's judgment of the soul.

Apart from divine inspiration, there are two other aspects of Lloyd-Jones's understanding of the Scriptures which are important to acknowledge. First of all, he believed that while the Bible was written over a long period of time ('at least sixteen hundred years') and by a great number of authors ('over forty'), yet it was totally without contradiction, recording just one 'doctrine' and one 'morality'.[19] It constituted the only account of God's plan of salvation and therefore contained all that was needed to know about it. Thus, he argued, the Scriptures were either to be accepted in their entirety or, in practice, they were not accepted at all. There could be no compromise over this, for Lloyd-Jones believed that the Bible presented humankind with eternal truths and demanded a response:

> The message of the Bible is not to urge us to try to find truth; it is to ask us to listen to the truth, to God's truth. For its whole point is to say that God, knowing Himself, knowing man, knowing everything, has devised and schemed a plan whereby men and women can be delivered out of their failure and sin and can be made citizens and worthy citizens of God's kingdom.[20]

This meant that a critical approach was inappropriate and misleading. Despite the fact that he laid particular importance on the ability to reason, and he employed the appeal to logic as a rhetorical tool in his sermons, ultimately all human thought was to be subordinated to the scriptural revelation. This, he insisted, was to approach the issue properly by means of faith rather than by means of human reason. The proper attitude to adopt, he maintained, was submission to 'the Book':[21]

> 'I do not understand, but I am content not to understand. I believe the word of God and I rest myself and my whole position entirely upon it.' That is the faith position.

---

18. The NEB version of the New Testament was published in 1961 and the whole Bible in 1970.
19. Lloyd-Jones, 'How can we see a return to the Bible?', pp. 30–31; see also Tony Sargent, *The Sacred Anointing: The Preaching of Dr Martyn Lloyd-Jones* (London: Hodder and Stoughton, 1994), p. 229.
20. D. M. Lloyd-Jones, *The Kingdom of God* (Wheaton, IL: Crossway Books, 1992), p. 15.
21. Lloyd-Jones, 'How can we see a return to the Bible?', p. 108.

> The moment that you begin to bring in your mind and natural arguments and say that you cannot see or understand something, you are turning from the revelation and are reverting back to the sinful position of putting your mind up as the supreme court of appeal.[22]

Second, and almost paradoxically given his assertion that the Bible was not concerned with world history, he affirmed the historicity of all the events recorded in the Bible. We will return to this below. For the moment it is important to remember that while he asserted that belief in the historicity of the Scriptures was subordinate to the belief in the revelation of God's salvation, he also chided his listeners who might not assent to the former view. Thus, while the Bible is not primarily interested in world history, for 'it has another object', yet 'it crowds two thousand years into just eleven chapters in Genesis'.[23] He asserted that any rejection of the historicity of the flood (Gen. 7) would mean a similar rejection of Jesus Christ and his gospel because Christ believed it to be literally true.[24] Likewise, the story of the tower of Babel 'literally happened'.[25]

Such a hermeneutical approach was clearly intended to promote the sense of an absolutely trustworthy Bible. It suggests, even if unintentionally, that a simple reading and acceptance of the words themselves is sufficient. However, it appeared at times that Lloyd-Jones went beyond the text itself. This can be demonstrated by reference to his attitude to the doctrine of the Trinity. As a *doctrine*, the Trinity is not to be found on the pages of Scripture and Lloyd-Jones was aware of this.[26] For example, he argued, 'You will not find the doctrine of the Trinity stated either implicitly or explicitly anywhere in the

---

22. Lloyd-Jones, *The Assurance of Our Salvation*, pp. 180–181.

23. Lloyd-Jones, *Great Doctrines of the Bible, Volume I*, p. 2.

24. D. M. Lloyd-Jones, *The Gospel in Genesis: From Fig Leaves to Faith* (Wheaton, IL: Crossway Books, 2009), p. 98.

25. Ibid., p. 119.

26. Christian theologians have long recognized the absence in Scripture of the *doctrine* of the Trinity, but this does not necessarily lead them to abandon it. For Karl Barth, for example, the Trinity is 'a document of how [the Church] knows God'. As such it is a dogma, an analysis or interpretation of the revelation found in Scripture. The doctrine is not, then, the result of philosophical speculation, but is an attempt to explain how the definitive revelation of God has been made known to the world in a particular person, Jesus of Nazareth, the *theos ensarkos*. See Karl Barth, *Church Dogmatics I/1: The Doctrine of the Word of God* (Edinburgh: T. & T. Clark, 1960), pp. 346–354.

Bible. But you will find that there are references to "God the Father", "God the Son", and "God the Holy Spirit".[27] Yet elsewhere he claimed, 'No-one can read the Bible without, of necessity, coming face to face with this doctrine of the Trinity.'[28] And again, 'Nowhere in the Bible will you find a statement that God is three Persons – Father, Son and Holy Spirit . . . But by implication the doctrine of the Trinity . . . is to be found in the Old Testament and the New.'[29]

Lloyd-Jones's affirmation appears to have been based on two important considerations. First of all, he clearly believed it necessary to uphold the church's historical confession in the Trinity because such belief was essentially linked to the doctrine of the atonement: only the Son of God could bear the sins of the world in order to present humanity without blemish to the Father. Second, Lloyd-Jones held the Scriptures to be the exclusive and adequate account of God's truth revealed to human beings for their salvation. The Trinity, then, could not be the result of human cogitation or reflection, it had to be something which God has revealed. Consequently he had to affirm that the doctrine was to be found – if only one were to look properly for it – in the Scriptures. Clearly Lloyd-Jones believed the doctrine of the Trinity to be an essential part of Christian faith and belief. He was forced to confirm the presence of the *doctrine* because of his understanding of *Scripture*.

We find, then, that Lloyd-Jones's approach to Scripture was not as straightforward as it might at first appear. Despite having declared at one point that 'whatever is asserted in the Scripture about creation, about the whole cosmos, is true because God has said it',[30] his exposition of Scripture was not straightforwardly literalist. He was, in practice, a foundationalist, emphasizing that all made complete logical sense providing certain basic and unquantifiable truths were accepted.[31] Indeed, on one occasion, he described his method as 'the result of an acceptance of certain truths, and the working out of a reasoned logical argument'.[32] Thus his hermeneutical method, namely the idea that Scripture should be interpreted by Scripture, must be qualified by the fact that

27. Lloyd-Jones, *Great Doctrines of the Bible, Volume I*, p. 43.

28. Ibid., p. 83.

29. Ibid., p. 85.

30. D. M. Lloyd-Jones, *What Is an Evangelical?* (Edinburgh: Banner of Truth, 1971), p. 78; see Harris, *Fundamentalism and Evangelicals*, p. 174.

31. See Harriet Harris, 'How Helpful is the Term "Fundamentalist"?', in Christopher Partridge (ed.), *Fundamentalisms* (Carlisle: Paternoster, 2001), pp. 3–18.

32. D. M. Lloyd Jones, *Why Does God Allow War?* (London: Hodder and Stoughton, 1939), p. 10; Brencher, *Lloyd-Jones*, p. 223.

each verse was interpreted in light of his understanding of the basic message of the gospel. Sophisticated as his interpretation might have been, it could appear to others as unambiguous literalism.

That this is problematic can be illustrated by the shocking and bizarre story recorded by Bethan Lloyd-Jones of her encounter with 'the strangest person I ever met in Aberavon', namely an elderly woman who wore an eye shade. The woman explained how she had arrived at such a condition:

> This was not an accident at all. I did it myself . . . Christ says in the Bible that 'if thy right eye offend thee, pluck it out and cast it from thee' – well, it did offend me and led me into sin, so I did that . . . Yes, I plucked it out and cast it from me. Don't you think I did the right thing?[33]

Bethan Lloyd-Jones's response shows that this particular verse, from the Sermon on the Mount (Matt. 5:29), should not be taken literally. Instead, she said, 'If only she had come to Christ in repentance, and told him of her problem, he would have given her forgiveness and freedom, and his own strength to fight temptation.' Not only was the woman herself unable to interpret the verse in anything but a literal way, but the response was not specifically the interpretation of Scripture by Scripture. Instead, Bethan Lloyd-Jones's response offered a *theological* framework in which all else should be understood. In other words, her response was no more than a declaration of the essential feature of the gospel that sin can be forgiven because of Jesus Christ and that forgiveness is appropriated by grace through faith.

This example is rather extreme, but it demonstrates that the Scriptures are often – if not always – interpreted according to a theological system. Despite Lloyd-Jones's protests that he was concerned merely with *biblical* doctrine and that therefore he needed only to refer to the biblical texts, he nevertheless applied a theological lens to Scripture based on an evangelical creed. His approach to Scripture demonstrated that the interpretation of the Bible was perhaps more subtle, not to mention difficult, than his proclamations might at times appear to suggest.

On the one hand, then, the affirmation of the infallibility and inerrancy of Scripture, as well as its plenary inspiration, certainly aligns Lloyd-Jones with the early fundamentalists of North American Protestantism. On the other hand, his assertion that the Bible was not a text book about the world

---

33. Bethan Lloyd-Jones, *Memories of Sandfields* (Edinburgh: Banner of Truth, 1983), pp. 25–26.

or natural history but the revelation of God's plan of salvation qualified his approach to Scripture in a way not always mirrored by his fundamentalist antecedents. Thus Lloyd-Jones's attitude to Scripture suggests that he was, at least in part, a fundamentalist, but because only 'in part' the question must be raised regarding the appropriateness of applying the epithet to him on these grounds alone. More evidence is required and, given the doctrinal nature of early fundamentalism, an overview of his doctrinal statements might offer further insight. So what were the main aspects of Lloyd-Jones's creed?

A fundamentalist creed?

On at least one occasion, Lloyd-Jones outlined his basic belief system following the formula of the traditional creeds but stepping slightly beyond their content. He confessed:

> I believe that he [Jesus Christ] is very God and very man. I believe that he came from the glory of eternity and was born of the Virgin Mary. I believe he demonstrated and manifested his deity in his miracles of power. I believe that when he died on the cross, he was dying in order that I might be forgiven. I believe that he was smitten with the stripes that were meant for me and that I do so richly deserve . . . I believe that he arose literally from the grave in his body – the same body, but one that was changed and glorified. I believe in the literal physical resurrection – I have no gospel apart from it, for I would not know that he conquered death apart from this . . . I believe that he will come again to receive those of us who belong to him unto himself, to judge the whole world in righteousness and to set up his eternal kingdom.[34]

Apart from the infallibility of Scripture, which he certainly believed but did not mention at this point, Lloyd-Jones's list mirrors exactly the beliefs identified as fundamental in early twentieth-century North American Protestantism. Furthermore, he appears to echo the exact expression of those beliefs, especially through the adoption of words such as 'literal' and 'physical' in relation to the atonement. He clearly believed that there were certain doctrines that were 'essential to the way of salvation' on which 'we are and must be absolutely final'. These he identified as 'the person of Christ', 'the miraculous and

---

34. D. M. Lloyd-Jones, *I Am Not Ashamed: Advice to Timothy* (London: Hodder and Stoughton, 1986), pp. 106–107; See also Sargent, *The Sacred Anointing*, p. 123.

the supernatural', 'the substitutionary death upon the cross' and 'the literal, physical resurrection'. He admitted that there were non-essential doctrines over which 'sympathy' and 'tolerance' could be exercised.[35] Unfortunately, it was not entirely clear which doctrines could be identified as 'non-essential'.

Christology was central to Lloyd-Jones's scheme, both the *person* and *work* of Christ. Christ's deity was clearly a 'fundamental' doctrine: Christ 'is not a man like other men, for he was not born in a natural manner. It was a Virgin Birth, a miraculous birth,' he asserted, and to deny Christ's deity was to deny the very foundations of Christian belief. 'If he regards Jesus of Nazareth as only a man,' he said, 'he is not a Christian. The Christian believes in the incarnation, he believes that almost two thousand years ago the Son of God came into this world and entered into time.'[36] Indeed, Lloyd-Jones's opposition to the ecumenical movement was driven, in part, by the perception that the theological liberalism of the age had denuded Christ of his divinity and that such liberalism appeared to dominate in the historic denominations. While Christ's divinity was crucial, it was the scheme of salvation, understood in terms of Christ's substitutionary atonement in place of sinful human beings, that governed his thought as the essence of the *good* news of the Christian gospel. Human beings are lost and helpless in their sin; God in Christ has acted to save them. Of course, there could be no salvation without incarnation and the virgin birth was intended to highlight that point, but these doctrines served to support the doctrine of the atonement rather than stand alongside it as being of equal importance. Lloyd-Jones's approach to creation and to eschatology – the doctrines of the first and the last things which constitute significant aspects of contemporary Christian fundamentalism – appear to be *secondary* to the primacy of the doctrine of salvation in his thought. And this is the case despite the fact that Lloyd-Jones held definite views about both.

Lloyd-Jones was keen to defend the doctrine of creation and there appear to be at least three reasons for this. First of all, creation is a biblical doctrine. While he confirmed that the creation stories were not intended to offer a mechanical or a technical or a biological explanation of the created order, he nevertheless held those accounts to be true and historical (regardless of obvious differences between the accounts found in Gen. 1 and 2). Creation was part of God's revelation: 'God gave an account of the creation to Moses or someone else; so it is not man's ideas or theories.'[37] He went further and

---

35. Lloyd-Jones, *Great Doctrines of the Bible, Volume I*, p. 46.

36. Lloyd-Jones, *The Assurance of Our Salvation*, pp. 259–260.

37. Lloyd-Jones, *Great Doctrines of the Bible, Volume I*, p. 26.

asserted that 'it seems perfectly clear that the last three days in the account in this first chapter of Genesis were determined by the sun and therefore were twenty-four hour days'.[38] And Scripture, he asserted, demonstrated that Christ believed the creation stories to be historical fact. To claim that the creation narrative is a myth which reveals theological meaning rather than an account of what historically happened was to be in conflict with the teaching of Christ, he said, 'because in His teaching about divorce, He referred to the creation of man and woman'. Indeed, Jesus 'based His whole argument upon the fact that this is literal history'.[39] Thus, he concluded, 'though Scripture may appear to conflict with certain discoveries of science at the present time . . . ultimately the scientists will discover that they have been in error at some point or other, and will eventually come to see that the statements of Scripture are true'.[40] At another time he declared, 'Let us never compromise the truth of God to fit any scientific theory. The time will soon come when that scientific theory, if it contradicts the Bible, will be replaced by another.'[41]

Second, at other times he argued that there was no conflict between the creation stories and what he called 'established scientific facts'. Indeed, 'the very order of creation which is given in the first chapter of Genesis is identical with the order that the modern scientist gives us'.[42] On another occasion he asked the straightforward question, 'Why should we be afraid of the scientist?' He responded to his own query by asserting that the scientist 'has no facts which interfere with this Book'.[43] He could not understand the apparent public trust in scientists *qua* scientists, for they, 'like the rest of us, are full of error and of failure. Indeed, they are some of the most opinionated people in the world today, dogmatism is certainly not confined to pulpits.'[44] Evolution, he maintained, is *only* a theory. 'Why should that undifferentiated slime or protoplasm become more complicated and involved; what made it do it? They do not know. There is a complete failure to explain the changes, still less to explain why the changes should always be upward.'[45] He concluded, 'Quite

38. Ibid., p. 131.

39. Ibid., p. 134.

40. Lloyd-Jones, *What Is an Evangelical?*, p. 78; Harris, *Fundamentalism and Evangelicals*, p. 174.

41. See Lloyd-Jones, *Great Doctrines of the Bible, Volume I*, p. 139.

42. Ibid., p. 134.

43. Lloyd-Jones, 'How can we see a return to the Bible?', p. 110.

44. Lloyd-Jones, *Great Doctrines of the Bible, Volume I*, p. 136.

45. Ibid., p. 137; see also Lloyd-Jones, *The Gospel in Genesis*, p. 11.

apart from my believing the Bible to be the inspired and authoritative word of God, on scientific grounds alone I have never been able to accept the theory of evolution.'[46] For Lloyd-Jones, the belief in and propagation of evolution as *true* was no more than the dogmatism of an 'anti-God religion'.[47]

Third, he believed that the teaching about evolution contradicted the biblical doctrine of salvation. This was, perhaps, the most crucial point and one that demonstrated the evolutionists' error. The Bible, he said, revealed that there was a time when humanity was perfect, created by and for a holy God. However, humankind fell from grace as recorded by Genesis 3. The fall was both an historical event and 'an actual account of what every one of us does'.[48] From Genesis 3:15, the gospel is announced and the rest of the Bible records the revelation of the gospel, the covenant of grace, God's way of salvation.[49] The movement, in the Bible, is from perfection to sin from which God will effect salvation. However, the theory of evolution runs in the opposite direction. 'The theory of evolution tells us that man has not only evolved, but that it is always an upward process, from the primitive and the simple to the more highly organised and involved, moving steadily in the direction of perfection.'[50] On another occasion he said, 'Now evolutionism tells us that man is just evolving out of the animal stage; he obviously has still a great deal of the bestial in him, but he is advancing up to perfection. The trouble is that he has not climbed high enough yet. But if that is true, then I have to cut out a great deal of my Bible.'[51] Indeed:

> The whole biblical case for salvation rests upon the fact that man, who was made perfect, fell and became imperfect – which is the exact opposite of evolution . . . The doctrine of evolution of man from the animals, and the denial of his special creation by God, involves us at once in a denial of the doctrine of the Fall, and therefore puts us in serious trouble with regard to the doctrine of salvation.[52]

Lloyd-Jones's approach to the doctrine of creation is important. He did not list belief in creation or the fall as essential doctrines. Nevertheless, he emphasized that the biblical witness maintains that Jesus and Paul both believed in

---

46. Lloyd-Jones, *Great Doctrines of the Bible, Volume I*, p. 138.

47. Ibid., p. 189.

48. Lloyd-Jones, *The Gospel in Genesis*, pp. 12, 21.

49. Lloyd-Jones, *Great Doctrines of the Bible, Volume I*, p. 228.

50. Ibid., p. 156.

51. Lloyd-Jones, *The Assurance of Our Salvation*, p. 131.

52. Lloyd-Jones, *Great Doctrines of the Bible, Volume I*, p. 156.

the creation as an historical event and therefore to reject the historical value of the creation accounts meant also the rejection of the teaching of Jesus and Paul.[53] So they may not have constituted *fundamental* Christian doctrines, but it was clearly necessary that Christians believe them to be true accounts of actual events. Once again, Lloyd-Jones's approach to the doctrine of creation was grounded in his belief about Scripture. The doctrine of creation was not in itself a fundamental doctrine, but the authority and inerrancy of Scripture certainly was. It was inevitable, then, that he would expect Christians to believe the creation stories as recorded in Scripture rather than as qualified by scientific theory.

Lloyd-Jones held a similar approach to the doctrine of the last things. Unlike contemporary fundamentalist Christian groups, it seems that Lloyd-Jones was not, for most of his ministry, particularly bothered by eschatology, except in as much as he was concerned with the personal fate of individual human beings. He emphasized the immortality of the soul and the need for faith in order that God's gracious salvation in Christ was efficacious in an individual's life, leading her or him to eternal life rather than to eternal punishment. Of the 'final judgment', for example, he said, 'It will be a great public occasion when the whole world will be assembled together and the fate of every single individual will be announced. It is, I repeat, the public pronouncement of the eternal and final judgment.'[54] He made very little of the 'new heaven' and virtually nothing of the 'new earth' of Revelation 21, apart from to say that 'everything will be glorified even nature itself'.[55]

Perhaps this was the result of what was basically an amillennial stance. Lloyd-Jones believed in the restoration of Israel, the conversion of the Jews and the physical and personal return of Christ to inaugurate the golden age.[56] He refuted the idea that there was a secret rapture or a millennium, either preceding or succeeding Christ's return. He asserted that the golden age would follow the return of Christ and that this would be preceded by a period of tribulation.[57] Alongside this, he avoided, prior to his retirement from Westminster Chapel,

---

53. See, e.g., Lloyd-Jones, *The Gospel in Genesis*, p. 98; Lloyd-Jones, *Great Doctrines of the Bible, Volume I*, pp. 134, 182.

54. Lloyd-Jones, *Great Doctrines of the Bible, Volume III: The Church and the Last Things* (Wheaton, IL: Crossway, 2003), p. 241.

55. Ibid., p. 247.

56. Sargent, *The Sacred Anointing*, p. 259; Lloyd-Jones, *Great Doctrines of the Bible, Volume III*, pp. 91, 100, 113.

57. See D. M. Lloyd-Jones, *Romans: An Exposition of Chapter 8:17–39: The Final Perseverance of the Saints* (Edinburgh: Banner of Truth, 1975), ch. 7. Tony Sargent

any speculation surrounding the timing of the eschaton. During his talks on the 'great doctrines of the Bible', for example, he told his listeners that there would be 'signs' preceding the return of Christ, but he refused to offer 'any help or indication whatsoever in a precise form as to when this second coming will take place'.[58]

Nevertheless, it seems that Lloyd-Jones's interest in eschatology increased as he approached the end of his life. Indeed, he began at that point to try to interpret the 'signs of the times'. In an interview with Carl Henry in 1980, Lloyd-Jones asserted that the 'signs' were pointing to an imminent end. 'I'm not sure at all that we have twenty years,' he said. He saw the expansion of Israel into the Gaza Strip, the Sinai Peninsula, the West Bank, East Jerusalem and the Golan Heights following the Six-Day War in 1967 as the fulfilment of Scripture: 'Jerusalem shall be trodden down of the Gentiles *until* the time of the Gentiles be fulfilled' (Luke 21:43).[59] But he also saw the dominance of democracy in the political realm, which he understood in terms similar to Reinhold Niebuhr as 'the ultimate position politically' but which remained in constant danger of disintegration into dictatorship or total chaos,[60] as reflecting the dominance of the human. Lloyd-Jones asserted, '666 is the number of man, and this is democracy – man worshipping himself, his own likeness.' As a result, he could see only 'collapse' in a 'dissolving world'. Yet he remained insistent that 'the only hope for the world is the return of Christ – nothing else', and concluded, 'All my life I've opposed setting "times and seasons", but I feel increasingly that we may be in the last times.'[61]

Proclamation and separation

Alongside his belief in the authority and inerrancy of Scripture and his identification of essential doctrine, it is important to recognize that Lloyd-Jones

---

maintains that Lloyd-Jones was 'consistent in his eschatology throughout his ministry'; see Sargent, *The Sacred Anointing*, p. 251.

58. Lloyd-Jones, *Great Doctrines of the Bible, Volume III*, p. 97.

59. Henry, 'An Interview', p. 105.

60. Niebuhr asserted, for example, that democracy 'is a principle of order and its power prevents anarchy; but its power is not identical with divine power'. See Reinhold Niebuhr, *The Nature and Destiny of Man: A Christian Interpretation*, 2 vols. (London: Nisbet, 1943), vol. 1, p. 279.

61. Henry, 'An Interview', pp. 104–108.

also had a particular method which he employed in his preaching and lecturing. He proclaimed his understanding of the gospel in assured terms and he used his formidable intellect as well as rhetorical skills in persuading congregations, from a quite logical point of view, that there was a single appropriate interpretation of the Scriptures. His method was to discuss a number of possible interpretations, to explain where they erred and then to offer his own explanation of the Bible's message as the most reasonable one. This, he explained during a rare television interview with the Welsh poet and broadcaster Aneirin Talfan Davies in 1970, was the role of the preacher:

> I am an expositor of the scriptures. I don't believe that it is the preacher's function
> to stand up and voice his own opinions and theories and ideas, but to expound and
> to bring out the message of the Bible. And I think it's this, and one does this in
> as reasonably and as logically a manner as one can to show the inevitability of the
> conclusion.[62]

While he believed that his congregations should be made aware of all kinds of possible interpretations – 'Nothing, to me, is more lamentable than that people should only know one view,' he declared[63] – in practice his approach had the effect of highlighting one explanation as being the most reasonable, if not the only accurate, understanding of the biblical message. The case may be overstated in John Brencher's claim that 'being the corrector of error and signpost of the truth became habitual and the danger was that, in the end, for all practical purposes Lloyd-Jones came to assume his own infallibility'.[64] Lloyd-Jones himself would undoubtedly have been horrified by such a statement. On one occasion he confessed, 'I am not big enough to be an authority; I am too fallible to be an authority. No man is capable of being such an

---

62. Interview with Aneirin Talfan Davies (1970), at www.youtube.com/user/
   mljrecordingstrust (accessed 6 April 2011). The interviewer is incorrectly identified
   as Aneirin Taflan Jones [sic].
63. Lloyd-Jones, *Great Doctrines of the Bible, Volume III*, p. 205. He also exclaimed, 'I am
   not a pope. I do not believe in popes, and I do not believe in making *ex cathedra*
   statements. It is the business of any man who tries to expound biblical truth and
   doctrine to justify what he is doing.' D. M. Lloyd-Jones, *Great Doctrines of the Bible,
   Volume II: God the Holy Spirit* (Wheaton, IL: Crossway, 1997) p. 62. This was clearly
   a rejection of statements that were not logically argued rather than opposition to
   authority *per se*.
64. Brencher, *Lloyd-Jones*, p. 177.

authority.'[65] Nevertheless, as a result of the relentless logic of his argument as well as by the sheer strength of personality – what J. I. Packer calls 'masterful personal magnetism'[66] – Lloyd-Jones became an authoritative figure to whom many looked for leadership and for a binding exposition of the Scriptures.

An authoritarian manner and absolute certitude in interpretation are held by some to be definite characteristics of leadership within movements identified as fundamentalist, where 'a leader-follower relationship' develops and a 'deep and complete understanding of sacred texts' is imputed to 'the minister'.[67] Some of this is undoubtedly attributable to Lloyd-Jones, or at least attributed to him by some who sat under his ministry. He was authoritarian and he certainly emphasized that the Bible was only properly understood in a particular way. He encouraged the identification of what amounted to a righteous remnant who would maintain a sharp distinction between the true believer and others who might claim the name Christian but whose doctrine was compromised by theological liberalism, biblical criticism or other commonly held philosophies.[68] Yet he eschewed every possibility of leading the evangelical movement in any other way than in teaching and preaching the gospel. He believed himself to be a humble expositor of the Scriptures whose vocation was the declaration of divine truth. This led to the maintenance of Westminster Chapel as a preaching station more than an ecclesial community,[69] and it also led to perhaps the most contentious aspect of Lloyd-Jones's ministry.

---

65. D. M. Lloyd-Jones, *Romans: An Exposition of Chapter 5: Assurance* (Edinburgh: Banner of Truth, 1971), pp. 221–222; also Sargent, *Gems from Martyn Lloyd-Jones*, p. 33.

66. See J. I. Packer, 'Foreword', in Sargent, *Gems from Martyn Lloyd-Jones*, p. ix.

67. See Gabriel A. Almond, Emmanuel Siva and R. Scott Appleby, 'Fundamentalism: Genus and Species', in Martin E. Marty and R. Scott Appleby (eds.), *Fundamentalism Comprehended* (Chicago: University of Chicago Press, 1995), p. 404.

68. The Fundamentalism Project of the early 1990s, based in the United States of America, called on an international team of scholars from various religious traditions in an attempt to understand the increase in militant religion in the 1970s and to see whether there were common characteristics to the various movements. Nine characteristics were initially identified, and Lloyd-Jones appears to display at least some of them. See Almond, Siva and Appleby, 'Fundamentalism: Genus and Species', pp. 399–424.

69. John Brencher quotes correspondence with R. T. Kendall in support of such a claim. Kendall recorded, 'I asked him [Lloyd-Jones] twice over on one occasion if

There has probably been more controversy over Lloyd-Jones's polemical stance towards the world, towards the church and towards fellow Christians than over any other aspect of his life's work. He asserted in 1963 that the world was in crisis, living under the possibility of impending destruction.[70] This was, in part, the result of reading 'the signs of the times' during the height of the Cold War, months after the Cuban missile crisis and at the very time that the Profumo affair came to light. But it also stemmed from his biblical exposition and his theological stance. He was convinced that, because existence was precarious and death could come at any moment, all human beings needed to be prepared to face their post-mortem judgment. Coupled with this was his view that the church was not fulfilling its proper task of proclaiming the gospel, resulting in the fact that men and women were not even aware of the eternal fate which they faced. Thus, he complained, there was 'so much tragic confusion as to what Christianity really is' and 'when it [the world] does turn to listen, it hears a confused sound',[71] largely because the church was not proclaiming the substitutionary atonement as the means to human salvation. He interpreted his own ministry as a correction to this trend, which inevitably led him to a separatist ecclesiology in which he opposed the ecumenical movement for failing to concentrate on the basic Christian message. It was not a *big* church that was required, he insisted, but a *pure* one.[72] He claimed that Christian history witnessed to the problems which developed when the church failed to remain true to its proper vocation.

> If you go back through the long history of the Christian Church, you will find that it
> has often counted most, and has been used most by God, when there have been just
> a handful of people who were agreed in spirit and in doctrine . . . But when there was

---

Westminster Chapel was a church and he answered, "just barely": those were his actual words.' See Brencher, *Lloyd-Jones*, p. 78.

70. Lloyd-Jones, *The Kingdom of God*, p. 11.

71. Ibid., p. 49. 'This Gospel is many-sided, it has many aspects, so that is not surprising. But I do suggest that it is indeed very surprising that at the end of the twentieth century, men and women should still be all wrong about what the Gospel is; wrong about its foundation; wrong about its central message; wrong about its objective and wrong about the way in which one comes into relationship with it.' Lloyd-Jones, *The Kingdom of God*, p. 8.

72. Lloyd-Jones, *The Assurance of Our Salvation*, p. 648. See also Lloyd-Jones, *Great Doctrines of the Bible, Volume III*, p. 8, where he emphasized that unity was a spiritual rather than physical reality.

only one Church in the whole of western Europe, what did she lead to? The Dark Ages.[73]

Lloyd-Jones was resolute in his opposition to what he considered to be churches whose doctrine had been compromised by theological liberalism. This led him into stern censure of the Church of England, to a severing of links with evangelicals who held different views of the church, and to his infamous call to evangelical Christians to leave what he considered to be doctrinally mixed denominations, uttered at the National Assembly of Evangelicals in Westminster Central Hall in October 1966. The call was to a righteous remnant to remain pure and unsullied by the impure majority and to separate from them.[74] He used certain biblical texts to highlight this position, such as 'Can two walk together unless they be agreed?' (Amos 3:3), or 'come out from among them, and be ye separate, saith the Lord and touch not the unclean [thing]; and I will receive you' (2 Cor. 6:17), or even 'And I heard another voice from heaven, saying, Come out of her, my people, that ye be not partakers of her sins, and that ye receive not of her plagues' (Rev. 18:4).[75] He also offered a careful exposition of John 17 in which he emphasized that the words of Jesus regarding the unity of his followers were addressed to those who shared true belief about his divinity[76] and whose unity was spiritual rather than physical.[77] Once again this highlights the importance of true doctrine for Lloyd-Jones. Christians were those who shared in the essential truths of God's revelation as they are safeguarded in Scripture. As a result, it was his uncompromising exposition of the gospel in terms of substitutionary atonement, his advocacy of an unerring Bible and his insistence that this had to be believed unquestioningly or else a person's faith was suspect, that more than anything else led to him being associated in some minds with fundamentalism. But is this justified?

---

73. Lloyd-Jones, *Great Doctrines of the Bible, Volume III*, p. 10.

74. See Bruce B. Lawrence's definition in *Defenders of God*, pp. 235–237; also the identification of calling an 'elect membership from the faithful remnant' as set out by the Fundamentalism Project. See Almond, Siva and Appleby, 'Fundamentalism: Genus and Species', pp. 407–408.

75. See, e.g., D. M. Lloyd-Jones, *Luther and His Message for Today* (London: British Evangelical Council, 1968), p. 26.

76. E.g., Lloyd-Jones, *The Assurance of Our Salvation*, p. 642.

77. E.g., ibid., pp. 633–648; Lloyd Jones, *Great Doctrines of the Bible, Volume III*, pp. 8–9.

Conclusion

Was Martyn Lloyd-Jones a fundamentalist? Some aspects of his ministry seem to lead towards an affirmative answer. He clearly asserted that there were certain essential doctrines that should be believed by the Christian, and he suspected the authenticity of the faith of those who could not confess such belief. Substitutionary atonement, secured by the incarnate Son of God and witnessed to in an infallible Scripture seem to have been the key doctrines in his scheme. His emphasis appears to have echoed that of the earliest 'fundamentalists' in North America and he publicly identified himself with their stance[78] in opposition to subsequent proponents of a fundamentalist point of view. According to Harriet Harris, 'full-fledged fundamentalism developed after World War I and was markedly more militant' than that represented by *The Fundamentals*.[79] On the surface, this could account for Lloyd-Jones's attitude. It is possible that he sought to distance himself from the militancy of subsequent fundamentalism in order to affirm the authenticity of the initial movement as a means of safeguarding pure doctrine. However, it is Harris's contention that post-1925 fundamentalism adopted a more aggressive approach towards modernism and ultimately became separatist in intention, forming either independent churches or new denominations, as well as Bible schools which offered 'a sound academic program built upon the old-time fundamentals of the Bible'.[80] There is clearly a similarity between this militant fundamentalism and Lloyd-Jones's advocacy of withdrawal from doctrinally compromised churches and his suspicion of academia, especially academic theology. This possibly supports the contention that Lloyd-Jones was a fundamentalist.

Yet it must be borne in mind that he refuted the term, embracing instead the word 'evangelical'. Indeed, when once asked, during his television interview with Aneirin Talfan Davies in 1970, 'Are you a fundamentalist?', he offered an intriguing response. 'Like many others,' he said, 'I don't like the term. I prefer to call myself a conservative evangelical. That is very largely because of the abuse of the term, I think, in the United States. But I am a conservative

---

78. As in his television interview with Aneirin Talfan Davies (1970) in which he confessed, 'I am a conservative evangelical . . . as most of those men who wrote the contributions to that symposium . . . were.' The symposium in question was *The Fundamentals*.

79. Harris, *Fundamentalism and Evangelicals*, p. 28.

80. Ibid., p. 42.

evangelical.'[81] In this he – wittingly or otherwise – followed J. I. Packer's advice and can be viewed as representative of the British scene generally where those who considered themselves to be true 'to the doctrinal content of the gospel' consistently avoided use of the term 'fundamentalist' because of its negative associations.[82]

During the same interview, Lloyd-Jones went on to elaborate on what he saw as the differences between his approach and that of the fundamentalists:

> I think our attitude is a little more intelligent. I mean, I have very little sympathy with the man who just holds up a Bible and says, 'I believe this from cover to cover, every comma and full stop', and all the rest of it. There's been a little bit too much of that and a refusal to use one's mind and to recognise figures of speech and so on. I think their danger has been to be literalistic, in a wrong sense. That would be the main difference, I think, between us.[83]

It is not entirely clear who Lloyd-Jones had in mind here, but perhaps that is not important. What is important is his desire to identify his own position as thoughtful, if not also reasonable, in contradistinction to what he identified as the literalistic and unthinking attitude of the fundamentalist. There is at least the suggestion here that Lloyd-Jones did not believe himself to be a literalist and that he upheld the role of the mind and of reason in biblical interpretation. However, reason and logic had a limited role: they could not be seen as in any way masters of Scripture; they were instead to be employed in its defence or, more accurately, in biblical defence of an evangelical creed.

This all reveals the complexity of the issue. There were similarities between Lloyd-Jones and the fundamentalists – even those in the United States whom he believed to be abusing the term. Yet the context in Britain made it difficult, almost meaningless, to employ the word unless the aim was to provoke a particularly hostile reaction. Perhaps it is better to allow him his self-designation as a 'conservative evangelical', the former appellation qualifying the latter sufficiently to recognize that 'evangelical' itself is a term which includes a range of opinion. This reflects the historical and contemporary disagreement between those who hail Lloyd-Jones as an expositor of gospel truth and those who see him as a dangerous and narrow fundamentalist. There remains, then,

---

81. Interview with Aneirin Talfan Davies (1970).
82. Packer, *'Fundamentalism' and the Word of God*, p. 38.
83. Interview with Aneirin Talfan Davies (1970).

something inscrutable, even enigmatic, about Lloyd-Jones as well as in the polarization of opinion about him between supporters and opponents. This, in part, contributes to the fact that, at least in some quarters and a generation after his death, his legacy continues to be the subject of debate.

© Robert Pope, 2011

8. LLOYD-JONES AND KARL BARTH

Robert Strivens

Barthian theology has tended to be met with suspicion and often outright hostility from conservative evangelicals, at least in Britain. In his recent analysis of the reception of Barth in the British Isles during the twentieth century, Densil Morgan attributes this phenomenon in part to the strong resistance to the Swiss theologian's thought which was mounted by conservative evangelicalism in the middle years of the past century, a resistance in which the Inter-Varsity Fellowship and its leaders, including at that time Martyn Lloyd-Jones, played a significant role.[1] Little work has been done on the reasons for Lloyd-Jones's hostility to Barthian theology, partly, no doubt, due to the scattered nature and relative paucity of evidence available to make any meaningful assessment. This chapter will seek to bring together what evidence there is and will also examine some new evidence in the form of an annotated copy of a short work of Karl Barth recently discovered in Lloyd-Jones's personal library, in order to try to identify more precisely the theological grounds of the Welsh preacher's objections to Barthian ideas.

Karl Barth died on 10 December 1968, at the age of eighty-two. The *Evangelical Times* of the following month carried an anonymous obituary of

---

1. D. Densil Morgan, *Barth Reception in Britain* (London: T. & T. Clark, 2010), pp. 244–256.

the Swiss theologian.[2] Its author was Martyn Lloyd-Jones[3] and in it Lloyd-Jones praises the older man's 'first-class intellect', his 'acute criticism of various theological outlooks' and his greatness of character, 'seen supremely in his heroic stand against Hitler and Nazism'. Barth, says Lloyd-Jones, was a 'theological giant' of the twentieth century. But Lloyd-Jones also had some searching questions to ask about Barth's legacy. While admitting that Barth's 'attacks on Liberalism and Modernism were devastating', Lloyd-Jones's 'great question' was: 'What has all this meant from the evangelical standpoint?' His startling answer was, 'Practically nothing!' In justification of this verdict, Lloyd-Jones cites Barth's critical approach to the Bible, his denial of propositional revelation, his view of the historicity of the foundational facts of the Christian faith and, most telling of all in Lloyd-Jones's estimation, the absence of true spiritual benefit from his theology: 'Though his works and influence have been in existence for 50 years, he has brought no revival to the church.' The reasons for this, in Lloyd-Jones's view, lay in the philosophical nature of his approach, the difficulty of his style and the intellectual character of preachers whom he influenced, who preached about the Word rather than the Word itself. In sum, although Barth was superb in his critique of 'the old Modernism', 'his positive contribution to the cause of the Gospel was virtually nil'. The obituary ends, 'All honour to a great man . . . but!'

Lloyd-Jones's early reaction to Barth

Karl Barth's ideas began to make an impact in Britain from about 1925. The first publication in Britain to address his writings came from the pen of his fellow countryman Adolf Keller (1872–1963), soon to be followed by analyses from scholars of many of the major denominations.[4] The translation of Barth's works into English began with the appearance of *The Word of God and the Word*

2. [D. M. Lloyd-Jones], 'The Significance of Karl Barth', *Evangelical Times* (January 1969), pp. 1, 6.

3. Editorial note by Peter Masters, *Sword and Trowel*, no. 2 (2009), p. 11.

4. Densil Morgan refers to the following British authors as amongst those, in addition to Keller, who published on Barth before 1930: John Phillips and J. D. Vernon Lewis (Congregational), John McConnachie (United Free Church of Scotland), Richard Birch Hoyle (Baptist), W. F. Lofthouse (Methodist) and C. J. Shebbeare (Anglican). Morgan, *Barth Reception in Britain*, pp. 9–118.

of Man in 1928.[5] Though not uncritically received, by 1930 Barth's thought had begun to make a significant impression on some parts of the church in Britain, especially in Scotland and Wales and within English Congregationalism.[6] Those who were searching for a theology that was more faithful to Scripture and less opposed to supernaturalism than the liberalism which was then dominant showed considerable interest and appreciation. For them, Barth's work brought a freshness and the hope of a return to a more fruitful, biblical approach. Drawing on his own experience as a minister, John McConnachie of the United Free Church of Scotland wrote in 1933 that 'the modern theology . . . has proved a broken reed to lean on in a time of crisis'.[7] Some who felt themselves failed by a dominant liberalism were finding in the theology of Karl Barth a fresh strength and renewed vigour.

Lloyd-Jones's view of Barth's influence in Britain at that time was not so favourable. Looking back from the vantage point of 1961, Lloyd-Jones spoke to an Inter-Varsity Fellowship meeting of the 'very subtle attack which came in the form of what has been known as "Barthianism"'. He continued, 'Here was a movement in theology which claimed that it was going back to the Bible and to true biblical theology. It seemed to be reasserting the great message of the Reformation and Reformed theology.' Lloyd-Jones went on to speak of 'friends of this Fellowship in prominent positions' who had 'failed to see the true character' of the new ideas and who had 'thought it was a return to evangelical Christianity'. These years, 'roughly speaking, from 1938 to 1940', said Lloyd-Jones, were 'some of the most critical years through which the IVF has ever passed'.[8] The strength of Lloyd-Jones's opposition to the new thought is clear. What is not so clear, however, is the extent and depth of his actual engagement with Barth's theology and, especially, the precise grounds of his opposition to it.

There is evidence, however, that from early in the time when Barth's ideas were beginning to become known in Britain, Lloyd-Jones made efforts to familiarize himself with them, as well as with the thought of Emil Brunner and

---

5. Karl Barth, *The Word of God and the Word of Man*, trans. Douglas Horton (London: Hodder and Stoughton, 1928).

6. Morgan, *Barth Reception in Britain*, pp. 25–99.

7. John McConnachie, *The Barthian Theology and the Man of Today* (London: Hodder and Stoughton, 1933), p. 34.

8. D. M. Lloyd-Jones, '"Beware That Thou Forget Not": A Message Given at the Dedication Service of the IVF New Office Building, 29 September 1961', *Christian Graduate*, vol. 15 (March 1962), p. 3.

other contemporary theologians, in order to assess their ideas and formulate his own considered response to them. Lloyd-Jones had in his personal library English translations of works of Barth published in Britain during that period: *The Word of God and the Word of Man* (1928), *Credo* (1936) and *The Doctrine of the Word of God*, the first part of the *Church Dogmatics* (1936).[9] It seems likely that he read these, as his reference to the writings of Barth and Brunner in a book review published in 1939 would suggest.[10]

That review, of *On to Orthodoxy* by fellow Welshman D. R. Davies, is suggestive of some of the concerns which Lloyd-Jones had about 'neo-orthodoxy' (as he there refers to it). In the review, he expresses his keen admiration for Davies' exposition of the shortcomings of liberal theology and commends the reading of the book. However, he fears that the shift which the author describes in his 'intellectual and philosophical' position from liberalism falls short of the 'spiritual and moral' change which 'traditional Protestant orthodoxy' has always stood for. Implicitly, Lloyd-Jones suggests that Davies had not provided an answer to the central problem facing the 'modern man', which is 'our ignorance of the power of God, especially in our own lives'. In a letter to his wife written

---

9. Barth, *The Word of God and the Word of Man*; *Credo: A Presentation of the Chief Problems of Dogmatics with Reference to the Apostles' Creed. Sixteen Lectures Delivered at the University of Utrecht in February and March, 1935*, trans. J. Strathearn McNab (London: Hodder and Stoughton, 1936); *The Doctrine of the Word of God*, trans. G. T. Thomson (Edinburgh: T. & T. Clark, 1936). Lloyd-Jones's copy of the first-mentioned work is inscribed with a personal greeting dated 1929. Later works of Barth in Lloyd-Jones's library are: *Dogmatics in Outline*, trans. G. T. Thomson (London: SCM, 1949); *A Shorter Commentary on Romans*, trans. D. H. Van Daalen (London: SCM, 1959); and *Christ and Adam: Man and Humanity in Romans 5*, trans. T. A. Smail (Edinburgh: Oliver and Boyd, 1956), on which see further below. Lloyd-Jones's library also contains books on Barth by Colin Brown, T. F. Torrance, Cornelius Van Til, Otto Weber and Gustaf Wingren. Lloyd-Jones's theological books are now at the London Theological Seminary.

10. D. M. Lloyd-Jones, 'The Story of a Spiritual Pilgrimage', *The Christian World*, 12 October 1939, a review of D. R. Davies, *On to Orthodoxy* (London: Hodder and Stoughton, 1939). See also Lloyd-Jones's review of Emil Brunner, *Man in Revolt: A Christian Anthropology*, trans. Olive Wyon (London: Lutterworth Press, 1939), in *Inter-Varsity Magazine*, vol. 12 (Lent Term 1940), pp. 29–30; and of Cornelius Van Til's critique of Barth, *Christianity and Barthianism* (Philadelphia, PA: Presbyterian and Reformed, 1962), in *Westminster Theological Journal*, vol. 27 (November 1964), pp. 52–55.

at about the same time, Lloyd-Jones comments that Davies, 'like Brunner and Barth, falls short of the real thing. I feel he has had some kind of "intellectual conversion" and nothing more. And yet – on the negative side [i.e. his critique of liberalism] he is excellent.'[11] These are indications that Lloyd-Jones was, from about 1930 onwards, formulating a considered and informed response to Barth.

These fragments of evidence are, however, frustratingly short on the details of Lloyd-Jones's precise theological objections to the new views. In his discussion of the strength of the opposition with which conservative evangelicalism met Barthian thought in the mid-twentieth century, Densil Morgan suggests that such a reaction might initially be a matter of some surprise, given the apparently shared emphases on Scripture, the centrality of Christ and an orthodox trinitarianism, together with a suspicion of liberal theology.[12] Morgan argues that the main points of contention were the doctrines of biblical inerrancy and limited atonement and that the opposition evidenced a tendency towards a rigid scholasticism and narrow interpretation of Calvinism pioneered by Barth's implacable opponent, Cornelius Van Til.[13] However, the evidence reviewed so far, together with that examined below, indicates that Lloyd-Jones's concerns may not have been so narrowly confined to certain specific doctrines and that, in his view, what was at stake went to the very heart of the gospel message.

Barth (and Lloyd-Jones) on Romans 5

Some further light may be thrown on the precise nature of Lloyd-Jones's objections by pencilled comments which he made in the margin of his copy of one of Barth's works, the latter's study of Romans 5, *Christ and Adam: Man and Humanity in Romans 5*, published in English translation in 1956.[14] There are

---

11. Martyn Lloyd-Jones to Bethan Lloyd-Jones, 21 September 1939, in Iain H. Murray (ed.), *D. Martyn Lloyd-Jones: Letters 1919–1981* (Edinburgh: Banner of Truth, 1994), p. 46. Murray writes that, during the 1930s, Lloyd-Jones was reading Barth and Brunner with the objective of warning ministers about their teachings and their deviation, as he saw it, from Reformed orthodoxy: Iain H. Murray, *D. Martyn Lloyd-Jones: The First Forty Years 1899–1939* (Edinburgh: Banner of Truth, 1982), pp. 290–291.

12. Morgan, *Barth Reception in Britain*, p. 244.

13. Ibid., pp. 252, 246–248.

14. Karl Barth, *Christ and Adam: Man and Humanity in Romans 5*, trans. T. A. Smail (Edinburgh: Oliver and Boyd, 1956).

manuscript annotations in this copy in two different hands. One hand is definitely not that of Lloyd-Jones – it would appear that Lloyd-Jones purchased
the book second hand and that this hand is that of the first owner. However,
the other hand appears certainly to be that of Lloyd-Jones. The comments are
concise and often trenchant; moreover, they give some assistance in understanding more precisely Lloyd-Jones's objections to Barth's theology.

The thrust of Barth's *Christ and Adam* is summarized in the foreword to the
English translation:

> Here is a penetrating account of the Biblical and Christian doctrine of man in the
> light of the saving humanity of Christ, in which Barth at the same time shows
> the profound unity of redemption and creation and reveals the foundation of the
> Christian life and Church in the human nature of the Son of God.[15]

The work focuses on the second half of Romans 5, from verse 12 onwards,
where the apostle Paul addresses the foundational importance of the figures of
Adam and Christ, the one bringing sin and judgment into the world, the other
righteousness and life. Barth takes up the themes of humanity's relationship to
Adam and to Christ and seeks to analyse, compare and contrast the two relationships. Barth's principal concern in the work seems to be to demonstrate
how Christ, and humanity's relationship to him, has priority in every sense
over Adam and our relationship to him; he seeks to locate the point of connection between Adam and Christ, with the emphasis firmly on the latter as
the one in whom all other persons and events are to be understood; and so to
show how it is Christ, not Adam, who reveals true humanity and how human
nature, even sinful human nature, finds its true reflection, not in Adam, but in
Christ. In the closing paragraph of the booklet, Barth asserts that Christ 'is true
man in an absolute sense, and it is in His humanity that we have to recognise
true human nature in the condition and character in which it was willed and
created by God'.[16] For Barth, the second half of Romans 5 demonstrates the
priority of Christ, rather than Adam, as the genuine human being, the epitome
of true human nature.

Lloyd-Jones's pencilled comments and markings are found mostly on pages
6–28 of this booklet of forty-five pages. The markings are of various kinds.
Some consist simply of underlinings of words and phrases and exclamation
marks in the margin. It is difficult to know how to interpret these and so they

---

15. T. F. Torrance and J. K. S. Reid, 'Editors' Foreword', in Barth, *Christ and Adam*.
16. Barth, *Christ and Adam*, p. 45.

are left out of this analysis. There are also some ticks in the margin, which may well be by Lloyd-Jones, but, as it is difficult to be sure, again no comment is made on these. There are, however, a number of substantive comments, as well as some pencilled question marks, in Lloyd-Jones's hand against various passages, which clearly indicate doubt or disagreement. The principal topics which are addressed by these markings are those of original sin, universalism and Christocentrism. Lloyd-Jones's comments on each of these matters will first be examined and then some proposals will be made about their significance for understanding the basis for Lloyd-Jones's objections to Barthian theology.

One set of comments clusters around the issue of original sin – in particular, Barth's characterization of the relationship between Adam's sin and the sins of the rest of humanity. In Lloyd-Jones's view, Barth's statements do not bring out sufficiently clearly Paul's focus on the one sin of Adam, as the sin in which all humanity participated and which resulted in their condemnation, a theme which comes out very clearly in Lloyd-Jones's own preaching on this passage in his Friday evening series on Romans 5 between October 1957 and May 1958.[17] So Barth argues that we have become guilty of Adam's sin 'by our sinning in Adam' and that 'by our sinning we also deserve to die' the death that Adam died.[18] Against this, Lloyd-Jones notes, 'Paul says it is because of Adam's sin.' The point comes clearly into focus where Barth explains Paul's statement in Romans 5:12 that all have sinned as meaning 'that all have repeated Adam's sinful act', against which Lloyd-Jones simply comments, 'No!!'[19] Romans 5, for Lloyd-Jones, concerns the consequences for all humanity of the one sin of Adam; by contrast, Barth was bringing into consideration the subsequent actual sins of humanity in a manner which Paul in that passage does not contemplate.

Another set of comments relates to the vexed issue of universalism. When Barth speaks of the cross as that on which Christ died 'for the sin of Adam and the sin of all men, and by which Adam and all men are reconciled and pardoned', Lloyd-Jones comments simply, 'Universalism.'[20] A little later, Barth discusses the parallel which Paul draws between the 'one' and the 'many', in relation to both Adam and Christ. Barth argues, on the basis of this parallel, that Christ has died for all who sinned in Adam:

---

17. D. M. Lloyd-Jones, *Romans. An Exposition of Chapter 5: Assurance* (Edinburgh: Banner of Truth, 1971).

18. Barth, *Christ and Adam*, p. 21.

19. Ibid., p. 26.

20. Ibid., p. 18.

The one Jesus Christ who took Adam's place in His death on the cross, has thereby
entered into the closest possible relationship with Adam, and, since, in dying for
the one Adam, He died also for the many who had sinned in Adam, He has thereby
entered into the closest possible relationship with them.[21]

Lloyd-Jones comments, 'Paul does not say all this. Only deduction from
this is universalism. It denies John 17:1–5.' In Lloyd-Jones's own exegesis of
the verses in question, the parallel is understood to be between all who are
in Adam and all who are in Christ, thereby avoiding a universalistic conclusion which Lloyd-Jones believes to be absolutely contrary to the teaching of
Scripture.[22] Again, he understands Barth to be teaching something entirely
different from that which Paul teaches in Romans 5.

Turning then to issues which are central to Barth's thesis in this booklet,
there are a number of marginal comments by Lloyd-Jones which make reference to Barth's insistence on the priority of Christ over against Adam, in the
parallel which Paul draws between the two. This theme is sounded early on
in the booklet, where Barth asserts that 'our relationship to Adam is only the
type, the likeness, the preliminary shadow of our relationship to Christ. The
same human nature appears in both, but the humanity of Adam is only real and
genuine in so far as it reflects and corresponds to the humanity of Christ.'[23]
Against this, Lloyd-Jones has marked two vertical lines in the margin and commented, 'Quite wrong.' A little further on, Barth develops his argument in a
discussion of the relationship between sin and grace. He concludes this section
by saying, 'Our relationship to Adam is a subordinate relationship, because the
guilt and punishment we incur in Adam have no independent reality of their
own but are only the dark shadows of the grace and life we find in Christ.'[24]
Lloyd-Jones's comment here is, 'Pure philosophy making cross without effect.'
Lloyd-Jones of course would never have disputed that Christ is superior, in
every sense, to Adam. The objection which underlies his comments is that
Barth's subordination of Adam to Christ is not something which concerns the
apostle in this chapter.

Barth develops his views on the relationship between Adam and Christ in a
manner which brings out more clearly the nature of Lloyd-Jones's objections.
It may be helpful to summarize Barth's argument at this point. He is dealing

---

21. Ibid.
22. Lloyd-Jones, *Romans 5*, pp. 225, 252.
23. Barth, *Christ and Adam*, p. 9.
24. Ibid., p. 11.

here with the central part of the passage, Romans 5:15–17, and in particular the phrase 'so much more', which he sees as fundamental to the import of this section. Barth's concern is to show how that phrase gives hope because it demonstrates that there is a connection between being in sin in Adam and being in grace in Christ. Without that phrase, says Barth, we would be at a loss to see how we might move from the one to the other: 'From the sin of Adam, as such, no way leads to the grace of Christ.'[25] But this phrase, he argues, shows that there is a connection – a way is found to move from 'our unhappy past', in sin and in Adam, to a present and future which

> belong to Christ and in belonging to Christ they are connected with the past, because the past contains not only Adam's sin and Adam's death, not only our weakness, sin, godlessness, and enmity, it contains also the crucifixion of Jesus Christ, and through it our reconciliation to God. It is because Christ has thus invaded the world of Adam and claimed it for Himself, that Paul can find a connexion between the two, a way that leads from Adam to Christ for himself and all believers.[26]

Lloyd-Jones objects to this line of argument with a string of comments, including, 'Pure philosophy & making the cross of none effect,' and, 'All alien to Paul's thought.' So, for Lloyd-Jones, Barth here is again simply expounding views of his own making, rather than exegeting the argument of the apostle. More specifically, Barth's Christocentrism, in the manner in which he develops it in this booklet, is very far removed, in Lloyd-Jones's view, from the Christocentrism which is taught by Paul.

Barth then writes, 'Christ has removed the barriers and opened the doors and Adam can pass from sin to pardon – from death to life.'[27] Lloyd-Jones has an extensive comment here, which is not entirely easy to read: 'According to this Christ has merely opened the door of possibility, whereas Paul's whole point is that as the one thing actually differed in Adam [illegible] Christ. Paul is concerned about assurance!' Whatever the precise words here, Lloyd-Jones's concern is clear: Barth's commentary obscures the certainty which Lloyd-Jones believes Paul to be here asserting, as to the finality of what Christ has done. Christ has not 'merely opened the door of possibility', he has completed the work of redemption for all who are in him. One of the principal emphases in Lloyd-Jones's sermons on this passage is the assurance which these verses bring

---

25. Ibid., p. 17.
26. Ibid.
27. Ibid., pp. 18–19.

to the believer, as he or she grasps the finality of Christ's work as taught by the apostle. This emphasis Lloyd-Jones failed to find in Barth's exposition of the passage. In summary, then, Lloyd-Jones took issue with Barth's view of original sin, with Barth's perceived universalism and with the particular nature of Barth's Christocentrism. On these central issues, Lloyd-Jones considered Barth to be teaching something entirely different from the message of the apostle Paul.

Assessment

In seeking to assess these fascinating comments, it is important to bear in mind that they were made by Lloyd-Jones for his own personal benefit, as he studied the booklet in which they were made. They were not intended for publication and Lloyd-Jones would never have envisaged that they would be the subject of discussion and analysis. It would be an error to treat them as if they were his fully digested considered thoughts on Barth's theology. Nevertheless, they are indicative of his views and therefore allow cautious conclusions to be drawn which, with the other evidence already cited, shed some light on Lloyd-Jones's view of certain aspects of Barth's thought.

It is worth noting, first, that the evidence of this copy of Barth's *Christ and Adam*, together with that cited earlier, demonstrates that Lloyd-Jones did indeed seek seriously to engage with Barth's thought and that this interest was an enduring one, beginning in 1929 or 1930 when Barth's ideas were starting to penetrate the consciousness of British evangelicalism and lasting through to some point after 1956, the year in which this booklet was published. It would appear that his engagement with Barth was at the level of the informed and concerned pastor, rather than of the academic theologian: there is no evidence, for example, of any extended discussion of whether Barth's theology was in fact universalistic – that is simply assumed on the basis of the apparent implications of what Barth writes about the status of humanity in Christ. Nor does there appear to be any engagement with the main thesis of Barth's booklet, that it is Christ, not Adam, who ultimately defines true humanity. Nevertheless, Lloyd-Jones cannot be accused of ignoring Barth, or, on the evidence of this booklet, of not taking his views seriously. His concerns, however, were not so much those of the professional theologian as of the pastor and preacher and, as the obituary quoted at the beginning of this chapter shows, they centred on the implications of Barth's teaching for the gospel in the world and in the life of the believer and the church.

Is it then possible, second, to identify some common strands which link the objections noted by Lloyd-Jones in his pencilled comments on Barth's booklet, in order to elucidate more clearly the negative comments that Lloyd-Jones made about Barth in his obituary? It would seem that it is, if the thrust of those comments is compared with the emphases in Lloyd-Jones's own sermons on the same passage in Romans 5. In his own preaching on Romans 5, Lloyd-Jones does not mention Barth by name at all, nor does he take up directly any of Barth's themes which he critiques in the booklet, with one exception – that of universalism. Lloyd-Jones spends some time exegeting the central portion of the passage, at verses 15–17, where in Barth he perceives a clear universalistic tendency. He admits in his sermons, without naming Barth, that this is a challenge which he needs to meet and he seeks to do so with the combination of careful, detailed exegesis and powerful rhetoric which is the hallmark of those sermons.[28]

Lloyd-Jones's conclusion on this issue is uncompromising: 'There is no universalism taught in the Scripture; the exact opposite is taught there.'[29] This question is evidently of very great concern to Lloyd-Jones and provides a key to understanding his great objection to Barth's approach to Romans 5. Leaving aside the controverted question whether Barth's teaching is or is not in fact universalistic, the issue for Lloyd-Jones was that Barth appeared to see the entirety of humanity as having been in Adam but as now being in Christ. Consequently, as Lloyd-Jones saw it, there could be no room in Barth's theology for drawing distinctions between the saved and the unsaved, or for issuing any challenge to the latter to find salvation. In stark contrast, Lloyd-Jones understood the apostle's message as forcing the question on each individual distinctly: are you yet in Christ? This was the central issue which any preacher was obliged to press on his congregation. To teach that all humanity is now in Christ was, for Lloyd-Jones, to rip out the very heart of the gospel, 'making the cross of none effect'.

Lloyd-Jones's own teaching on Romans 5 is quite different from Barth's: Paul there demonstrates that all humanity is, from the start, in Adam and so now shares in Adam's sin and the death and judgment which necessarily follow. Given that horrific situation, the great issue for Lloyd-Jones, in his understanding of Paul's message, is for each individual to find the only antidote to their desperate plight, which consists in evangelical repentance and a personal faith in Jesus Christ. Lloyd-Jones was always conscious, as a preacher and pastor, that his audiences were likely to include at least some who did not have this faith. So a constant theme of his sermons on Romans 5, as well as of his

---

28. Lloyd-Jones, *Romans 5*, pp. 225, 240–252.

29. Ibid., p. 252.

preaching generally, is the distinction which must be drawn between those who are saved, through faith in Christ alone, and those who are lost, because they remain in Adam. Lloyd-Jones worked hard in his preaching to press this distinction on his congregation and to challenge each individual with it, in order to exhort the unbeliever urgently to turn to Christ. The preacher who failed to do this would, in Lloyd-Jones's estimation, fail in the most basic of his duties. It would seem that Lloyd-Jones's frustration with Barth's booklet lay largely in the fact that he did not find there this distinguishing note and so no ground on which to issue the challenge that the unbeliever much needed to hear.

The strength of Lloyd-Jones's objections to Barth's approach, then, centres ultimately on the implications of that approach for preaching. Lloyd-Jones lamented in his obituary of Barth that preaching based on the Swiss theologian's thought was, in the end, sterile. Similar comments have been made more recently by evangelicals reviewing the effects of Barthian preaching over the whole course of the twentieth century. Carl Trueman refers to 'the failure of Barthianism to stem the collapse of Europe's churches, both numerically and doctrinally' as 'perhaps, the greatest elephant in the room when it comes to discussing how Barth's thought impacts preaching and the Christian life'.[30] Henri Blocher affirms that 'during the short-lived Barthian era, preachers in mainline churches had again substance to preach', but adds that, as he had himself observed in French Protestantism, 'the effect did not last'.[31]

For Lloyd-Jones, Barthian preaching was, in the last analysis, an intellectual and philosophical exercise, rather than the truly spiritual experience which Lloyd-Jones believed fervently should lie at the heart of all true Christian preaching. Preaching, for Lloyd-Jones, must be full of individual challenge: the call to repentance and faith in Jesus Christ, based on the reality of conscious everlasting punishment in hell for all who reject him, lies at the very heart of the gospel message. The lack of this note in Barth's writings, as Lloyd-Jones saw it, was at the root of his objections to Barth's exposition of Romans 5 – indeed, of Barth's theology generally. Ultimately, for Lloyd-Jones, Barthianism failed because it lacked the challenge to the individual to leave sin and to fly to Jesus Christ for salvation.

© Robert Strivens, 2011

---

30. Carl R. Trueman, 'Foreword', in David Gibson and Daniel Strange (eds.), *Engaging with Barth: Contemporary Evangelical Critiques* (Nottingham: Apollos, 2008), p. 14.

31. Henri Blocher, 'Karl Barth's Christocentric Method', in ibid., p. 46.

9. LLOYD-JONES AND ROMAN CATHOLICISM

John Maiden

'I would not hesitate to assert that this system, known as Roman Catholicism, is the devil's greatest masterpiece. It is such a departure from the Christian faith and the New Testament teaching, that I would not hesitate with the Reformers of the sixteenth century to describe it as "apostasy".'[1] An unambiguous aspect of Lloyd-Jones's thought was his opposition to Catholicism, both the Church of Rome and catholicizing tendencies within the Protestant denominations. Yet his prevailing influence within British evangelicalism coincided with a transformative epoch for Protestant–Catholic relations.[2] The imperative to confront Rome had been a core component of the evangelical psyche until the 1950s, although popular British anti-Catholicism had declined steadily since the late nineteenth century.[3] In 1928, when Lloyd-Jones transitioned from medicine to ministry, Anglican and Free Church evangelicals successfully

---

1. D. M. Lloyd-Jones, *Roman Catholicism* (London: Evangelical Press, 1966), p. 2.
2. I use the terms 'Catholic' and 'anti-Catholic' in relation to Catholicism of both the Anglican and Roman varieties. This reflects the historical evangelical tendency towards elision.
3. See Hugh McLeod, 'Protestantism and British National Identity, 1815–1945', in Peter van der Veer and Hartmut Lehman (eds.), *Nation and Religion: Perspectives on Europe and Asia* (Princeton: Princeton University Press, 1999), pp. 60–65; John

campaigned for a second parliamentary defeat of the revised Prayer Book, largely on the basis of a fear of Catholic influence. During the middle years of the Welshman's ministry at Westminster Chapel, Rome displayed a new warmness towards the ecumenical movement, coining the kindly phrase 'separated brethren' to replace the intransigent term 'schismatic', and Protestant leaders contemplated closer relations. In 1966 Archbishop Ramsey and Pope Paul VI exchanged the kiss of peace in Rome, symbolic of a breakthrough achieved. The traditional anti-Romanism of the Free Churches, so influential during the interwar years, appeared to wane. During the 1960s it became apparent that evangelicals were not impervious to the ecumenical spirit of the age. Anglican evangelicalism experienced a reconfiguration, a reawakening of ecclesiology that, to adopt Christopher Cocksworth's extended metaphor, developed embryonically in the 1950s, was finally born in the 1960s and was baptized at the National Evangelical Anglican Congress in 1967.[4]

This chapter will argue that a crucial influence on Lloyd-Jones's thought, ministry and steering of the 'non-participatory'[5] evangelical ship was his conscientious refusal to compromise traditional Reformed anti-Romanism.[6] Valuable studies by Iain Murray and John Brencher have acknowledged the importance of such positioning, yet neither reflects fully on Lloyd-Jones's anti-Roman thought or gives much attention to the significance of Lloyd-Jones's Protestant posturing for relations between evangelicals.[7] Furthermore, anti-Romanism has been strangely underemphasized in assessments of the defining 'moment' for postwar British evangelical historical consciousness, Lloyd-Jones's 'secessionist peroration' of 1966.[8] What follows is divided into

---

Maiden, *National Religion and the Prayer Book Controversy, 1927–1928* (Woodbridge: Boydell Press, 2009).

4. Christopher J. Cocksworth, *Evangelical Eucharistic Thought in the Church of England* (Cambridge: Cambridge University Press, 1993), p. 103.

5. A term used by Paul Helm in 'A Pure Church?', *The Banner of Truth*, no. 45 (November – December 1966), pp. 1–3.

6. The terms 'anti-Romanism' and 'anti-Catholicism' are used throughout this paper. Where Lloyd-Jones is concerned, this is not to suggest that his views were held militantly.

7. John Brencher, *Martyn Lloyd-Jones (1899–1981) and Twentieth-Century Evangelicalism* (Carlisle: Paternoster, 2002), ch. 4; Iain H. Murray, *D. Martyn Lloyd-Jones: The Fight of Faith 1939–1981* (Edinburgh: Banner of Truth, 1990), see esp. pp. 305–308, 444–448, 514.

8. Brencher, *Lloyd-Jones*, p. 95.

three sections. To provide contextualization the chapter will assess the background of evangelical anti-Catholicism and its contribution to church–chapel unity. It then surveys the frame of reference for Lloyd-Jones's thinking regarding Roman Catholicism and the ecumenical movement. Finally, it examines the phases of anti-Romanism in Lloyd-Jones's ministry, arguing that just as anti-Catholicism had been a defining feature of historical evangelical identity, so the question of Rome brought about the polarization of the movement in the 1960s.

Background: anti-Catholicism in England and Wales

Anti-Catholicism had deep roots in evangelicalism. The movement, of course, traced its lineage to the Reformers, and aversion to Roman Catholicism was a feature of eighteenth-century transatlantic evangelicalism. The rise of Tractarianism meant a new 'popish' threat, against which evangelicals devoted significant energy from the mid-nineteenth century.[9] By the early twentieth century, anti-ritualism remained, in the judgment of one historian, a 'neurosis' for Anglican evangelicals.[10] Yet this was no mere Anglican concern: as David Bebbington describes, by the late nineteenth century 'anti-Catholicism had put down deep roots in Nonconformity'.[11] The disestablishmentarianism of Nonconformists made genuine cooperation in anti-Catholic campaigns problematic.[12] However, as opposition to the established church declined, anti-Catholicism became more markedly a pan-denominational rallying point. As already mentioned, when Anglicans attempted to revise the Prayer Book in a moderately Catholic direction in 1927–8, evangelicals across the divide united in a national campaign against the 'return of the Mass'. Thomas Nightingale (General Secretary of the National Council of the Evangelical Free Churches) assured his Anglican counterparts that the Free Churches would 'roll up our forces and stand

---

9. See James C. Whisenant, *A Fragile Unity: Anti-Ritualism and the Division of Anglican Evangelicalism in the Nineteenth Century* (Milton Keynes: Paternoster, 2003).

10. J. W. Walmsley, 'The History of the Evangelical Party in the Church of England between 1906 and 1928' (unpublished PhD thesis, University of Hull, 1980), p. 227.

11. David W. Bebbington, *The Nonconformist Conscience: Chapel and Politics, 1870–1914* (London: George Allen & Unwin, 1982), p. 90.

12. Denis G. Paz, *Popular Anti-Catholicism in Mid-Victorian England* (Stanford, CA: Stanford University Press, 1992), pp. 158–163, 188.

with you shoulder to shoulder, different regiments but one army'.[13] In England, official bodies of all but the Presbyterian Church of England and the Unitarians passed resolutions against revision. The Evangelical Alliance provided machinery for a national anti-revision campaign. The climax came in the House of Commons, where Anglican and Free Church MPs, mobilized by varying degrees of Protestant attachment, rejected the bishops' book.[14] The controversy underlined the durability of a shared anti-Catholicism among church and chapel evangelicals.

Enmity towards Rome was embedded in the Welsh national and religious culture. Trystan Owain Hughes's work on twentieth-century Welsh religion reveals a flourishing of anti-Romanism, with causal factors paralleling those in nineteenth-century England, such as Irish immigration, the visibility of Roman Catholicism and the perception of Protestant decline.[15] 'Such was the strength of prejudice in 1914', explains Densil Morgan, 'that the ancient Christianity of the Church of Rome was seen by many of the Welsh to be worldly and unregenerate if not, indeed wholly reprobate.' The Irish Catholic stood opposite to the Nonconformist religious culture: 'For Welsh chapel-goers they represented everything which Protestant evangelicalism existed to counter: clericalism, a sacramentalism so primitive as to be superstitious and a morality impervious to the blandishments of teetotalism and the keeping of the sabbath.'[16] Anti-Catholic sentiment flowed from Nonconformist pulpit orations during this period and the Calvinistic Methodist circles in which Lloyd-Jones was raised were, of course, strongly Reformed and Protestant. There was also some anxiety over high-profile conversions to Roman Catholicism in the first half of the twentieth century, particularly among the leadership of the infant Welsh nationalist movement.[17] While Lloyd-Jones's actual earlier experiences of Roman Catholicism are unclear, his later views were surely influenced by the

---

13. 'Notes of the Week', *Record*, 25 November 1926, p. 813.

14. Maiden, *National Religion*.

15. Trystan Owain Hughes, 'Anti-Catholicism in Wales, 1900–1960', *Journal of Ecclesiastical History*, vol. 53 (April 2002), pp. 313–322.

16. D. Densil Morgan, *The Span of the Cross: Christian Religion and Society in Wales, 1914–2000* (Cardiff: University of Wales Press, 1999), p. 8.

17. The number of Roman Catholics in the movement has tended to be exaggerated, but influential converts included Saunders Lewis (the playwright and founder of Plaid Cymru), R. C. Richards (one of the editors of the *Welsh Nationalist*) and Victor Hampson-Jones. On this see Trystan Owain Hughes, 'An Uneasy Alliance?

ecclesiastical and cultural setting in which he was formed and with which he
kept close connections after leaving.

Rome in Lloyd-Jones's thought

While the same cannot be said for all British evangelicals in the twentieth
century, there is no evidence that Martyn Lloyd-Jones's opposition to Rome
was based on anything other than theological conscience and intellectual
conviction. This point was made with clarity in a 1961 sermon: 'Let me make
it abundantly clear that I am not concerned with individuals. There are, of
course, individuals who are both Roman Catholics and Christians.'[18] It is
noteworthy that Lloyd-Jones's brother Vincent, while he never converted
to Rome, developed an intellectual attachment to Catholic authors such as
Chesterton, Belloc, Waugh and Ronald Knox while at Oxford. However, this
does not appear to have strained the brothers' relationship.[19] Personal interac-
tions with Catholics were perfectly amiable, as Iain Murray illustrates in the
case of H. W. J. Edwards's visit to Westminster Chapel.[20] Lloyd-Jones was
certainly conversant with modern Roman Catholicism – he was a reader of the
monthly New Blackfriars and kept abreast of Hans Küng's work.[21] He respected
his theological foe and, unsurprisingly considering his systematic and logical
preferences, admitted a grudging admiration for the integrated intellectual
approach of Roman Catholicism. Paradoxically, while he could describe Rome
in the most diabolical of terms, he also spoke freely of Rome's 'comprehensive' system, arguing that its theologians had 'worked out their theology all
along the line to cover the whole of life'.[22] The heavyweight rival expressions
of Christianity were to be found in the systematized works of Rome and the
Reformers. Throughout his ministry Lloyd-Jones maintained that Roman
Catholics should be the objects of evangelism, encouraging efforts towards
this. In later years his support for such schemes, for example his chairing in

---

Welsh Nationalism and Roman Catholicism', *North American Journal of Welsh Studies*,
vol. 2, no. 2 (2002), pp. 1–6.

18. Lloyd-Jones, *Roman Catholicism*, p. 2.

19. Brencher, *Lloyd-Jones*, p. 143.

20. Murray, *Lloyd-Jones: Fight of Faith*, p. 446.

21. Ibid.

22. D. M. Lloyd-Jones, 'Address', in *Annual Meeting of the Evangelical Library* (1961), pp.
19–20.

April 1970 of a rally with ex-priests at the Welsh Church, London, would have appeared to some as oddly anachronistic.[23]

As will be shown, the main intellectual tributaries flowing into Lloyd-Jones's anti-Romanism were the thinking of the Reformers, the Puritans and early Nonconformists, and additionally the amillennial tradition and Protestant interpretations of national history. Analysis of his sermons and other publications indicates a coherent framework of thought, based around the issues of authority, ecclesiology, worship, eschatology and temporal concern. His clearest extended statement on the topic came in *Roman Catholicism* (1966), a published version of a sermon preached in 1961 in his marathon series on Ephesians. While the final section of this chapter describes important phases of Lloyd-Jones's anti-Romanism, there was also considerable consistency in his thought on the issue.

Authority

Lloyd-Jones's theological critique of Rome was wide ranging; however, his controlling criticism of the Catholic system was its usurpation of the authority of Christ. In *Roman Catholicism* he expressed this by referring to the Vatican's claim to 'totalitarian allegiance'.[24] Such claims of authority undermined the saving work and divine Lordship of Christ. The Catholic system stood between humanity and the divine Saviour. It approved the worship of images, statues and relics and so encouraged idolatry and superstition. It superseded Christ's authority, claiming the binding control of its tradition, the salvific necessity of the church, the miracle working of the priest, the absolute power of the pope and the mystical lineage of the bishops. Teachings on baptism and the Mass corroded the Christian doctrines of justification and sanctification.[25] Such authoritarianism robbed Christ of his divine pre-eminence and plundered his church of the knowledge of the full completeness of salvation. Furthermore, Rome undercut the authority of Christ in Scripture. Lloyd-Jones would freely identify the aspects of Catholic theology he deemed 'sound', notably the person of Christ, the virgin birth, the incarnation, miracles, the substitutionary work of the cross and the ascension, yet would denounce Rome because 'to all that she "adds", with a damnable plus, things which are

23. 'Ex-Priests Tour Britain', *Evangelical Times* (April 1970), p. 5. See also 'Annual Letter, 1954', in Iain H. Murray (ed.), *D. Martyn Lloyd-Jones: Letters 1919–1981* (Edinburgh: Banner of Truth, 1994), pp. 93–95.

24. Lloyd-Jones, *Roman Catholicism*, p. 7.

25. Ibid., pp. 6–13.

utterly unscriptural and which, indeed, become a denial of Scripture'.[26] The Reformation, he asserted, saw the rejection of the authority of a 'visible institution' over biblical 'truth': Luther had 'refused to be bound by that mighty institution, the Roman Catholic Church, with her long centuries of history'[27] and had come to recognize that to uphold the primacy of Scripture meant that there could be 'no possible compromise' with a Church of Rome that taught a different gospel.[28] Similarly, Lloyd-Jones articulated that the early Nonconformist leaders followed the same dictum that truth should come before tradition.[29]

Ecclesiology

Lloyd-Jones's stand against Rome and ecumenism was based partly on ecclesiology, in particular the questions of what constituted the true church and the definition of schism. Here he became influenced particularly by John Owen (whose motto on the matter was, 'Believers are not made for churches, but churches are appointed for believers') and spoke on his views at the 1963 Puritan Conference.[30] He subscribed to Owen's particularity rather than Richard Baxter's flexibility on the matter of essentials of the faith. The most lucid explanation of Lloyd-Jones's understanding of the church was given in two sermons on John 17 and Ephesians 4 preached in 1962 and published that year as *The Basis of Christian Unity*. The church was pneumatically founded, an association of regenerated persons united by true doctrine. He was, therefore, concerned with the local assembly, rather than associations of those 'who happen to have been brought up in a certain country, or who happen to belong to a given race or nation or a particular visible church',[31] and opposed efforts

---

26. Ibid., p. 3. See also D. M. Lloyd-Jones, 'What is an Evangelical?', in D. M. Lloyd-Jones, *Knowing the Times: Addresses Delivered on Various Occasions, 1942–1977* (Edinburgh: Banner of Truth, 1989), p. 321.

27. D. M. Lloyd-Jones, *The Basis of Christian Unity* (London: Inter-Varsity Fellowship, 1962), p. 59.

28. D. M. Lloyd-Jones, *Luther and His Message for Today* (Foxton: Burlington Press, 1967), p. 26.

29. D. M. Lloyd-Jones, 'Division – True and False', *Westminster Record*, vol. 38 (July 1963), p. 103.

30. D. M. Lloyd-Jones, 'John Owen on Schism', in D. M. Lloyd-Jones, *The Puritans: Their Origins and Successors: Addresses Delivered at the Puritan and Westminster Conferences 1959–1978* (Edinburgh: Banner of Truth, 1987), pp. 73–100.

31. Lloyd-Jones, *The Basis of Christian Unity*, p. 11.

to foster a wider Christian, as opposed to evangelical, unity. Sharp distinction was drawn between a restricted and particular 'evangelical' view of the church and a 'Catholic view, the comprehensive view, the all-inclusive view'.[32] Evangelicals could not support an ecumenical enterprise because it was based on flawed first principles. Here, the language of the remnant was also an associated aspect of Lloyd-Jones's thinking on ecumenical aspirations: evangelicals should trust in the faithfulness of the Holy Spirit rather than rely on 'expediency and expedients'.[33] On occasion he reminded listeners that in the United States it was the most exclusivist churches that were growing most rapidly.[34]

Important to Lloyd-Jones's apologia for Christian exclusivism was a defence of the Reformation as a non-schismatic event. He held the view that schism was a 'deadly sin',[35] but that the Protestants were right to separate, although they had subsequently been sinful in dividing from each other.[36] In the former case Protestants were not chargeable with schism, but rather the Roman Catholic Church was guilty of apostasy.[37] Furthermore, following the precedent of the early Nonconformist leaders, Lloyd-Jones maintained that it was always right to separate from any church returning to the Roman Catholic position, saying that 'any returning to the practices of Rome, her sacramental teaching and so on, is something which more than justifies division'.[38] This justification for separation was particularly salient to some evangelicals in the climate of the 1960s.

Worship

Lloyd-Jones had an antipathy for 'formalism', describing it in an Ephesians series sermon entitled 'Quenching the Spirit' (May 1961) as 'the greatest curse

---

32. D. M. Lloyd-Jones, 'Can We Learn from History?', in Lloyd-Jones, *The Puritans*, p. 231.

33. D. M. Lloyd-Jones, 'Ecclesiola in Ecclesia', in ibid., p. 147. See also D. M. Lloyd-Jones, *Authority* (Edinburgh: Banner of Truth, 1964), pp. 70–71; Lloyd-Jones, *The Basis of Christian Unity*, p. 59.

34. Lloyd-Jones, 'Ecclesiola in Ecclesia', p. 147.

35. Lloyd-Jones, 'Can We Learn from History?', p. 230.

36. Owen, of course, made the same distinction between schism and separation. See Lloyd-Jones, 'John Owen on Schism', p. 89. On Protestant divisions see Lloyd-Jones, 'Can We Learn from History?', p. 219.

37. D. M. Lloyd-Jones, 'Schism', *Westminster Record*, vol. 38 (June 1963), pp. 85–86.

38. D. M. Lloyd-Jones, 'Division – True and False', p. 105. See also D. M. Lloyd-Jones, *From Puritanism to Nonconformity* (2nd ed., Bridgend: Evangelical Press of Wales, 1991), pp. 46–47.

of the Church'.[39] The tendency towards 'religious' ritual had never, he claimed, been fully dismantled within the Church of England. In the seventeenth century lack of freedom in worship had been adequate grounds for division;[40] and during the nineteenth century with the rise of the Oxford Movement a Catholic formalism had risen again to the surface.[41] However, for Lloyd-Jones:

> Formalism is seen at its zenith again in Roman Catholicism – the pomp, the ceremony and the circumstance, and everything worked out to the minutest detail with the processions and the vestments, etc., and the people sitting back doing nothing while the great performance takes place before them. The people really do not enter into the service. There has never been a revival in the Roman Catholic church; there cannot be, there is no room left for it.[42]

Formalism at its most spiritually suffocating, he claimed, would always be found in the Roman Catholic Church.

Eschatology

Lloyd-Jones's views on eschatology were closest to the amillennial position, though on occasion he used the term 'spiritual interpretation'.[43] Like the Protestant Reformers he identified the scriptural prophecies of deception in the Last Days with the papacy. In a postwar talk on the subject of the Antichrist, he stated that while there may have been numerous manifestations of this in human history, he 'would reach his fullest power immediately before the end of this age'.[44] During the presentation he considered the various possible identities of the Antichrist described in 2 Thessalonians 2 and, though ambiguous, he gave most attention to the witness of the Reformers.[45] In a later talk, 'The Final Judgment', he made his own position explicit, arguing that 'here we have a description of the papacy with its curious attempt to combine secular and spiritual power, something which has also been imitated by other

---

39. D. M. Lloyd-Jones, 'Quenching the Spirit', *Westminster Record*, vol. 39 (September 1964), p. 139.
40. Lloyd-Jones, 'Division – True and False', p. 103.
41. See Brencher, *Lloyd-Jones*, p. 166.
42. Lloyd-Jones, 'Quenching the Spirit', p. 139.
43. D. M. Lloyd-Jones, *Great Doctrines Series: The Church and the Last Things* (London: Hodder and Stoughton, 1997), p. 218.
44. Ibid., p. 118.
45. Ibid., pp. 117–118.

religions'.[46] He then went on to identify the second beast of Revelation 13 with false religion, and more particularly with the Roman Catholic Church and also liberal Christianity. Applying these apocalyptic symbols to the ecumenical call, Lloyd-Jones commented, 'Patently . . . we cannot stand together with all these so-called Christians because to align ourselves with false religion is simply to put ourselves into the camp of our ultimate enemy, the devil, who uses the one antagonist exactly as he uses the other.'[47] In *Roman Catholicism* he applied a range of prophetic pictures to the counterfeit Rome, claiming it was a form of Antichrist, in the spirit of the 'man of lawlessness', the second beast, and adding that Rome's deception was prophesied in Revelation 17, 'in the picture of "the great whore" sitting on those seven hills, as Rome does and always has done'.[48] Tellingly, he concluded the sermon, 'There is no difficulty about this; this is a counterfeit, a sham; this is prostitution of the worst and most diabolical kind. It is indeed a form of the antichrist, and it is to be rejected, it is to be denounced; but above all it is to be countered.'[49] This aspect of Lloyd-Jones's views has often been overlooked, but there is no doubt that eschatology informed his attitude towards both Roman Catholicism and the ecumenical movement.

Temporal concerns

Evangelical opposition towards Rome had often included non-theological dimensions, with assertions regarding the Vatican's political, social and moral record. Importantly, Lloyd-Jones was clear that while a political critique of Rome's power was important, this was better left to Christian laymen and statesmen rather than preachers, and that his priority was the 'spiritual aspect'.[50] However, he did on occasion refer to traditional claims about Rome's apparently malign temporal influence. He was uncompromising in his view that Rome was chameleon-like with her use of power, claiming that in some countries she was 'utterly intolerant, vicious and vile in her persecuting zeal'.[51] Such assertions about persecution in 1961 would have resonated with contemporary evangelical concerns about Catholic militancy in places such as Spain, Malta and Columbia. The Evangelical Alliance lobbied the British

---

46. Ibid., p. 195.

47. Ibid.

48. Lloyd-Jones, *Roman Catholicism*, p. 5.

49. Ibid., p. 15.

50. Ibid., p. 2.

51. Ibid., p. 5. See also D. M. Lloyd-Jones, 'The Weapons of our Warfare', in Lloyd-Jones, *Knowing the Times*, p. 202.

Foreign Secretary on the matter[52] and the international secretary of the World
Evangelical Fellowship claimed in 1961 that the 'dictatorial church is no less
a menace to the evangelical cause than the dictatorial state'.[53] Furthermore,
Lloyd-Jones appealed to a Protestant interpretation of national histories. He
associated Roman Catholic influence with material and moral poverty. While
holidaying in Donegal in 1949 he expressed private sadness at what he perceived as economic, intellectual and cultural poverty and blamed Rome: 'it is
a more powerful argument against that vicious system than anything I have
ever read or even heard before.'[54] He claimed the transformative effect of the
Reformation on nations. In a 1960 address commemorating the Reformation
in Scotland, he claimed that it had given 'life-blood to the whole democratic
notion in the realm of politics, and the consequences, as judged from a social
and moral standpoint, simply baffle description'.[55] In a period in which ideas
of Protestant heritage were losing their currency, Lloyd-Jones continued to
recite Protestant national narratives.

Anti-Romanism and Lloyd-Jones's ministry

It is evident that the structure of Lloyd-Jones's thought on Rome constituted
a range of interlocking doctrinal, ecclesiological, eschatological, ecclesiastical and historical arguments built on Reformed Protestant and evangelical
intellectual foundations. As this section shows, anti-Romanism was a latent
feature of Lloyd-Jones's ministry until around 1960. Then, from the turn of the
decade, his anti-Roman polemic became more pronounced and from 1966 his
views on Catholicism contributed significantly to the shaping of his separatist
policy and the polarization of the evangelical movement.

Postwar years: 'positive Protestantism'
In the long postwar period ecumenism entered a new phase of momentum.
In Britain, the British Council of Churches (BCC) was founded in 1942 and
then in 1948 the World Council of Churches (WCC) was officially established,

---

52. London, Evangelical Alliance Archives, Minutes of the Executive Council of the
    Evangelical Alliance (1955–1964), 28 June 1956.
53. 'The Field is the World', *Evangelical Alliance Broadsheet* (Winter 1960), p. 1.
54. Quoted in Murray, *Lloyd-Jones: Fight of Faith*, p. 212.
55. D. M. Lloyd Jones, 'Remembering the Reformation', in Lloyd-Jones, *Knowing the
    Times*, p. 96.

representing all the mainstream British denominations. However, at this point, while the instruction from the Holy See, *Ecclesia Catholica*, had in 1949 recognized the desire of many 'outside the Church' for reunion, Rome had no official ecumenical involvement. Evangelicals also were largely unmoved by the developing ecumenical mood. Furthermore, pre-war feelings of animosity towards Roman and Anglican Catholics proved resilient. Within the Church of England many conservative-leaning evangelicals were still preoccupied with concerns about 'catholicization', in this case with regards to canon law revision from 1953 and then new proposals for Prayer Book revision.[56] Under the leadership of Gilbert W. Kirby (also honorary secretary of the United Protestant Council) the Evangelical Alliance kept a close eye on such Anglican developments in the late 1950s.[57] However, there were also evangelical ambiguities concerning both ecumenism and Catholicism. The Evangelical Alliance did not take an obstructionist line on ecumenism, adopting a policy of 'benevolent neutrality' regarding the World Council of Churches. In 1952 came a portent of future evangelical division when E. J. Poole-Connor, founder of the Fellowship of Independent Evangelical Churches and friend of Lloyd-Jones, resigned his membership of the Alliance over concerns about their flexibility on the matter.[58] There were some signs that the new generation of Anglican leaders might not so willingly volunteer for the anti-ritualistic conflicts of their fathers. In a period of embryonic renewal the older defensive mentality was beginning to change. In 1958, for example, the *Churchman* questioned whether the church could afford a 'new ritual war at this juncture' and suggested a cross-party truce in order that Anglicans could fight 'a vital battle for the soul of the nation'.[59]

While Lloyd-Jones was concerned by ecumenical trends, as long as Rome was a non-participant and evangelical anti-ritualism seemed reasonably solid, the movement did not yet constitute a menace. The threat of Rome was not an important theme of his ministry during this period. Looking back at these years, Lloyd-Jones claimed that his sole focus had been to

---

56. See John Maiden and Peter Webster, 'Parliament, the Church of England and the Last Gasp of Political Protestantism, 1961–64', *Parliamentary History* (forthcoming).

57. London, Evangelical Alliance Archives, Minutes of the Executive Council of the Evangelical Alliance (1955–1964), 24 May 1956 and 22 October 1959; *Evangelical Alliance Broadsheet* (Summer 1961), p. 2.

58. Murray, *Lloyd-Jones: Fight of Faith*, pp. 299–300.

59. 'Editorial', *Churchman*, vol. 72 (March 1958), p. 3.

preach a 'positive Protestantism',[60] a phrase conceivably borrowed from
fellow Congregationalist William Selbie's 1926 work of the same name.
Lloyd-Jones was content to articulate Reformed truths rather than clash
with Rome. There were few direct attacks on 'false' Catholic beliefs in his
preaching during these years, his mention of the 'spurious doctrine' of
apostolic succession in his addresses on authority given at the International
Fellowship of Evangelical Students in Ontario in 1957 being a rare exception.[61] The seeds of later anti-ecumenical themes were evident on occasion:
in 1952 he cautioned the Inter-Varsity Fellowship against the growing
outlook, warning of 'false prophets' in the church and those willing 'to
barter away their birthright by capitulating to the unreformed Church'.[62]
During the same address he set up Martin Luther as an historical exemplar
for evangelicals to follow.[63]

However, anti-Romanism was not accented in Lloyd-Jones's ministry. As
Brian Stanley has pointed out, during these years Lloyd-Jones was by no means
an intransigent exclusivist. Notably, in 1948 he allowed W. R. Matthews, Dean
of St Paul's, to chair an Evangelical Alliance meeting at Westminster Chapel,
and in the same year only illness prevented him from joining Alec Vidler, the
liberal Anglo-Catholic, as a missioner to the University of Edinburgh.[64] From
1957 to 1961 he participated as a critical voice in private meetings convened
by the British Council of Churches to discuss ecumenical cooperation in evangelism.[65] Given the robustness of Lloyd-Jones's opposition to the ecumenical
movement in the 1960s, it is difficult to understand how he could stomach
even unsympathetic participation in British Council of Churches-sponsored
dialogue only a few years earlier. Perhaps these meetings persuaded him that
the ecumenical enterprise was pointless? However, more likely the stiffening
of his resolve against ecumenism came as a result of the surprise entrance of
Rome onto the ecumenical stage.

---

60. Lloyd-Jones, *Roman Catholicism*, p. 2.

61. Lloyd-Jones, *Authority*, p. 59.

62. D. M. Lloyd-Jones, 'Maintaining the Evangelical Faith Today', in Lloyd-Jones,
    Knowing the Times, p. 46.

63. Ibid., p. 40.

64. Brian Stanley, 'Post-War British Evangelicalism: Shifting Identities and Global
    Trajectories' (unpublished paper, Evangelicalism and Fundamentalism in Britain
    conference, June 2009).

65. Murray, *Lloyd-Jones: Fight of Faith*, pp. 314–320.

Early 1960s: developing controversy

In 1928 the encyclical *Mortalium Animos* had underlined Rome's historic position with regard to other churches, condemning involvement in 'pan-Christian' activities. Yet the reign of Pope John XXIII marked the beginning of a period of ecumenical involvement and *aggiornamento*. Four Vatican observers attended the third assembly of the World Council of Churches at New Delhi in 1961, where the Russian, Bulgarian and Romanian Orthodox Churches also joined the Council. The Second Vatican Council had important ecumenical dimensions and in preparation a newly appointed Secretariat for Promoting Christian Unity set about inviting observers from other churches and the World Council. In 1960 and 1962 remarkable developments occurred when Archbishop Geoffrey Fisher and A. C. Craig, Moderator of the General Assembly of the Church of Scotland, met the Pope in Rome. The Anglican primate would later ruffle Protestant feathers by suggesting that the terms 'Protestant' and 'Catholic' were outdated and 'almost used now entirely for propaganda purposes'.[66] Maurice Wood, Principal of Oak Hill College, detected an 'anxiety' within his evangelical circles about the 'new impetus of relations between the Church of England and the Church of Rome'.[67] Some conservative evangelicals looked on with concern at liturgical and ceremonial developments within their denominations. Within Anglicanism canon law revision brought controversies about the Eucharist into focus, particularly with relation to Mass vestments, while the process of Prayer Book revision began once again. In Methodism a liturgical movement began to make inroads and in 1963 the Methodist Conference recommended the rewriting of its Book of Offices.

In 1962 Gilbert Kirby admitted that there was now a 'considerable difference of opinion within the evangelical ranks regarding the ecumenical movement'.[68] *Evangelicals and Unity*, a collection of papers published in 1964, underlined a growing interest in unity between Christians during the period.[69] In the same year, following attendance at the British Council of Churches conference, John Wenham, the rising young scholar, informed the leadership of the Federation of Diocesan Evangelical Unions that Anglican evangelicals

---

66. 'Dr Fisher says "Out of Date"', *The Times* (11 January 1961), p. 14.

67. Watford, Church Society Archives, Federation of Diocesan Evangelical Unions Minute Book (November 1956 – October 1962), 10 May 1961.

68. Gilbert W. Kirby, 'Foreword', in Leith Samuel, *Evangelicals and the Ecumenical Movement* (London: Evangelical Alliance, 1962), p. 1.

69. J. D. Douglas (ed.), *Evangelicals and Unity* (Appleford: Marcham Manor Press, 1964).

should 'strengthen the cords' of unity and reconsider attitudes to those usually regarded as enemies, stretching out hands of 'warm fellowship to people on all sides'.[70] Two years earlier, A. T. Houghton, General Secretary of the Bible Churchmen's Missionary Society and Keswick luminary, produced an influential apologetic for evangelical testimony within the World Council of Churches on the grounds of 'comprehension without compromise'.[71] Significantly, for some the door was left ajar for Rome's involvement, subject to certain criteria. Houghton stressed that Rome's participation depended on her conforming to the aims and basis of the World Council of Churches and reneging her historic ecclesial claims; but if Rome complied then there could be 'no logical objection' to her involvement in the World Council.[72]

In the midst of such developments Lloyd-Jones's anti-Romanism moved to the foreground of his ministry and his anti-ecumenical resolve hardened. As early as 1960 he warned Scottish evangelicals that Protestant ecumenists were endeavouring to heal the Reformation and form a single global church.[73] The next year the anti-Roman flavour of his opposition to the World Council of Churches was apparent in his address to the Evangelical Library. He highlighted the significance of New Delhi, accusing ecumenical leaders of having 'their eye on this question of joining up again with Rome'.[74] He spoke of resisting current tendencies towards Rome, 'even unto blood, because if the drift to Rome prevails . . . everything is lost'.[75] However, the clearest indication of Lloyd-Jones's growing concern was the sermon already mentioned on Roman Catholicism, preached on 29 January 1961. In a crucial passage at the beginning of the sermon he described contemporary ecclesiastical changes such as the movements to bring 'a kind of rapprochement between Roman Catholicism and Protestantism' and the rise of Roman Catholicism in different global contexts. 'From all standpoints', he argued, 'it is imperative that we should look at this position and at this great fact which is confronting us.' He then explained that he had never spoken on the topic before, had not been a member of a Protestant society, and that his preferred emphasis was positive

---

70. Watford, Church Society Archives, Federation of Diocesan Evangelical Unions Minute Book (May 1963 – October 1978), 1 October 1964.

71. A. T. Houghton, *Evangelicals and the World Council of Churches* (London: World Dominion Press, 1962), pp. 7–10.

72. Ibid., pp. 19–20.

73. Lloyd-Jones, 'Remembering the Reformation', p. 91.

74. Lloyd-Jones, 'Address', p. 19.

75. Ibid., p. 20.

Protestantism, but that 'whether we like it or not this is something we have to do'. 'Our text compels me to deal with this,' he asserted, and he continued to read the apostle Paul's warnings about schemes of spiritual deception through the lenses of the supposed contemporary drift towards the Vatican.[76] Additionally, during this period Lloyd-Jones's assessment of the religious situation in Wales was that Roman Catholicism was becoming the greatest rival to evangelicalism, at the expense of comprehensive Anglicanism. In 1963 he wrote, 'I venture to prophesy that the great battle of the future in Wales will be the battle between the Roman Catholics and the despised Evangelical people – the only two groups which know where they stand and what they believe.'[77]

Three important motifs materialized in Lloyd-Jones's public statements on ecumenism during this period. First, in response to the increasing openness to the 'new' Catholicism, he asserted Rome's changelessness. In the final talk of the Campbell Morgan Lectureship series in 1964, he dissected the view that fundamental differences between Protestantism and Rome were disappearing, referring also to the popularity of the media-friendly Pope John XXIII.[78] The suggestion that there was 'no longer a warfare to wage' with Rome was the most 'subtle and dangerous thing of all' confronting evangelicals: she would deceive with her outward behaviour, but the fundamental conflict between Protestant and Catholic theology remained.[79] Rome was impervious to real change.

Second, a common theme found expression in Lloyd-Jones's preaching in the Christian warfare series between October 1960 and July 1961: the 'wiles of the devil' and the danger of the church falling victim to the subtlety of the principalities and powers, and 'the spirit of antichrist, seducing spirits'.[80] In 'Heresies' (January 1961) he spoke of the pressure to avoid preaching a 'negative' gospel and instead a positive, simple Christianity. Yet, he argued, heresy was 'caused and produced, undoubtedly, by the devil and his powers' and the

---

76. Lloyd-Jones, *Roman Catholicism*, pp. 1–2.

77. Martyn Lloyd-Jones to the editor of *Barn*, April 1963, in Murray (ed.), *Lloyd-Jones: Letters 1919–1981*, pp. 143–146. See also his letter in June 1963, ibid., pp. 157–163.

78. Lloyd-Jones, 'The Weapons of our Warfare', p. 200.

79. Ibid., p. 202. See also Lloyd-Jones, *Roman Catholicism*, pp. 1–2, 15; Martyn Lloyd-Jones to the editor of *Barn*, June 1963, in Murray (ed.), *Lloyd-Jones: Letters 1919–1981*, pp. 157–163.

80. D. M. Lloyd-Jones, 'The Wiles of the Devil', *Westminster Record*, vol. 36 (July 1962), p. 98.

analogy of warfare was appropriate in such circumstances.[81] A later sermon, 'The Christian Soldier: Applying the Doctrine' (March 1962), spoke of the devil's deception of the church, arguing that while Protestant churches were 'hurtling their way back to Rome and all that that represents', true Christians were to 'stand and to fight, whatever the cost'.[82] If apostasy was one diabolical 'wile', another was schism; however, in this series Lloyd-Jones asserted that the Reformation had been entirely justified and that the Roman Catholic Church had been guilty of apostasy.[83] This was a claim explored in greater depth in his lecture on John Owen and schism at the Puritan Conference in 1963.[84] The sermon on Roman Catholicism gave the wiles of the devil a definite focus, arguing that the divide of Christendom was more fundamental than the divide between democracy and communism that dominated the decade. Like the barbaric ideologies of the twentieth century, Rome was a totalitarian system, binding 'the souls of her people absolutely, as much as communism does, as much as Hitler did under his horrible system'.[85] Yet Rome was a greater threat because, instead of 'atheistical godlessness', it deceived in the name of Christ.[86] There could be no thawing of relations between Protestantism and the Vatican. Thus, as church leaders prepared to discuss Christian unity in New Delhi, Lloyd-Jones's message from the Westminster Chapel pulpit was of the fundamental incompatibility of Protestantism and Rome.

Third, the uncompromising defence of the Reformation and the idea that the theological battles of the Reformation were being refought came to increasing prominence. This would remain an important motif of Lloyd-Jones's leadership in the succeeding years. In his 1960 address commemorating the Reformation in Scotland he spoke of the theological, social and moral benefits which came from the sixteenth century. The apparent Romeward tendencies of the ecumenical movement and so-called catholicizing trends within the Protestant denominations were denounced. 'We are fighting for a heritage' was the *cri de coeur*.[87] *Roman*

---

81. D. M. Lloyd-Jones, 'Heresies', *Westminster Record*, vol. 38 (April 1963), pp. 50–53.

82. D. M. Lloyd-Jones, 'The Christian Soldier: Applying the Doctrine', *Westminster Record*, vol. 44 (October 1966) pp. 158–159.

83. D. M. Lloyd-Jones, 'Schism', *Westminster Record*, vol. 38 (June 1963), p. 85. See also D. M. Lloyd-Jones, 'Division – True and False', p. 104.

84. Lloyd-Jones, 'John Owen on Schism'.

85. Lloyd-Jones, *Roman Catholicism*, p. 7.

86. Ibid., p. 14.

87. Lloyd-Jones, 'Remembering the Reformation', p. 94.

Catholicism ended with rhetoric that would have befitted the platform of any Protestant society: 'Let me warn you very solemnly that if you rejoice in these approaches to Rome you are denying the blood of the martyrs! Never go near Smithfield if you believe that kind of thing [that Rome is changing]. Those men were burnt at the stake there in Smithfield, John Bradford and the rest, because of their denunciation of Roman Catholicism.'[88] Lloyd-Jones was developing a heightened feeling of Protestant consciousness, not only a keen awareness of Reformed history, but a sense that his own times and challenge were inextricably bound up with the era and legacy of the Reformers.

By the early 1960s Lloyd-Jones had moved beyond 'positive Protestantism'. The language of warfare and struggle and the references to spiritual deception in his polemic are telling. During the same period came signs of polarization among evangelicals concerning Catholicism. In 1961 the House of Lords held a six-hour debate on Christian unity at which Viscount Alexander of Hillsborough, the Labour Baptist peer, gave a stinging speech on the doctrinal differences between Canterbury and Rome. The response to Hillsborough's oration, widely reported in the British press, was such that the Evangelical Alliance wrote a general letter to its members on the matter. However, while Gilbert Kirby characteristically claimed that 'it is quite clear that Britain is at heart still very much a Protestant country', the correspondence received by Hillsborough indicates that anti-Romanism was becoming largely the preoc-cupation of separatist evangelicals and members of Protestant societies.[89] A significant number of letters expressing gratitude for the peer's defence of Protestantism came from those who presumably admired Lloyd-Jones.[90] More widely during these years, non-participatory evangelicals warned against cooperation with Rome. Leith Samuel wrote a booklet published by the Evangelical Alliance in 1962 criticizing evangelical involvement in the ecu-menical movement, giving particular focus to catholicizing trends.[91] In 1964, Herbert Carson, who later served for two years as an assistant to Lloyd-Jones at Westminster Chapel, published *Roman Catholicism Today*, a critique of both

---

88. Lloyd-Jones, *Roman Catholicism*, p. 14.
89. Cambridge, Churchill Archives Centre, Lord Alexander of Hillsborough Papers, AV11/2, Gilbert W. Kirby to Evangelical Alliance members, May 1961.
90. Cambridge, Churchill Archives Centre, Lord Alexander of Hillsborough Papers, AV11/2. See various letters in this archive collection. One correspondent with Lord Alexander was Iain Murray.
91. Samuel, *Evangelicals and the Ecumenical Movement*.

traditional Catholic dogma and the 'new Catholicism', which was revised and republished after the Second Vatican Council.[92] Robust opposition to ecumenical trends and contemporary Catholicism was becoming a hallmark of Lloyd-Jones and his circle. However, ecumenically minded evangelicals, and most strikingly the emerging leadership of Anglican evangelicalism, were moving in a different direction.

Mid-1960s onwards: Rome and separatism

The prospects for ecumenical relations between Protestants and Catholics seemed to be rapidly improving by the conclusion of the Second Vatican Council and its decree *Unitatis Reintegratio* of November 1964. Two years later, Pope Paul VI confirmed that the Secretariat for Promoting Christian Unity would remain as a permanent dicastery of the Holy See. Then in March 1966 the visit of Archbishop Michael Ramsey to Rome, where he and Paul VI exchanged the kiss of peace, further heightened expectation about the possibility of reunion.[93] While aspects of Vatican II appeared underwhelming to some Protestant commentators, the representative bodies of mainstream denominations responded with a greater openness to the idea of Christian unity. When Anglican-Methodist reunion discussions began again in 1965, for example, a Roman Catholic observer was invited to attend the commission's meetings.

Also significant was a remarkable shift in evangelical relations with Anglo-Catholics. The passing of the Vesture of Ministers Measure in 1964 saw many evangelicals finally reject a policy of Erastianism.[94] Influential figures began to suggest that evangelicals must accept Anglican comprehensiveness. *All in Each Place: Towards Reunion in England* (1965), edited by theologian J. I. Packer, emphasized that future proposals for Anglican and Methodist reunion should not 'create conscientious difficulties for Anglo-Catholics'.[95] This conciliatory mindset was evident in the Church Assembly, where evangelicals regarded themselves as

---

92. Herbert Carson, *Roman Catholicism Today* (London: Inter-Varsity Fellowship, 1964); revised as *Dawn or Twilight? A Study of Contemporary Roman Catholicism* (London: Inter-Varsity Press, 1966).

93. 'The Pope and Dr Ramsey in Kiss of Peace', *The Times* (24 March 1966), p. 12.

94. See Maiden and Webster, 'Parliament, the Church of England and the Last Gasp of Political Protestantism'.

95. J. I. Packer, 'Wanted: A Pattern for Union', in J. I. Packer (ed.), *All in Each Place: Towards Reunion in England* (Appleford: Marcham Manor Press, 1965), pp. 29–30.

'statesmanlike'.[96] However, the National Evangelical Anglican Congress in 1967 was the defining moment for Anglican evangelicalism. The presence of Archbishop Ramsey, as well as of observers from various Anglo-Catholic bodies and, remarkably, a Roman Catholic, underlined an 'official' policy of participation in the wider church.[97] This was given substance in the congress statements, which spoke of greater Anglican involvement, and which some Free Churchmen deemed would come at the expense of pan-denominational evangelical cooperation. However, the statement on Roman Catholicism was arguably the most radical in the document, recognizing the 'many fundamental doctrines' held in common and cautiously welcoming the potentialities of dialogue 'on the basis of Scripture'.[98]

From the mid-1960s, Lloyd-Jones's concerns regarding the influence of Rome on the ecumenical movement affected his ministry beyond mere polemics and became a primary factor in his policy of separatism. This policy was evident in Westminster Chapel's decision not to join the proposed Congregational Church in England and Wales in 1966; in his speech to the second National Assembly of Evangelicals; and in his public support for the British Evangelical Council from 1967. The first Westminster Chapel members' meeting of 1966 provides insights into Lloyd-Jones's preoccupations. The proposed new Congregational Church (with a strongly ecumenical constitution) was the pressing issue, and Lloyd-Jones also described an 'anti-evangelical' ecumenical movement and a 'fraternization that was taking place between the World Council of Churches and the Church of Rome'. He discussed the mutual exchange of observers between Rome and the World Council of Churches, the proposed visit of Archbishop Ramsey to Rome and plans for a Jesuit priest to preach at Westminster Abbey during a proposed week of prayer for Christian unity. Also mentioned were the various ecumenical developments between Protestant denominations in England. He concluded that 'the ultimate object was to have a single comprehensive church in this country and that would obviously include the Church of Rome, basically unreformed though perhaps modified in certain outward

---

96. Gervase Duffield, 'Evangelical Involvement', in John C. King, *Evangelicals Today: 13 Stock-taking Essays* (London: Lutterworth Press, 1973), p. 167.

97. See Andrew Atherstone, 'The Keele Congress of 1967: A Paradigm Shift in Anglican Evangelical Attitudes', *Journal of Anglican Studies*, vol. 9 (November 2011), pp. 175–197.

98. Philip Crowe (ed.), *Keele '67: National Evangelical Anglican Congress Statement* (London: Falcon Books, 1967), p. 39.

respects'.[99] It was in this year that Lloyd-Jones's 1961 sermon 'Roman Catholicism', which had already appeared in the *Westminster Record*, was published as a stand-alone booklet.

It is hardly surprising, but largely overlooked, that before his secessionist *denouement* in the address to the National Assembly of Evangelicals in October 1966, Lloyd-Jones's description of the situation facing evangelicals was framed in strongly Protestant terms. As he had previously, Lloyd-Jones warned that the ecumenical movement was willing to 'throw everything into the melting pot' in order to form a new world church.[100] To this end Protestant denominations were revising traditional attitudes towards Rome. 'A change, a profound change, has taken place in the attitude of Protestants towards the Roman Catholic Church. The situation is indeed so novel that I am afraid that many of us as evangelicals do not yet quite realize it and are not aware of what is happening.'[101] There was criticism of the silence of evangelicals in the past year, where 'certain visits' were made to 'certain places' (presumably a reference to Ramsey's meeting in Rome) – a hush that Lloyd-Jones blamed on the denominational disunity of evangelicalism.[102] He also alluded to improving relations between Anglican evangelicals and Anglo-Catholics, relating this to supposed ecumenical trends. Were evangelicals content with 'just being an evangelical wing in a territorial church that will eventually include, and must, if it is to be a truly national and ecumenical church, the Roman Catholic Church?' He criticized experts who created formulas to satisfy the interpretation of both evangelicals and Anglo-Catholics.[103] A critical section of the oration before his final secessionist appeal went as follows:

> My friends, we are not only the guardians and custodians of the faith of the Bible; we are the modern representatives and successors of the glorious men who fought this same fight, the good fight of faith, in centuries past. Surely, as evangelicals, we ought to feel this appeal. We are standing in the position of the Protestant reformers. Are we accepting this modern idea that the Reformation was the greatest

99. London, Westminster Chapel Archives, Church Meeting Minute Book (January 1959 – May 1977), 20 January 1966.

100. D. M. Lloyd-Jones, 'Evangelical Unity: An Appeal', in Lloyd-Jones, *Knowing the Times*, p. 248.

101. Ibid., p. 249.

102. Ibid., p. 250.

103. Ibid., p. 251.

tragedy that ever happened? If you want to say that it was a tragedy, here was the tragedy, that the Roman Church had become so rotten that it was necessary for the reformers to do what they did. It was not the departure of the reformers that was the tragedy. It was the state of the Roman Church that was the tragedy. We are the modern representatives of these men, and of the Puritans, the Covenanters, the early Methodists, and others. Can you not see the opportunity?[104]

The subtext to Lloyd-Jones's speech was the movement of the churches towards Rome: evangelicals were called to reject compromise and defend the Reformation outside the mixed denominations. Clear evidence of this is found in the annual letter to Westminster Chapel members in January 1967. Again, Lloyd-Jones surveyed the wider ecclesiastical scene: the covenanting together of English congregational churches; the sermon by a Roman Catholic at Westminster Abbey; Ramsey's meeting with the Pope; and an ecumenical service at Westminster Cathedral with Anglican and Free Church participation. 'All these and many other publicised meetings and conferences', he argued, 'are but moves in the direction of the formation of a single world church including the Roman Catholics.' He then disclosed that it was 'in the light of all this' that he had made his speech to the National Assembly of Evangelicals.[105]

In the same letter Lloyd-Jones explained that 'truth' could not be maintained in isolation. A division of evangelicalism occurred in 1967, with Lloyd-Jones throwing his influence behind the little-known British Evangelical Council. Separatist and non-participatory evangelicals set up the *Evangelical Times*, with Peter Masters as editor. This was strongly anti-ecumenical in basis and unashamedly anti-Roman on principle.[106] In March it reprimanded G. R. Beasley-Murray, Principal of Spurgeon's College, for sharing a platform with a Roman Catholic.[107] The following month Herbert Carson, a member of the editorial board, claimed it was 'no longer a wild Protestant alarm which speaks of a return to Rome. It is facing sober facts. I cannot see anything in this country but a steady movement back towards Rome.'[108] The newspaper was highly critical of the Keele Congress and the involvement of Archbishop Ramsey,

---

104. Ibid., p. 255.

105. London, Westminster Chapel Archives, D. M. Lloyd-Jones to the congregation of Westminster Chapel, 1 January 1967.

106. 'Why the *Evangelical Times*?', *Evangelical Times* (February 1967), p. 2.

107. 'Indignation', *Evangelical Times* (March 1967), p. 2.

108. Herbert Carson, 'The ECU menace', *Evangelical Times* (April 1967), p. 18.

arguing that Anglican evangelicals were 'drifting from their moorings' and beckoning the rest 'along a path of denominational involvement – with Rome as the inevitable goal'.[109] Some articles were more alarmist: for example, E. G. Dyer appeared to suggest that a united Church of Rome and a unified Europe would fulfil the prophecy of the scarlet woman in the book of Revelation.[110]

The reinvigorated British Evangelical Council served as a separatist Protestant counterblast to the National Evangelical Anglican Congress. While Keele had reassessed traditional evangelical attitudes towards Catholicism, the British Evangelical Council's annual gathering in 1967 celebrated the four hundred and fiftieth anniversary of Luther's presentation of his ninety-five theses. The front page of the *Evangelical Times* report on Lloyd-Jones's address carried the headline 'Here I Stand', implying a parallel between the speaker and his subject.[111] His talk gloried in the political, social, cultural and scientific legacies of the Reformation.[112] Lloyd-Jones compared the situations faced by the Reformers and contemporary evangelicals. Both had to decide on ecclesiological first principles, a choice between 'religious motive and ecclesiasticism'. Like Luther, evangelicals were called to prioritize gospel truth over 'unity' and reject the idea of 'one great world-church'.[113] In another stinging rebuke of Keele Anglicans, he warned listeners to repudiate the kind of inclusive, participatory evangelicalism which sought to find 'formulas' which satisfied Anglo-Catholics, mentioning Church Assembly discussions, in which evangelicals were actively involved, on prayers for the dead and Anglican-Methodist reunion conversations.[114] The ultimate peril faced by both Luther and modern evangelicals was the apostasy of Rome. The ecumenical movement was 'travelling in the direction' of a Catholicism that remained in apostasy. The so-called 'new' Catholic currents were moving towards modernism and liberalism rather than evangelicalism.[115] The uncompromising lecture concluded with an appeal to churches to join the British Evangelical Council. Similar themes were apparent in other speeches. Roland Lamb, later General Secretary of the British Evangelical Council, spoke on the theme 'Revival and Reformation', contending that the two were mutually linked. The Reformation was a revival

---

109. 'What Sort of History Is This?', *Evangelical Times* (May 1967), p. 2.

110. 'Isn't It Obvious?', *Evangelical Times* (March 1967), p. 12.

111. 'Here I Stand', *Evangelical Times* (November 1967), p. 1.

112. Lloyd-Jones, *Luther and His Message*, pp. 4–5.

113. Ibid., p. 23.

114. Ibid., p. 24.

115. Ibid., pp. 26–27.

that 'freed multitudes from bondage to the superstition and ritualism of an apostate papacy and converted them to God and true godliness'.[116] It is surely no coincidence that the British Evangelical Council had a significant Ulster Protestant presence among its leadership. Alongside Lloyd-Jones on the platform at the meeting were Herbert Carson, who later returned to minister in Northern Ireland, W. J. Grier of the Evangelical Presbyterian Church and Norman Porter, director of the Belfast-based Evangelical Protestant Society, among the more belligerently anti-Catholic of the British Protestant organizations.[117]

Those years, 1966–7, were the period in which evangelical unity was broken, and the issue of Rome was critical to the division. Though the context of his public ministry changed from 1968, Lloyd-Jones continued to shape the anti-Roman dimensions of the movement until his death. The divergence of evangelical attitudes widened in the late 1960s when theological dialogue between leading evangelical and Anglo-Catholic theologians produced *Growing into Union: Proposals for Forming a United Church in England* (1970), authored by J. I. Packer, Colin Buchanan, Graham Leonard and Eric Mascall, each of whom had agreed on the whole text.[118] This publication and the response of separatist evangelicals saw the last vestiges of cooperative unity between leading members of the divided evangelical movement disappear.[119] That year Lloyd-Jones wrote to Packer on behalf of the Free Church members of the council of the Puritan Conference, telling him the event would be suspended on the grounds that there could be no cooperation following *Growing into Union*, a book the Welshman argued 'cannot be regarded as being evangelical'.[120] When

116. Roland Lamb, 'Revival and Reformation', in *The Challenge of the Reformation for Today: Addresses given at the 1967 Conference of the British Evangelical Council* (London: Evangelical Press, 1968), p. 46.

117. Writing in 1966, Porter argued that 'Romanism is still public enemy number one and she must be resisted'; Norman Porter, *Rome's Harvest: A Challenge to Faithful Protestants* (Belfast: Evangelical Protestant Society, 1966).

118. J. I. Packer, et al., *Growing into Union: Proposals for Forming a United Church in England* (London: SPCK, 1970). See Andrew Atherstone, 'A Mad Hatter's Tea Party in the Old Mitre Tavern? Ecumenical Reactions to *Growing into Union*', *Ecclesiology*, vol. 6 (January 2010), pp. 39–67.

119. See the response of Peter Masters, in 'Evangelicals in Surprise Scheme with Catholics', *Evangelical Times* (June 1970), p. 1.

120. D. M. Lloyd-Jones to J. I. Packer, 7 July 1970, in Iain H. Murray, *Lloyd-Jones: Messenger of Grace* (Edinburgh: Banner of Truth, 2008), pp. 205–207.

the event was reconstituted as the Westminster Conference in 1971, Packer was conspicuous by his absence.

The Pentecostal and charismatic movements built bridges between Protestant and Catholic Christians, both in global contexts and in Britain; the Holy Spirit, so it was argued, was no respecter of denominational divides. In 1975 the Anglican evangelical Oxford Conference was resumed for a dialogue with Roman Catholics, and many speakers were participants in the charismatic renewal.[121] David Watson, by now an enthusiast for charismatic cooperation, began to argue that the Reformation had had unfortunate consequences for the church.[122] However, Lloyd-Jones warned against the doctrinal ambiguities in the charismatic movement and the assumption that someone baptized in the Spirit was not necessarily required to reconsider his Roman Catholic beliefs.[123] The trajectory of Anglican evangelicalism was confirmed in the official statement of the National Evangelical Anglican Congress at Nottingham in 1977, with Roman Catholics described as 'fellow Christians' and repentance made for previous denials of this fact, implicit support given for the Anglican–Roman Catholic International Commission, and agreement to 'work towards full communion between our two churches'.[124] In contrast, British Evangelical Council leaders remained vocal in their opposition to local examples of cooperation between evangelicals and Catholics on evangelism and moral issues.[125] Herbert Carson continued in his role as the Reformed critic-in-chief of contemporary Catholicism, maintaining that the destination of the ecumenical movement was Rome.[126]

The London Theological Seminary, established in 1977 with Lloyd-Jones's encouragement, was intended to be an institution that would articulate the points of difference between Protestantism and Rome. In his address to mark

---

121. *Agreement in the Faith: Talks between Anglicans and Roman Catholics: The Oxford Conference 1975* (London: Church Book Room Press, 1975).

122. He claimed that while the break-up with Rome might have been inevitable, it was unfortunate, and that a 'divided Christianity is . . . a scandal for which all Christians need deeply to repent'; David Watson, *I Believe in the Church* (London: Hodder and Stoughton, 1978), p. 27.

123. On this, see Murray, *Lloyd-Jones: Fight of Faith*, pp. 661–662.

124. *The Nottingham Statement: The Official Statement of the Second National Evangelical Anglican Congress* (London: Falcon, 1977), paras. M1–M3.

125. Roland Lamb, *The State of the Church* (London: Evangelical Press, 1972), pp. 4–5.

126. Herbert Carson, *United We Fall: A Study of Current Ecumenical Pressures* (Haywards Heath: Carey Publications, 1975), p. 16.

the opening of the institution, Lloyd-Jones explained that the sponsoring committee, which he had chaired, envisioned the college – which shared a site with the Kensit Memorial College, Finchley, where the Protestant Truth Society's Wycliffite preachers were trained – as not merely an evangelical but a definitely Protestant institution. This was partly in response to rumours that pan-denominational, amalgamated colleges were to be formed which would include Roman Catholics. 'We are living in days, unfortunately, when it is no longer sufficient to talk about being evangelical. We must emphasize Protestant as well as evangelical, because we stand not only against ecumenicity but very definitely, and in particular, against Roman Catholicism. We are Protestants and this is to be a Protestant evangelical college.'[127] Thus Lloyd-Jones's Protestant convictions achieved a legacy in the training of future Reformed pastors.

Conclusion

Martyn Lloyd-Jones's anti-Romanism was based on principle and conviction rather than on bigotry or malice. He regarded Roman Catholicism as a 'terrible' system, yet it seems he harboured no personal animosity towards individual Roman Catholics.[128] His anti-Romanism must be understood in the long view of his evangelical tradition. Hostility towards Catholicism was a fundamental aspect of evangelical identity in England and Wales until the 1950s and formed an important basis of their shared church–chapel identity. Lloyd-Jones's phase of influence came during a transformative period in broader Christian relations and a time of uncertainty as far as traditional evangelical attitudes towards Catholicism were concerned, and this chapter has argued that diverging attitudes towards Catholicism caused a fissure in the movement in the 1960s. However, Lloyd-Jones – even considering the anti-Rome dimensions of his 1966 secessionist appeal – cannot be blamed alone for this division. The deep-rootedness of opposition towards Rome in the evangelical psyche, intellectual tradition and historical imagination meant that such a paradigmatic shift in attitudes towards Rome and Anglo-Catholicism within the movement was likely to disturb its larger unity.

The issue of Rome, both in terms of its influence on the ecumenical

---

127. D. M. Lloyd-Jones, 'A Protestant Evangelical College', in Lloyd-Jones, *Knowing the Times*, p. 357.

128. D. M. Lloyd-Jones, 'Address', *Annual Meeting of the Evangelical Library* (1966), p. 30.

movement and 'sacramentalist' developments within the denominations, became the crucial factor in the development of Lloyd-Jones's separatist thinking and policy. How might Lloyd-Jones's Protestant positioning be evaluated in hindsight? By the early 1960s he was convinced that the ecumenical movement was aiming at not just single territorial churches but a global united church. He did not predict the exact configuration of this church, but it was to include Rome within its bounds, and considering Lloyd-Jones's views on the authoritarian nature of Roman Catholicism and its role in biblical apocalyptic literature, he likely assumed that the papacy would have a controlling function. This, however, seems to have been based on a flawed estimation of the ecumenical movement and the World Council of Churches. Ecumenical enthusiasm for the glittering prize of reunion proved to be a chimera. From the end of the 1960s global centripetal trends, of which the World Council of Churches was part, gave way to a rise of 'centrifugality'. There was cooperation in evangelism and social justice, and bilateral discussions on doctrine, including between Canterbury and Rome, but less emphasis on reunion.[129] Importantly, while there was talk of Rome joining the World Council of Churches in 1968, the 'unresolved tensions' within Roman Catholicism regarding its ecclesial status prevented progress on the issue of reunion.[130] The primacies of Paul VI and John Paul II saw strongly conservative doctrinal and ethical tendencies within the Roman Catholic Church.[131] Lloyd-Jones underestimated the intrinsic impediments to reunion within Roman Catholicism itself.

Lloyd-Jones and others misinterpreted the aims of the World Council of Churches. While no doubt the triumphal pronouncements of some of its leadership fed anxieties, the World Council of Churches was not, constitutionally at least, a movement for organizational union of churches. That the World Council of Churches was not intended to be a 'super-church' was clarified in the Toronto Statement (1950).[132] A key document published by the Baptist Union in 1969 explained that 'large numbers of enthusiastic supporters of the World Council of Churches have never been convinced

129. Martin E. Marty, 'The Global Context of Ecumenism, 1968–2000', in John Briggs, et al. (eds.), *A History of the Ecumenical Movement, Volume 3: 1968–2000* (Geneva: World Council of Churches, 2004), pp. 3–22; Michael Kinnamon, 'Assessing the Ecumenical Movement', ibid., pp. 51–81.

130. Lukas Vischer, 'Major Trends in the Life of the Churches', ibid., p. 30.

131. Ibid., pp. 28–29.

132. Dale T. Irwin, *Hearing Many Voices: Dialogue and Diversity in the Ecumenical Movement* (Lanham, MD: University Press of America, 1994), p. 38.

of the desirability of unity in terms of organisational union, or believe in its
feasibility'.[133] Furthermore, Lloyd-Jones seems to have overlooked the levels
of doctrinal conviction within the World Council of Churches.[134] The Faith
and Order discussions, as various Protestant participants gave testimony, were
of a contested rather than conciliatory character.[135] Furthermore, the ecumenical movement was not, as G. R. Beasley-Murray commented sarcastically, a
'popish plot to take over Protestantism'.[136] A statement made by the World
Council of Churches' central committee in 1963 spoke of Protestant and
Catholic developments in guarded terms: 'This does not mean that the great
issues of faith and order upon which we are divided have been settled, or are
on the way to settlement. On the contrary, they remain realities which must
be faced.'[137] In the aftermath of the Second Vatican Council, many prominent Protestants, while welcoming improving relations with Rome, remained
ambivalent about the possibility of Protestant–Catholic rapprochement. For
example, Stephen Neill (General Secretary of the World Council of Churches
from 1948 to 1951) wrote in 1967 of his 'uncertainty' regarding Rome, candid
in the fact that reunion would be a 'long and difficult business'.[138] Various
Protestants made clear that there would be no doctrinal truckling to Rome.[139]
Did separatist evangelicals attack a straw man? It should be stressed again that
some involved in the World Council of Churches gave mixed messages on
the matter of reunion, but it seems that Lloyd-Jones and others misjudged the
threat of Rome. This may have clouded Lloyd-Jones's judgment with regard
to his separatist policy in 1966–7.

The nature of Lloyd-Jones's anti-Romanism was complex. He was an
evangelical leader who was willing to defend the division between Rome and

---

133. *'Baptists and Unity' Reviewed* (London: Baptist Union of Great Britain and Ireland,
      1969), p. 5.
134. A. T. Houghton, 'Truth, Unity and Mission', in Douglas (ed.), *Evangelicals and Unity*,
      p. 42.
135. See Ernest A. Payne, *Baptists and Church Relations* (London: Baptist Union of
      Great Britain and Ireland, 1964), pp. 10–11; G. R. Beasley-Murray, *Reflections on the
      Ecumenical Movement* (London: Baptist Union, 1966), p. 8.
136. Beasley-Murray, *Reflections*, p. 11.
137. Quoted in *'Baptists and Unity' Reviewed*, p. 5.
138. Stephen Neill, *Rome and the Ecumenical Movement* (Grahamstown, South Africa:
      Rhodes University, 1967), p. 22.
139. See James Atkinson, *Rome and Reformation: A Stubborn Problem Re-examined* (London:
      Hodder and Stoughton, 1966), p. 81; Beasley-Murray, *Reflections*, p. 10.

Protestantism 'to the death',[140] but never a member of a Protestant society. He gained a reputation for fighting Rome tooth and nail, even as a modern-day Luther, but said little about Roman Catholicism before ecumenical relations with the Vatican began to improve around 1960. He displayed few, if any, signs of militant or vindictive opposition to Rome. However, during the 1960s anti-Romanism became one of the defining features of Lloyd-Jones's ministry and leadership, and this contributed to the visible division of evangelicalism from 1966. In this sense, Lloyd-Jones deserves a title that may be judged an accolade by some and will be seen as outmoded by others: outside Ulster at least, he was the last truly influential anti-Catholic leader within British evangelicalism.

© John Maiden, 2011

---

140. Lloyd-Jones, 'Can We Learn from History?', p. 219.

10. LLOYD-JONES AND THE ANGLICAN SECESSION CRISIS

Andrew Atherstone

Martyn Lloyd-Jones's address at the National Assembly of Evangelicals at Westminster Central Hall in October 1966 has attained what Carl Trueman calls 'legendary, perhaps even mythical' status.[1] His appeal for a radical rethink of evangelical ecclesiology and his call for secession from doctrinally mixed denominations has become an established part of evangelical folklore, as has the dramatic intervention of John Stott (rector of All Souls, Langham Place). In retrospect, the public clash between Lloyd-Jones and Stott, the two leading figureheads of British evangelicalism in the 1960s, has been seen as a parting of the ways. This chapter seeks to re-examine the event, especially from the viewpoint of evangelicals in the Church of England. It sets the debate within the broader context of the Anglican evangelical secession crisis and the controversy over evangelical identity provoked by the 1967 Keele Congress and the publication of *Growing into Union* in 1970.

---

1. Carl R. Trueman, 'J. I. Packer: An English Nonconformist Perspective', in Timothy George (ed.), *J. I. Packer and the Evangelical Future: The Impact of his Life and Thought* (Grand Rapids, MI: Baker, 2009), p. 120.

The Anglican seceders

The vociferous Anglican evangelical reactions to Lloyd-Jones's unity appeal cannot be understood without first appreciating the internal debates over secession from the Church of England which had been gathering pace for several years. John Brencher's biography of Martyn Lloyd-Jones states that the number of Anglican seceders was only two, a claim apparently based on the selective memories of Alec Motyer, J. I. Packer and R. T. France.[2] In fact, the number was nearly ten times as large. Evangelical ministers left the Church of England for various forms of independency almost every year between 1964 and 1974, sometimes two or three within the space of a few months. It is no exaggeration to speak of an Anglican 'secession crisis'. Several of these ex-Anglicans received personal encouragement from Lloyd-Jones and he sometimes preached at their inductions into their new pastorates.[3]

From an evangelical perspective, there were many reasons to despair at developments within the national church. In 1963 Bishop John Robinson scandalized evangelical opinion with the publication of *Honest to God*, for which he was lauded rather than disciplined by the Anglican hierarchy. In 1964 parliament legalized Mass vestments and stone tables, despite a concerted evangelical campaign of resistance.[4] Two years later prayers for the dead were reintroduced, using an ambiguous liturgical formula, and the Reformation heritage of *The Book of Common Prayer* was undermined by a bevy of new experimental services. The Paul Report threatened to erase all theological distinctives in the Church of England, blending parishes and theological colleges into a bland middle-of-the-road Anglicanism.[5] Anglicans also played a full part in

---

2. John Brencher, *Martyn Lloyd-Jones (1899–1981) and Twentieth-Century Evangelicalism* (Carlisle: Paternoster, 2002), p. 100.

3. Lloyd-Jones preached at the inductions of Herbert Carson to Hamilton Road Baptist Church, Bangor, Northern Ireland in 1967, and of Barry Shucksmith to Binscombe Evangelical Church, Godalming in 1972; see *English Churchman* (20 October 1967), p. 10; 'Ex-Anglican Inducted at Binscombe', *Evangelical Times* (April 1972), p. 3. He also preached at the inauguration of Clay Cross Evangelical Church, Derbyshire in 1974, of which John Rosser was the first pastor; information from John Rosser, April 2009.

4. John Maiden and Peter Webster, 'Parliament, the Church of England and the Last Gasp of Political Protestantism 1961–64', *Parliamentary History* (forthcoming).

5. Leslie Paul, *The Deployment and Payment of the Clergy: A Report* (London: Church Information Office, 1964).

the British Council of Churches which resolved at its 1964 Faith and Order Conference in Nottingham to seek one united territorial church in Britain by Easter Sunday 1980.[6] The Anglican and Methodist denominations seemed certain to merge, with the help of an ambiguous 'service of reconciliation',[7] and meanwhile Archbishop Michael Ramsey was feting the Pope in Rome, the first Archbishop of Canterbury to be received officially at the Vatican since the Reformation. In this fast-changing ecclesiastical context, the possibility of secession was never far below the surface in Anglican evangelical discourse.

The first clergyman to announce his resignation was Eric Lane (vicar of All Saints, Leyton) in July 1964, driven partly by despair at the rapid deterioration of the Church of England. In a letter of explanation to his parishioners he asked:

> If there is room for heresy, tyranny and idolatry (and I mean these words) in the Church of England, there is no room for me . . . How can I remain in communion with men who are doing the opposite of what I am, and even undoing the work I am addressing myself to? How can I promise obedience to Bishops and Archbishops who refuse to prohibit error in the Church, but rather encourage it?[8]

He pointed to Psalm 11:3 as a summary of his verdict on the Church of England: 'If the foundations be destroyed, what can the righteous do?'[9] Although some Anglicans, like Raymond Johnston, praised Lane's courage and integrity, others warned at the dilution of evangelical influence in the national church.[10] For example, Michael Keulemans (a young lay-reader in Bermondsey) cautioned, 'If Evangelicals of Mr Lane's calibre go wandering off into Nonconformist backwaters, with their inevitable lack of outreach and influence, there will be few voices of God left to guide the laity in the parishes, and the cause of the Gospel will take a very severe knock.'[11] Lane thought this attitude was typical of

---

6. *Unity Begins at Home: A Report from the First British Conference on Faith and Order, Nottingham, 1964* (London: SCM, 1964).

7. See further, Andrew Atherstone, 'Evangelical Dissentients and the Defeat of the Anglican-Methodist Unity Scheme', *Epworth Review*, vol. 35 (October 2008), online edition.

8. *Truth and Light: All Saints Church, Leyton Parish Magazine* (July 1964), Waltham Forest Archives.

9. Letter from G. E. Lane, *Church of England Newspaper* (17 July 1964), p. 5.

10. Letter from O. R. Johnston, *Church of England Newspaper* (10 July 1964), p. 5.

11. Letter from Michael Keulemans, *Church of England Newspaper* (10 July 1964), p. 5.

'Anglican snobbishness' and affirmed, 'I would rather be on a backwater sailing on a biblical compass than drifting down the mainstream towards Rome.'[12]

Meanwhile, Herbert Carson was on the brink. He was vicar of St Paul's, Cambridge and had a wide ministry outside the parish as a conference speaker, author and editor of the *Gospel Magazine*. The turning point in his relationship with the Church of England came while listening to Lloyd-Jones deliver the annual lecture at the Evangelical Library in July 1962, commemorating three hundred years since the Great Ejection. Lloyd-Jones rehearsed the history of this mass departure of Puritans from the national church, praising their godliness and fortitude and observing, 'Schism is always a grievous sin, but separation is sometimes a Christian's duty.'[13] He ended with some sharp application aimed at evangelicals in mixed denominations:

> Which comes first: Is it the position in which we find ourselves as a result of the accident of birth and upbringing and tradition? Or is it the Truth of God? . . . Is it right and honest to make mental reservations, or to give my private interpretation, to Articles or Confessions of faith to which I am asked to subscribe? . . . Are we always to abide by majority decisions, and to say when we are out-voted, that though we think the majority is quite wrong, it is still our business to stay inside and bear our witness to the Truth and try to influence the others in that direction? . . . When do we come to the position of 1662? At what point do we feel that we are compromising the Truth and violating conscience? . . . As in 1662, the choice before us today is – conformity or purity?[14]

Carson recalled that Lloyd-Jones's lecture 'bit into my conscience' and was 'the beginning of the end' on his journey to secession. He was forced to face the question: 'Could I remain as an admirer of the Puritans and one who expounded their theology but failed to follow their example?'[15] In September 1964 Carson chaired a private meeting in the crypt of St Paul's, Portman Square, for Anglican evangelical clergy who felt 'sincerely burdened' by the possibility of secession, and he led the way in mid-November by announcing his resignation.[16] The next month others followed suit. George Forester (vicar of St Paul's, Beckenham), whose congregation had been one of the first

12. Letter from G. E. Lane, *Church of England Newspaper* (17 July 1964), p. 5.

13. D. M. Lloyd-Jones, *1662–1962: From Puritanism to Nonconformity* (London: Evangelical Library, 1962), p. 8.

14. Ibid., pp. 46–47.

15. H. M. Carson, *Farewell to Anglicanism* (Worthing: Henry Walter, 1969), p. 20.

16. Letter from H. M. Carson, N. L. Dunning, D. L. Gardner, D. R. Hill and A. W.

in the Church of England to experience charismatic renewal and 'speaking in tongues', departed in a crisis of conscience over baptism.[17] David L. Gardner (vicar of Alne near York) seceded in protest at Anglicanism's anti-Reformation trend.[18]

As these clergymen drifted away from the Church of England one by one, there were calls for united action. H. J. W. Legerton (General Secretary of the Lord's Day Observance Society) asked:

> Must Mr Gardner be allowed to go out alone . . . whilst the rest of us dilly-dally and eventually perhaps back out of the Church one by one with little impact upon the Church or Nation? . . . A secession of clergy and laity in some numbers and as a concerted action, would, I believe, be used of God mightily and could very well go down in history as that of 1662 has done, as a blessing to the Cause of Christ and to the Nation.[19]

Likewise Geoffrey Carr (rector of Aborfield near Reading) argued that if secession was really necessary, then 'the whole body of dissentients should leave together' in a coordinated protest.[20] Another wrote that it was foolish to remain inside such a 'corrupt, idolatrous, amorphous' denomination:

> I believe that God is calling His faithful people out of the Church in the same way that He called Lot from Sodom before the terrible destruction of that city . . . What is clear is this – 'Be not yoked with unbelievers'. I say 'out', and leave them to their Ecumenical wanderings, their Romeward trends, their new morality and the rest.[21]

In view of these sudden departures, the Islington Clerical Conference in January 1965 was on tenterhooks to hear the verdict of the leading Anglican evangelical spokesmen. One participant reported:

> The air was thick . . . with protestations of undying loyalty to 'our beloved Church'. Several times our favoured place in the divine scheme of things was touched

---

Rainsbury, *Church of England Newspaper* (4 September 1964), p. 6; Carson, *Farewell to Anglicanism*, pp. 22–23.

17. '"Tongues" Vicar Resigns', *Church of England Newspaper* (11 December 1964), p. 1.

18. 'Vicar of Alne Resigns', *English Churchman* (18 December 1964), p. 12.

19. Letter from H. J. W. Legerton, *English Churchman* (8 January 1965), p. 9.

20. Letter from Geoffrey Carr, *Church of England Newspaper* (18 December 1964), p. 6.

21. Letter from B. S. J. Clifford, *English Churchman* (3 July 1964), p. 9.

upon, especially to be contrasted with those poor nonconformists. Any amateur psychologist could explain it, one supposes. One hopes that all the pink-faced young curates, secret thoughts of spectacular secession lurking in their breasts, felt suitably chastened for their cogitated disloyalty.[22]

In his presidential address Peter Johnston (vicar of St Mary's, Islington) appealed for those troubled by secession 'not to take too narrow a view of the present situation. The situation is fluid: we do not know what the future holds. The Church of England is its constitution, and not the opinion of individuals, whatever their position.'[23] Elsewhere he called on Anglican evangelicals 'to stand fast and to stand together', observing that in the New Testament secession was not commanded even from churches infiltrated by immorality (like Corinth) or heresy (like Pergamum and Thyatira).[24]

There was a concerted effort to dampen secessionist ardour. Maurice Wood (Principal of Oak Hill Theological College) warned that secession would have 'tragic consequences' for evangelical witness and must be resisted.[25] Roger Beckwith (librarian of Latimer House, Oxford) maintained that the situation for Anglican evangelicals in the 1960s was like that of Archbishop Cranmer under Henry VIII. Although they faced frequent set-backs and might be 'tempted to secede out of sheer impatience', they should remain within the national church however slow the progress of reform.[26] Likewise John Pearce (rector of St Paul's, Homerton in East London) declared:

> Surely it is time that Evangelicals realised that separation is no solution. On the contrary it may be the Devil's way to make one's work of non-effect. Let us stay in the C. of E. and *change* it. This is what the Tractarians and their successors did with conspicuous success. Let us do the same . . . It is surely significant that just at the moment when, in my view, we are on the brink of a real Evangelical renewal

---

22. 'Islington, 1965', *Church of England Newspaper* (15 January 1965), p. 16.

23. 'Islington Conference Presidential Address', *English Churchman* (15 January 1965), p. 12.

24. R. Peter Johnston and John F. Sertin, 'Foreword', in Roger T. Beckwith, *Time for Secession?* (London: Church Book Room Press, 1964), p. 5.

25. Maurice Wood, 'Some Considerations for Evangelicals', in Peter Morgan (ed.), *The Anglican-Methodist Conversations: An Evangelical Approach* (London: SPCK, 1964), p. 13.

26. Beckwith, *Time for Secession?*, p. 9.

in England disunity amongst Evangelicals is increasing. Let us stay in the C. of E., change it and change England.[27]

Others argued that evangelical ministers should not leave the denomination until they were 'driven out'.[28] They should instead adopt the approach of Bishop J. C. Ryle to 'unite, and fight, before flight'.[29] If the shepherds fled their congregations 'at the howling of the wolf', what would become of the sheep in evangelical parishes?[30] When John Stott addressed the annual meeting of the Church Society in June 1965, he too expressed his abhorrence of secession:

> Some Evangelicals of the Free Churches are talking of seceding from their different Churches in order to form a United Evangelical Church. I, for one, ardently hope they will not do so. I believe that history as well as Scripture is against them, and I am quite sure that they would not carry more than a small handful of Anglican Evangelicals with them.[31]

This statement is strikingly similar to Stott's famous intervention at the National Assembly of Evangelicals the following year, to the effect that history and Scripture were against Lloyd-Jones. It reveals that although Stott may not have been planning to oppose the Doctor on that occasion, his words were not entirely off the cuff.

Still the secessions continued. In September 1965, R. C. P. Hunt (vicar of Colston Bassett near Nottingham), who had been in Anglican ministry for twenty-three years, resigned in protest at the legalization of Mass vestments and became a Nonconformist pastor.[32] These concerns were much in evidence at the 'Facing the Future' conference at Swanwick in March 1966, organized by Latimer House and the Eclectic Society, and attended by two hundred younger evangelical clergymen. The key motifs of the papers by George Marchant (vicar of St Nicholas, Durham) and J. I. Packer (warden of

---

27. Letter from John Pearce, *Church of England Newspaper* (18 December 1964), p. 6.
28. Letter from C. W. Finney, *English Churchman* (29 January 1965), p. 9.
29. Letter from Charles H. Vigar, *English Churchman* (19 June 1964), p. 9.
30. Letter from F. H. Flood, *English Churchman* (26 June 1964), p. 9.
31. Quoted in Alister Chapman, 'John R. W. Stott and English Evangelicalism, 1938–84' (unpublished PhD thesis, University of Cambridge, 2004), p. 141. Stott's copy of this address mistakenly has 'structure' instead of 'Scripture'.
32. 'Vestments Protest', *Church of England Newspaper* (20 August 1965), p. 3; *Evangelical Magazine*, no. 37 (November – December 1965), pp. 35–36.

Latimer House) were 'involvement not isolation' and 'cooperation without compromise'.[33] One participant recalled, 'It was clear that every speaker had been told, whatever his subject, to make the point that Evangelicals must not secede from the Church of England.'[34] There were complaints that the question had been 'swept under the carpet'.[35]

Tensions were heightened by the impression that some in Lloyd-Jones's circle were trying to woo evangelicals away from the national church. After departing Cambridge in February 1965, Carson walked straight into a new post as assistant minister at Westminster Chapel.[36] He was assailed in the Anglican press for throwing over his needy parishioners simply to 'satisfy his own ego' by preaching to a large congregation of suburban Christians,[37] and Bishop Williams of Leicester accused him of joining a 'sect'.[38] Carson remained as Lloyd-Jones's adjutant for two and a half years, until he was appointed as pastor of Hamilton Road Baptist Church in Bangor, Northern Ireland in September 1967. Meanwhile, Iain Murray (minister of Grove Chapel, Camberwell and Lloyd-Jones's former assistant) published *The Reformation of the Church* (1965) to aid ecclesiological discussion in ministers' fraternals. He spoke of 'denominational apostasy' and urged evangelicals to come together on a scriptural basis, not just in para-church societies.[39] His chosen texts from Reformation and Puritan authors illustrated that the Church of England had never been thoroughly reformed. The following year Murray's short paperback *The Forgotten Spurgeon* (1966) drew lessons from the Downgrade Controversy of the 1880s with clear contemporary application to mixed denominations in the 1960s. He summarized Spurgeon's position as a conviction that, 'For Christians to be linked in association with ministers who do not preach the gospel of Christ is to incur moral guilt . . . It is error which breaks the unity of

----

33. 'Get Involved' and 'We Must Cooperate, says Dr Packer', *Church of England Newspaper* (11 March 1966), p. 3.

34. Michael Walker to Timothy Dudley-Smith, 8 October 1997, in Timothy Dudley-Smith, *John Stott: A Global Ministry* (Leicester: Inter-Varsity Press, 2001), p. 81.

35. Letter from O. C. Leigh-Williams, *Church of England Newspaper* (25 March 1966), p. 7.

36. London, Westminster Chapel Archives, Church Meeting Minute Book (January 1959 – May 1977), 21 January 1965.

37. Letter from J. C. Meers, *Church of England Newspaper* (22 January 1965), p. 6.

38. 'The Bishop's Letter', *Leicester Diocesan Leaflet*, vol. 39 (January 1965).

39. Iain H. Murray (ed.), *The Reformation of the Church: A Collection of Reformed and Puritan Documents on Church Issues* (London: Banner of Truth, 1965), p. 10.

churches, and to remain in a denominational alignment which condones error is to support schism.'[40] He also reprinted Spurgeon's challenge to Ryle to come out from the corruption of the established church, a telling Victorian parallel to Lloyd-Jones's criticism of John Stott.[41] Murray's critique of contemporary Anglicanism was made explicit when a chapter of the book was republished as *Spurgeon and the Church of England*, with a photograph of Lambeth Palace on the front cover.[42]

The National Assembly of Evangelicals

In that context, Lloyd-Jones's address at the opening rally of the second National Assembly of Evangelicals in October 1966 was bound to be explosive. He had already presented his views to the Evangelical Alliance's unity commission and was asked to reiterate them in this public forum, though Iain Murray observes that the organizers 'clearly underestimated the difference between hearing the Doctor's views in private and the same views *preached* at the Central Hall'.[43] *Crusade* magazine reported that Lloyd-Jones 'unburdened his heart' of a vision for evangelical unity.[44] Another witness described his laying down of the gauntlet as 'a lutheran act', reminiscent of the great Wittenberg Reformer.[45] Packer suggests that he gave his 'opportunist instincts full rein' and 'pulled out all the stops in making this plea', believing he had been briefed to do so.[46]

At the heart of Lloyd-Jones's address was a call for visible unity among evangelicals to match their spiritual unity. He lamented that they were divided among themselves and 'scattered about in the various major denominations . . . weak and ineffective'. Anglicans, Presbyterians and Congregationalists

40. Iain H. Murray, *The Forgotten Spurgeon* (London: Banner of Truth, 1966), pp. 164–165.

41. Ibid., p. 143.

42. Iain H. Murray, *Spurgeon and the Church of England* (London: Banner of Truth, 1966).

43. Iain H. Murray, *D. Martyn Lloyd-Jones: The Fight of Faith 1939–1981* (Edinburgh: Banner of Truth, 1990), p. 526.

44. 'Evangelicals Confer', *Crusade*, vol. 12 (December 1966), p. 33.

45. David R. Smith, 'Authority and Power: British Evangelical Council Conference', *Life of Faith* (9 November 1967), p. 1092.

46. J. I. Packer, 'A Kind of Puritan', in Christopher Catherwood (ed.), *Martyn Lloyd-Jones: Chosen by God* (Crowborough: Highland Books, 1986), p. 45.

often claimed that their denominations were constitutionally evangelical, on the basis of the Thirty-Nine Articles, the Westminster Confession or the Savoy Declaration, but in practice they were little better than 'a paper church', because most members now rejected those doctrinal foundations. Nevertheless, Lloyd-Jones proclaimed, the ecumenical turmoil of the 1960s presented 'a most remarkable opportunity' to rethink evangelical ecclesiology along New Testament lines.[47] He appealed:

> You and I are evangelicals. We are agreed about these essentials of the faith, and yet we are divided from one another. We meet like this, I know, in an occasional conference, but we spend most of our time apart from one another, and joined to and united with people who deny and are opposed to these essential matters of salvation. We spend our time with them. We have our visible unity with them. Now, I say, that is sinful . . . I am arguing that for us to be divided – we who are agreed about everything that really matters – for *us* to be divided from one another in the main tenor of our lives and for the bulk of our time, is nothing but to be guilty of the sin of schism. And we really must face this most urgently. Let me therefore make an appeal to you evangelical people here present this evening. What reasons have we for not coming together?[48]

He described those in mixed denominations as in a 'contradictory position', forced often to dissociate themselves from the decisions of their own church. Lloyd-Jones asked:

> What cogent reason have we for staying as we are when we have this new, and as I regard it, heaven-sent opportunity for doing something new? What are our reasons for rejecting and refusing the need for change? Let me put it positively. Do we not feel the call to come together, not occasionally, but *always*? It is a grief to me that I spend so little of my time with some of my brethren. I want to spend the whole of my time with them. I am a believer in ecumenicity, evangelical ecumenicity.[49]

He proclaimed that evangelicals had no right to ask God's blessing on churches which denied the essentials of the faith, but if they stood together

---

47. D. M. Lloyd-Jones, 'Evangelical Unity: An Appeal', in D. M. Lloyd-Jones, *Knowing the Times: Addresses Delivered on Various Occasions 1942–1977* (Edinburgh: Banner of Truth, 1989), pp. 250–251.

48. Ibid., p. 254.

49. Ibid., p. 255.

they could expect the Holy Spirit to fall 'in mighty revival and re-awakening'. The preacher concluded:

> My dear friends, we are living in tremendous times. We are living in one of the great turning points of history. I have said already and I say it again, there has been nothing like this since the sixteenth century. It is a day of glorious opportunity . . . And who knows but that the ecumenical movement may be something for which, in years to come, we shall thank God because it has made us face our problems on the church level instead of on the level of movements, and really brought us together as a fellowship, or an association, of evangelical churches. May God speed the day.[50]

The excitement of the evening was not yet over. When Stott rose to announce the closing hymn, he first interjected, 'I hope no one will make a precipitate decision after this moving address. We are here to debate this subject and I believe that history is against Dr Jones in that others have tried to do this very thing. I believe the Scripture is against him in that the remnant was within the Church and not outside it.'[51] Iain Murray described the intervention as nothing less than 'sensational'.[52] Although Stott later apologized to Lloyd-Jones for misusing the chair, the situation was now polarized and the rift could no longer be ignored.[53]

Press coverage of the address only muddied the waters. For example, David Winter (Editorial Secretary of the Evangelical Alliance) summarized it as 'an eloquent plea to Evangelicals to leave their denominations and join a United Evangelical Church'.[54] This summary has often been repeated, but bears two significant mistakes – an error of fact (that Lloyd-Jones wanted to establish a united evangelical church) and an error of emphasis (that his focus was on secession). Winter admitted he was guilty of 'careless journalism',[55] but this sloppy style of reporting has been in circulation ever since, despite the attempts by Lloyd-Jones's friends to correct the misunderstandings.

---

50. Ibid., pp. 256–257.

51. 'Evangelicals – Leave Your Denominations', *The Christian* (21 October 1966), p. 9.

52. Murray, *Lloyd-Jones: Fight of Faith*, p. 526.

53. John Stott, 'An Appreciation', in Catherwood (ed.), *Lloyd-Jones: Chosen by God*, p. 207.

54. David Winter, 'The Church and the World', *Life of Faith* (27 October 1966), p. 1127.

55. Letter from David Winter, *Life of Faith* (16 November 1967), p. 1127.

Leith Samuel (minister of Above Bar Church, Southampton) quickly pointed out that Lloyd-Jones 'did *not* suggest the launching of yet another denomination', but a fellowship of local evangelical congregations.[56] Packer queried this distinction, portraying it as 'in effect, the founding of a new, loose-knit, professedly undenominational denomination'.[57] No blueprint was provided. Packer later complained at Lloyd-Jones's 'lack of realism' and his 'campaign of words without plans'. He wondered whether Lloyd-Jones 'was not more interested in making the gesture of calling for separation', with its prophetic criticism of Anglican evangelicals, 'than he was in seeing the gesture succeed'.[58] Alister McGrath follows Packer in this apophatic interpretation: 'We shall never know what Lloyd-Jones intended his address to achieve.'[59] Most provocatively, Trueman accuses the Doctor of ecclesiological naïveté and compares him unfavourably with the vigorous confessional stance of the Presbyterian seceder J. Gresham Machen in the 1930s. In Trueman's view, although the call to 'come out' was legitimate, Lloyd-Jones's vague alternative to Anglicanism was 'a nonecclesiastical, non-confessional disaster'.[60] Nevertheless, one of those who heard the original address, Gordon Murray (an Anglican clergyman and editor of the *English Churchman* from 1965), insisted that the lack of a blueprint was no reason nonchalantly to reject the appeal: 'It is too easy simply to dismiss his vision as unrealistic and impossible of realisation, but we cannot afford to mis-read the signs of the times and so lose the opportunity which God in His mercy has given us.'[61]

The question of emphasis has also been the subject of much debate. *The Christian* magazine summed up Lloyd-Jones's address with the banner headline, 'Evangelicals – Leave Your Denominations',[62] which has been rightly criticized by Iain Murray as a distraction from the crux of the message.[63] Yet

---

56. Letter from Leith Samuel, *Life of Faith* (3 November 1966), p. 1150.

57. J. I. Packer, 'David Martyn Lloyd-Jones', in *Honouring the People of God: The Collected Shorter Writings of J. I. Packer*, vol. 4 (Carlisle: Paternoster, 1999) p. 79.

58. Packer, 'A Kind of Puritan', pp. 49–50.

59. Alister McGrath, *To Know and Serve God: A Biography of James I. Packer* (London: Hodder and Stoughton, 1997), p. 125.

60. Trueman, 'J. I. Packer: An English Nonconformist Perspective', p. 122.

61. 'Secession? Not Yet', *English Churchman* (4 November 1966), p. 6.

62. 'Evangelicals – Leave Your Denominations', *The Christian* (21 October 1966), p. 1.

63. Iain H. Murray, *Evangelicalism Divided: A Record of Crucial Change in the Years 1950 to 2000* (Edinburgh: Banner of Truth, 2000), pp. 48, 283.

Murray goes too far in playing down this emphasis almost to vanishing point. Although Lloyd-Jones never used the words 'secede' or 'secession', it was the inevitable implication of his unity plan. He stated, for example, that 'to leave a church which has become apostate is not schism. That is one's Christian duty and nothing else.' He also acknowledged that responding to his call would mean 'great and grievous difficulties', including financial hardship for some families – a clear reference to the economic sacrifice required when ministers resigned their posts in mixed denominations.[64] Nonetheless, this was secondary, not the main point. Gordon Murray observed, 'The emphasis on secession has tended to give a negative and destructive air to something which came over to us as essentially positive and constructive.'[65] Lloyd-Jones was offering a grander vision. Writing his annual letter to the congregation at Westminster Chapel at New Year 1967, he gave his own authoritative summary of his recent address in Westminster Central Hall:

> An appeal . . . to all truly Evangelical people in all the denominations to come together and to form local independent Evangelical churches which should be in a loose fellowship together in order that the world might hear and see a living witness to the truth of the Gospel . . . We are living in momentous times, undoubtedly one of the great turning-points of history. The opportunity for Evangelical witness is unique, the possibilities are tremendous. Are we equal to the times?[66]

Gordon Murray concurred:

> He was not putting forward some negative scheme into which we are reluctantly forced, but rather was he pointing us to the glorious opportunity of taking positive action in the ecumenical sphere, of coming together as Christians, not because other people's errors demand it, but because we want to and we realise we ought to if we are to be true to our Evangelical convictions.[67]

David Winter welcomed the fact that the public 'pyrotechnics' between Lloyd-Jones and Stott brought into the open key differences which 'could not be papered over – primarily, of course, the really fundamental one of "gathered

---

64. Lloyd-Jones, 'Evangelical Unity', pp. 253, 256.
65. 'Striving Together', *English Churchman* (13 January 1967), p. 6.
66. London, Westminster Chapel Archives, D. M. Lloyd-Jones to the congregation of Westminster Chapel, 1 January 1967.
67. 'Misunderstandings', *English Churchman* (28 October 1966), p. 6.

church" versus "national church"'.[68] This was made clear on the second day of
the Assembly by a paper from one of Stott's former curates, Julian Charley (tutor
at the London College of Divinity from 1964). He argued that the Bible's ecclesiology was not gathered but territorial, and affirmed the statement of the 1961
New Delhi Assembly of the World Council of Churches that the local church
should include 'all in each place who are baptized into Jesus Christ and confess
Him as Lord and Saviour'. This view had previously been promulgated in the
controversial Anglican evangelical symposium *All in Each Place* (1965), edited
by Packer, which Iain Murray correctly identifies as a turning point in Packer's
ecclesiology from exclusivism to ecumenism.[69] The implication of a territorial
church was to make secession illogical. Like Stott, Charley emphasized that in
Scripture the 'godly remnant' was always within the visible church, not separate
from it. Caleb and Joshua did not secede from disobedient Israel, nor did the
Rechabites in Jeremiah's day. The few godly people in Sardis (Rev. 3:4) were not
instructed by the risen Jesus to leave their degenerate church. Charley continued:

> Why, the very idea of doing so betrays a failure to understand the nature of God's
> Church. You do not leave it because it is not perfect, or even when it is invaded by
> heresy and immorality . . . Secession is unthinkable *till it has altogether ceased to be the
> Church at all* . . . Secession is the result of a confused theology of the Church.

He argued that Richard Baxter and John Wesley had departed the Church of
England reluctantly, in effect expelled, but, 'The spirit of secession is quite different. This is a denial of the principle of a territorial Church. This is what has
led to the fragmentation of Protestantism with its damaging effects upon the
Church's witness.'[70] Charley was confident that very few Anglican evangelicals
would heed Lloyd-Jones's call. On the contrary, he ended his address in deliberately provocative style by urging Free Church evangelicals to return to the
national church, an invitation which was 'greeted with growls and mutterings
of "Never!" from several quarters'.[71]

Charley followed up his Assembly address with an article in the *Church
of England Newspaper* reiterating that the call to secede and form a united
evangelical church

---

68. Winter, 'The Church and the World', p. 1127.

69. Murray, *Evangelicalism Divided*, pp. 90–91.

70. Julian Charley, 'Church Order', in *Unity in Diversity: Evangelicals, the Church and the
     World* (London: Evangelical Alliance, 1967), pp. 22–23.

71. Winter, 'The Church and the World', p. 1127.

betrays a singular lack of historical proportion and absence of honest realism . . .
The point is that the visible community of the Church is basically *inclusive* and not
exclusive. It takes men at their word. It does not arrogate to itself the prerogative
of God to discuss the thoughts and intentions of the heart. Such is the Anglican
understanding of the Scriptural teaching on the Church – a territorial Church,
accepting what men profess, over against a gathered Church with its individualist and
perfectionist tendencies.[72]

He claimed that the only biblical example of voluntary secession was that of
the northern kingdom of Israel, not a happy precedent. Charley concluded:

The task of the godly is to reform from *within*, not to opt out of their responsibilities
. . . It is not a lack of moral courage that makes Anglican Evangelicals stay where
they are, nor do they remain with a bad conscience. Their compelling motive is a
deep-seated theological conviction concerning the nature of the national, territorial
Church. The determination to influence the Anglican Communion from within
requires courage and patience, and it is the Biblical pattern. The fruits of such a policy
are beginning to be apparent to those with eyes to see them.[73]

Charley set the tone for other Anglicans to follow, among whom Lloyd-
Jones's appeal met with widespread criticism. One columnist in the *Church of
England Newspaper* described the proposal as 'nothing short of harebrained'.[74]
Another pugnacious correspondent wrote:

Secede? How on earth was the Reformation won? By writing cry-baby letters, as some
do, to Evangelical newspapers threatening to run out if this or that isn't prevented?
The enemies of Christ would only laugh! And are we to leave the nominally Christian,
who attend only from habit, entirely to the mercy of the wolves? The reformation was
achieved through Christians putting up a fight – often at the cost of their lives . . . As
one of the determined stay-putters, I can only assert, 'Let 'em all come!' Certainly we
could all retire, if we wished, to a large live Church, but cosy hothouse atmospheres
never breed saints. Saints are tough. Let those who are fight-shy get out. The Church
will be richer without them![75]

---

72. Julian Charley, 'Come Out From Among Them?', *Church of England Newspaper* (11
   November 1966), p. 7.
73. Ibid.
74. 'Dr Lloyd-Jones's Plea', *Church of England Newspaper* (28 October 1966), p. 5.
75. Letter from Edward Atkinson, *Church of England Newspaper* (28 October 1966), p. 6.

Keith Weston (rector of St Ebbe's, Oxford) was more eirenic, writing in his parish magazine of his 'deep love and respect' for Lloyd-Jones, 'a God-used and doughty warrior for the Gospel'. Yet he rejected Lloyd-Jones's appeal as 'mis-founded and most unwise':

> I am innocent enough to believe that the Church of England needs its committed Evangelicals now probably as never before. It would be a terrible tragedy if we were all to leave now. As one respected Evangelical in this City once said, 'Only rats leave a sinking ship!' Has not God put us here (with all the resulting problems) precisely because He has a job for us here? – to uphold the Truth of the Gospel for which our Church of England Martyrs died. I will not leave the Church of England, my spiritual home which I love, until I am forced out – and I pray God that will never be.[76]

Likewise, Tony Turner (vicar of Christ Church, Macclesfield) argued that it was much more profitable for evangelicals to work from inside the church than 'retreating into their own little corner'.[77]

There were, however, a minority of Anglicans who responded positively to Lloyd-Jones's call. The correspondence columns of the *English Churchman* were filled with so many letters that one clergyman feared 'secessionitis' was sweeping through evangelical ranks.[78] Most vocal was Legerton, writing under the pseudonym '*Prokletos*' ('Call Forth'), who proclaimed that the time had finally arrived for evangelicals to separate from the de-reformed Church of England:

> No longer can we use the by now old excuse: 'If such and such a thing happens, if the Articles are tampered with, if we are prevented from preaching the Gospel, *then* we secede.' Far too many stages have been passed, apostacy [sic] has been reached, the secession of every faithful Evangelical clergyman, layman and woman is due. Let it be done quickly – not hastily – before further 'involvement' submerges us all in sinful association with a most dreadful blasphemy, ripe for judgement.[79]

Gordon Murray was more cautious, but still sympathetic. He described the opening rally of the National Assembly of Evangelicals as a bittersweet moment:

---

76. *News from St Ebbe's Oxford* (November 1966), St Ebbe's Church Archives, Oxford.

77. Letter from Tony Turner, *Church of England Newspaper* (25 November 1966), p. 6.

78. Letter from Henry Brierly, *English Churchman* (13 January 1967), p. 7.

79. 'Secession? Yes!', *English Churchman* (4 November 1966), p. 4.

The sweetness was to listen to the type of Biblical leadership which Evangelicals need in these confusing days, to hear a man not afraid to face the reality of present-day church issues and to show the way forward to those whose one desire is to remain loyal to Scripture . . . Here, we felt, was the God-given answer to our predicament. Here was the way in which we could surely demonstrate the power of the Gospel and its reality in our own lives. Despite the difficulties, despite the cost, here was a Scripturally founded call which we could answer with enthusiasm. The bitterness came with the realisation that the call had fallen on deaf ears where most Evangelical Anglicans were concerned. Denominationalism appeared to mean more than real unity. What the Doctor said at Westminster has still to be refuted.[80]

Distressed by the inaction of his Anglican evangelical colleagues, Murray himself seceded from the Church of England four years later and went on to be pastor of Bethesda Baptist Church in Felixstowe.[81]

The vast new housing development at Thamesmead in south London presented an ideal opportunity to put into action precisely the sort of local evangelical unity which Lloyd-Jones was advocating. The Greater London Council initially planned to provide one ecumenical centre for use by all the Christian denominations, under the leadership of Nicolas Stacey (Anglican rector of Woolwich), a maverick pioneer of South Bank Religion. The local Strict Baptists saw their chapel demolished under a compulsory purchase order and it was rumoured that no space would be set aside for a new evangelical church. In March 1967 more than a thousand people gathered to protest at the intransigence of the council and Lloyd-Jones addressed the crowd, urging evangelicals to 'come together and stand together' by establishing a united evangelical congregation.[82] Nevertheless, the *Church of England Newspaper* continued to assail him. It instructed Anglican evangelicals to throw their energies into the ecumenical centre and dismissed Lloyd-Jones's idea for a united evangelical congregation at Thamesmead as 'divisive, obscurantist and impracticable' and even 'repugnant'.[83]

---

80. 'What Next?', *English Churchman* (30 December 1966), p. 4.

81. As Principal of Kensit Memorial College in Finchley from 1968, Gordon Murray did not hold a bishop's licence, so he marked his secession by resigning in January 1971 as editor of the *English Churchman* (an Anglican newspaper) and relinquishing his place on the Church of England Evangelical Council.

82. George Stirrup, 'Over a Thousand at Woolwich Protest Meeting', *Life of Faith* (9 March 1967), p. 220. For the response of the Greater London Council, see John McNicol, 'Comment from Official Standpoint', *Life of Faith* (9 March 1967), p. 220.

83. 'Woolwich Protest', *Church of England Newspaper* (10 March 1967), p. 1.

Meanwhile, Lloyd-Jones's Westminster Fellowship was reconstituted along anti-ecumenical lines. Its new Statement of Principles affirmed that there was 'no hope whatsoever' of winning doctrinally mixed denominations to an evangelical position, so secession was 'inevitable'.[84] Faced by predictable hostility and misunderstanding in the Anglican press,[85] the conveners explained the redrawn boundaries of the Fellowship: 'The new meeting . . . is *not* only for ministers outside the main denominations. Nor does attendance imply the intention to secede at any given date. The only Evangelical ministers not invited are those determined to stay in their denominations whatever happens.'[86] On this basis, most Anglican clergymen were excluded, but one of the few who chose to remain within the Westminster Fellowship was Moshe Radcliff, a Messianic Jew. After the 1938 *Anschluss* his family had fled from Vienna, Austria to Sydney, Australia, where he came to faith in Christ aged twenty and joined an Anglican evangelical congregation.[87] After training at Moore College, Radcliff was ordained in England in 1960, but had now reached the conclusion that the mixed denominations were 'corrupt beyond reformation', so he seceded in October 1967.[88]

The Keele Congress

The widening gulf between Anglican evangelicals and Lloyd-Jones's circle was further entrenched by the National Evangelical Anglican Congress (NEAC) held at Keele University in April 1967.[89] It had been planned for two years and was by no means intended as a response to the National Assembly of Evangelicals, though arguments about ecumenical dialogue and church purity

---

84. Murray, *Lloyd-Jones: Fight of Faith*, pp. 536–537.

85. 'Puritan Enthusiasts Disband – Or Do They?', *Church of England Newspaper* (9 December 1966), p. 5.

86. Letter from T. H. Bendor-Samuel, David Mingard and Leith Samuel, *Church of England Newspaper* (23 December 1966), p. 4.

87. Moshe Radcliff, 'My Testimony', *Presbyterian Standard*, no. 11 (July – September 1998), pp. 22–29.

88. Letters from H. R. M. Radcliff, *Church of England Newspaper* (16 December 1966), p. 14; *English Churchman* (10 November 1967), p. 7.

89. See further Andrew Atherstone, 'The Keele Congress of 1967: A Paradigm Shift in Anglican Evangelical Attitudes', *Journal of Anglican Studies*, vol. 9 (November 2011), pp. 175–197.

were inevitably to the fore.[90] The *Evangelical Times* believed that the Congress represented 'the parting of the ways'.[91] The 10,000-word Keele Statement set the agenda for Anglican evangelicalism for a generation and included a significant paragraph dismissing secession out of hand:

> We are deeply committed to the present and future of the Church of England. We believe that God has led us to this commitment, and we dare to hope and pray that through it God will bring His Word to bear with new power upon this Church. We do not believe secession to be a live issue in our present situation. Only if the Church of England ceased to exhibit the marks of a true Church (see Article XIX of the 39 Articles) could such a step be contemplated.[92]

For the sake of factual accuracy, one young ordinand at the congress attempted in debate to replace 'secession is not a live issue' with 'secession is not a wise option' – because it patently *was* a live issue – but he was overruled.[93] When it came to relationships with Free Church evangelicals, the statement was terse to the point of coldness, but it was effusive about the opportunities for ecumenical dialogue, even with Roman Catholicism and Eastern Orthodoxy. It explicitly affirmed the World Council of Churches' definition of Christianity and declared:

> Polemics at long range have at times in the past led us into negative and impoverishing 'anti'-attitudes (anti-sacramental, anti-intellectual, etc.), from which we now desire to shake free. We recognize that in dialogue we may hope to learn truths held by others to which we have hitherto been blind, as well as to impart to others truths held by us and overlooked by them.[94]

One observer at Keele, Sir John Lawrence, summed up the paradigm shift as 'Pietism is out, ecumenism is in'.[95] The *Church of England Newspaper* celebrated, 'We Anglicans should be the last people to stand aloof from other Christians.

---

90. For the initial announcement of the Congress, see 'Keele, 1967', *Church of England Newspaper* (30 July 1965), p. 5.

91. 'What Sort of History Is This?', *Evangelical Times* (May 1967), p. 3.

92. Philip Crowe (ed.), *Keele '67: The National Evangelical Anglican Congress Statement* (London: Falcon Books, 1967), para. 87.

93. Letter from David W. A. Gregg, *Church of England Newspaper* (5 May 1967), p. 6.

94. Crowe (ed.), *Keele '67*, para. 84.

95. 'From the Editors', *Frontier*, vol. 10 (Summer 1967), p. 82.

By definition we are committed to a comprehensive Church.'[96] As proof of this new ecumenical attitude, Archbishop Ramsey was invited to give the opening address, though as Iain Murray ruefully observes, on this occasion there was no attempt by John Stott to dissociate himself from the speaker's remarks.[97] The *Evangelical Times* chastised the NEAC organizers for welcoming onto the platform 'an avowed enemy of fundamentalism, and a man who is a committed advocate of harmony with Rome'.[98]

Morgan Derham (General Secretary of the Evangelical Alliance) warned that Keele's advocacy of ecumenism and its broadening definition of 'Christianity' were seen by independent evangelicals as 'something near to treachery'.[99] A minority of Anglicans felt the same way. Brian Basted (rector of Leverton in Lincolnshire) asked, 'Is Evangelical Christianity the truth, or not? . . . What significant aspect of the "old, old story" are the ritualists and rationalists going to teach us? Is the gospel we preach defective in any substantial matter?' He insisted that if evangelicals already believed the true gospel, then their ecumenical conversations should not be called 'dialogue' but 'witness'.[100] Disillusioned with Anglican ministry and longing for a 'return to New Testament Christianity', Basted resigned his parish in October 1967 and returned to secular employment.[101] Other clergymen raised similar concerns about Keele's new ecumenical policy. For example, A. G. Pouncy (vicar of Woking) asked:

> Does this mean that we are now to accept the basic assumptions of Tract XC as true? Does it mean in practice that we must, for example, share a common evangelistic

---

96. 'Keele and Unity', *Church of England Newspaper* (30 June 1967), p. 1.

97. Murray, *Lloyd-Jones: Fight of Faith*, p. 554.

98. 'What Sort of History Is This?', *Evangelical Times* (May 1967), p. 2. In November 1974 Lloyd-Jones said of a speaker at a recent evangelical congress that he was not sure the man was 'really a Christian in the New Testament sense of the term'. Brencher identifies this as Ramsey at the 1967 Keele Congress, but it was more likely a reference to the 1974 Lausanne Congress. See D. M. Lloyd-Jones, 'Fight for Survival', *Dedication*, vol. 7 (January – February 1975), p. 12; Brencher, *Lloyd-Jones*, p. 168.

99. A. Morgan Derham, 'Evangelical Fellowship Keele-Halled', *Church of England Newspaper* (28 April 1967), p. 12.

100. Letter from B. R. Basted, *Evangelical Magazine*, no. 49 (December 1967), p. 42.

101. 'Rector's Decision to Quit Shocks Parish', *Lincolnshire Standard* (20 October 1967), p. 1.

platform with our neighbours if they teach baptismal regeneration? . . . I am finding modern Evangelical gymnastics most confusing.

Pouncy wondered whether it would be more honest to tell the Free Church evangelicals that their Anglican brethren could no longer be relied on 'for a definite stand upon absolute truth'.[102]

Likewise, John Rosser (Director of Irish Evangelistic Treks) asked in the *Church of England Newspaper*:

> Many of us find the Church of England a doubtful enough institution to belong to at the best of times but to help us we were taught that authentic Biblical Anglicanism was Evangelical Anglicanism. Now it seems that we can learn from others. From whom? Anglo-Catholics with their views of the Mass; middle churchmen with their prayers for the dead; liberals with their rejection of orthodoxy? Could someone tell me please?

Rosser insisted that wise evangelicals had always sought to learn 'not from an apostate section of a spiritually weak Church but from God Himself, through His revealed Word'.[103] Such sentiment provoked a fierce response. Four young students from Cranmer Hall, Durham (including John Gladwin, later Bishop of Chelmsford) attacked Rosser as 'foolish' and 'offensive', guilty of 'spiritual arrogance' for refusing 'to hear the Word of God wherever it is truly ministered'.[104] Another chastised his 'narrow-minded intolerance': 'How superior can we get? . . . Small wonder if critics ask Mr Rosser what on earth he is doing in the Church of England. Is not a greater loyalty expected – a broader love demanded?'[105] Paul Hunt (curate of St Paul's, Widnes) asserted, 'To be willing to learn from others is not a sign of weakness but of strength.' He saw the Keele Congress as the beginning of a recognition among Anglican evangelicals that they possessed 'only a part of the truth'.[106] Meanwhile, Michael Botting (vicar of St Matthew's, Fulham) resisted the call to 'pull out and just shout from the touch-line' when so many 'tremendous opportunities' existed for evangelical witness in the national church. Arguing *ad hominem*, he

---

102. Letter from A. G. Pouncy, *Church of England Newspaper* (4 August 1967), p. 4.
103. Letter from John Rosser, *Church of England Newspaper* (12 May 1967), p. 6.
104. Letter from William A. Stewart, Geoffrey Crees, Jennifer H. Crees and John Gladwin, *Church of England Newspaper* (19 May 1967), p. 6.
105. Letter from Bryan Morris, *Church of England Newspaper* (19 May 1967), p. 6.
106. Letter from Paul Hunt, *Church of England Newspaper* (19 May 1967), p. 6.

wondered 'whether those, like Mr Rosser, who are so afraid of compromise did not compromise themselves when they entered the Church of England ministry'.[107]

Nevertheless, Rosser continued to lament 'the doctrinal anaemia that infects our Church today' and warned, 'When Evangelicals get involved in the wider life of the Church of England so often their testimony is in danger of being blunted and their doctrinal position compromised.'[108] In an article on 'The Case for Separation' in September 1967, he asked:

> What are the future prospects for Evangelicals who are unhappy with the present trend of involvement? . . . The believer must leave the erring church. To decide when the crisis point has been reached is no easy matter, but for many of us it can surely not be far away.[109]

Rosser himself reached that crisis point six years later, at Easter 1973, when he resigned from ministry in the Church of England.[110] He was one of more than a dozen Anglican evangelical clergymen who seceded in the decade after the Keele Congress, several citing the theological trends promoted by Keele as the reason for their departure. For example, Peter Beale (vicar of St Stephen's, Cambridge), who resigned in November 1973, called Keele 'the beginning of the end' so far as his Anglican ministry was concerned.[111]

Reflecting on the Keele Congress, J. D. Douglas (editor of *The Christian*) observed that Anglican evangelicals 'seemed to be following Erasmus almost to a man: the call was for reform from within'.[112] In November 1967 Lloyd-Jones offered an alternative vision of Lutheran rather than Erasmian reform in his address to the closing rally of the British Evangelical Council's annual conference, marking 450 years since Luther nailed up his ninety-five theses in Wittenberg. He argued that the vital question for Luther was not 'How can we

---

107. Letter from Michael Botting, *Church of England Newspaper* (22 September 1967), p. 6.

108. Letter from John Rosser, *Church of England Newspaper* (26 May 1967), p. 6.

109. John Rosser, 'The Case for Separation', *Church of England Newspaper* (8 September 1967), p. 7.

110. 'Years of Agonizing Over', *Evangelical Times* (January 1973), p. 13.

111. Peter Beale, 'Why I Resigned the C of E', *Evangelical Times* (January 1974), p. 5. See also Peter James, 'Six Years of Change', *Evangelical Times* (February 1970), pp. 13–14; 'Ex-Anglican Inducted at Binscombe', *Evangelical Times* (April 1972), p. 3.

112. 'Hereafter Known as Keele 1967', *The Christian* (14 April 1967), p. 2.

have one territorial church?', but 'What is a Christian?' Lloyd-Jones mocked the idea that evangelicals could reform any established church from the inside as 'midsummer madness' and his call for secession became much more explicit, quoting Revelation 18:4, 'Come out of her, my people!'[113] Most controversial was his talk of 'guilt by association', though Iain Murray plays it down as no more than 'a passing reference'.[114] The Doctor maintained that it was impossible for evangelicals to be 'yoked together' either with the Church of Rome or with those who rejected the fundamentals of the faith, 'who seem to deny the very being of God and who convey the impression that the Lord Jesus Christ was a homosexual'. This was a thinly veiled allusion to the recent proclamations of two Anglican dignitaries, Bishop John Robinson and Canon Hugh Montefiore. In the published version of the address, Lloyd-Jones insisted, 'There is no agreement between evangelicals and such teaching, for it is a question of light and darkness! The very desire to hold such groups together in one territorial church is surely a virtual denial of the Christian faith. It also raises the question of guilt by association.'[115] His actual words spoken at the rally were rather sharper: 'It is guilt by association.' *The Christian* rejected the idea as 'an appallingly bad argument' and 'a thoroughly irresponsible charge'. It accused separatists like Lloyd-Jones of 'a divisive and disruptive spirit'.[116]

Once again, as with his address at the National Assembly of Evangelicals, there was confusion over what precisely Lloyd-Jones intended. Derham took him to mean that Anglican evangelicals were 'now denying the Faith'.[117] Packer was still under the same impression when addressing the Reform Conference in 1995, where he recalled that Lloyd-Jones was 'a great man, but great men can be enmeshed in bad arguments. Bad argument number one was that if we stay in the Church of England we're guilty by association of all the theological errors that any Anglican may be propagating anywhere at all.'[118] However, those closer to Lloyd-Jones, like Leith Samuel and Elizabeth Braund (editor of the *Evangelical Magazine*), understood it as a future reference – not that any evangelicals were guilty by association *now*, but that they would be if

---

113. D. M. Lloyd-Jones, *Luther and His Message for Today* (London: Evangelical Press, 1968), pp. 23–25, 29.

114. Murray, *Evangelicalism Divided*, p. 95.

115. Lloyd-Jones, *Luther and His Message for Today*, p. 26.

116. 'Separated – or Guilty?', *The Christian* (24 November 1967), p. 2.

117. Letter from A. Morgan Derham, *Evangelical Magazine*, no. 54 (October 1968), p. 37.

118. Quoted in Roger Steer, *Church on Fire: The Story of Anglican Evangelicals* (London: Hodder and Stoughton, 1998), p. 288.

they remained within the one vast ecumenical church when it eventually came into existence.[119]

Rocking the boat

The divisions within the evangelical movement were rapidly worsening. The *English Churchman* was alarmed at the 'widening breach' over the issue of separation and warned that correspondence in the evangelical press had turned into 'a slanging match'.[120] Likewise, as Winter looked back in November 1967 on the turmoil which had followed Lloyd-Jones's appeal at the National Assembly of Evangelicals, he protested:

> It seems a pity that, more than a year after the event, the old ashes of controversy are still being raked over. The view of the present EA Council and secretariat is that there is a most important role for the British Evangelical Council to play in the current evangelical situation, and we have no desire to perpetuate the notion of rival 'camps'. I hope that those who write in our evangelical periodicals will now turn their fire on the real enemies, rather than on their friends – and this goes for extremists at *both* ends of the evangelical spectrum.[121]

Efforts at rapprochement were few and far between. A dialogue planned for the spring of 1968 between rival delegations from the British Evangelical Council (BEC) and the Church of England Evangelical Council (CEEC) had to be shelved because of Lloyd-Jones's sudden illness and hospital treatment.[122] It did not take place until a year later, after the Doctor had sufficiently recovered and retired from Westminster Chapel. He met with Stott and Packer, alongside eight others, in March 1969 at All Souls, Langham Place. On the agenda was the concept of a national church, the principles of separation, the limits of comprehensiveness and the meaning of guilt by association. It was hoped the discussion would foster greater respect between the two sides and

---

119. Leith Samuel, 'Fellowship: The Perils of Inclusivism and of Exclusivism', *Evangelical Magazine*, no. 53 (August 1968), p. 22; comment by Elizabeth Braund, *Evangelical Magazine*, no. 54 (October 1968), p. 38.

120. 'United We Stand . . .', *English Churchman* (8 December 1967), p. 6.

121. Letter from David Winter, *Life of Faith* (16 November 1967), p. 1127.

122. London, Latimer Trust Archives [LTA], CEEC Minutes, 2 November 1967, 1 February and 7 March 1968, 2 January 1969.

'the renunciation of mutual sniping'.[123] Stott declared it 'a very useful essay in personal relations' and believed the BEC representatives had been 'reassured of our genuine evangelicalism'.[124] Nevertheless, there was scant evidence to support Stott's sanguine assessment. The mutual sniping continued unabated and the divisions deepened.

Were both sides equally to blame? Christopher Catherwood asserts that it was his grandfather who 'drove a wedge' among British evangelicals by his Westminster Central Hall address and so 'created the very schism that he was so anxious to avoid'.[125] Similarly, Packer maintains that Lloyd-Jones's emphasis on separatism, and in particular the pressure he put on Anglicans, 'led to individual estrangements' and 'disrupted evangelical community'.[126] This has become a common refrain among recent commentators. McGrath claims that it was Lloyd-Jones who 'shattered' evangelicalism's 'peaceful coexistence'.[127] Rob Warner asserts that Lloyd-Jones led his followers 'into the separatist wilderness of an extreme and exclusive Reformed isolationism'.[128] Trueman concurs, 'The spirit of 1966 left English nonconformity in particular in a highly weakened, fissiparous, intellectually impoverished, and increasingly fragmented condition.'[129]

The leaders of the Evangelical Alliance in the late 1960s also placed the responsibility squarely on the Lloyd-Jones camp. It was tragic, Derham lamented, for evangelicals to divide 'on the basis of secondary associations and spend our energies in mutual recriminations'. He believed the separatists were chiefly to blame for the rift, because they determined the bounds of fellowship by attitudes to ecumenism, not by common concern for the gospel.[130] Derham appealed:

---

123. LTA, CEEC Minutes, 6 March 1969. The dialogue comprised Lloyd-Jones, T. H. Bendor-Samuel, John Caiger, Roland Lamb, David Mingard and Leith Samuel (BEC), with Stott, Packer, Michael Benson, Timothy Hoare and Peter Johnston (CEEC).

124. LTA, CEEC Minutes, 17 April 1969.

125. Christopher Catherwood, *Martyn Lloyd-Jones: A Family Portrait* (Eastbourne: Kingsway, 1995), pp. 106, 141–142.

126. Packer, 'A Kind of Puritan', p. 46.

127. McGrath, *To Know and Serve God*, p. 123.

128. Rob Warner, *Reinventing English Evangelicalism, 1966–2001: A Theological and Sociological Study* (Milton Keynes: Paternoster Press, 2007), p. 215.

129. Trueman, 'J. I. Packer: An English Nonconformist Perspective', p. 125.

130. A. Morgan Derham, 'We Need One Another: A Comment in Current Trends', *Life of Faith* (15 June 1967), p. 556.

There are more ways than one of strengthening the cause of the Gospel: some will do it by separating from denominational structures; some will do it by working within them . . . No one should claim a monopoly here; and what worries many of us is the implied claim of the extreme separatists that they are the *only* people who are doing anything effective in the cause of defending and upholding the Gospel today: this is nonsense, at best.[131]

Similarly, in a polemical article entitled '"Separation" is Separating Evangelicals', Gilbert Kirby (Principal of London Bible College and Derham's predecessor as General Secretary of the Evangelical Alliance) asked, 'Is the hallmark of orthodoxy no longer to be one's adherence to a Biblical faith, or does it also involve repudiation of all who have links, however tenuous, with the ecumenical movement?' He mourned the 'bitterness and rancour' which now existed between evangelicals and looked back wistfully to the days when they enjoyed 'real fellowship in the Gospel'.[132] Lloyd-Jones told the annual BEC conference at Westminster Chapel in October 1969, in some bemusement, that he was being accused of dividing evangelicalism simply because he had appealed for evangelical unity. Indeed, one British evangelist had reportedly called him 'the devil's instrument'.[133] To this Douglas drolly replied, 'While the charge of diabolical involvement is unsubstantiated, it is irrefutable that the veteran Welsh preacher's views on separation *have* split evangelical ranks.'[134]

Herbert Carson believed there was a McCarthy-esque witch hunt against the separatists, who were being blamed for the ills of the church. In the *Gospel Magazine* he complained:

So the ugly intolerance encountered in the ecumenical movement is now coming into evangelical circles. The new policy apparently is, tolerate anything – Rome, the Bishop of Woolwich, Lord Soper, the lot – all except those separatists who seek to call a halt to the present drift towards final apostasy.[135]

---

131. Letter from A. Morgan Derham, *Life of Faith* (6 July 1967), p. 630.
132. Gilbert W. Kirby, '"Separation" is Separating Evangelicals', *Life of Faith* (25 January 1968), pp. 73, 96.
133. D. M. Lloyd-Jones, 'Sound an Alarm', in Hywel Rees Jones (ed.), *Unity in Truth: Addresses Given by Dr D. Martyn Lloyd-Jones at Meetings Held under the Auspices of the British Evangelical Council* (Darlington: Evangelical Press, 1991), p. 66.
134. J. D. Douglas, 'Who is Dividing British Evangelicals?', *Christianity Today*, vol. 14 (19 December 1969), p. 35.
135. H. M. Carson, 'Editorial', *Gospel Magazine* (March 1968), p. 98.

Elsewhere Carson suggested that it was in fact ecumenism which was hindering true unity, 'for it has driven a wedge between those who are spiritually and theologically one. It has put back the clock, in that the hopes of closer unity between true evangelicals are receding fast.'[136] Likewise, Omri Jenkins (General Secretary of the European Missionary Fellowship and a member of Westminster Chapel) maintained that one of the lessons of history was 'the failure of evangelicalism within the main-line denominations'. He continued:

> Believing what we do, we must rebut any suggestion that we are dividing the
> evangelical camp: on the contrary, our profound desire is to ensure that a camp which
> is truly evangelical will continue. Neither are we 'rocking the boat': rather there is
> a case for saying that it is compromise with non-evangelical religion which is really
> rocking the boat.[137]

Peter James (rector of Little Leighs, near Chelsmford) agreed. He blamed the rift on the evangelical ecumenists, whom he likened to John Bunyan's Mr Facing-Both-Ways.[138] Unwilling to run in two directions at once, James joined the growing ranks of Anglican seceders in February 1970 and became pastor of Bristol Road Baptist Church, Weston-super-Mare.[139]

The boat was rocked to the point of capsizing by the publication in May 1970 of *Growing into Union*, an ecumenical tract co-authored by J. I. Packer and Colin Buchanan (tutor at the London College of Divinity) in harness with two traditional Anglo-Catholics, Eric Mascall and Bishop Graham Leonard.[140] Their primary aim was to sink the Anglican-Methodist Unity Scheme, but they claimed to have reached doctrinal agreement in the process. Though lauded among ecumenists, the response from Free Church evangelicals was devastating. In Packer's words, they were accused 'of being either knaves or fools, according to whether we trimmed our sails consciously or unconsciously!'[141]

---

136. Letter from Herbert Carson, *Life of Faith* (2 November 1967), p. 1072.

137. Letter from T. Omri Jenkins, *Life of Faith* (6 July 1967), p. 630.

138. Letter from Peter H. James, *Church of England Newspaper* (15 December 1967), p. 14.

139. Peter James, 'Why I Am Leaving the Church of England Ministry', *English Churchman* (13 February 1970), p. 5; James, 'Six Years of Change', pp. 13–14.

140. See further, Andrew Atherstone, 'A Mad Hatter's Tea Party in the Old Mitre Tavern? Ecumenical Reactions to *Growing into Union*', *Ecclesiology*, vol. 6 (January 2010), pp. 39–67.

141. J. I. Packer, '"Growing into Union": A Reply to Some Criticisms', *Evangelical Magazine*, no. 66 (April 1971), p. 6.

In *The Banner of Truth*, Paul Helm (philosophy lecturer at Liverpool University) warned that the book was 'muffled and muted' on the central doctrine of justification by faith alone.[142] *Peace and Truth* (the journal of the Sovereign Grace Union, edited by Anglican seceder Eric Lane) claimed that the evangelical authors had 'cut loose from their moorings' and that their book was an insult to Protestantism.[143] According to the *Evangelical Magazine of Wales*, *Growing into Union* had 'done well-nigh irretrievable damage within that which used to be called Evangelicalism, but which cannot without serious re-definition of terms be so called any longer'. Packer and Buchanan had 'dragged their anchors' and departed from 'historic, biblical Evangelicalism'.[144] The magazine spoke of its 'tremendous sense of sadness':

> We had thought (and still hope) that these Evangelicals and the party they lead were our brethren. Some of us would readily testify to the immense help the earlier labours of such men have been to us in our own spiritual and ministerial lives. And it is hard when old friends resolutely and deliberately turn their backs on you by taking a course which they know full well you cannot *in all conscience* follow. One feels betrayed and abandoned.[145]

Likewise, Michael Buss (pastor of Tollington Park Baptist Church, Islington) feared that *Growing into Union* would break unity, not create it, 'that at a time when evangelicals are just beginning to draw closer this book may drive a wedge into their own ranks'.[146] In the British Evangelical Council's newsletter, Buss asserted that 'if these men are truly evangelical we are tempted to say the word has lost all its meaning'. He believed the book would end hopes of unity with evangelicals in the Church of England, serving only 'to entrench these brethren deeper in a position of unscriptural ecumenicity'.[147]

A minority of Anglican evangelicals shared these concerns. One shocked reader prophesied that the book would hasten evangelical divisions, and asked in bewilderment:

---

142. Paul Helm, 'Reunion – Another Scheme', *The Banner of Truth*, no. 81 (June 1970), p. 16.

143. 'The National Church', *Peace and Truth*, vol. 49 (October 1970), p. 78.

144. 'Unity: At a Price', *Evangelical Magazine of Wales*, vol. 9 (August – September 1970), p. 3.

145. Ibid., p. 5.

146. Michael Buss, 'Count Me Out!', *English Churchman* (12 June 1970), p. 3.

147. *BEC Newsletter*, no. 5 (July 1970).

What has happened? Can it really be true that evangelical Anglicans prefer the church fellowship of anglo-catholics to that of the evangelical Free Churchmen with whom they have worked for so long in organisations such as Scripture Union, Inter-Varsity Fellowship and many others? I am still pinching myself to make sure I am awake![148]

Beckwith called the book 'deplorably weak',[149] while David Samuel (rector of the Ravendale group of parishes near Grimsby) lambasted Packer and Buchanan for having 'bartered away' the precious Reformation heritage of the Church of England.[150] Stott acknowledged that the increasing sense of 'alienation' between Anglican and independent evangelicals since the Keele Congress had been exacerbated by *Growing into Union*. He told the Church of England Evangelical Council:

> We must be clear that what many Free Church (and some Anglican) evangelicals are questioning is neither just our post-Keele *policy* of involvement in the wider church; nor our *approach* to Catholic Christians which is now more eirenical than polemical; nor our seeming *preoccupation* with secondary ecclesiastical and denominational questions, which we have previously neglected in favour of primary issues; but our *theology* itself. It is suspected that these other phenomena are signs and symptoms of an underlying doctrinal compromise. We must not blind ourselves to the fact that our theological orthodoxy and integrity as evangelicals are being called in question.

Stott affirmed the desire of the CEEC 'not only to maintain the faith of the gospel, but if possible to heal the breach which has arisen between us'.[151] Alan Stibbs (former Vice-Principal of Oak Hill Theological College), a close friend of both Lloyd-Jones and Packer, was said to be 'very upset' by the whole affair.[152] Stibbs, together with Oliver Barclay (General Secretary of

---

148. Letter from John Ratcliffe, *Church of England Newspaper* (3 July 1970), p. 9.
149. Roger Beckwith, '"Growing Into Union" – Why the Split?', *English Churchman* (28 August 1970), p. 3.
150. David Samuel, 'Evangelical Catholicity', *Evangelical Magazine*, no. 72 (November 1972), p. 14. Samuel's critiques from the *Evangelical Magazine* were published together as David Samuel, *The New Evangelicalism in the Church of England* (Barnet: Protestant Reformation Society, 1973).
151. John Stott, 'Growing into Union: The Internal Evangelical Debate' (memorandum, 17 December 1970), LTA, CEEC Minutes.
152. Martyn Lloyd-Jones to Philip E. Hughes, 22 December 1970, in Iain H. Murray (ed.), *D. Martyn Lloyd-Jones: Letters 1919–1981* (Edinburgh: Banner of Truth, 1994),

Inter-Varsity Fellowship) and Nigel Sylvester (General Secretary of Scripture Union), warned:

> Most evangelical Anglican clergy are now so committed to the Church of England that they are unwilling to fix certain points beyond which they cannot go. They give the impression that they would stay in it however far its official formularies and structures were altered . . . Denominational loyalties, which are without clear biblical warrant, seem to take precedence over questions of truth.[153]

They pleaded for the strictures from independent evangelicals to be taken seriously and for Anglican evangelicals to make it clear that 'loyalty to biblical doctrine and full fellowship with all who share that faith must be more important than denominational loyalty in a mixed Church'.[154] Stibbs and Barclay were invited to address the CEEC, but they did not win a sympathetic hearing and Packer said their attitude reflected 'a siege mentality'.[155] The visitors asked how bad the Anglican situation would need to be before the bulk of evangelical clergy considered secession, but Buchanan retorted that this was 'comparable to asking a man under what circumstances he would contemplate divorce, when he is, in fact, happily married'.[156] Barclay recalled that Stibbs left the meeting 'almost in tears', distressed at the drift of the Anglican evangelical movement.[157]

Another casualty of this controversy was the Puritan Studies Conference, in which Lloyd-Jones and Packer had collaborated since 1950. It was planned as usual for December 1970 and speakers were booked, but Lloyd-Jones took

---

p. 182. On Stibbs see further, Andrew Atherstone, 'Alan Stibbs (1901–1971): Missionary, Preacher, Theologian', in Andrew Atherstone (ed.), *Such a Great Salvation: The Collected Essays of Alan Stibbs* (Fearn: Mentor, 2008), pp. 9–24.

153. Oliver Barclay, Alan Stibbs and Nigel Sylvester, 'Evangelical Witness and Unity' (memorandum, December 1970), LTA, CEEC Minutes.

154. Oliver Barclay, Alan Stibbs and Nigel Sylvester, 'Some Notes on J. R. W. S.'s Memo' (memorandum, March 1971), LTA, CEEC Minutes.

155. LTA, CEEC Minutes, 4 March 1971.

156. Colin Buchanan, 'Evangelical Witness and Unity' (memorandum, 1 December 1970), LTA, CEEC Minutes. For Packer's use of the same analogy, see J. I. Packer, *The Evangelical Anglican Identity Problem: An Analysis* (Oxford: Latimer House, 1978), p. 30.

157. Oliver Barclay, *Evangelicalism in Britain 1935–1995: A Personal Sketch* (Leicester: Inter-Varsity Press, 1997), p. 85.

the unilateral decision (with his Free Church colleagues John Caiger and David Fountain) to cancel the event and break with their Anglican co-organizers, Packer and Geoffrey Cox. They reached this conclusion during the monthly meeting of the Westminster Fellowship in July 1970, when *Growing into Union* was the topic of discussion and the unanimous verdict was that 'the doctrinal position outlined in that book cannot be regarded as being evangelical, still less puritan'. Lloyd-Jones hoped the separation would not damage their personal friendship, but lamented Packer's embroilment in ecumenical politics as 'nothing less than a great tragedy and a real loss to the Church'.[158] Packer acquiesced in the death of the Puritan Conference, appealing in vain for the Doctor to reconsider his decision.[159] Lloyd-Jones resolutely told Philip E. Hughes, 'It would be a farce in the light of that book to continue, for I felt that such concessions had been made to the Catholics that our friend was no more either Evangelical or Puritan.'[160] Packer also lost his place on the editorial board of the *Evangelical Magazine* as a result of the furore. Nevertheless, he continued to insist that *Growing into Union* was 'as faithful and responsible an evangelical effort after the renewing of the church as is (for instance) any public activity of the British Evangelical Council'. Although the treatise had aroused 'painful suspicions' and the attacks from fellow evangelicals had been 'pretty unpleasant',[161] he still hoped

for a genuine meeting of minds some day between those who espouse different hopes for the future of evangelicalism in English church life – for such a meeting is, in my judgment, long overdue, and has not yet begun. During the past five years, alternative strategies have been formulated, and there has been a lot of propaganda, browbeating, appealing to prejudice, and playing to galleries – but fear, mistrust, and various fixations have effectively kept the parties involved from the sympathy that leads to mutual understanding. The great advance of the past decade has been a dawning realization among Evangelicals generally that tomorrow's strategy must centre, not on inter-denominational 'movements', but on the church itself. Is this gain to be lost in a new outbreak of sectarian bitterness? 'If you bite and devour one

---

158. Martyn Lloyd-Jones to J. I. Packer, 7 July 1970, in Iain H. Murray, *Lloyd-Jones: Messenger of Grace* (Edinburgh: Banner of Truth, 2008), pp. 205–206.

159. J. I. Packer to Martyn Lloyd-Jones, 9 July and 18 October 1970, Aberystwyth, National Library of Wales, Lloyd-Jones Papers 13/8 and 13/10.

160. Martyn Lloyd-Jones to Philip E. Hughes, 22 December 1970, in Murray (ed.), *Lloyd-Jones: Letters 1919–1981*, p. 182.

161. Packer, 'Growing into Union', pp. 3, 10.

another take heed that you are not consumed by one another' (Galatians 5:15). Will this warning be heeded?[162]

Who was to blame for shattering British evangelicalism's peaceful coexistence? Responsibility for this painful rupture is still unevenly apportioned by the two sides. Was it Lloyd-Jones in his 1966 appeal at the National Assembly of Evangelicals, or was it Stott in his uncharacteristic intervention? Was it Lloyd-Jones in his 1967 address on Martin Luther at the BEC conference, or was it Anglican evangelicals like Stott, Packer and Buchanan at the Keele Congress and in *Growing into Union*? As this chapter has demonstrated, the division was not a clean break along denominational lines. There were a number within the Church of England, albeit a beleaguered minority among the evangelical clergy, whose sympathies lay more with Lloyd-Jones and the Westminster Fellowship than with John Stott and the Church of England Evangelical Council. They resisted the post-Keele trends and some felt conscience-bound to resign their ministry in the national church. The testimony of these Anglican evangelical seceders of the 1960s and early 1970s has been largely airbrushed from the history books, resulting in a skewed and simplistic picture of exclusivist independents versus ecumenical Anglicans. In fact, as has been shown, Lloyd-Jones's heartfelt appeals for evangelical unity in the face of ecumenical confusion had a stronger groundswell of support within the Church of England than has previously been recognized. Lloyd-Jones's teaching had a significant impact on intra-Anglican debates concerning evangelical identity. It was for this very reason that his public pronouncements generated such passionate reactions among Anglican evangelicals, as they continue to do more than a generation later.

© Andrew Atherstone, 2011

---

162. Ibid., p. 10.

11. LLOYD-JONES AND THE PROTESTANT PAST[1]

John Coffey

Collective identities are powerfully shaped by stories. The histories we tell shape who we are. This is true of nations, political parties, ethnic groups and religious movements. Modern evangelicals are no exception. Evangelical identity has been consolidated through tales of the Reformation or the 'Great Revivals'. Evangelicals name institutions after famous figures in the Protestant past: Wycliffe Hall, Tyndale House, Latimer Trust, Rutherford House, the Wesley Owen bookstores. Student ministries like the Cambridge Inter-Collegiate Christian Union (CICCU) and the Universities and Colleges Christian Fellowship (UCCF) build a cohesive identity through telling a particular kind of story (what some might call an origin myth) about the split between the Inter-Varsity Fellowship and the Student Christian Movement.[2]

---

1. I am most grateful to Christopher Catherwood, Paul Helm and Tony Lane for critical comments on this chapter. They bear no responsibility for its shortcomings or its interpretation of Lloyd-Jones.
2. See, e.g., Oliver Barclay and Robert Horn, *From Cambridge to the World: 125 Years of Student Witness* (Leicester: Inter-Varsity Press, 2002). For an alternative view, see Justin Thacker and Susanna Clark, 'A Historical and Theological Exploration of the 1910 Disaffiliation of the Cambridge Inter-Collegiate Christian Union from the Student Christian Movement', www.eauk.org (accessed 28 July 2011).

Because the past is so important for shaping identity, it is also frequently a battleground. For some, evangelicalism originates in the eighteenth-century awakenings, for others in the sixteenth-century Reformation, and each of these versions of history carries implications for the present.[3] Baptists have argued over whether their tradition originates among the Puritans or the Anabaptists, whether it is at root Calvinist or Arminian.[4] Doctrinal debates about penal substitutionary atonement or open theism inevitably have an important historical component, as Christians assess the status of these positions within their theological tradition. And for many years now there has been a struggle to gain control of the narrative history of British evangelicalism since 1945, especially the events of 1966.[5]

Martyn Lloyd-Jones recognized that history matters. Whoever controls the past shapes the present. And because he understood this, he devoted a great deal of energy and time to an historical project. This project had two major components: retrieval and interpretation. Lloyd-Jones and his wider circle sought to retrieve the forgotten resources of the Protestant past in order to renew modern evangelicalism. And in his public lectures, he crafted an account of church history that was designed to govern the way evangelicals thought about themselves.

In many respects, this project was very successful, but it was not without its ironies. The return to history – and especially Puritanism – was designed to create a cohesive new Reformed Protestantism. But Puritanism itself (despite the 'ism') was never monolithic, and as conservative evangelical Calvinists dived into the Puritan past looking for treasures on the seabed, they came up with very different versions of Puritanism. Immersion in the Puritan past actually contributed to two painful splits within the Lloyd-Jones circle, leading to the ostracizing of J. I. Packer and R. T. Kendall. In what follows, I will begin by examining the project of retrieval in which Lloyd-Jones was such a central figure, before turning to his interpretation of church history.

---

3. See Michael Haykin and Kenneth Stewart (eds.), *The Emergence of Evangelicalism: Exploring Evangelical Continuities* (Nottingham: Apollos, 2008).

4. See David W. Bebbington, *Baptists through the Centuries: A History of a Global People* (Waco: Baylor University Press, 2010), chs. 2–4.

5. Compare Oliver Barclay, *Evangelicalism in Britain, 1935–1995: A Personal Sketch* (Leicester: Inter-Varsity Press, 1997); Iain H. Murray, *Evangelicalism Divided: A Record of Crucial Change in the Years 1950 to 2000* (Edinburgh: Banner of Truth, 2000); Alister McGrath, *To Know and Serve God: A Biography of James I. Packer* (London: Hodder and Stoughton, 1997); Rob Warner, *Reinventing English Evangelicalism, 1966–2001: A Theological and Sociological Study* (Milton Keynes: Paternoster, 2007).

Retrieval

During the mid-nineteenth century, British publishers churned out numerous multi-volume sets of collected works by Puritan divines: Richard Sibbes (7 vols.), Richard Baxter (23 vols.), John Owen (24 vols.), John Bunyan (4 vols.), Thomas Manton (22 vols.), Thomas Goodwin (12 vols.), Thomas Brooks (6 vols.), John Howe (6 vols.), John Flavel (6 vols.), Edward Reynolds (6 vols.), William Bridge (5 vols.), George Swinnock (4 vols.) and David Clarkson (3 vols.). The greatest Nonconformist preacher of the nineteenth century, the Baptist C. H. Spurgeon, had a vast personal library filled with such Puritan and Reformed works.[6]

Yet these writings fell out of fashion with alarming rapidity in the last four decades of the nineteenth century. Liberal Protestants were avowedly modernist and tended to the view that older Puritan and Reformed literature was not fit for purpose in the post-Enlightenment world of higher criticism and scientific progress. At the same time, 'conservative' Protestants were also swept up in enthusiasm for new movements, including dispensationalism, Keswick and holiness teaching. The Puritans were thoroughly eclipsed. By the early twentieth century, British Protestants had forgotten (or mislaid) the riches of their theological heritage. They were suffering from a severe case of collective amnesia.

As a young minister among the Welsh Calvinistic Methodists, Lloyd-Jones himself was almost entirely ignorant of the Puritans. He surely knew of Bunyan and Cromwell, but he had no inkling of the massive theological output of the Puritan divines. The land of early modern Reformed divinity was *terra incognita*. Lloyd-Jones first stumbled upon the Puritans at second hand. In 1925, he saw a publisher's advertisement for a new abridgement of the *Autobiography of Richard Baxter* and this led him to read a biography of the Puritan by F. J. Powicke. He was so taken by Baxter that he delivered an address on 'Puritanism' to the literary and debating society at his home church at Charing Cross in March 1926. At this stage, his seventeenth-century reading was limited to *The Pilgrim's Progress* and lives of Baxter and George Fox, and he showed no awareness that this trio made very odd bedfellows. His focus was on 'the spirit which animated the old Puritans', and like many Nonconformists in the late nineteenth and early twentieth centuries he found that same spirit

6. For a brief survey of the reception of Puritan texts, see John Coffey, 'Puritan Legacies', in John Coffey and Paul C. H. Lim (eds.), *The Cambridge Companion to Puritanism* (Cambridge: Cambridge University Press, 2008), pp. 333–340.

in disparate seventeenth-century figures who disagreed profoundly on matters of doctrine and ecclesiology.[7]

Over the next decade, Lloyd-Jones's understanding of Reformed theology firmed up considerably. He purchased other Puritan works from London's second-hand bookstores and received second-hand editions of the works of Baxter and Owen as wedding presents. In 1929, while waiting for a train, he visited a bookshop in Cardiff and fell upon a two-volume edition of the works of Jonathan Edwards which he purchased for five shillings. 'I devoured these volumes', he later recalled, 'and literally just read and read them.' On a visit to Canada in 1932, he poured over the writings of the Princeton theologian B. B. Warfield, who had rearticulated early modern Reformed orthodoxy for a modern audience.[8] In January 1939, Lloyd-Jones was introduced to Geoffrey Williams's Beddington Free Grace Library, a collection of around 20,000 Puritan and Reformed books, and recorded that he felt like the Queen of Sheba visiting King Solomon.[9] He also borrowed piles of old books from Sion College Library and Dr Williams's Library.[10] He was busy excavating the Reformed theological tradition.

By the later 1940s, the young J. I. Packer was embarked on the same exercise, after he came across the works of John Owen, uncut and unread, in the library of the Oxford Inter-Collegiate Christian Union.[11] For both men, this encounter with the Puritans struck them with the force of a revelation. In particular, they were impressed by the theological and spiritual depth of these old books. Like the children who stepped through the wardrobe into Narnia, they were introduced to a new world.[12] Armed with these old texts, they set about transforming the evangelical subculture. Lloyd-Jones's son-in-law, Sir Fred Catherwood, explained his impact:

7. Iain H. Murray, *D. Martyn Lloyd-Jones: The First Forty Years 1899–1939* (Edinburgh: Banner of Truth, 1982), pp. 97–100.

8. Ibid., pp. 155–156, 253–254, 285, 287–296.

9. See Iain H. Murray, *D. Martyn Lloyd-Jones: The Fight of Faith 1939–1981* (Edinburgh: Banner of Truth, 1990), pp. 81–83.

10. Personal communication from Christopher Catherwood, January 2011.

11. McGrath, *To Know and Serve God*, pp. 24–26.

12. The analogy would appeal more to Packer, a firm admirer of Lewis, than to Lloyd-Jones, who remained a Lewis-sceptic. See John Brencher, *Martyn Lloyd-Jones (1899–1981) and Twentieth-Century Evangelicalism* (Carlisle: Paternoster, 2002), p. 168.

He showed our generation clearly that the strand of pietistic evangelicalism, the muscular Christianity of the varsity and public school camps, the devotional piety of the Brethren, the emotional dedication at the great conventions, the revivalism of the big interdenominational missions, was not enough . . . He led the evangelical wing of the church back into the centre of theological argument, not by conceding a thing, but by going back to its foundation in the Reformation. He, almost alone to begin with, wove in again the strong central strand of reformed theology to evangelical teaching – a strand which had almost snapped off in the late nineteenth century, when Spurgeon seemed to lose to the rising tide of liberalism in the 'downgrade' controversy.[13]

While Lloyd-Jones was most famous for promoting the Reformed cause through his preaching, his role in disseminating Puritan books was almost equally important in the longer run. At times he did this through personal conversation, as when he recommended Puritan writings to the Christian Brethren founder of the International Fellowship of Evangelical Students (IFES), C. Stacey Woods.[14] But it was the institutional structures that had the greatest impact. Lloyd-Jones was a key figure in the establishment of the Evangelical Library (the former Beddington Free Grace Library) which opened in 1945 and lent out tens of thousands of Reformed books to pastors in Britain and overseas. In 1950, at the prompting of Packer, he co-founded the Puritan Conference, which met annually over two days just before Christmas every year to discuss papers on Protestant church history and theology, with a particular focus on the seventeenth century. Most importantly, Lloyd-Jones helped to establish the Banner of Truth Trust in 1957, which became the most important publisher and promoter of Puritan and Reformed literature in the English-speaking world.

In publicizing and republishing Puritan and Reformed works, Lloyd-Jones and his circle were engaged in what Bruce Hindmarsh has called a project of 'retrieval and renewal'. Hindmarsh draws an analogy with the *resourcement* movement among Roman Catholic theologians associated with the *nouvelle théologie* from the 1920s onwards. Figures like Jean Daniélou, Yves Congar, Louis Bouyer and Hans Urs von Balthasar wanted to renew Catholic theology by going behind neo-Thomism and recovering the riches of patristic thought.

---

13. Frederick and Elizabeth Catherwood, *Martyn Lloyd-Jones: The Man and his Books* (Bridgend: Evangelical Library of Wales, 1982), p. 5.

14. A. Donald Macleod, *C. Stacey Woods and the Evangelical Rediscovery of the University* (Downers Grove, IL: InterVarsity Press, 2007), pp. 102–103.

British evangelicals too were attempting to go behind recent Protestant teaching in order to retrieve older aspects of their tradition.[15]

The comparison, however, involves a mismatch, one that goes beyond the obvious contrast between high church Roman Catholics and low church evangelical Protestants. The evangelicals were starting from a far lower base than their Catholic counterparts and suffered from a daunting erudition gap. Von Balthasar was later described by his friend Joseph Ratzinger as 'the most learned man in Europe', and he epitomized the sophisticated, multilingual ethos of Catholicism's intellectual elite. With the high culture of the West at their fingertips, these figures created perhaps the most intellectually powerful theological movement of the twentieth century.[16] Conservative evangelicals, by contrast, inhabited a much more cramped mental world, one with narrower horizons, and it is little wonder that they focused on the somewhat parochial project of recovering their own Protestant tradition, while leaving the Fathers of the Church to the Catholics. This was ironic, because the Reformers themselves had been among the leading scholars and intellectuals of their day, trained in the latest humanist techniques and immersed in patristic and medieval texts. While a few evangelical scholars were engaged with patristic sources from the 1950s, it would take several decades before evangelicals began to rediscover the Fathers and re-engage with 'the Great Tradition' of the church alongside Roman Catholic and Eastern Orthodox theologians.[17]

But if the project of retrieving patristic thought would have to wait, mid-twentieth-century British evangelicals did give themselves wholeheartedly to a revival of conservative biblical scholarship. This, too, can be seen as a project of retrieval and renewal, though its relationship to the Reformed project was ambivalent. It seems clear that there were divergent views on this among the conservatives who supported the founding of Tyndale House. For Lloyd-Jones, the 'technical scholar' was to be subordinate to the 'biblical theologian' when it came to formulating doctrine. The task of evangelical biblical scholarship was essentially apologetic – to defend established conservative positions on the historicity of biblical narrative, the authorship of biblical books and the doctrine of the biblical authors as it was understood by 'systematic biblical theology'. F. F.

---

15. Bruce Hindmarsh, 'Retrieval and Renewal', in Timothy George (ed.), *J. I. Packer and the Evangelical Future* (Grand Rapids, MI: Baker, 2009), ch. 7.

16. See the recent study by Hans Boersma, *Nouvelle Théologie and Sacramental Ontology: A Return to Mystery* (Oxford: Oxford University Press, 2009).

17. See Kenneth Stewart, 'Evangelicalism and Patristic Christianity: 1517 to the Present', *Evangelical Quarterly*, vol. 80 (October 2008), pp. 307–321.

Bruce, on the other hand, while being personally sympathetic to Reformed teaching, had a somewhat more open-ended view of what evangelical biblical scholarship might achieve. As a member of the Brethren, he had a less deferential view of church tradition and allowed greater room for a spirit of enquiry. Biblical scholarship could, in principle, challenge and correct received wisdom, for God always had 'new light' to break forth from his Word. Under Bruce's editorship, the *Evangelical Quarterly* shifted from being a journal dominated by articles on Reformed theology to one chiefly devoted to biblical studies. Bruce's own flexibility on issues of biblical authorship and historicity meant that he was conspicuously absent from James Barr's *Fundamentalism* (1978), a polemical attack on Inter-Varsity's biblical scholarship. Thus two of the major leaders of the postwar evangelical resurgence – Lloyd-Jones and F. F. Bruce – established divergent paths for evangelical biblical scholarship.[18] The gap between these trajectories was to grow wider from the 1970s onwards, as evangelical biblical scholars questioned standard conservative positions.

Although biblical scholarship was unquestionably the most important retrieval project of postwar evangelicalism, the work of the Banner of Truth Trust was also to have a profound impact. So it is worthwhile reflecting on what was retrieved and what was not.

While the Banner of Truth Trust is widely known as a 'Puritan publisher', it actually published a much wider range of Reformed literature. It promoted the writings of nineteenth-century Calvinist theologians like the Americans Robert L. Dabney, Charles Hodge, W. T. Shedd and James Henry Thornwell, and the Scot William Cunningham. It also disseminated the literature of the eighteenth-century evangelical revivals, including the *Journals* and *Letters* of George Whitefield, the works of Jonathan Edwards and John Gillies' *Historical Collections of Accounts of Revival* which construed Protestant history in terms of successive waves of revival. These texts, as will be seen, reflected the deepest passions of Martyn Lloyd-Jones.

At the same time, the Trust did publish a broad swathe of seventeenth-century Puritan literature across a variety of genres: sermons, treatises, evangelistic tracts, biblical commentaries, letters, histories and biographies. The authors published included early Stuart Puritans (Richard Sibbes),

---

18. This paragraph draws on Thomas Noble, *Tyndale House and Fellowship: The First Sixty Years* (Leicester: Inter-Varsity Press, 2006), pp. 37–40, 51–53, 70, 98, 101–102, 152–154, 176–183, 242–243. See also F. F. Bruce, *In Retrospect: Remembrance of Things Past* (London: Pickering and Inglis, 1980); W. W. Gasque, 'F. F. Bruce', in Timothy Larsen (ed.), *Biographical Dictionary of Evangelicals* (Leicester: Inter-Varsity Press, 2003), pp. 85–88.

Presbyterians (Thomas Manton), Congregationalists (John Owen), Baptists (John Bunyan) and even the odd Restoration conformist (William Gurnall). For the most part, the works of these writers were simply reprints of the nineteenth-century editions mentioned above, but recognizing the daunting weight of these volumes and their often small typeface, the publishers also produced a series of user-friendly 'Puritan Paperbacks', reformatted and abridged for modern readers who lacked either stamina or time.

Although this represented a major publishing effort, a great deal of Puritan writing was left on the shelf. Given the sheer bulk of the Puritans' output and the reliance on nineteenth-century editions, this was inevitable, but it also reflected a very deliberate policy of exclusion. In choosing which works to publish, the Banner of Truth Trust stuck to a staunchly orthodox agenda, eschewing radical Puritanism and omitting any works emanating from the Puritan milieu that strayed from the path of Dortian Calvinism. Their catalogue had no space for the polemical theology of the 'Neonomian' Richard Baxter, the Arminian John Goodwin or the Antinomian Tobias Crisp. Also excluded were the prophecies of Anna Trapnel, the works of John Milton or Roger Williams and everything by General Baptists or other sects. Even the somewhat mystical divinity of Welsh Puritans like Walter Cradock and Morgan Llwyd found no place in the Trust's catalogue. And since those around Lloyd-Jones were deeply shaped by a pietistic reaction against the social gospel, they displayed little interest in retrieving the riches of Puritan political thought.

In making these choices, the publishers (advised by Lloyd-Jones himself) created a Puritan canon. Thanks to the Banner of Truth Trust, Puritanism was largely shorn of its many unruly outgrowths. This was understandable, since the retrieval project had been driven by theological convictions more than historical curiosity, but it meant that a wider body of Puritan texts was lost to view and it had the effect of turning the Puritans into the property of one particular tribe within evangelicalism (the conservative Calvinists).[19] Of course, the Banner's books did sometimes reach readers far beyond conservative Reformed circles. One of them was endorsed by the American Pentecostal leader David Wilkerson, whose book *The Cross and the Switchblade* (1963) was a key text in the early years of the charismatic movement.[20] But as a general

---

19. For an outsider's wry perspective on the Anglican members of this Puritan tribe, see Michael Saward, *Evangelicals on the Move* (Oxford: Mowbray, 1987), p. 70.

20. Wilkerson wrote the foreword to the Banner's paperback abridgement of William Gurnall's *The Christian in Complete Armour* (3 vols., Edinburgh: Banner of Truth, 1987–9).

rule, some evangelicals read little but the Puritans, while most ignored them altogether. In the eighteenth century, by contrast, different wings of the evangelical movement had engaged with Puritan writings. John Wesley reprinted the Puritans alongside a wide variety of other authors in his *Christian Library*. Of course, Wesley heavily edited texts to fit with his own theological position, but his project did ensure that Puritan works were digested by non-Calvinists and that ordinary Christians read classics from different streams of Christianity. His conception of the Christian tradition was arguably broader and deeper than that of Lloyd-Jones.[21]

If it is easy to find faults with the Lloyd-Jones project of retrieval, we should remember the place from which he started. In overcoming the collective amnesia that afflicted much of English-speaking Protestantism in the early twentieth century, he and his circle launched a major project of *resourcement* that is still flourishing.

Interpretation

The second part of Lloyd-Jones's historical project was his interpretation of church history. Throughout his ministry he displayed an interest not just in older works of theology, but also in the history of Protestant Christianity. 'There is something wrong', he asserted, 'with an evangelicalism that is not interested in church history.'[22] Reading works of history and historical biographies was a favourite hobby, and he set aside two days every year to chair the Puritan Conference (later the Westminster Conference), devoting further time to preparing his own closing address. Few pastors have displayed such a sustained interest in both reading and promoting church history, though a similar emphasis can be seen in the writings of the contemporary American Reformed pastor John Piper, who shares many of the same passions as Lloyd-Jones.[23]

---

21. See R. C. Monk, *John Wesley: His Puritan Heritage* (Nashville, TN: Abingdon Press, 1966); Ted Campbell, *John Wesley and Christian Antiquity* (Nashville, TN: Abingdon Press, 1990).

22. D. M. Lloyd-Jones, 'John Calvin and George Whitefield', in D. M. Lloyd-Jones, *The Puritans: Their Origins and Successors: Addresses Delivered at the Puritan and Westminster Conferences 1959–1978* (Edinburgh: Banner of Truth, 1987), p. 106.

23. See further, John Piper, *The Legacy of Sovereign Joy: God's Triumphant Grace in the Lives of Augustine, Luther and Calvin* (Leicester: Inter-Varsity Press, 2000); *Tested by Fire: The Fruit of Suffering in the Lives of John Bunyan, William Cowper and David Brainerd*

Moreover, Lloyd-Jones went to the trouble of keeping up to date with some of the latest scholarship on aspects of church history. When he discussed the nature of Puritanism, a topic that has long divided historians, he surveyed the contrasting opinions of Basil Hall, M. M. Knappen, William Haller, C. H. George, Patrick Collinson and John F. New. In his 1962 lecture on the Great Ejection, he utilized the latest monograph on the subject by Robert Bosher. When exploring eighteenth-century Methodism, he turned to the works of Geoffrey Nuttall, Gordon Rupp and Rupert Davies. He admired the writings of Professor Owen Chadwick, especially *The Secularization of the European Mind* (1975).[24] He enjoyed the classicist Peter Brown's 'excellent biography', *Augustine of Hippo* (1967).[25] And he was delighted when his grandson Christopher Catherwood won a place to read history at Balliol College, Oxford. The Master of Balliol was the Marxist historian Christopher Hill, whose books on Puritanism and the English Revolution were avidly read by the Doctor.[26] Although more recent scholarship is often at odds with Lloyd-Jones's interpretation of the Protestant past, he cannot be blamed for ignoring books published after his death. He made a genuine effort to read widely in the historical literature.

Yet as a pastor, Lloyd-Jones constantly stressed that his interest in history was not driven by 'a mere antiquarian interest' or 'historical curiosity'.[27] Indeed, he warned ominously against a purely academic interest in the

---

(Leicester: Inter-Varsity Press, 2001); *The Roots of Endurance: Invincible Perseverance in the Lives of John Newton, Charles Simeon and William Wilberforce* (Leicester: Inter-Varsity Press, 2003); *Contending for Our All: Defending Truth and Treasuring Christ in the Lives of Athanasius, John Owen and J. Gresham Machen* (Leicester: Inter-Varsity Press, 2006); *Filling Up the Afflictions of Christ: The Cost of Bringing the Gospel to the Nations in the Lives of William Tyndale, Adoniram Judson and John Paton* (Nottingham: Inter-Varsity Press, 2009).

24. See the index to Lloyd-Jones, *The Puritans*; Catherwood and Catherwood, *Martyn Lloyd-Jones: The Man and his Books*, p. 26.

25. D. M. Lloyd-Jones, 'A Protestant Evangelical College', in D. M. Lloyd-Jones, *Knowing the Times: Addresses Delivered on Various Occasions, 1942–1977* (Edinburgh: Banner of Truth, 1989), p. 373.

26. Personal information from Christopher Catherwood, January 2011. See D. M. Lloyd-Jones, 'The Christian and the State in Revolutionary Times', in Lloyd-Jones, *The Puritans*, p. 342.

27. D. M. Lloyd-Jones, 'Luther and His Message for Today', in Hywel Rees Jones (ed.), *Unity in Truth: Addresses Given by Dr D. Martyn Lloyd-Jones at Meetings Held under the Auspices of the British Evangelical Council* (Darlington: Evangelical Press, 1991), p. 38.

subject. He had known three (unnamed) historians of the eighteenth century who studied the evangelical revival but were entirely untouched by its spiritual passion.[28] Warnings against 'intellectualism' and 'scholasticism' recurred throughout Lloyd-Jones's lectures and addresses. They might be seen as part of a consistently anti-establishment ethos, which made him suspicious of the English metropolitan elite, state churches, high culture and the ivory towers of academia. Invoking the fideism of Tertullian and Pascal, he decried the mixing of theology and philosophy which he detected in the early Christian apologists and the pre-Reformation church, as well as in Lutheran and Reformed scholasticism. He worried that '"Athens" is coming back into evangelicalism', and went so far as to say that 'the evangelical distrusts scholarship'.[29]

Because of this acute ambivalence towards academic scholarship, the most gifted writers in Lloyd-Jones's circle showed little interest in writing for the academy. Iain Murray often reiterated the Doctor's ominous warnings about academia, and while he wrote well-researched historical studies, their argument was heavily shaped by contemporary agendas. Among historians, Murray's histories and biographies were generally eclipsed by scholarship with a stronger sense of their intellectual, social and political context.[30] J. I. Packer wrote his Oxford doctorate on the theology of Richard Baxter under the leading historian of Puritanism, Geoffrey Nuttall, but the work was not published until decades later.[31] It was, in fact, a very fine piece of research, but Packer saw himself as a theologian writing for the church, not an historian writing for the academy. While he did not share Lloyd-Jones's suspicion of scholarship, intellectualism and scholasticism, Packer never published his work in historical journals and his many essays on the Puritans are almost never cited by academic historians.

The only figure close to Lloyd-Jones who made a significant impact on historical scholarship was R. T. Kendall. His monograph *Calvin and English Calvinism*

---

28. D. M. Lloyd-Jones, 'Knowledge – False and True', in Lloyd-Jones, *The Puritans*, pp. 30–31.

29. See Lloyd-Jones, *Knowing the Times*, pp. 97–98, 207–213, 270, 283, 301, 324–329, quotations at 210, 327.

30. E.g., George Marsden's *Jonathan Edwards: A Life* (New Haven, CT: Yale University Press, 2003) presents a far more rounded and richly contextualized account of its subject than does Murray's *Jonathan Edwards: A New Biography* (Edinburgh: Banner of Truth, 1987).

31. J. I. Packer, *The Redemption and Restoration of Man in the Thought of Richard Baxter* (Carlisle: Paternoster, 2003).

(1979) was a revised version of his Oxford doctorate and was published by the highly prestigious Oxford University Press.[32] It was a problematic book and made an overdrawn contrast between the teaching of Calvin and his later followers on the doctrine of assurance and the extent of the atonement. This 'Calvin versus the Calvinist' paradigm was seriously undermined by Richard Muller's massive works on Reformed orthodoxy some years later. But Kendall's book has been very widely cited in the academic literature and its suggestive distinction between 'credal' and 'experimental' predestinarians is still invoked by some of the leading figures in the field.[33] However, Kendall lost contact with academia after becoming pastor of Westminster Chapel. The Puritan/Westminster Conference and the Institute of Historical Research were worlds apart.

So while Lloyd-Jones had an eye on academic history, his own brand of historical reflection had little time for scholarly concerns. Instead, it was unabashedly utilitarian. Determined to draw lessons from history, the Doctor worked on the assumption that there were direct analogies between past and present crises. Anniversaries became very important to him, especially at the height of his fame and influence, when he gave lectures to mark the quatercentenary of the Scottish Reformation (1960), the tercentenary of the Great Ejection (1962), the four hundred and fiftieth anniversary of Luther's Reformation (1967), and the three hundred and fiftieth anniversary of the Pilgrim Fathers (1970). He was inclined to discern 'a very close parallel' between these momentous historical turning points and the crisis of the 1960s.[34] The modern church, he declared, was confronted by 'the very same problems' as Christians on the eve of the Reformation.[35] This approach injected the present with intense (even epic) significance and suggested that the need of the hour was to stand

---

32. R. T. Kendall, *Calvin and English Calvinism to 1649* (Oxford: Oxford University Press, 1979).

33. Richard Muller, *The Unaccommodated Calvin* (Oxford: Oxford University Press, 2001), ch. 9; Richard Muller, *Post-Reformation Reformed Dogmatics*, 4 vols. (Grand Rapids, MI: Baker, 2003). A search on Google Scholar reveals scores of references to Kendall's book in both academic journals and evangelical publications. Kendall's distinction between 'credal' and 'experimental' predestinarians has an important function in the argument of Peter Lake's influential essay, 'Calvinism and the English Church, 1570–1635', *Past and Present*, vol. 114 (February 1987), pp. 39–40.

34. See, e.g., D. M. Lloyd-Jones, 'The Mayflower Pilgrims', in Jones (ed.), *Unity in Truth*, p. 85.

35. D. M. Lloyd-Jones, 'Remembering the Reformation', in Lloyd-Jones, *Knowing the Times*, p. 94.

firm for the old paths rather than find new ways to tackle new problems. During a decade of unprecedented cultural upheaval, Lloyd-Jones was dwelling on the past. The perils of the ecumenical movement loomed larger than the challenge of secularism. Despite Vatican II, he thought that little had changed; contemporary Protestants faced a Catholic Church that was at least as bad as in Luther's day.[36] Rome was not allowed to shift its ground and evangelicals did not need to adapt.

Lloyd-Jones's account of history was avowedly partisan. He found it impossible to be objective about Anglicanism. He declared that the sermons of the Caroline divines 'consisted very largely of strings of classical allusions'. He recycled the old cliché that the Church of England in the early eighteenth century 'was dead; you know about the pluralities of livings, you know about the drunkenness and the fox-hunting – it has all been described so often'. The strange appeal of Anglicanism he could only explain by resort to national stereotypes: 'The via media appeals to the Englishman,' he suggested, and, 'The typical Englishman has a dislike of definitions.'[37]

While the Doctor was quite prepared to work alongside Arminian evangelicals, his history had a firm Calvinist bias. He maintained that 'every single person who was involved in the beginning of the great missionary enterprise in the 1790s was what is called a Calvinist', a verdict that ignores the role of Arminians like William Wilberforce in setting up the Church Missionary Society and misses entirely the role of the Moravians in launching 'the great missionary enterprise'.[38] He thought that Calvinists tend to be 'less interested in advertising' than Arminians, a view that can hardly accommodate the savvy promotional techniques of George Whitefield and the early Methodists.[39] He maintained that it was only since the decline of Calvinism that revivals have become 'less and less frequent', a claim that hardly fits with the remarkable global revivals of the twentieth century.[40]

---

36. Lloyd-Jones, 'Luther and His Message for Today', p. 41.

37. Lloyd-Jones, *The Puritans*, pp. 42, 108, 221. One wonders where this leaves Dr Johnson and his famous dictionary!

38. See J. C. S. Mason, *The Moravian Church and the Missionary Awakening in England, 1760–1800* (Woodbridge: Boydell and Brewer, 2001).

39. David Ceri Jones, *'A Glorious Work in the World': Welsh Methodism and the Evangelical Revival, 1735–1750* (Cardiff: University of Wales Press, 2004).

40. Lloyd-Jones, *The Puritans*, pp. 42, 107, 211. On twentieth-century revivals, mostly non-Calvinist, see Mark Shaw, *Global Awakening: How 20th-Century Revivals Triggered a Christian Revolution* (Downers Grove, IL: InterVarsity Press, 2010).

Of course, such bold claims arose because Lloyd-Jones was painting on a large canvas with broad brushstrokes. Like his contemporary Francis Schaeffer, he had neither the training nor the resources of a professional historian. Uninhibited by the discipline of footnotes and concerned to communicate with a popular audience, both men offered sweeping historical overviews and reacted sharply when challenged by sympathetic but critical scholars.[41] Lloyd-Jones's collected lectures from the Puritan and Westminster Conferences were published under the title *The Puritans: Their Origins and Successors*. Yet because of their scope, they could have been called *An Interpretation of Protestant History*. Together with his other historical lectures, they sketch out a distinctive vision of the Protestant tradition. In keeping with his wide-angle view, Lloyd-Jones thought in centuries and focused on major turning points, moments of crisis and division: the sixteenth-century Reformation split between Catholic and Protestant; the seventeenth-century conflict between Anglican and Puritan; the eighteenth-century parting between critics and proponents of the evangelical revival; and the nineteenth-century departure of both liberal and evangelical modernizers from the old Calvinist paths. At each of these turning points he took sides, identifying emphatically with the Reformers, the Puritans, the awakeners and the conservative Calvinists.

The sixteenth century: Protestants versus Catholics

Lloyd-Jones's 1967 lecture on 'Luther and His Message for Today' was delivered to a packed audience of 2,500 people in Westminster Chapel. He noted that 'Luther's action in 1517 has changed the entire course of history'. Luther had 'in a sense created the German language', and 'you would never have had modern science were it not for the Reformation'. The Reformer had struck a great blow for liberty and individual conscience and one could not understand the modern United States without understanding his achievement.[42] This was a ringing endorsement of the Whig interpretation of history. Like many conservative Protestants, Lloyd-Jones combined a rather

---

41. See Francis Schaeffer, *How Should We Then Live?* (Grand Rapids, MI: Fleming H. Revell, 1976). For Schaeffer's testy exchanges with George Marsden and Mark Noll, see Barry Hankins, *Francis Schaeffer and the Shaping of Evangelical America* (Grand Rapids, MI: Eerdmans, 2008), pp. 209–227; for the bruising encounter between Lloyd-Jones and Basil Hall, see McGrath, *To Know and Serve God*, p. 121.

42. Lloyd-Jones, 'Luther and His Message for Today', pp. 21–23.

glum anti-modernist outlook with a Whiggish celebration of modernity's Reformation roots.[43]

But this was a mere prologue. What really mattered about Luther was his theology and his break with Rome. Lloyd-Jones retold the familiar story of Luther's spiritual journey and concluded by drawing out the 'message for today'. Since he was speaking a year after his famous altercation with John Stott, he drove home his separatist point, even ending with the words of Revelation 18:4: 'Come out of her my people.' The ecumenical movement, he warned, was 'travelling in the direction of Rome' and the only hope was for evangelicals to leave compromised territorial churches and 'come into an association such as this British Evangelical Council'.[44]

With hindsight, Lloyd-Jones's fear of an ecumenical juggernaut trundling towards Rome seems misplaced, but it was not implausible in the context of the Second Vatican Council. Lloyd-Jones did appreciate Catholic authors like Pascal and he read modern Catholic theologians like Hans Küng.[45] In his final Welsh-language sermon, delivered at Aberystwyth in May 1980, he cited Aquinas, Pascal, Cardinal Newman and Francis Thompson alongside the lone Protestant George Matheson.[46] But he would have deplored Packer's involvement in Evangelicals and Catholics Together (as he did Packer's cooperation with the Anglo-Catholic wing of the Church of England). And he would have known the answer to Mark Noll's question, *Is the Reformation Over?* In his 1966 address at the second National Assembly of Evangelicals, Lloyd-Jones criticized Protestants who suggested that the Reformation was a tragedy. Conservative evangelicals, he insisted, were 'standing in the position of the Protestant Reformers', as well as being the representatives of 'the Puritans, the Covenanters, the early Methodists'.[47]

---

43. In an earlier lecture, Lloyd-Jones announced that the Reformers had 'laid the foundation of the whole democratic view of government'. See Lloyd-Jones, 'Remembering the Reformation', in Lloyd-Jones, *Knowing the Times*, pp. 95–96.

44. Lloyd-Jones, 'Luther and His Message for Today', pp. 42–43.

45. See D. M. Lloyd-Jones, 'William Williams and Welsh Calvinistic Methodism', in Lloyd-Jones, *The Puritans*, p. 205; D. M. Lloyd-Jones, 'The Weapons of our Warfare', in Lloyd-Jones, *Knowing the Times*, p. 220; Murray, *Lloyd Jones: Fight of Faith*, p. 446.

46. The sermon was published in a special commemorative issue of the Evangelical Movement of Wales's Welsh-language magazine, D. M. Lloyd-Jones, 'A Jacob a Adawyd ei Hunan', *Y Cylchgrawn Efengylaidd*, cyfrol 19, rhif 5 (Rhifyn Arbennig 1981), pp. 42–46. I am grateful to E. Wyn James for this reference.

47. D. M. Lloyd-Jones, 'Evangelical Unity: An Appeal', in Lloyd-Jones, *Knowing the Times*, p. 255.

At the same time, he tended to remake the Reformers in the image of later evangelicals. 'At the very heart and centre of the story of Martin Luther', he asserted, was 'this volcanic element, this living element, this experimental element, this experiential element'. Luther's high church sacramentalism, his commitment to baptismal regeneration, consubstantiation and a territorial *volkskirche*, and his debt to medieval traditions of academic theology were passed over in silence. On Lloyd-Jones's account, the Reformation was led by a Spirit-filled man, whereas the modern ecumenical movement was 'a movement of professors and ecclesiastics'.[48] This resonated with pietist evangelicals, but it was dubious history. Lloyd-Jones confessed to being 'a hero worshipper' and he reduced the Reformation to the story of 'big men', 'great men', 'giants', ignoring the broader intellectual and religious currents that shaped them.[49] He did not explain that the Reformation began its life among scholars and professors, Europe's intellectual elite. He did note Luther's engagement with Augustine and in classic Protestant fashion he traced a continuous evangelical 'remnant' through the Waldensians, the Hussites and the Lollards. But he seriously underplayed the debt owed by the Reformation to medieval scholasticism, medieval devotional traditions and humanist textual scholarship. Viewing the Reformers through modern evangelical spectacles, he missed their intellectualism and their catholicity.[50]

At times, Lloyd-Jones did recognize his own distance from the Reformers. While he sometimes claimed that they fought for 'a pure church', a church with 'no room for all and sundry', he elsewhere admitted that 'one of the tragedies of the Reformation was the way in which Luther, Calvin and Zwingli tended to take over the notion of the state church'. On this point, Lloyd-Jones confessed sympathy with the Anabaptists.[51]

---

48. Lloyd-Jones, 'Luther and His Message for Today', p. 37.

49. Lloyd-Jones, 'Remembering the Reformation', p. 97.

50. On the Reformation's patristic, medieval and Renaissance roots, see Heiko Oberman, *Forerunners of the Reformation* (London: Lutterworth Press, 1967); Muller, *Post-Reformation Reformed Dogmatics*; Alister McGrath, *The Intellectual Origins of the European Reformation* (2nd ed., Oxford: Blackwell, 2004); Dennis E. Tamburello, *Union with Christ: John Calvin and the Mysticism of St Bernard* (Louisville, KY: Westminster John Knox Press, 1994); Anthony Lane, *John Calvin: Student of the Church Fathers* (Grand Rapids, MI: Baker, 2000); Carl Trueman, *John Owen: Reformed Catholic, Renaissance Man* (Aldershot: Ashgate, 2007).

51. Lloyd-Jones, *Knowing the Times*, pp. 101, 194.

The seventeenth century: Puritans versus Anglicans

Indeed, by the latter part of his ministry, Lloyd-Jones inclined to a separatist ecclesiology that prevented his loyalists from engaging fully with either the wider church or the ancient church. His critique of Anglicanism fitted well with this separatist tendency. Around half of his church history lectures were devoted to the conflict between Anglicans and Puritans. This theme preoccupied Lloyd-Jones throughout the 1960s and well into the 1970s. Indeed, one of the most striking features of *The Puritans* is that whenever he gave lectures on the Puritans proper (as opposed to the eighteenth-century evangelicals), he was almost always addressing ecclesiology. He drew his spirituality from Jonathan Edwards and the Calvinistic Methodists and rarely discussed Puritan practical divinity in any depth.

J. I. Packer, on the other hand, did the opposite. Packer's collected essays on the Puritans were almost entirely devoted to their practical divinity and simply ignored ecclesiological issues.[52] The two key figures behind the Puritan Conference had quite different visions of Puritanism. For Lloyd-Jones, Puritanism was the drive for a pure church, while for Packer, it was a renewal movement within the church. At the Puritan Conference, the two men promoted their rival visions in very different ways. Lloyd-Jones chose the path of confrontation, giving polemically charged lectures that directly challenged the Anglican vision. Packer, by contrast, accentuated the positive, ignoring the separatist vision as if it was an irrelevance and focusing relentlessly on Puritanism as a devotional and theological renewal movement within the Church of England. In a lecture at Oak Hill College in 2009, Packer recalled how he had 'collaborated on certain matters with the late, great, Martyn Lloyd-Jones and he, I will tell you, put me under pretty heavy pressure to stop being an Anglican'.[53] Elsewhere he talked about how Lloyd-Jones 'occasionally put the boot into me' during the 1960s.[54] While Packer was clearly referring to personal conversations, the pressure was also applied through Lloyd-Jones's closing addresses at the annual Puritan Conference. Other sessions of the

---

52. J. I. Packer, *Among God's Giants: The Puritan Vision of the Christian Life* (Eastbourne: Kingsway, 1991); published in the United States as *A Quest for Godliness: The Puritan Vision of the Christian Life* (Wheaton, IL: Crossway Books, 1990).

53. J. I. Packer, 'Church and Schism' (2009), www.oakhill.org (accessed 12 January 2011).

54. J. I. Packer, 'A Kind of Puritan', in Christopher Catherwood (ed.), *Martyn Lloyd-Jones: Chosen by God* (Crowborough: Highland Books, 1986), p. 46.

conference were followed by vigorous discussions, but not the closing address. Here Lloyd-Jones always had the last word.

As early as 1959, in a lecture on revival, we see him delivering well-aimed jabs at the Anglican vision of Puritanism as a movement of renewal. Lloyd-Jones asserted that there had never been a general revival within the Church of England, probably because liturgical, parochial, state churches inhibit the free movement of the Spirit. And he also suggested that 'the Puritans themselves do not seem to teach us anything about revival', a view at odds with Packer's later claim that Puritanism should be seen as a movement of revival.[55]

But it was from 1962 onwards that Lloyd-Jones really trained his guns on Anglicanism. This was, of course, the tercentenary of the Great Ejection of Puritan ministers from the Church of England and the Doctor delivered two lectures to commemorate the event, one at the Puritan Conference, the other for the Evangelical Library.[56] He had become increasingly worried by the growing influence of the ecumenical movement and as he reflected on 1662, he became convinced that the same scenario would be played out once again three hundred years later. By drawing this historical analogy, Lloyd-Jones imbued the present situation with an ominous sense of crisis, one that demanded a new parting of the ways between Puritanism and Anglicanism: 'I predict that we are going to pass through a period in which probably every one of us in this room will have to make as vital and as drastic a decision as did those men of 1662.' He seized on the latest monograph on the Restoration religious settlement by the historian Robert Bosher, which argued that it was a 'counter-Reformation' coup by the Laudian party.[57] This meshed nicely with Lloyd-Jones's own understanding of the Church of England, suggesting that Puritanism and Anglicanism were incompatible.[58] Evangelicals should learn from the Puritans 'the all-importance of the purity of the church, especially in the matter of doctrine'.[59]

----

55. D. M. Lloyd-Jones, 'Revival: An Historical and Theological Survey', in Lloyd-Jones, *The Puritans*, pp. 3, 10. Cf., Packer, *Among God's Giants*, ch. 3.

56. D. M. Lloyd-Jones, *1662–1962: From Puritanism to Nonconformity* (London: Evangelical Library, 1962); D. M. Lloyd-Jones, 'Puritan Perplexities – Some Lessons from 1640–1662', in Lloyd-Jones, *The Puritans*, pp. 54–72.

57. Lloyd-Jones, 'Puritan Perplexities', pp. 57–58, 59.

58. Recent historiography has challenged this account, emphasizing the strongly Protestant identity of the Restoration church and the continuing presence of Calvinists within it. See Stephen Hampton, *Anti-Arminians: The Anglican Reformed Tradition from Charles II to George I* (Oxford: Oxford University Press, 2008).

59. Lloyd-Jones, 'Puritan Perplexities', p. 69.

A year later, in 1963, Lloyd Jones gave an address entitled 'John Owen on Schism', in which he read out long sections from Owen's defence of independency. He offered remarkably little commentary, letting the text speak for itself. It is hard not to see this as a rather pointed appeal to Packer, who revered Owen as a theologian but had not followed his ecclesiology. Lloyd-Jones ended with the suggestion that 'John Owen speaks very directly and immediately to our situation at this very moment'. As in the 1650s, the godly faced a choice between what Owen called 'external uniformity' (known now as the ecumenical movement) and 'evangelical union'.[60] The implication was clear: instead of joining the World Council of Churches, evangelicals should forge a union among themselves on lines suggested by the Cromwellian church.

In 1965, the year before his famous clash with John Stott, Lloyd-Jones gave a lecture on 'Ecclesiola in Ecclesia', surveying the attempts to renew state churches from within by forming 'little churches within the church'. He pronounced the project a resounding failure and warned once more that the godly must withdraw from fellowship with heretics. The challenge of the ecumenical movement meant that 'every one of us' would have to 'decide one way or the other, and that very soon'.[61] A year later, some months after his Westminster Central Hall appeal had tried to force the issue, Lloyd-Jones addressed the Puritan Conference on Henry Jacob, the first English congregationalist. The Puritans, he noted, 'were not only interested in pastoral problems . . . they were also tremendously, and indeed even primarily, interested in the doctrine of the nature of the Christian church'. That remark would have made Packer wince, and as in the Owen lecture, he was forced to sit through long readings from a seventeenth-century congregationalist, including all twenty-eight points of Jacob's church platform. 'I am simply reporting', said Lloyd-Jones somewhat disingenuously, 'and not expressing my own opinion.'[62]

In 1969, the Puritan Conference met for the last time. For twenty years, Packer and Lloyd-Jones had met to discuss the Puritans, but in 1970, the Free Church trustees of the conference would write to Packer explaining that they were closing it down in protest at his ecumenical concessions to liberal and high church Anglicans. In his 1969 lecture on 'Learning from History' (a closing lecture in more senses that one), Lloyd-Jones pulled no punches. He laid into ecumenism, ecclesiastical hierarchies, state churches, the *via media*, the

---

60. D. M. Lloyd-Jones, 'John Owen on Schism', in Lloyd-Jones, *The Puritans*, pp. 97, 99.

61. D. M. Lloyd-Jones, 'Ecclesiola in Ecclesia', in Lloyd-Jones, *The Puritans*, p. 148.

62. D. M. Lloyd-Jones, 'Henry Jacob and the First Congregational Church', in Lloyd-Jones, *The Puritans*, pp. 150, 168.

compromising English temperament and Richard Baxter's minimalist criteria for Christian unity. That final point was perceptive, because Packer himself was an odd amalgam of Baxter (the subject of his doctorate) and Owen (his favourite theologian). Like Owen, he was a doughty champion of Reformed orthodoxy, renowned for defending biblical inerrancy, penal substitution and even limited (or definite) atonement. Yet like Baxter, who once protested that some of the godly wanted to 'shut up the church of God in a nutshell', Packer was surprisingly broad in his sympathies.[63] In the latter part of his career he would be a key figure in Evangelicals and Catholics Together and would write glowing blurbs for a remarkable range of Christian books.

For Packer, the experience of sitting through Lloyd-Jones's closing addresses may well have been acutely uncomfortable. Both parties, perhaps, were a little relieved when their strained cooperation came to an end. When the conference was reconvened in 1971 as the Westminster Conference, Lloyd-Jones gave a closing address on 'Puritanism and its Origins'. Here he rejected 'the Anglican view' of Puritanism as 'essentially practical theology' (the view that Packer espoused). Instead, Lloyd-Jones praised the rather extreme position of the historian J. F. H. New, who detected fundamental differences between the Puritan and the Anglican over a wide range of doctrinal matters. 'True Puritanism', Lloyd-Jones insisted, 'can never rest content with being a mere wing or emphasis in the comprehensive episcopal Church, but must always end in Presbyterianism or Independency.' To suggest otherwise was to depart from 'the true Puritan attitude, the Puritan outlook, the Puritan spirit, and the Puritan understanding'.[64] The subtext to this address was unmissable: Lloyd-Jones and his party were the true Puritans.

The next year, in 1972, he reinforced this message with a lecture on 'John Knox, the Founder of Puritanism'. This was a much more personal address. What is striking is Lloyd-Jones's obvious identification with Knox. The Scottish Reformer was the subject of 'vitriolic attacks' in 'these days of ecumenicity'. He was 'a strong man . . . a stern man, a courageous man', 'an heroic, rugged character', characteristically vehement in his preaching, an anti-establishment man, 'a model of moderation' over against his bitter Anglican critics. At Frankfurt his Anglican critic Richard Cox behaved in a way that was 'quite abominable, intransigent and rude – not the last time Puritans have

63. On Baxter's ecumenicity, see Paul Lim, *In Pursuit of Purity, Unity, and Liberty: Richard Baxter's Puritan Ecclesiology in its Seventeenth-Century Context* (Leiden: Brill, 2004), ch. 6.

64. D. M. Lloyd-Jones, 'Puritanism and its Origins', in Lloyd-Jones, *The Puritans*, pp. 239–240, 255, 259.

had to suffer in that way at the hands of Anglicans'.[65] By this stage, shades of grey had largely disappeared from Lloyd-Jones's telling of the story. English Protestant history was now a tale of struggle between Puritan heroes and Anglican villains and there was simply no room for Packer's, for Puritans who tried to work within Anglicanism.

Yet around this time, another figure was emerging as the leading historian of Puritanism, someone who would seriously undermine the view that Puritanism and Anglicanism were destined to diverge. Patrick Collinson had been raised in the conservative evangelical subculture and had been a CICCU leader at Pembroke College, Cambridge during the 1950s.[66] After graduation he moved away from conservative evangelicalism towards a more liberal, high church Anglicanism, while writing a massive doctoral thesis at London University which eventually became *The Elizabethan Puritan Movement* (1967). In this book and his subsequent writings, Collinson would make a powerful case for seeing Puritanism as Packer saw it, as an energetic tendency within the Church of England. He showed how the leading clergy of the church, under both Elizabeth and James I, were self-consciously Reformed Protestants, committed to Calvinist doctrine and a preaching ministry and sympathetic to the evangelical labours of moderate 'Puritan' pastors. Although some Puritan clergy refused to conform to certain ceremonies and a minority flirted with Presbyterianism or separatism, Puritanism as a whole was not heading inexorably towards either revolution or dissent; instead it was absorbed within the bloodstream of the Church of England. Only the contingency of Charles I's accession and his promotion of the ideologue Archbishop Laud turned the church sharply away from Reformed Protestantism and alienated the godly. 'Anglicanism', on this reading, was a seventeenth-century invention.[67]

If rival interpretations of Puritanism fuelled the split between Packer and Lloyd-Jones, they also fed another major controversy in the last decade of

---

65. D. M. Lloyd-Jones, 'John Knox, the Founder of Puritanism', in Lloyd-Jones, *The Puritans*, pp. 262, 279, 265–266, 274.

66. See his memoir, Patrick Collinson, *The History of a History Man: or, The Twentieth Century Viewed from a Safe Distance* (Woodbridge: Boydell/Church of England Record Society, 2011), p. 68.

67. See especially Patrick Collinson, *The Religion of Protestants, 1559–1625* (Oxford: Oxford University Press, 1982). The broad lines of this account are now endorsed by the leading historians of the post-Reformation English Church, including Kenneth Fincham, Peter Lake, Diarmaid MacCulloch, Anthony Milton, Jean-Louis Quantin and Nicholas Tyacke.

Lloyd-Jones's life. In the mid-1970s, the young American scholar R. T. Kendall wrote an Oxford doctoral thesis on Calvin and the English Calvinists which argued that the Reformer taught believers to look for assurance in Christ's atoning death for all men, whereas later Puritans (with a few exceptions) told Christians to find assurance through a painful process of self-examination.[68] Kendall was known to say (according to Iain Murray) that 'the Puritans were a miserable lot', prone to legalism, but his free grace emphasis on full assurance through the Spirit's testimony was warmly welcomed by Lloyd-Jones.[69] In his 1960 lecture on the Reformation, he himself had identified a shift between the Reformers' emphasis on 'full assurance' and the more cautious statement of the Westminster Confession.[70] The Doctor also sympathized with Kendall's critique of limited (or particular) atonement as taught by John Owen and endorsed by J. I. Packer. Kendall claims that the Doctor 'loved my thesis' and encouraged its publication, and he adds that his mentor 'was not particularly fond of the arid and scholastic teaching of the seventeenth-century Puritans, except for Thomas Goodwin'.[71] While Iain Murray takes issue with this, he admits that Lloyd-Jones was attracted to Kendall because he confirmed his own teaching about the baptism or sealing of the Spirit, which left a door open to the charismatic movement, a door through which 'the "Irvingite disaster" was to be repeated, even within Westminster Chapel itself'.[72]

    This was a reference to the charismatic outbursts that attended both the ministry of Edward Irving in the 1820s and that of R. T. Kendall in the 1980s, when he was pastor of Westminster Chapel. In the mid-1970s, Kendall was not yet involved in the charismatic movement, but the shape of things to come was presaged in a statement he made in a paper at the Westminster Conference in 1976:

> If our doctrine of salvation is not accused of being antinomian, it is likely that we
> have not really preached justification by faith . . . if our doctrine of the immediate
> witness of the Spirit is not accused of being charismatic, we probably have not really
> held to a robust doctrine of the Spirit. This is neither to condone antinomianism nor

---

68. Kendall, *Calvin and English Calvinism*.
69. Iain H. Murray, '"Openness to the Holy Spirit": How Westminster Chapel was Turned Around', *The Banner of Truth*, no. 486 (March 2004), pp. 25–32.
70. Lloyd-Jones, 'Remembering the Reformation', pp. 100–101.
71. R. T. Kendall, *In Pursuit of His Glory: My 25 Years at Westminster Chapel* (London: Hodder and Stoughton, 2002), p. 30.
72. Iain H. Murray, *Lloyd-Jones: Messenger of Grace* (Edinburgh: Banner of Truth, 2008), p. 159.

the charismatic movement (for I have no sympathy for either), but is to suggest that we must become far more vulnerable than most of us have been to these charges if we really desire to see something unusual happen in our churches.[73]

Something unusual did indeed happen in the following decade, when Kendall hosted the colourful evangelist Arthur Blessitt and the charismatic prophet Paul Cain at Westminster Chapel. Already, towards the end of his life, Lloyd-Jones had become wary of Kendall and his construal of Puritanism. A year after the Doctor's death, the Banner of Truth Trust published Paul Helm's vigorous refutation of Kendall, *Calvin and the Calvinists* (1982).

Although Kendall misconstrued Calvin and the broader Reformed tradition, he was picking up on a particular strand within Puritanism, one uncannily close to that of the antinomian Anne Hutchinson, who in New England in the mid-1630s had denounced most of the Puritan ministry as legalists and declared that only her own pastor, John Cotton, preached the gospel of grace. Hutchinson also claimed immediate revelations from God and her charismatic, free grace version of radical Puritanism would re-emerge in the ministry of R. T. Kendall, who also extolled John Cotton. Thus Kendall was taking sides in the antinomian controversies that had once convulsed both London and Massachusetts Puritanism, and setting out his own distinctive vision of true evangelical religion.[74]

There is a case for saying that Lloyd-Jones himself was always somewhat ambivalent about the mainstream Puritans. He once said that 'the Puritans were primarily teachers, in my opinion, not preachers'. Their learned expositions stood in contrast to the passionate, extemporary sermons of his hero Whitefield.[75] He worried that some young Reformed preachers were so

---

73. R. T. Kendall, 'John Cotton – First English Calvinist?', in *The Puritan Experiment in the New World: Westminster Conference 1976* (Ripon: Evangelical Press, 1977), p. 48.

74. See Janice Knight, *Orthodoxies in Massachusetts: Re-Reading American Puritanism* (Cambridge, MA: Harvard University Press, 1994); Michael Winship, *Making Heretics: Militant Protestantism and Free Grace in Massachusetts, 1636–1641* (Princeton: Princeton University Press, 2002); T. D. Bozeman, *The Precisianist Strain: Disciplinary Religion and Antinomian Backlash in Puritanism to 1638* (Chapel Hill: University of North Carolina Press, 2004); David Como, *Blown by the Spirit: Puritanism and the Emergence of an Antinomian Underground in Pre-Civil-War England* (Stanford: Stanford University Press, 2004).

75. D. M. Lloyd-Jones, 'What is Preaching?', in Lloyd-Jones, *Knowing the Times*, pp. 269, 272–273.

slavishly devoted to the Puritans that they had started to speak 'as if they lived in the seventeenth century', preaching for at least an hour with strange phrasing and mannerisms. The Puritans needed to be used with discernment and the ones Lloyd-Jones preferred were those closest in spirit to the revivalists of the next century. 'There are Puritans and Puritans!' he remarked. 'John Owen on the whole is difficult to read; he was a highly intellectual man. But there were other Puritan writers who were warmer, and more direct, and more experimental.' Two particular favourites were Richard Sibbes and Thomas Goodwin, 'one of the greatest of the Puritans', whom Lloyd-Jones admired for his doctrine of the sealing of the Spirit subsequent to conversion.[76]

In the end, then, Lloyd-Jones offered a version of Puritanism that was both separatist and pietist. His pietist emphasis would make him attractive to Protestants outside conservative Reformed circles. For example, Lloyd-Jones recalled the pleasure of meeting with the renowned American pastor A. W. Tozer, who hailed from the holiness tradition. He agreed with Tozer's observation that they had both reached 'just about the same position on spiritual matters' via different routes – Tozer by way of the mystics, Lloyd-Jones by way of the Puritans.[77]

The eighteenth century: awakeners versus formalists

While Lloyd-Jones revered the Reformers and admired the Puritans, his greatest affection was reserved for the awakeners of the eighteenth century. If ecclesiology was the first grand theme of his lectures, the second theme was revival and for this he turned to the early evangelicals. Almost half of his 'Puritan' lectures touched on revival and a number were wholly devoted to it: 'Revival: An Historical and Theological Survey' (1959); 'John Calvin and George Whitefield' (1964); 'William Williams and Welsh Calvinistic Methodism' (1968); 'Howell Harris and Revival' (1973); 'Jonathan Edwards and the Crucial Importance of Revival' (1976). One of his few forays into the world of television was to make a documentary about Whitefield. He advised that one could 'test the quality of a man's evangelicalism' by gauging 'his interest in revival'.[78]

---

76. D. M. Lloyd-Jones, *Preaching and Preachers* (London: Hodder and Stoughton, 1971), pp. 175, 218.

77. James L. Snyder, *A. W. Tozer: In Pursuit of God* (Oxford: Monarch, 2009), p. 152.

78. D. M. Lloyd-Jones, 'What Is an Evangelical?', in Lloyd-Jones, *Knowing the Times*, p. 334.

Lloyd-Jones was a passionate defender of what the American church historian Douglas Sweeney has called the 'eighteenth-century twist'.[79] He realized that revival was a new concept, an idea unfamiliar to both the Reformers and the Puritans. It was promoted by the pietists like Philip Jakob Spener and August Hermann Francke (whom Lloyd-Jones believed should be much better known among English-speaking Christians), and it was experienced by the Methodists. Like the later historian David Bebbington, Lloyd-Jones insisted on the novelty of the eighteenth-century revival.[80] 'Calvinistic Methodism', he declared, 'was not a mere continuation of Puritanism. A new element has come in – this emphasis upon the feeling aspect, the revival aspect, and this whole matter of assurance.' Puritans had emphasized obedience to the Law, but Methodism emphasized 'experience'.[81]

This new accent on experience, feeling, assurance and revival was a thoroughly good thing, for 'Calvinism without Methodism tends to produce a joyless, hard, not to say a harsh and cold type of religion'. Indeed, Lloyd-Jones could insist that 'John Calvin needs George Whitefield' and that the Methodist societies of the eighteenth century were closer to the New Testament than were the Puritan churches of the seventeenth century.[82] 'I am myself an eighteenth-century man,' he explained, 'not seventeenth-century; but I believe in using the seventeenth-century men [i.e. the Puritans] as the eighteenth-century men used them.'[83] His daughter recalled, 'How often have we heard him say, "I am an eighteenth century man".'[84]

Lloyd-Jones's passion for revival resonated with Pentecostals and charismatics, including Michael Harper and Terry Virgo, but it was precisely his heavy stress on revival and experience that has made him look rather dubious in the eyes of some conservative Reformed theologians. Carl Trueman has alleged that Lloyd-Jones and his followers were not 'really Reformed'. They thought that to be Reformed meant embracing the Five Points of Calvinism, the Calvinist revival tradition and 'an almost mystical concern for Christian

---

79. Douglas A. Sweeney, *The American Evangelical Story: A History of the Movement* (Grand Rapids, MI: Baker, 2005), pp. 24–25.

80. See David W. Bebbington, *Evangelicalism in Modern Britain: A History from the 1730s to the 1980s* (London: Unwin Hyman, 1989), ch. 2.

81. D. M. Lloyd-Jones, 'William Williams and Welsh Calvinistic Methodism', in Lloyd-Jones, *The Puritans*, pp. 204–205.

82. Ibid., pp. 210, 213.

83. Lloyd-Jones, *Preaching and Preachers*, p. 120.

84. Catherwood and Catherwood, *Martyn Lloyd Jones: The Man and his Books*, p. 33.

experience'. 'Lloyd-Jones', continues Trueman, 'read the Reformed tradition through the grid of eighteenth-century revivalism; and so the ideal of a learned ministry and the importance of ecclesiology, sacraments, creeds, confessions and liturgy all tended to be marginalised in his thinking and critiqued through the lens of his pneumatology.' Viewing modern evangelicalism as a wrong turn – a 'lowest common-denominator, conservative, experiential evangelicalism' – Trueman and other confessional Presbyterians like Darryl Hart and Scott Clark want to undo the eighteenth-century twist and take evangelicals back to the era of Reformed orthodoxy.[85]

It has to be said that Trueman is partly right in his historical analysis. The eighteenth-century twist can be seen as a downgrade movement that undermined aspects of the orthodox Reformed tradition. It downgraded confessionalism in favour of a doctrinal minimalism based around what were later called 'the 3 Rs' (ruin by sin, redemption by Christ, regeneration by the Holy Spirit). It downgraded Calvinism by accepting Wesleyan Arminians and Moravians within the pale of evangelical Protestantism. It downgraded ecclesiology by suggesting that what mattered was heart experience not formal churchmanship. It downgraded sacramental routine by elevating the crisis experience of revival. It downgraded the ideal of a learned ministry by fostering populist preaching by unlettered men. And it downgraded tradition by encouraging naïve biblicism and primitivism. Of course, moderate evangelicals like Jonathan Edwards tried their hardest to hold back this tide, but as Thomas Kidd suggests, they unleashed a radical and populist evangelicalism that they could not control, the precursor of later Pentecostalism.[86]

---

85. Carl Trueman, 'J. I. Packer: An English Nonconformist Perspective', in George (ed.), *J. I. Packer and the Evangelical Future*, pp. 126–127. See also Darryl Hart, *Deconstructing Evangelicalism: Conservative Protestantism in the Age of Billy Graham* (Grand Rapids, MI: Baker, 2004); R. S. Clark, *Recovering the Reformed Confession* (Philadelphia: Presbyterian and Reformed, 2008). For a similar critique of the 'new Calvinists' from different sectors of the Reformed world, see Todd Billings, 'Calvin's Comeback', *Christian Century*, 1 December 2009; James K. A. Smith, *Letters to a Young Calvinist: An Invitation to the Reformed Tradition* (Grand Rapids, MI: Brazos Press, 2010). Both argue that in reducing 'Calvinism' to TULIP (i.e., Total depravity, Unconditional election, Limited atonement, Irresistible grace, Perseverance of the saints), the new Calvinists overlook the catholicity, sacramentalism and transformative social vision of the Reformed tradition.

86. Thomas S. Kidd, *The Great Awakening: The Roots of Evangelical Christianity in Colonial America* (New Haven, CT: Yale University Press, 2007).

Yet it is easy to overplay the eighteenth-century twist by ignoring the way it built on earlier developments.[87] Dogmaticians like Trueman and Clark operate with a top-down picture of the early Reformed tradition, one that owes more to the study of intellectuals, official confessions and theological treatises than it does to the study of lived religion. The Reformed movement within Protestantism branched out into diverse streams and it contained strong pietist, populist and even revivalist undercurrents. In the British Isles it could be especially boisterous. In England, Puritanism has been described as 'the first Protestant Pietism' and the godly subculture would throw up an extraordinary array of sectarian lay preachers, prophets (and prophetesses), exorcists and mystics.[88] Several recent historians have traced the origins of the American revival tradition back to the fervent communion festivals of Scots and Ulster Presbyterians in the 1620s. These occasions were marked by shouting, trembling, falling, weeping and ecstasies not dissimilar to those seen in the Great Awakening.[89]

Lloyd-Jones recognized some of the problems associated with revivalism, but unlike his recent critics he appreciated the achievements that followed in the wake of the pietist turn. If psalms were the secret weapon of the Protestant Reformation, then the evangelical revival was borne along on a wave of hymns. To his dying day, Lloyd-Jones prized the hymns of the eighteenth-century revival, especially those of William Williams. And he recognized that revival was a powerful new concept that injected fresh dynamism into Protestantism. The great global expansion of evangelical religion began in the eighteenth century with the dramatic birth of a new black Christianity in the Caribbean and North America through the revivalism of the Moravians, Whitefield, Baptists and Methodists (both Calvinistic and Wesleyan).[90] The Protestant missionary

---

87. See John Coffey, 'Puritanism, Evangelicalism and the Evangelical Protestant Tradition', in Haykin and Stewart (eds.), *The Emergence of Evangelicalism*, ch. 11.

88. See Bozeman, *The Precisianist Strain*; David Como, 'Radical Puritanism, c. 1558–1660', in Coffey and Lim (eds.), *The Cambridge Companion to Puritanism*, pp. 241–258.

89. See especially Leigh Eric Schmidt, *Holy Fairs: Scotland and the Making of American Revivalism* (Grand Rapids, MI: Eerdmans, 2001).

90. See Sylvia Frey and Betty Wood, *Come Shouting to Zion: African American Protestantism in the American South and British Caribbean to 1830* (Chapel Hill: University of North Carolina Press, 1998); Jon Sensbach, *Rebecca's Revival: Creating Black Christianity in the Atlantic World* (Cambridge, MA: Harvard University Press, 2005); Joanna Brooks, *American Lazarus: Religion and the Rise of African American and Native American Literatures* (New York: Oxford University Press, 2003).

movement of the modern era was driven by societies inspired by the new-style evangelicalism. And the explosive growth of non-Western Christianity in the twentieth century owed far more to Pentecostals than to Presbyterians (though the revivalist Presbyterians of South Korea deserve an honourable mention). Lloyd-Jones's accent on 'the crucial importance of revival' is arguably vindicated by recent work on the history of evangelical expansion.[91]

The nineteenth century: Calvinists versus modernizers

Ironically, Lloyd-Jones took a dim view of nineteenth- and twentieth-century evangelicalism, despite its dramatic global expansion. 'The sooner we forget the nineteenth-century and go back to the eighteenth the better,' he once announced.[92] Unlike the American Baptist historian Kenneth Latourette, who thought of the nineteenth century as 'the great century', Lloyd-Jones paid relatively little attention to the history of missions.[93] His focus was mainly on Britain and America, and there he found declension.

Charles Finney was a key culprit, both for his deviation from the Calvinist orthodoxy of Jonathan Edwards and for turning 'revival' into 'revivalism'. For both Lloyd-Jones and Iain Murray, Whitefield's revival was a supernatural phenomenon sent down from heaven, whereas Finney's revivalism was all too human, something worked up by the technique of the 'new methods'.[94] Historians like Harry Stout and Frank Lambert have demonstrated that the contrast between the First and the Second Great Awakenings is not as stark as Lloyd-Jones tended to suggest. Whitefield was a brilliant publicist who relentlessly advertised his campaigns in the press, networked furiously and held crowds spellbound not just by his intense spiritual passion but also by his powers of oratory and theatrical performance.[95] Stout's account of Whitefield

---

91. See Shaw, *Global Awakening*. Note also David Bebbington's eagerly anticipated history of global revivals in the nineteenth century.

92. Lloyd-Jones, *Preaching and Preachers*, pp. 265–266.

93. Several volumes of Kenneth Scott Latourette's *A History of the Expansion of Christianity* were published under the subtitle *The Great Century* (New York: Harper, 1941–4).

94. See Lloyd-Jones, *The Puritans*, pp. 5, 18–19, 314–316; Iain H. Murray, *Revival and Revivalism: The Making and Marring of American Evangelicalism, 1750–1858* (Edinburgh: Banner of Truth, 1994).

95. See Harry Stout, *The Divine Dramatist: George Whitefield and the Rise of Modern Evangelicalism* (Grand Rapids: Eerdmans, 1991); and Frank Lambert, '*Pedlar in*

as a 'divine dramatist' provoked a sharp exchange with Iain Murray, who levelled charges of irreverence at the distinguished American historian (himself
a Reformed evangelical and a key figure in the revival of Jonathan Edwards
studies).[96] But what was most troubling about the new scholarship was that it
disturbed a very important storyline established by Lloyd-Jones himself.

If Finney had begun the rot, others had continued it. Lloyd-Jones once
complained about 'an evangelicalism that seems to think that evangelical
history began with the first visit to this country of D. L. Moody about 1873'.[97]
Moody was a culprit because he was theologically lightweight, an exponent of
mass evangelism, 'easy-believism', anti-intellectualism, humorous anecdotal
preaching, popular choruses and prophecy conferences. His mission to the
British Isles coincided with the start of the Keswick Convention and the rise
of the holiness movement, and Lloyd-Jones devoted his lecture on 'Living the
Christian Life' to exposing the slippery slope that ran from the evangelical perfectionism of Wesley, through the ethical perfectionism of Finney, to the psychological perfectionism of Keswick and holiness teachers like Phoebe Palmer
and Hannah Pearsall Smith. This telling of recent evangelical history flew in
the face of conventional wisdom among English conservative evangelicals,
who were far more inclined to quote Moody than Edwards. When the Doctor
provided his diagnosis of evangelicalism's ills at the Kingham Conference that
established the Tyndale Fellowship in 1941, G. T. Manley slowly turned his
back to the speaker in silent protest.[98]

But Lloyd-Jones had other targets beside newfangled popular evangelicalism. He was critical of developments among the Protestant intelligent-
sia, both conservative and progressive. Seminary education had failed the
churches, partly because the conservative Presbyterian seminaries had turned
against revival. He felt that Charles Hodge advocated a rather dry Reformed

Divinity': George Whitefield and the Transatlantic Revivals, 1737–1770 (Princeton: Princeton
University Press, 2002). Others suggest that in some respects Finney remained
quite Edwardsian: see Allen Guelzo, 'Oberlin Perfectionism and its Edwardsian
Origins', in Stephen Stein (ed.), Jonathan Edwards's Writings (Bloomington: Indiana
University Press, 1996), ch. 10.

96. For this exchange, see review of Stout's Divine Dramatist by David White,
    The Banner of Truth, no. 366 (March 1994), p. 29; Iain H. Murray, 'Explaining
    Evangelical History', The Banner of Truth, no. 370 (July 1994), pp. 8–14; 'Reviewers
    Reviewed', The Banner of Truth, no. 378 (March 1995), pp. 7–11.

97. Lloyd-Jones, 'John Calvin and George Whitefield', p. 106.

98. Noble, Tyndale House and Fellowship, pp. 34–35.

orthodoxy, lacking in revival fire, and he was dismayed to find that Lewis Sperry Chafer's work on the Holy Spirit contained no mention of revival.[99]

But far graver problems lay with the modernists who abandoned orthodox doctrine and undermined biblical authority, all in the name of accommodating modern thought. On them, Lloyd-Jones's verdict was the same as that of his heroes, B. B. Warfield and J. Gresham Machen. He claimed that pious moderates like the Scottish Free Church scholar A. B. Davidson had been more dangerous conduits for higher criticism than its extreme proponents. Spurgeon had stood out against the 'Downgrade', only to be 'ferociously attacked by evangelical people'.[100] For Lloyd-Jones, the social gospel was part and parcel of apostate Protestant liberalism. As Fred Catherwood notes, he had, 'throughout his life, attacked the social gospel' and 'tended to the view that there was no Christian attitude to politics'.[101] Though fascinated by politics, he thought that it was a corrupting business. The 'admixture of religion and politics' had bedevilled Puritan history and 'the preacher-politician' was 'the curse of the nonconformist churches' in the generation or so before 1914.[102] Quite what Lloyd-Jones made of Martin Luther King and the civil rights movement is unclear. But at Westminster Chapel he had disbanded many of the social programmes that had flourished under Campbell Morgan, and there are grounds for seeing him as part of 'the great reversal' that saw twentieth-century evangelicals shying away from the social and political involvement of their forebears.[103]

By the early 1970s, however, evangelicals were starting to rediscover the social vision of Reformed Christianity, thanks to the writings and lectures of Francis Schaeffer and Hans Rookmaaker. Lloyd-Jones's son-in-law, Fred Catherwood, was at the forefront of those urging Christian involvement,[104] and in 1975 the Doctor himself gave a lecture to the Westminster Conference on 'The Christian and the State in Revolutionary Times'. Yet even here he was deeply ambivalent about Christian politics. While paying lip service to the Kuyperian vision and suggesting (in good dissenting fashion) that Christians must not be stooges of the establishment, he also declared that 'the Christian must never get excited about reform, or about political action'.[105] This was

---

99. Lloyd-Jones, 'Revival: An Historical and Theological Survey', pp. 7–8.

100. Lloyd-Jones, 'What Is an Evangelical?', pp. 302–303.

101. Catherwood and Catherwood, *Martyn Lloyd-Jones: The Man and his Books*, p. 8.

102. Lloyd-Jones, 'Puritan Perplexities', pp. 60–61.

103. See Brencher, *Lloyd-Jones*, pp. 63–66.

104. Fred Catherwood, *The Christian in Industrial Society* (Cambridge: Tyndale Press, 1966).

105. Lloyd-Jones, 'The Christian and the State in Revolutionary Times', p. 345.

not the attitude of Christian abolitionists like William Wilberforce, but Lloyd-Jones himself was always interested in the piety and theology of evangelicalism and gave little attention to the social dimensions of Christianity. He worried that those who read Rookmaaker or Schaeffer would become too engrossed in 'the political and social and cultural implications of the gospel'.[106]

Conclusion

The historical project of Martyn Lloyd-Jones enjoyed mixed results. On the one hand, it was profoundly influential. If *Time* magazine is correct to see Calvinism as one of the ten big ideas shaping the world in the early twenty-first century,[107] then Lloyd-Jones (and the institutions he helped to found) was a major contributor to its resurgence. Through the Banner of Truth Trust he helped to popularize older Reformed literature and in doing so he undoubtedly deepened and enriched the thinking and spirituality of postwar evangelicalism. By establishing a canon of 'sound' books, the Trust played a major role in the resurgence of Calvinism across the English-speaking world and prepared the way for organizations that would define gospel unity in Calvinist terms. In Lloyd-Jones's lifetime the great obstacle to that project was the success and prestige of Billy Graham's pan-evangelicalism; the Doctor disliked Graham's drive to seek 'the widest possible sponsorship'.[108] When Graham's influence finally waned in the United States and elsewhere, the way was open for the rise of the Gospel Coalition and Together for the Gospel, movements which drew the boundaries of fellowship more tightly than the National Association of Evangelicals, or the Evangelical Alliance in the United Kingdom. Their leaders (including the Presbyterian Tim Keller and the Baptists John Piper, Mark Dever, Al Mohler and Don Carson) revered Lloyd-Jones as one of the great Christian leaders of the twentieth century. Like him, they treated differences over baptism, the millennium and charismatic gifts as 'non-essential', though they were arguably more inclined than Lloyd-Jones to exclude evangelical Arminians.[109] To varying degrees, many conservative Reformed leaders also

---

106. D. M. Lloyd-Jones, 'How to Safeguard the Future', in Lloyd-Jones, *Knowing the Times*, p. 286.

107. David van Biema, 'The New Calvinism', *Time* (12 March 2009), www.time.com.

108. Lloyd-Jones, 'What Is an Evangelical?', p. 310.

109. Lloyd-Jones included predestination and sanctification among the 'secondary issues not essential to unity'. See Lloyd-Jones, 'What Is an Evangelical?', pp. 351–354.

embraced the basic shape of the story Lloyd-Jones told about Protestantism. His rejection of Rome, his critique of mixed denominations, his praise for the Puritans, his passionate endorsement of revival and his attack on both liberal and evangelical modernizers gained an eager hearing.

Yet Lloyd-Jones's historical project also failed to command universal respect among evangelicals. Within popular evangelicalism – both in the West and in the rest of the world – there was much enthusiasm for revival but little appetite for old books and meaty Reformed theology. Among evangelical intellectuals there was bemusement and frustration at the nostalgic reverence of conservative Calvinists for the Protestant past, and a fear that this entailed an ostrich-like posture towards the challenges of modern science, scholarship and philosophy. The world's most influential evangelical biblical scholar, N. T. Wright, had admired Lloyd-Jones's preaching and even published his first book (a multi-authored defence of five-point Calvinism) with the Banner of Truth Trust.[110] But he remained firmly on the Anglican side of the Packer–Lloyd-Jones dispute and attracted much criticism from conservative evangelicals for promoting the new perspective on Paul. By the twenty-first century, evangelical projects of historical retrieval were also pushing beyond the Reformation itself, especially by delving deeply into the patristic tradition, something encouraged by Packer's friend, the Wesleyan theologian Thomas Oden.[111]

Even within neo-Puritan circles, Lloyd-Jones's vision of the Protestant past failed to win unanimous approval. Puritanism itself had been marked by significant tensions, and these tensions were reproduced in the new Puritans of the late twentieth and early twenty-first centuries. At least four competing versions of true Puritanism emerged. For Lloyd-Jones himself, Puritanism was essentially the anti-Anglican drive for a pure church, combined with warm experimental Calvinist piety (the Puritanism of the Cromwellian Congregationalists). For J. I. Packer, Puritanism was a theological and spiritual renewal movement (a continuation of early Stuart moderate Puritanism). For R. T. Kendall, Puritanism at its best was a charismatic, free grace movement (the Puritanism of the New England 'antinomians' led by John Cotton). And for Carl Trueman, the pinnacle of the Puritan achievement was to be found in scholastic Reformed orthodoxy – catholic, learned, churchly and sacramental

110. John Cheeseman, Philip Gardner, Michael Sadgrove and Tom Wright, *The Grace of God in the Gospel* (London: Banner of Truth, 1972).

111. See the volumes in the *The Ancient Christian Commentary on Scripture* series edited by Thomas Oden and published by InterVarsity Press in the United States.

(the Puritanism of the major British and Dutch Reformed theologians). Each of these visions produced a distinct kind of churchmanship and could even generate divergent spiritualities. While Lloyd-Jones's historical project was a powerful influence within evangelicalism, it was in competition with rival understandings of the Protestant past.

© John Coffey, 2011

BIBLIOGRAPHY: LLOYD-JONES AND HIS WRITINGS

Andrew Atherstone and David Ceri Jones

New material from the ministry of Martyn Lloyd-Jones continues to be published regularly and this bibliography does not claim to be comprehensive, but it is the most complete compilation of his English language publications to date. A bibliography of Lloyd-Jones's Welsh language writings has already been published in *Llais y Doctor* (Pen-y-bont yr Ogwr: Gwasg Bryntirion, 1999), pp. 156–159.

We have included only first editions of Lloyd-Jones's works, not the multiple reprints or translations. Likewise, the many newspaper and magazine extracts from his books are not listed. Individual sermons and addresses from the *Westminster Record*, the monthly magazine of Westminster Chapel, are given in chronological order, but his longer sermon series from the *Westminster Record* are listed at the end of the bibliography.

Chief biographical studies

John Brencher, *Martyn Lloyd-Jones (1899–1981) and Twentieth-Century Evangelicalism* (Carlisle: Paternoster, 2002).

Christopher Catherwood (ed.), *Martyn Lloyd-Jones: Chosen by God* (Crowborough: Highland Books, 1986).

Christopher Catherwood, *Martyn Lloyd-Jones: A Family Portrait* (Eastbourne: Kingsway, 1995).

Gaius Davies, 'Physician, Preacher and Politician: Dr D. Martyn Lloyd-Jones (1899–
    1981)', in Gaius Davies, *Genius, Grief and Grace: A Doctor Looks at Suffering and Success*
    (Fearn: Christian Focus, 2001), pp. 331–378.

Iain H. Murray, *D. Martyn Lloyd-Jones: The First Forty Years 1899–1938* (Edinburgh: Banner
    of Truth, 1982).

Iain H. Murray, *D. Martyn Lloyd-Jones: The Fight of Faith 1939–1981* (Edinburgh: Banner of
    Truth, 1990).

Iain H. Murray, *Lloyd-Jones: Messenger of Grace* (Edinburgh: Banner of Truth, 2008).

John Peters, *Martyn Lloyd-Jones, Preacher* (Exeter: Paternoster, 1986).

Tony Sargent, *The Sacred Anointing: The Preaching of Dr Martyn Lloyd-Jones* (London: Hodder
    and Stoughton, 1994).

Chronological bibliography

1929

Reviews
A. T. Schofield, *Christian Sanity* (London: Marshall, Morgan and Scott, 1926), in *Yr
    Efengylydd*, vol. 20, no. 1 (15 January 1929), pp. 6–8.

1933

Articles
'The Lordship of Christ', *Yr Efengylydd*, vol. 25, no. 1 (15 January 1933), pp. 7–8.

1935

Sermons, lectures and addresses
'Have Mercy On Us', *Sunday Companion*, vol. 82 (16 March 1935), p. 265.

1936

Medical writings
Charles B. Perry, *Bacterial Endocarditis . . . With an Appendix on an Experimental Study on
    Malignant Endocarditis by D. M. Lloyd-Jones* (Bristol: J. Wright and Sons, 1936).

328 ENGAGING WITH MARTYN LLOYD-JONES

Sermons, lectures and addresses

Proclaiming Eternal Verities: The Addresses Delivered at the Thirteenth Great Demonstration Organised by the Bible Testimony Fellowship in Support of the Full Inspiration of the Bible at the Royal Albert Hall on December 3rd 1935 (London: Marshall, Morgan and Scott, 1936), pp. 17–29.

'True Christian Discipleship', *Christian World Pulpit*, vol. 129 (16 January 1936), pp. 30–33.

'The Hope of the Christian', *Christian World Pulpit*, vol. 130 (10 September 1936), pp. 129–131.

'The Narrowness of the Gospel', *Westminster Record*, vol. 10, no. 4 (April 1936), pp. 70–77.

1937

Sermons, lectures and addresses

'Psalm 107', *Westminster Record*, vol. 11, no. 8 (August 1937), pp. 149–158.

'How to be a Happy Christian', *Christian Herald* (5 August 1937), pp. 97–98.

'A Cheerful Song for Depressed People', *Christian Herald* (2 September 1937), pp. 185–186.

1938

Sermons, lectures and addresses

'Zeal without Knowledge', *Westminster Record*, vol. 12, nos. 8–9 (August – September 1938), pp. 150–155, 170–174.

'The Lordship of Christ in the Life of Today', *Westminster Record*, vol. 12, no. 10 (October 1938), pp. 191–196.

'The Shunammite Woman', *Westminster Record*, vol. 12, no. 12 (December 1938), pp. 230–233, and vol. 13, no. 1 (January 1939), pp. 10–16.

'The Problem of Miracles', *Christian Herald* (17 March 1938), p. 245.

'The Vital Principle of Religion', *Christian Herald* (27 October 1938), pp. 334–335.

'The Miracle of Grace', *Christian World Pulpit*, vol. 134 (13 October 1938), pp. 174–177.

'The Problem of Suffering', *Christian World Pulpit*, vol. 134 (29 December 1938), pp. 301–303.

1939

Sermons, lectures and addresses

'The Inestimable Value of Prayer: A New Year Reminder', *Evangelical Christendom* (January – February 1939), pp. 1–3.

'The Irreligion of Self-Content', *Christian World Pulpit*, vol. 135 (23 March 1939), pp. 138–140.

'The Motives and Methods of the Missionary Enterprise', *Christian World Pulpit*, vol. 135 (25 May 1939), pp. 241–244.

'The Corner-Stone of the Christian Faith', *Christian World Pulpit*, vol. 136 (13 July 1939), pp. 13–15.

'The Lordship of Christ', *Inter-Varsity Magazine*, vol. 12, no. 1 (Michaelmas Term 1939), pp. 5–8.

'Life's Preparatory School', *Westminster Record*, vol. 13, no. 3 (March 1939), pp. 51–57.

'The Final Consolation', *Westminster Record*, vol. 13, no. 5 (May 1939), pp. 90–96.

'The Motives and Methods of the Missionary Enterprise', *Westminster Record*, vol. 13, no. 8 (August 1939), pp. 150–158.

'The Nature of Prayer', *Westminster Record*, vol. 13, no. 11 (November 1939), pp. 206–211.

'Facing the Unexpected', *Westminster Record*, vol. 13, no. 12 (December 1939), pp. 222–231.

Why Does God Allow War? (London: Hodder and Stoughton, 1939).

Forewords and introductions

J. C. M. Conn, *The Menace of the New Psychology* (London: Inter-Varsity Fellowship, 1939).

Reviews

D. R. Davies, *On to Orthodoxy* (London: Hodder and Stoughton, 1939), in *Christian World* (12 October 1939), p. 4.

R. E. D. Clark, *The Universe and God: A Study of the Order of Nature in the Light of Modern Knowledge* (London: Hodder and Stoughton, 1939), in *Inter-Varsity Magazine*, vol. 11, no. 3 (Easter Term 1939), p. 40.

1940

Sermons, lectures and addresses

'Christ our Sanctification', in *Christ our Freedom: The Message of the Fourth International Conference of Evangelical Students, Cambridge, 1939* (London: Inter-Varsity Fellowship, 1940), pp. 54–78.

'The Mystery of God's Ways', *Westminster Record*, vol. 14, no. 1 (January 1940), pp. 6–15.

'Why Does God Allow War?', *Westminster Record*, vol. 14, no. 2 (February 1940), pp. 22–33.

'The Final Answer to All Our Questions', *Westminster Record*, vol. 14, no. 3 (March 1940), pp. 43–54.

'The Science of Sin', *Westminster Record*, vol. 14, no. 4 (April 1940), pp. 62–68.

'The Divine Wisdom', *Westminster Record*, vol. 14, no. 7 (July 1940), pp. 103–108.

'A Little Maid's Testimony', *Westminster Record*, vol. 14, no. 12 (December 1940), pp. 169–175.

'The Science of Sin', *Christian World Pulpit*, vol. 137 (8 February 1940), pp. 61–63.

'The Divine Wisdom', *Christian World Pulpit*, vol. 137 (20 June 1940), pp. 289–291.

'A Little Maid's Testimony', *Christian World Pulpit*, vol. 138 (21 November 1940), pp. 246–247.

'One Supreme Need Today', *Christian Herald* (31 October 1940), p. 285.

Reviews

Emil Brunner, *Man in Revolt: A Christian Anthropology*, trans. Olive Wyon (Cambridge: Lutterworth Press, 1939), in *Inter-Varsity Magazine*, vol. 12, no. 2 (Lent Term 1940), pp. 29–30.

1941

Sermons, lectures and addresses

'The Signs of the Times', *Westminster Record*, vol. 15, no. 1 (January 1941), pp. 6–13.

'Christ our Sanctification', *Westminster Record*, vol. 15, nos. 2–4 (February – April 1941), pp. 22–28, 34–39, 46–48.

'Why I Believe the Cross Is God's Way of Saving Men', *Westminster Record*, vol. 15, no. 5 (May 1941), pp. 57–63.

'Ye Are the Light of the World', *Westminster Record*, vol. 15, no. 7 (July 1941), pp. 82–85.

'The Nature of Sin', *Westminster Record*, vol. 15, no. 8 (August 1941), pp. 98–104.

'The Preaching of the Cross', *Christian World Pulpit*, vol. 139 (15 May 1941), pp. 232–233.

'Sin and its Consequences', *Christian World Pulpit*, vol. 140 (24 July 1941), pp. 25–26.

'Asleep in the Hour of Crisis', *Christian Herald* (3 April 1941), p. 224.

Reviews

Jacob T. Hoogstra (ed.), *The Sovereignty of God* (Grand Rapids, MI: Zondervan, 1941), in *Inter-Varsity Magazine*, vol. 14, no. 1 (Michaelmas Term 1941), p. 31.

1942

Sermons, lectures and addresses

The Plight of Man and the Power of God (London: Hodder and Stoughton, 1942).

The Presentation of the Gospel (London: Crusaders Union, 1942); reprinted in *Westminster Record*, vol. 16, nos. 4–5 (April – May 1942), pp. 47–52, 58–64.

'The Bible and Today', in *There Is But One! A Series of Addresses Issued by the Bible Witness Rally* (Stirling: Drummond Tract Society, 1942), pp. 29–39; reprinted in *Westminster Record*, vol. 17, no. 7 (July 1943), pp. 49–54.

'Religion and Morality (Romans 1:18)', *Evangelical Quarterly*, vol. 14, no. 1 (January 1942), pp. 9–21; reprinted in *Westminster Record*, vol. 16, nos. 2–3 (February – March 1942), pp. 23–28, 34–39.

'The Meaning of the Resurrection', *Christian World Pulpit*, vol. 141 (23 April 1942), pp. 132–134.

'Sounding the Alarm', *Christian World Pulpit*, vol. 142 (27 August 1942), pp. 68–70.

'The Fact of the Resurrection', *Westminster Record*, vol. 16, no. 7 (July 1942), pp. 73–80.

Reviews

C. S. Lewis, *The Screwtape Letters* (London: Geoffrey Bles, 1942), in *Inter-Varsity Magazine*, vol. 14, no. 3 (Summer Term 1942), p. 23.

T. C. Hammond, *Fading Light* (London: Marshall, Morgan and Scott, 1942), in *Inter-Varsity Magazine*, vol. 14, no. 2 (Lent Term 1942), pp. 31–32.

1943

Sermons, lectures and addresses

'Paul's Order of the Day – "Watch Ye"', *Inter-Varsity Magazine*, vol. 15, no. 2 (Lent Term 1943), pp. 2–4.

Reviews

'More Studies of the Disruption', *Evangelical Quarterly*, vol. 15, no. 4 (October 1943), pp. 309–310.

1944

Sermons, lectures and addresses

'Spirit, Soul and Body: Problems Confronting Christians in a Time of War', *Westminster Record*, vol. 18, no. 5 (May 1944), pp. 33–41.

'Hearkening to the Gospel', *Westminster Record*, vol. 18, no. 6 (June 1944), pp. 47–50.

Forewords and introductions

G. N. M. Collins, *Donald Maclean* (Edinburgh: Lindsay, 1944).

1945

Sermons, lectures and addresses

'The Conquest of the Fear of Death', *Westminster Record*, vol. 19, no. 1 (January 1945), pp. 1–7.

'The Evangelical Library', *Evangelical Quarterly*, vol. 17, no. 3 (July 1945), pp. 223–225.

Articles

'The Late Professor D. M. Blair', *Evangelical Quarterly*, vol. 17, no. 1 (January 1945), pp. 3–4.

'Tribute to Dr G. Campbell Morgan', *Westminster Record*, vol. 19, no. 7 (July 1945), pp. 60–64.

Reviews

A. D. Lindsay, Emil Brunner, A. M. Murray, et al., *The Predicament of the Church: Contemporary Essays* (London and Redhill: Lutterworth Press, 1944), in *Inter-Varsity Magazine*, vol. 17, no. 2 (Spring Term 1945), pp. 23–24.

Franz Hilderbrandt, *This Is the Message: A Continental Reply to Charles Raven* (London and Redhill: Lutterworth Press, 1944), in *Inter-Varsity Magazine*, vol. 17, no. 2 (Spring Term 1945), p. 23.

Forewords and introductions

Duncan M. Blair, *The Beginning of Wisdom* (London: Inter-Varsity Fellowship, 1945).

1946

Sermons, lectures and addresses

'The Wider Evangelism: The Uniqueness of the Gospel', *Evangelical Christendom* (January – March 1946), pp. 1–2.

'Christ and the Wisdom of this World', *Westminster Record*, vol. 20, no. 10 (October 1946), pp. 73–80.

'Advent and History', *Westminster Record*, vol. 20, no. 12 (December 1946), pp. 89–96.

1947

Sermons, lectures and addresses

'Jesus Christ the Same Yesterday, and Today, and For Ever', *Westminster Record*, vol. 21, no. 1 (January 1947), pp. 1–8.

'"He Comes Himself to Save You": A Christmas Message', *Westminster Record*, vol. 21, no. 12 (December 1947), pp. 89–96.

Forewords and introductions
Philip Edgcumbe Hughes, *Revive Us Again* (London: Marshall Morgan and Scott, 1947).

1948

Sermons, lectures and addresses
Christ our Sanctification (London: Inter-Varsity Fellowship, 1948).
'"The Mirage Shall Become a Pool": A New Year Message', *Westminster Record*, vol. 22, no. 1 (January 1948), pp. 1–9.
'The Christian View of the Universe', *Christian Graduate*, vol. 1, no. 4 (December 1948), pp. 6–8.
'The Universal Week of Prayer', *Evangelical Christendom* (January – March 1948), pp. 13–16.

Articles
'Know Thyself', *Spurgeon's College Magazine* (Midsummer 1948), pp. 2–4.
'Notes on Two Stimulating Discussions', *Christian Graduate*, vol. 1, no. 1 (March 1948), pp. 21–22.
'The Position of Evangelicals in their Churches', *Westminster Record*, vol. 22, nos. 3–5 (March – May 1948), pp. 33–35, 36–38, 57–59.

Correspondence
'Medical Missions', letter to the editor, *The Times* (15 September 1948), p. 6.

1949

Sermons, lectures and addresses
'Christ and the Unconscious Mind', *Christian Graduate*, vol. 2, no. 3 (September 1949), pp. 81–84.

Forewords and introductions
Mrs Howard Taylor, *Pastor Hsi: Confucian Scholar and Christian* (London: China Inland Mission, 1949).

1950

Sermons, lectures and addresses

'The Wondrous Cross', *Westminster Record*, vol. 24, no. 3 (March 1950), pp. 25–33.

'Illusion and Reality', *Westminster Record*, vol. 24, no. 4 (April 1950), pp. 37–46.

1951

Sermons, lectures and addresses

'Healing: Miraculous and Psychotherapeutic: Notes of a discussion conducted by Dr
    Martyn Lloyd-Jones', *Christian Graduate*, vol. 4, no. 1 (March 1951), pp. 22–24.

Truth Unchanged, Unchanging (London: James Clarke, 1951).

'Mr E. Emlyn Davies, F.R.C.O.: Memorial Service', *Westminster Record*, vol. 25, no. 7 (July
    1951), pp. 83–87.

Forewords and introductions

Henry W. Frost, *Miraculous Healing* (London: Marshall, Morgan and Scott, 1951).

E. J. Poole-Connor, *Evangelicalism in England* (London: Fellowship of Independent
    Evangelical Churches, 1951).

1952

Sermons, lectures and addresses

Honour to whom Honour: Sermon Preached on the Death of King George VI (London:
    Westminster Chapel, 1952).

Maintaining the Evangelical Faith Today (London: Inter-Varsity Fellowship, 1952).

The Place of the Law in the Divine Economy (London: Lawyers' Christian Fellowship, 1952).

Forewords and introductions

J. C. Ryle, *Holiness: Its Nature, Hindrances, Difficulties and Roots* (Cambridge: James Clarke,
    1952).

Reviews

B. B. Warfield, *Biblical and Theological Studies*, ed. Samuel G. Craig (Philadelphia:
    Presbyterian and Reformed Publishing Co., 1952), in *Inter-Varsity Magazine* (Summer
    Term 1952), pp. 27–28.

1953

Sermons, lectures and addresses
From Fear to Faith (London: Inter-Varsity Press, 1953).

Correspondence
'Fair and Kind', letter to the editor, *British Weekly* (26 March 1953), p. 9.

Reviews
'Professor Berkouwer's Theology', *Evangelical Quarterly*, vol. 25, no. 2 (April 1953), pp. 107–110.

1954

Sermons, lectures and addresses
'Living Near to God', *Christian World Pulpit*, vol. 166 (11 November 1954), pp. 154–156.
'The Doctor Himself', *In the Service of Medicine*, no. 3 (February 1954), pp. 1–4.

1955

Sermons, lectures and addresses
'Address', *Annual Meeting of the Evangelical Library* (1955), pp. 11–16.

1956

Sermons, lectures and addresses
'Address', *Annual Meeting of the Evangelical Library* (1956), pp. 12–16.

Reviews
'Works of Professor Berkouwer', *Evangelical Quarterly*, vol. 28, no. 1 (January – March 1956), pp. 46–48.

1957

Sermons, lectures and addresses
'Evangelical Principles Essential to Revival', *Life of Faith* (7 February 1957), pp. 89–90.

'Stock-Taking', *Westminster Record*, vol. 31, no. 2 (February 1957), pp. 13–23.
'"But I Say Unto You": The True Exposition of the Law, Quotations from sermons
    preached in Westminster Chapel, London, by the Rev. Dr D. Martyn Lloyd-Jones on
    Matthew 5, vs 21 and 22, 38 and 39', *Evangelical Magazine of Wales*, vol. 1, no. 7 (Spring
    – Summer 1957), pp. 36–45.
'His Kingdom Is Forever', *Christianity Today*, vol. 2, no. 5 (9 December 1957), pp. 3–6.
'Medicine and "The Whole Man"', *In the Service of Medicine*, no. 9 (March 1957), pp. 1–7.
Sound an Alarm (London: Westminster Chapel, 1957).

1958

Sermons, lectures and addresses

Authority (London: Inter-Varsity Press, 1958).
'The Christian and the State – With Special Reference to Medicine', *In the Service of
    Medicine*, no. 12 (January 1958), pp. 1–14.
'A Christmas Message', *Westminster Record*, vol. 32, no. 12 (December 1958), pp. 133–143.

Forewords and introductions

B. B. Warfield, *Biblical Foundations* (London: Tyndale Press, 1958).
George Burrows, *The Song of Solomon* (London, Banner of Truth, 1958).
George Whitefield, *Select Sermons* (London: Banner of Truth, 1958).
Robert Haldane, *Exposition of the Epistle to the Romans* (London: Banner of Truth, 1958).
Ned B. Stonehouse and Paul Woolley (eds.), *The Infallible Word* (Grand Rapids, MI:
    Eerdmans, 1958).
Searching the Word: A Method for Personal Bible Study (Bala: Evangelical Press of Wales,
    1958).
Vincent Edmunds and C. Gordon Scorer (eds.), *Ideals in Medicine: A Christian Approach to
    Medical Practice* (London: Tyndale Press for the Christian Medical Fellowship, 1958).
William B. Sprague, *Lectures on Revivals of Religion* (London: Banner of Truth, 1958).

1959

Sermons, lectures and addresses

Conversions: Psychological and Spiritual (London: Inter-Varsity Press, 1959).
'A New Heaven and a New Earth: A New Year Message', *Westminster Record*, vol. 33, no. 1
    (January 1959), pp. 1–11.
'Address', *Annual Meeting of the Evangelical Library* (1959), pp. 3–8.
Studies in the Sermon on the Mount (Matthew 5), vol. 1 (London: Inter-Varsity Press, 1959).

Forewords and introductions

William Hendriksen, *Commentary on the Gospel of John* (London: Banner of Truth, 1959).

1960

Sermons, lectures and address

'Revival: An Historical and Theological Survey', in *How Shall They Hear? A Symposium of Papers Read at the Puritan and Reformed Studies Conference, December 1959* (London: Evangelical Magazine, 1960), pp. 38–56.

Studies in the Sermon on the Mount (Matthew 6 & 7), vol. 2 (London: Inter-Varsity Press, 1960).

'Address', *Annual Meeting of the Evangelical Library* (1960), pp. 12–15.

1961

Sermons, lectures and addresses

'Knowledge – False and True', in *Increasing in the Knowledge of God: Papers Read at the Puritan and Reformed Studies Conference, 20th and 21st December 1960* (London: Evangelical Magazine, 1961), pp. 47–63.

'Address', *Annual Meeting of the Evangelical Library* (1961), pp. 16–22.

1962

Sermons, lectures and addresses

1662–1962: From Puritanism to Non-conformity (London: Evangelical Library, 1962).

'Summing Up', in *Press Towards the Mark: Papers Read at the Puritan and Reformed Studies Conference, 19th and 20th December 1961* (London: Evangelical Magazine, 1962), pp. 74–80.

'Beware that Thou Forget Not: A Message Given at the Dedication Service of the I.V.F. New Office Building, 29 September 1961', *Christian Graduate*, vol. 15, no. 1 (March 1962), pp. 1–6.

'Man in the Presence of God', *Evangelical Magazine of Wales*, vol. 2, no. 2 (July – August 1962), pp. 36–40.

The Basis of Christian Unity: An Exposition of John 17 and Ephesians 4 (London: Inter-Varsity Fellowship, 1962).

'Truth Unchanged' (National Bible Rally address), *Free Grace Record*, vol. 2, no. 11 (Summer 1962), pp. 322–335; reprinted in *Evangelical Magazine of Wales*, vol. 2, no. 5 (February – March 1963), pp. 8–10; vol. 2, no. 6 (April – May 1963), pp. 6–9.

'Address', *Annual Meeting of the Evangelical Library* (1962), pp. 13–20.

Forewords and introductions
Richard Bennett, *The Early Life of Howell Harris* (London: Banner of Truth, 1962).

1963

Sermons, lectures and addresses
'Puritan Perplexities – Some Lessons from 1640–1662', in *Faith and a Good Conscience: Papers Read at the Puritan and Reformed Studies Conference, 18th and 19th December 1962* (London: Evangelical Magazine, 1963), pp. 64–80.

The Approach to Truth: Scientific and Religious (London: Tyndale Press for the Christian Medical Fellowship, 1963).

'Address', *Annual Meeting of the Evangelical Library* (1963), pp. 9–16.

1964

Sermons, lectures and addresses
'John Owen on Schism', in *Diversity in Unity: Papers Read at the Puritan and Reformed Studies Conference, December 1963* (London: Evangelical Magazine, 1964), pp. 59–80.

The Weapons of our Warfare, Campbell Morgan Memorial Lecture (London: Westminster Chapel, 1964).

'Address', *Annual Meeting of the Evangelical Library* (1964), pp. 15–24.

Reviews
Cornelius Van Til, *Christianity and Barthianism* (Philadelphia: Presbyterian and Reformed Publishing Co., 1962), in *Westminster Theological Journal*, vol. 27 (November 1964), pp. 52–55.

Forewords and introductions
J. H. Alexander, *More Than Notion* (London: Fauconberg Press, 1964).

1965

Sermons, lectures and addresses
Faith on Trial (London: Inter-Varsity Press, 1965).

'John Calvin and George Whitefield', in *Able Ministers of the New Testament: Papers Read at the Puritan and Reformed Studies Conference, December 1964* (London: Evangelical Magazine, 1965), pp. 75–96.

The Mirage Shall Become a Pool (London: Evangelical Press, 1965).
Spiritual Depression: Its Causes and Cure (London: Pickering and Inglis, 1965).
The Centenary of Westminster Chapel, 1865–1965 (London: Westminster Chapel, 1965).
'Address', *Annual Meeting of the Evangelical Library* (1965), pp. 15–24.

Articles

'Why I am a Christian . . .', in *This I Believe . . .* (London: Pickering and Inglis, 1965), pp. 5–6.

1966

Sermons, lectures and addresses

'Ecclesiola in Ecclesia', in *Approaches to Reformation of the Church* (London: Evangelical Magazine, 1966), pp. 57–72.
Roman Catholicism (London: Evangelical Press, 1966).
'The Problem of Diagnosis', *In the Service of Medicine*, no. 44 (January 1966), pp. 1–6.
'Address', *Annual Meeting of the Evangelical Library* (1966), pp. 25–30.

Forewords and introductions

David Fountain, *Contender for the Faith: E. J. Poole-Connor, 1872–1962* (Worthing: Henry Walter, 1966).

1967

Sermons, lectures and addresses

'Henry Jacob and the First Congregational Church', in *One Steadfast High Intent* (London: Evangelical Magazine, 1967), pp. 56–72.
'Man Himself – The Vital Factor', in Vincent Edmunds and C. Gordon Scorer (eds.), *Ethical Responsibility in Medicine: A Christian Approach* (Edinburgh and London: E. & S. Livingstone, 1967), pp. 181–197.
'The Evangelical Library Address', *Annual Meeting of the Evangelical Library* (1967), pp. 13–22.

Forewords and introductions

John Wilmot, *Inspired Principles of Prophetic Interpretation* (Toronto: Gospel Witness, 1967).

1968

Sermons, lectures and addresses

'Address and Appeal', in *Why the Evangelical Library Must Go On: An Urgent Appeal*
(London: Evangelical Library, 1968), pp. 5–16.

Luther and His Message for Today (London: Evangelical Press for the British Evangelical
Council, 1968).

'Sandemanianism', in *Profitable for Doctrine and Reproof* (London: Evangelical Magazine,
1968), pp. 54–71.

Forewords and introductions

John Fletcher, *Christ Manifested* (London: Christian Literature Crusade, 1968).

Klaas Runia, *Reformation Today* (London: Banner of Truth, 1968).

Peter M. Masters, *Men of Destiny* (London: Evangelical Times, 1968).

Correspondence

'To the Church at Westminster Chapel, 30 May 1968', in *The Banner of Truth*, no. 57 (June
1968), pp. 4–5.

1969

Sermons, lectures and addresses

'The Making or Breaking of a Registrar: A Study of Stress: A Minister's View', *In the
Service of Medicine*, no. 58 (July 1969), pp. 15–22.

Will Hospital Replace the Church? (London: Christian Medical Fellowship, 1969).

'William Williams and Welsh Calvinistic Methodism', in *The Manifold Grace of God: Papers
Read at the Puritan and Reformed Studies Conference, 1968* (London: Evangelical Magazine,
1969), pp. 76–95.

What Is the Church? (London: Evangelical Press for The British Evangelical Council, 1969).

'Address', *Annual Meeting of the Evangelical Library* (1969), pp. 12–24.

Articles

'The Significance of Karl Barth', *Evangelical Times* (January 1969), pp. 1, 6.

'Emyn' (translation of H. Elvet Lewis's hymn 'Rho im yr hedd'), *Evangelical Library
Bulletin*, no. 42 (Spring 1969), p. 14.

Interviews

Gaius Davies and Martyn Lloyd-Jones, 'Nationalism, Tradition and Language', *Evangelical
Magazine of Wales*, vol. 8, no. 4 (August – September 1969), pp. 5–11.

Forewords and introductions

Eifion Evans, *The Welsh Revival of 1904* (Port Talbot: Evangelical Movement of Wales, 1969).

1970

Sermons, lectures and addresses

'Can We Learn from History?', in *By Schisms Rent Asunder: Papers Read at the Puritan and Reformed Studies Conference, 1969* (London: Evangelical Magazine, 1970), pp. 69–86.

Romans: An Exposition of Chapters 3.20 – 4.25: Atonement and Justification (Edinburgh: Banner of Truth, 1970).

'The Awakener' (George Whitefield), *Evangelical Times* (November 1970), pp. 12–13.

Articles

'Problem Texts: 1 Samuel 28:7–20', *Evangelical Magazine of Wales*, vol. 9, no. 3 (June – July 1970), p. 12.

Interviews

'Preaching and Preachers: An Interview Given to One of the Editors by Dr Martyn Lloyd-Jones', *Evangelical Magazine of Wales*, vol. 9, no. 4 (August – September 1970), pp. 9–10.

Forewords and introductions

Arnold Dallimore, *George Whitefield: The Life and Times of the Great Evangelist of the Eighteenth Century Revival*, vol. 1 (London: Banner of Truth, 1970).

Mari Jones, *Trwy Lygad y Bugail* (Port Talbot: Mudiad Efengylaidd Cymru, 1970).

1971

Sermons, lectures and addresses

Preaching and Preachers (London: Hodder and Stoughton, 1971).

Romans: An Exposition of Chapter 5: Assurance (Edinburgh: Banner of Truth, 1971).

The Supernatural in the Practice of Medicine (London: Christian Medical Fellowship, 1971).

The State of the Nation (London: Evangelical Press for The British Evangelical Council, 1971).

Articles

'Tributes to Warfield: Defender of the Faith', *The Banner of Truth*, no. 89 (February 1971), pp. 16–18.

Correspondence

'Lord Northcliffe's Death', letter to the editor, *The Times* (11 December 1973), p. 13.

1972

Sermons, lectures and addresses

God's Way of Reconciliation: Studies in Ephesians Chapter Two (London: Evangelical Press,
    1972).

'On Treating the Whole Man', in R. E. Tunbridge, A. S. Aldis and D. M. Lloyd-Jones, *On
    Treating the Whole Man* (London: Christian Medical Fellowship, 1972), pp. 6–16.

'Puritanism and its Origins', in *The Good Fight of Faith: Papers Read at the Westminster
    Conference, 1971* (London: Westminster Conference, 1971), pp. 72–90.

Romans: An Exposition of Chapter 6: The New Man (Edinburgh: Banner of Truth, 1972).

The Doctor as Counsellor, Guidelines, no. 45 (London: Christian Medical Fellowship,
    1972).

Forewords and introductions

Lewis Lupton, *History of the Geneva Bible, Volume 4: Travail* (London: Olive Tree, 1972).

Mari Jones, *In the Shadow of Aran*, trans. Bethan Lloyd-Jones (Port Talbot: Evangelical
    Movement of Wales, 1972).

1973

Sermons, lectures and addresses

'John Knox: The Founder of Puritanism', in *Becoming a Christian* (London: Westminster
    Conference, 1973), pp. 95–111.

Romans: An Exposition of Chapter 7:1 – 8:4: The Law: Its Functions and Limits (Edinburgh:
    Banner of Truth, 1973).

'The Altar and the Fire: Notes of an Address by Dr D. M. Lloyd-Jones', *The Banner of
    Truth*, no. 122 (November 1973), pp. 1–5.

Interviews

'Lloyd-Jones Talks to Joan Bakewell', *Evangelical Magazine of Wales*, vol. 12, no. 1
    (February – March 1973), pp. 8–11.

Forewords and introductions

William Williams, *The Experience Meeting*, trans. Bethan Lloyd-Jones (Port Talbot:
    Evangelical Movement of Wales, 1973).

1974

Sermons, lectures and addresses

'Closing Address', *Evangelical Library Bulletin*, no. 52 (Spring 1974), pp. 9–10.

'Howell Harris and Revival', in *Adding to the Church* (London: Westminster Conference, 1974), pp. 66–81.

'This Man Was a Spiritual Statesman' (funeral tribute for W. T. H. Richards), *Dedication*, vol. 6, no. 6 (November – December 1974), pp. 20–21.

Life in the Spirit: In Marriage, Home and Work: An Exposition of Ephesians 5:18 to 6:9 (Edinburgh: Banner of Truth, 1974).

Romans: An Exposition of Chapter 8:5–17: The Sons of God (Edinburgh: Banner of Truth, 1974).

1975

Sermons, lectures and addresses

'Closing Address', *Evangelical Library Bulletin*, no. 54 (Spring 1975), p. 6.

'Fight for Survival' (memorial address for W. T. H. Richards), *Dedication*, vol. 7, no. 1 (January – February 1975), pp. 11–16.

'Tribute to Mr Geoffrey Williams', *Evangelical Library Bulletin*, no. 55 (Autumn 1975), pp. 2–3.

'New Developments in the 18th and 19th Century Teaching', in *Living the Christian Life* (London: Westminster Conference, 1975), pp. 82–99.

Romans: An Exposition of Chapter 8:17–39: The Final Perseverance of the Saints (Edinburgh: Banner of Truth, 1975).

Interviews

'Twenty-Five Years On', *Evangelical Magazine of Wales*, vol. 14, no. 2 (April – May 1975), pp. 8–9, 11; *The Banner of Truth*, no. 141 (June 1975), pp. 17–21; *Westminster Record*, vol. 50, nos. 8–9 (August – September 1975), pp. 93–96, 106–108.

Forewords and introductions

Peter Lewis, *The Genius of Puritanism* (Haywards Heath: Carey, 1975).

1976

Sermons, lectures and addresses

'Closing Address', *Evangelical Library Bulletin*, no. 56 (Spring 1976), pp. 5–7.

'Emotion', *Evangelical Magazine of Wales*, vol. 15, no. 5 (October – November 1975), pp. 20–22.

'The French Revolution and After', in *The Christian and the State in Revolutionary Times* (London: Westminster Conference, 1976), pp. 94–110.

The Christian Warfare: An Exposition of Ephesians 6:10 to 13 (Edinburgh: Banner of Truth, 1976).

Forewords and introductions

Thelma H. Jenkins, *John Bunyan's 'The Holy War' – A Version for Today* (London: Evangelical Press, 1976).

1977

Sermons, lectures and addresses

'Jonathan Edwards and the Crucial Importance of Revival', in *The Puritan Experiment in the New World* (London: Westminster Conference, 1977), pp. 103–121.

The Christian Soldier: An Exposition of Ephesians 6:10 to 20 (Edinburgh: Banner of Truth, 1977).

1978

Sermons, lectures and addresses

'Address by the Chairman', *Evangelical Library Bulletin*, no. 60 (Spring 1978), pp. 7–10.

God's Ultimate Purpose: An Exposition of Ephesians One (Edinburgh: Banner of Truth, 1978).

London Theological Seminary Inaugural Address (London: London Theological Seminary, 1978).

'Preaching', in *Anglican and Puritan Thinking* (London: Westminster Conference, 1978), pp. 89–102.

1979

Sermons, lectures and addresses

'John Bunyan: Church Union', in *Light from John Bunyan and other Puritans* (London: Westminster Conference, 1979), pp. 86–102.

The Unsearchable Riches of Christ: An Exposition of Ephesians 3:1 to 21 (Edinburgh: Banner of Truth, 1979).

1980

Sermons, lectures and addresses
Christian Unity: An Exposition of Ephesians 4:1 to 16 (Edinburgh: Banner of Truth, 1980).

Interviews
'Martyn Lloyd-Jones: From Buckingham to Westminster: An Interview with Carl F. H. Henry', *Christianity Today*, vol. 24, no. 3 (8 February 1980), pp. 27–34; reprinted in *The Banner of Truth*, no. 200 (May 1980), pp. 18–20; *Evangelical Magazine of Wales*, vol. 19, no. 3 (June – July 1980), pp. 9–12, 15.

1981

Sermons, lectures and addresses
'Jesus Christ and Him Crucified', *Evangelical Magazine of Wales*, vol. 20, no. 2 (April 1981), pp. 4–13.
'Paradise Lost and Regained', *Evangelical Magazine of Wales*, vol. 20, no. 2 (April 1981), pp. 27–35.
The Cross: The Vindication of God (Edinburgh: Banner of Truth, 1981).

1982

Sermons, lectures and addresses
Darkness and Light: An Exposition of Ephesians 4:17 to 5:17 (Edinburgh: Banner of Truth, 1982).
The Doctor Himself and the Human Condition (London: Christian Medical Fellowship, 1982).

1983

Sermons, lectures and addresses
Evangelistic Sermons at Aberavon (Edinburgh: Banner of Truth, 1983).
Expository Sermons on 2 Peter (Edinburgh: Banner of Truth, 1983).

1984

Sermons, lectures and addresses
Joy Unspeakable: The Baptism with the Holy Spirit (Eastbourne: Kingsway, 1984).

1985

Sermons, lectures and addresses

Prove All Things: The Sovereign Work of the Spirit (Eastbourne: Kingsway, 1985).
Romans: An Exposition of Chapter 1: The Gospel of God (Edinburgh: Banner of Truth,
    1985).

1986

Sermons, lectures and addresses

I Am Not Ashamed: Advice to Timothy (London: Hodder and Stoughton, 1986).
Revival (London: Marshall Pickering, 1986).
The Cross: God's Way of Salvation (Eastbourne: Kingsway, 1986).
The Miracle of Grace and Other Messages (Grand Rapids, MI: Baker, 1986).
'Don't Go By the Label', *Evangelicals Now* (July 1986), pp. 10–11.

Articles

'The Wisdom of Martyn Lloyd-Jones', *The Banner of Truth*, nos. 275–276 (August –
    September 1986), pp. 7–12.

1987

Sermons, lectures and addresses

Out of the Depths: Studies in Psalm 51 (Bridgend: Evangelical Press of Wales, 1987).
*The Puritans: Their Origins and Successors: Addresses Delivered at the Puritan and Westminster
    Conferences, 1959–1978* (Edinburgh: Banner of Truth, 1987).
Faith Tried and Triumphant (Leicester: Inter-Varsity Press, 1987).
Healing and Medicine (Eastbourne: Kingsway, 1987).

1988

Sermons, lectures and addresses

Saved in Eternity (Eastbourne: Kingsway, 1988).
Safe in the World (Eastbourne: Kingsway, 1988).

1989

Sermons, lectures and addresses

Growing in the Spirit (Eastbourne: Kingsway, 1989).

Knowing the Times: Addresses Delivered on Various Occasions, 1942–1977 (Edinburgh: Banner of Truth, 1989).

Romans: An Exposition of Chapter 2:1 to 3:20: The Righteous Judgment of God (Edinburgh: Banner of Truth, 1989).

Sanctified Through the Truth (Eastbourne: Kingsway, 1989).

The Life of Joy: Philippians Volume One, Chapters One and Two (London: Hodder and Stoughton, 1989).

1990

Sermons, lectures and addresses

The Life of Peace: Philippians Volume Two, Chapters Three and Four (London: Hodder and Stoughton, 1990).

'The Skeletons in Dr Lloyd-Jones' Cupboard', *The Banner of Truth*, no. 320 (May 1990), pp. 8–14.

1991

Sermons, lectures and addresses

Enjoying the Presence of God: Studies in the Psalms (Eastbourne: Crossway, 1991).

Hywel Rees Jones (ed.), *Unity in Truth: Addresses Given by Dr D. Martyn Lloyd-Jones at Meetings Held under the Auspices of the British Evangelical Council* (Darlington: Evangelical Press, 1991).

Romans: An Exposition of Chapter 9: God's Sovereign Purpose (Edinburgh: Banner of Truth, 1991).

The Heart of the Gospel: Who Jesus Is and Why He Came (Eastbourne: Crossway, 1991).

1992

Sermons, lectures and addresses

The Kingdom of God (Cambridge: Crossway, 1992).

1993

Sermons, lectures and addresses

Fellowship with God: Life in Christ, Volume 1: Studies in 1 John (Cambridge: Crossway, 1993).

Walking with God: Life in Christ, Volume 2: Studies in 1 John (Cambridge: Crossway, 1993).

Children of God: Life in Christ, Volume 3: Studies in 1 John (Cambridge: Crossway, 1993).

1994

Sermons, lectures and addresses

The Love of God: Life in Christ, Volume 4: Studies in 1 John (Cambridge: Crossway, 1994).

Articles

'A Summer Visit to Germany and Scotland', *The Banner of Truth*, nos. 371–372 (August – September 1994), pp. 49–54.

Correspondence

D. Martyn Lloyd-Jones: Letters 1919–1981, selected with notes by Iain H. Murray (Edinburgh: Banner of Truth, 1994).

1995

Sermons, lectures and addresses

Life in God: Life in Christ, Volume 5: Studies in 1 John (Cambridge: Crossway, 1995).

Love So Amazing: The Life-Changing Power of the Gospel (Eastbourne: Kingsway, 1995).

Old Testament Evangelistic Sermons (Edinburgh: Banner of Truth, 1995).

The Quiet Heart (Cambridge: Crossway, 1995).

1996

Sermons, lectures and addresses

Great Doctrines Series, Volume 1: God the Father, God the Son (London: Hodder and Stoughton, 1996).

1997

Sermons, lectures and addresses

A Nation under Wrath: Studies in Isaiah 5 (Eastbourne: Kingsway, 1997).

Great Doctrines Series, Volume 2: God the Holy Spirit (London: Hodder and Stoughton, 1997).

Great Doctrines Series, Volume 3: The Church and the Last Things (London: Hodder and Stoughton, 1997).

Romans: An Exposition of Chapter 10: Saving Faith (Edinburgh: Banner of Truth, 1997).

True Happiness: An Exposition of Psalm One (Bridgend: Bryntirion Press, 1997).

1998

Sermons, lectures and addresses

Christmas Sermons: An Exposition of the Magnificat (Luke 1:46–55) (Bridgend: Bryntirion Press, 1998).

God's Way Not Ours: Sermons on Isaiah 1:1–18 (Edinburgh: Banner of Truth, 1998).

Romans: An Exposition of Chapter 11: To God's Glory (Edinburgh: Banner of Truth, 1998).

1999

Sermons, lectures and addresses

Authentic Christianity: Sermons on the Acts of the Apostles, Volume 1: Acts 1 – 3 (Edinburgh: Banner of Truth, 1999).

Jesus Christ and Him Crucified (Edinburgh: Banner of Truth, 1999).

Let Everybody Praise the Lord: An Exposition of Psalm 107 (Bridgend: Bryntirion Press, 1999).

'Righteousness, Temperance, and Judgement to Come', *The Banner of Truth*, no. 435 (December 1999), pp. 4–18.

Spiritual Blessing: The Path to True Happiness (Eastbourne: Kingsway, 1999).

2000

Sermons, lectures and addresses

Heirs of Salvation: Studies in Biblical Assurance (Bridgend: Bryntirion Press, 2000).

Romans: An Exposition of Chapter 12: Christian Conduct (Edinburgh: Banner of Truth, 2000).

2001

Sermons, lectures and addresses

Authentic Christianity: Sermons on the Acts of the Apostles, Volume 2: Acts 4 – 5 (Edinburgh: Banner of Truth, 2001).

Not Against Flesh and Blood: The Battle against Spiritual Wickedness in High Places (Bridgend: Bryntirion Press, 2001).

Articles

'This Evangelical Faith', *Evangelical Magazine of Wales*, vol. 40, no. 2 (April – May 2001), pp. 18–20.

2002

Sermons, lectures and addresses

Romans: An Exposition of Chapter 13: Life in Two Kingdoms (Edinburgh: Banner of Truth, 2002).

2003

Sermons, lectures and addresses

Authentic Christianity: Sermons on the Acts of the Apostles, Volume 3: Acts 5 – 6 (Edinburgh: Banner of Truth, 2003).

Romans: An Exposition of Chapter 14:1–17: Liberty and Conscience (Edinburgh: Banner of Truth, 2003).

Singing to the Lord (Bridgend: Bryntirion Press, 2003).

2004

Sermons, lectures and addresses

Authentic Christianity: Sermons on the Acts of the Apostles, Volume 4: Acts 7:1–29 (Edinburgh: Banner of Truth, 2004).

2005

Sermons, lectures and addresses

The All-Sufficient God: Sermons on Isaiah 40 (Edinburgh: Banner of Truth, 2005).

2006

Sermons, lectures and addresses

Authentic Christianity: Sermons on the Acts of the Apostles, Volume 5: Acts 7:30–60 (Edinburgh: Banner of Truth, 2006).

Authentic Christianity: Sermons on the Acts of the Apostles, Volume 6: Acts 8:1–35 (Edinburgh: Banner of Truth, 2006).

'Learning to be Content', *The Banner of Truth*, no. 508 (January 2006), pp. 8–11.

2007

Sermons, lectures and addresses

The Christian in an Age of Terror: Selected Sermons of Dr Martyn Lloyd-Jones 1941–1950, ed. Michael Eaton (Chichester: New Wine Press, 2007).

Raising Children God's Way (Edinburgh: Banner of Truth, 2007).

2008

Sermons, lectures and addresses

'Raising the Standard of Preaching', in Iain H. Murray, *Lloyd-Jones: Messenger of Grace* (Edinburgh: Banner of Truth, 2008), pp. 99–106.

2009

Sermons, lectures and addresses

Living Water: Studies in John 4, 2 vols. (Eastbourne: David C. Cook, 2008).

2010

Sermons, lectures and addresses

The Gospel in Genesis: From Fig-Leaves to Faith (Leominster: Day One, 2010).

2011

Sermons, lectures and addresses

'Something Elemental', *Evangelical Times*, vol. 45, no. 3 (March 2011), p. 5.
John Knox and the Reformation, with Iain H. Murray (Edinburgh: Banner of Truth, 2011).

Sermon series first published in the *Westminster Record*

'Persecution of the Church' (Acts 12)

Preached between 3 and 31 August 1941. First published in *Westminster Record*, vol. 15,
   no. 9 (September 1941) to vol. 16, no. 1 (January 1942). Republished as *The Christian
   in an Age of Terror: Selected Sermons of Dr Martyn Lloyd-Jones 1941–1950*, ed. Michael Eaton
   (Chichester: New Wine Press, 2007), chs. 1–5.

1. Religious Persecution
2. The Nature of the Conflict
3. God Answering Prayer
4. Where Miracle Ends
5. The Church Triumphant

'Paul's Order of the Day' (1 Corinthians 16:13–14)

Preached on Sunday mornings between 2 and 30 August 1942. First published in
   Westminster Record, vol. 16, no. 9 (September 1942) to vol. 17, no. 5 (May 1943).
   Republished as *The Christian in an Age of Terror: Selected Sermons of Dr Martyn Lloyd-Jones
   1941–1950*, ed. Michael Eaton (Chichester: New Wine Press, 2007), chs. 20–24.

1. General Introduction and Strategy
2. 'Watch Ye'
3. 'Stand Fast in the Faith'
4. 'Quit You Like Men, Be Strong'
5. 'Let All Things Be Done With Charity'

'A Synopsis of Christian Doctrine: Studies in Hebrews 1:1–3'

Preached on Sunday mornings between 6 and 27 December 1942. First published in
   Westminster Record, vol. 17, no. 9 (September 1943) to vol. 18, no. 3 (March 1944).
   Republished as *The Christian in an Age of Terror: Selected Sermons of Dr Martyn Lloyd-Jones
   1941–1950*, ed. Michael Eaton (Chichester: New Wine Press, 2007), chs. 6–9.

1. Revelation

2.   The Value of the Old Testament
3.   From Glory – to Glory
4.   God's Supreme Revelation in Christ

'Advent and the Idea of Judgment'

Preached on Sunday mornings between 5 and 19 December 1943. First published in
Westminster Record, vol. 18, no. 7 (July 1944); vol. 18, no. 9 (September 1944); vol. 18, no.
11 (November 1944).

1.   General Consideration
2.   The Nature of Judgment
3.   The Judge

'God's Plan for World Unity: Studies in the Epistle to the Ephesians'

Preached on Sunday mornings between 1 October and 26 November 1944. First
published in *Westminster Record*, vol. 19, no. 3 (March 1945) to vol. 20, no. 8 (August
1946).

1.   General View of the Plan
2.   The Centrality of Christ
3.   The Cause of the Discord
4.   Original Sin
5.   The World into which Christ Came
6.   The Only Hope
7.   The Wondrous Cross
8.   The New Kingdom
9.   God Over All

'A Preview of History' (Revelation 4 – 5)

Preached on Sunday mornings between 16 April and 7 May 1944. First published
in *Westminster Record*, vol. 21, nos. 2–5 (February – May 1947). Republished as *The
Christian in an Age of Terror: Selected Sermons of Dr Martyn Lloyd-Jones 1941–1950*, ed.
Michael Eaton (Chichester: New Wine Press, 2007), chs. 16–19.

1.   The Right Perspective
2.   The Throne of Heaven
3.   The Two Types of History
4.   The Lord of History

'What is a Christian? Studies in Romans 8'

Preached on Sunday mornings between 23 June and 28 July 1946. First published in
Westminster Record, vol. 21, nos. 6–11 (June – November 1947). Republished as *The
Christian in an Age of Terror: Selected Sermons of Dr Martyn Lloyd-Jones 1941–1950*, ed.
Michael Eaton (Chichester: New Wine Press, 2007), chs. 10–15.

1.   Having the Spirit of Christ
2.   Having the Mind of the Spirit
3.   Loving God
4.   The Test of Conduct
5.   Assurance of Salvation
6.   The New View of Life

'Light in a Dark Place: Studies in the Second Epistle of Peter'

Preached on Sunday mornings between 6 October 1946 and 30 March 1947. First
published in *Westminster Record*, vol. 22, no. 2 (February 1948) to vol. 24, no. 2
(February 1950). Republished as D. M. Lloyd-Jones, *Expository Sermons on 2 Peter*
(Edinburgh: Banner of Truth, 1983).

1.   Precious Faith
2.   Exceeding Great and Precious Promises
3.   The Balanced Life
4.   Assurance of Salvation
5.   Life and Death
6.   Things We Must Never Forget
7.   The Doctrine of the Second Advent
8.   The Message of the Second Advent
9.   The Apostolic Testimony
10. The Authority of Scripture
11. Fulfilled Prophecy – the Message of Christmas
12. The Gleam in the Gloom
13. False Prophets and their Teachings
14. False Teaching and its Consequences
15. The Examples of Noah and Lot
16. The Sovereignty of God
17. The Vital Importance of Biblical History
18. God and Time
19. The Biblical View of History
20. The Blessed Hope
21. The Consolation of the Scriptures

22.   Growing in Grace (I)
23.   Growing in Grace (II)
24.   Growing in Grace (III)
25.   The Lord of Glory

'De Profundis: Four Studies in Psalm 51'

Preached on Sunday evenings between 9 and 30 October 1949. First published in
Westminster Record, vol. 24, nos. 5–8 (May – August 1950). Republished as D. M. Lloyd-
Jones, *Out of the Depths: Studies in Psalm 51* (Bridgend: Evangelical Press of Wales,
1987).

1.   The Sinner's Confession
2.   The Sinner's Helplessness
3.   The Sinner's Central Need
4.   Deliverance and New Life

'Comfort in Perplexity: Six Studies in the Book of Habakkuk'

Preached on Sunday mornings between 11 June and 16 July 1950. First published in
Westminster Record, vol. 24, no. 9 (September 1950) to vol. 25, no. 2 (February 1951).
Republished as D. M. Lloyd-Jones, *From Fear to Faith* (London: Inter-Varsity Press,
1953).

1.   The Strangeness of God's Ways
2.   How to Face the Problem
3.   Waiting for God's Answer
4.   'The Just Shall Live by Faith'
5.   How to Pray
6.   How to Rejoice in Tribulations

'The Sermon on the Mount'

Preached on Sunday mornings between 1 October 1950 and 6 April 1952. First published
in *Westminster Record*, vol. 25, no. 3 (March 1951) to vol. 30, no. 2 (February 1956).
Republished as D. M. Lloyd-Jones, *Studies in the Sermon on the Mount*, 2 vols. (London:
Inter-Varsity Press, 1959–60).

1.   General Introduction
2.   General View and Analysis
3.   The Beatitudes
4.   Blessed are the Poor in Spirit
5.   Blessed are They that Mourn

6. Blessed are the Meek

7. Righteousness and Blessedness

8. The Tests of Spiritual Appetite

9. Blessed are the Merciful

10. Blessed are the Pure in Heart

11. Blessed are the Peacemakers

12. The Christian and Persecution

13. Rejoicing in Tribulations

14. The Salt of the Earth

15. The Light of the World

16. Let Your Light So Shine

17. Christ and the Old Testament

18. Christ Fulfilling the Law, and the Prophets

19. Righteousness Exceeding that of Scribes and Pharisees

20. The Letter and the Spirit

21. Thou Shalt Not Kill

22. The Exceeding Sinfulness of Sin

23. The Mortification of Sin

24. Christ's Teaching on Divorce

25. The Christian and the Taking of Oaths

26. 'Eye for an Eye and Tooth for a Tooth'

27. The Cloak and the Second Mile

28. Denying Self and Following Christ

29. Love Your Enemies

30. 'What Do Ye More than Others?'

31. 'Living the Righteous Life'

32. How to Pray

33. Fasting

34. 'When Ye Pray'

35. Prayer – Adoration

36. Prayer – Petition

37. Treasures on Earth and in Heaven

38. God or Mammon

39. Sin's Foul Bondage

40. Be Not Anxious

41. Birds and Flowers

42. Little Faith

43. Increasing Faith

44. Worry – Its Causes and Cure

45. 'Judge Not'

46. The Mote and the Beam
47. Spiritual Judgment and Discrimination
48. Seeking and Finding
49. The Golden Rule
50. The Strait Gate
51. The Narrow Way
52. False Prophets
53. The Tree and the Fruit
54. False Peace
55. Unconscious Hypocrisy
56. The Signs of Self-Deception
57. The Two Men and the Two Houses
58. Rock or Sand?
59. The Trial and the Tests of Faith
60. Conclusion

'A Soul's Conflict: Studies in Psalm 73'

Preached on Sunday mornings between 4 October 1953 and 3 January 1954. First
    published in *Westminster Record*, vol. 30, no. 3 (March 1956) to vol. 31, no. 1 (January
    1957). Republished as D. M. Lloyd-Jones, *Faith on Trial* (London: Inter-Varsity
    Fellowship, 1965).

1.   The Problem Stated
2.   Getting a Foot-Hold
3.   The Importance of Spiritual Thinking
4.   Facing All the Facts
5.   Beginning to Understand
6.   Self-Examination
7.   Spiritual Allergy
8.   'Nevertheless'
9.   'The Final Perseverance of the Saints'
10. The Rock of Ages
11. The New Resolution

'Spiritual Depression: Its Causes and Cure'

Preached on Sunday mornings between 10 and 17 May 1953 and between 10 January and
    11 July 1954. First published in *Westminster Record*, vol. 31, no. 3 (March 1957) to vol.
    32, no. 11 (November 1958). Republished as D. M. Lloyd-Jones, *Spiritual Depression: Its
    Causes and Cure* (London: Pickering and Inglis, 1965).

1.   General Consideration
2.   The True Foundation
3.   Men as Trees Walking
4.   Mind, Heart and Will
5.   That One Sin
6.   Vain Regrets
7.   Fear of the Future
8.   Feelings
9.   Labourers in the Vineyard
10. 'Where is Your Faith?'
11. Looking at the Waves
12. The Spirit of Bondage
13. False Teaching
14. Weary in Well Doing
15. Discipline
16. Trials
17. Chastening
18. In God's Gymnasium
19. The Peace of God
20. Learning to be Content
21. The Final Cure

'The Word of Reconciliation: Studies in Ephesians 2'

Preached on Sunday mornings between 22 October 1955 and 15 July 1956. First
   published in *Westminster Record*, vol. 33, no. 2 (February 1959) to vol. 36, no. 1 (January
   1962).

*Republished as D. M. Lloyd-Jones, *God's Way of Reconciliation: Studies in Ephesians Chapter
   2* (London: Evangelical Press, 1972).

1.   *Introduction
2.   *Man in Sin
3.   *Original Sin
4.   *Life Without God
5.   *The Wrath of God
6.   *The Christian Message to the World
7.   *'In Christ Jesus'
8.   *Risen With Christ
9.   *In the Heavenly Places
10. *The Exceeding Riches of his Grace
11. *'Through Christ Jesus' – A Christmas Meditation

12. *'By Grace Through Faith'
13. *'His Workmanship'
14. *Jew and Gentile
15. *'Without Christ'
16. *'Made Nigh'
17. *'The Blood of Christ'
18. *'He is Our Peace'
19. *'Christ's Way of Making Peace'
20. *'The One Mediator'
21. *'Peace With God'
22. *'Access to the Father'
23. *'Lord, Teach Us to Pray'
24. *'Praying in the Spirit'
25. *Christian Unity
26. *'No More Strangers'
27. *Heavenly Citizenship
28. *Privileges and Responsibilities
29. *'Of the Household of God'
30. *'A Habitation of God'
31. * 'The Only Foundation'
32. *'Fitly Framed Together'
33. *'The Growth of the Church'
34. 'Diversity in Unity'
35. 'Being and Doing'
36. 'Christian Activity'

'The Christian Warfare: Studies in Ephesians 6:10–13'

Preached on Sunday mornings between 2 October 1960 and 9 July 1961. First published
   in *Westminster Record*, vol. 36, no. 2 (February 1962) to vol. 40, no. 3 (March 1965).
*Republished as D. M. Lloyd-Jones, *The Christian Warfare: An Exposition of Ephesians 6:10 to
   13* (Edinburgh: Banner of Truth, 1976).
**Republished as D. Martyn Lloyd-Jones, *Not Against Flesh and Blood: The Battle Against
   Spiritual Wickedness in High Places* (Bridgend: Bryntirion Press, 2001).
***Republished as D. M. Lloyd-Jones, *Roman Catholicism* (London: Evangelical Press,
   1966).

1. *Introduction
2. *The Only Way
3. *The Enemy
4. *The Enemy Described

5.   *The Origin of Evil
6.   *The Wiles of the Devil
7.   **The Causes of War
8.   **Demonology
9.   **Spiritism
10. **Devil Possession
11. The Grace of God
12. The Mighty Conqueror
13. The Christian Vantage Ground
14. *The Subtle Foe
15. *Heresies
16. ***Roman Catholicism
17. Schism
18. Division – True and False
19. *Cults
20. *Counterfeits
21. *Watchfulness
22. *'Philosophy and Vain Deceit'
23. *'Knowledge Puffeth Up!'
24. Denying the Lord
25. Denying the Resurrection
26. *Faith and Experience
27. *Physical, Psychological, Spiritual
28. *True and False Assurance
29. *Attacks upon Assurance (1)
30. *Attacks upon Assurance (2)
31. *Quenching the Spirit (1)
32. *Quenching the Spirit (2)
33. *Temptation and Sin
34. *Discouragement
35. *Worry and Anxiety
36. *Self
37. *True and False Zeal
38. *Worldliness

'The Christian Soldier: Studies in Ephesians 6:10–20'

Preached on Sunday mornings between 9 October 1961 and 8 July 1962. First published
in *Westminster Record*, vol. 40, no. 4 (April 1965) to vol. 43, no. 1 (January 1968).

*Republished as D. M. Lloyd-Jones *The Christian Soldier: An Exposition of Ephesians 6:10 to
20* (Edinburgh: Banner of Truth, 1977).

1. *The Call to Battle
2. *God's Battle, Not Ours
3. *Who Does the Fighting?
4. *Morale
5. *Food and Drink
6. *Exercise
7. *Discipline
8. *The Promises
9. *'Trust in God and . . .'
10. *Things to Avoid
11. *'Stand Therefore'
12. *The Whole Armour of God
13. *'Loins Girt about with Truth'
14. *The Only Authority
15. *The Scripture of Truth
16. Truth Unchanged Unchanging
17. Propositional Truth
18. Knowing the Doctrine
19. Applying the Doctrine
20. *The Breastplate of Righteousness
21. *'The Righteousness which is of God by Faith'
22. *Putting on the Breastplate
23. Resisting Temptation
24. 'Stand Fast in the Liberty . . .'
25. 'Looking Unto Jesus'
26. 'Alive Unto God'
27. *Marching Orders
28. *Stand Fast
29. *Mobility
30. *The Shield of Faith
31. *'The Helmet of Salvation'
32. *'The Sword of the Spirit'
33. *Praying in the Spirit
34. *Praying for All Saints

'Walking in the Light: Studies in Ephesians 5:14 – 6:9'

Preached on Sunday mornings between 4 October 1959 and 27 March 1960. First
published in *Westminster Record*, vol. 43, no. 2 (February 1968) to vol. 44, no. 12
(December 1969).

*Republished as *Darkness and Light: An Exposition of Ephesians 4:17 to 5:17* (Edinburgh: Banner of Truth, 1982), chs. 34–36.

**Republished as *Life in the Spirit in Marriage, Home and Work: An Exposition of Ephesians 5:18 to 6:9* (Edinburgh: Banner of Truth, 1974), chs. 1–15.

***Republished as *Singing to the Lord* (Bridgend: Bryntirion Press, 2003).

1. The Call
2. *The Primary Need of Wisdom
3. *Walking Circumspectly
4. *Redeeming the Time
5. **The Flesh and the Spirit
6. **The Only Hope
7. **Filled with the Spirit
8. ***Christian Praise
9. ***Melody and Harmony
10. ***'The Universal Song'
11. ***'Giving Thanks Always'
12. **'Submitting Yourselves One to Another'
13. **'In the Fear of Christ'
14. **Facing Problems
15. **Man and Woman
16. **Obedience
17. **'Even as Christ'
18. **Christ's Love for the Church
19. **Sanctification
20. **'The Marriage-Supper of the Lamb'
21. **'A Great Mystery'
22. **The Bride's Privileges
23. **'Nourishing and Cherishing'

The remaining twelve sermons in this series were not published in the *Westminster Record*, which from January 1970 carried instead the sermons of Lloyd-Jones's successor at Westminster Chapel, Glyn Owen.

© Andrew Atherstone and David Ceri Jones, 2011

INDEX

Alderson, Richard 137
Alexander, Eric 135
Alington, C. A. 40
Andrewes, Lancelot 51, 162
Anselm 191
Arnold, Thomas 169
Atherstone, Andrew 36–37
Atherton, Henry 45–50
Augustine of Hippo 23, 50, 308

Bailie, Ben 36
Bala Conference 32, 76–78, 84
Banner of Truth magazine 13, 29, 38, 58, 141,
    144, 148, 154, 186, 249, 288
Banner of Truth Trust 13, 17, 23, 58, 72, 115,
    118, 120, 129, 145, 153, 297, 299–300, 315,
    323–324
baptism of the Spirit 36, 66, 99–100,
    102–105, 108, 113–117, 120, 123–132,
    139–144, 147, 154, 256, 314
Baptist Revival Fellowship 103, 110, 134
Barclay, Oliver 194, 289–290

Barcombe Baptist Chapel 13, 151
Barr, James (d. 1949) 41
Barr, James (d. 2006) 299
Barry Bible College 185, 194
Barth, Karl 37, 54–56, 66–67, 184, 189–190,
    204, 220–231
Basted, Brian 280
Baxter, Richard 238, 274, 295–296, 300, 303,
    312
Beale, Peter 282
Beasley-Murray, G. R. 253, 259
Bebbington, David 35–36, 234, 317
Beckwith, Roger 22, 266, 289
Beecher, Henry Ward 165
Belloc, Hilaire 236
Bennett, Dennis 115
Benton, John 151
Binfield, Clyde 31, 33
Blanchard, John 135–136
Blessitt, Arthur 137, 140, 315
Blocher, Henri 231
Bosher, Robert 302, 310

Botting, Michael 281
Bouyer, Louis 297
Bowra, Maurice 39
Bradford, John 124, 249
Braund, Elizabeth 283
Bray, Gerald 19
Breed, Charles 38–39
Brencher, John 13, 25, 31–35, 61, 176, 198, 213, 233, 262
Bridge, William 295
British Council of Churches (BCC) 242, 244–245, 263
British Evangelical Council (BEC) 24, 32–33, 82–83, 109, 130–131, 136, 191, 251, 253–256, 282, 284–286, 288, 291–292, 307
Brooks, Thomas 132, 295
Brown, Callum 156
Brown, Peter 302
Bruce, F. F. 16, 53, 299
Brunner, Emil 66, 184, 190, 222–224
Buchanan, Colin 21, 255, 287–290, 292
Budgen, Victor 146, 149–150
Bunyan, John 26, 287, 295, 300
Burleigh, J. H. S. 52–53
Buss, Michael 288

Caiger, John 194, 291
Cain, Paul 137, 140, 315
Calvin, John 24, 39–40, 42, 49–52, 54, 56, 144, 304, 308, 314–317
Calvinism 36, 38–58, 65, 86, 95, 103, 180, 189, 224, 300, 320, 323
Calvinistic Methodism 41, 62, 66–67, 69, 81, 90, 97, 107, 110–111, 182, 190, 235, 295, 309, 317
Campbell, Duncan 102
Campbell, John 187
Campbell, Murdo 42
Campbell, R. J. 61
Canty, George 118
Carr, Geoffrey 265
Carson, Don 323

Carson, Herbert 149, 151–152, 194, 249, 253, 255–256, 262, 264, 268, 286–287
Carwardine, Richard 33
Catherwood, Christopher 13, 17–20, 23, 31, 35, 93, 107, 130, 141, 143, 285, 302
Catherwood, Elizabeth 17
Catherwood, Frederick 17, 152, 194, 296, 322
Chadwick, Owen 302
Chafer, Lewis Sperry 322
Chalmers, Thomas 23
Chapman, John 127
charismatic movement 36, 68, 89, 99, 103, 108, 111, 114–155, 194, 256, 265, 300, 314–315, 317–318, 320, 323–324
Charley, Julian 274–275
Chesterton, G. K. 236
Chilvers, H. Tydeman 43
Christenson, Larry 117
Chrysostom 23
Church of England Evangelical Council (CEEC) 277, 284, 289, 290, 292
Church of England Newspaper 15, 274–275, 277, 279, 281
Clark, Scott 318–319
Clark, Stephen 29, 34
Clarkson, David 295
Clements, Roy 149–150, 152
Cocksworth, Christopher 233
Coffey, John 37
Cole, Henry 45
Colijn, Hendrik 49
Collins, John 116
Collinson, Patrick 302, 313
Congar, Yves 297
Cotton, John 315, 324
Cox, Geoffrey 291
Cox, Richard 312
Cradock, Walter 300
Craig, A. C. 245
Cranmer, Thomas 266
Crieff Brotherhood 39
Crisp, Tobias 300
Cromwell, Oliver 295, 311

Crosslinks 22
Cunningham, William 300

Dabney, Robert 299
Dale, R. W. 66
Dallimore, Arnold 149
Daniélou, Jean 297
Davidson, A. B. 322
Davies, Andrew 195
Davies, Aneirin Talfan 213, 217
Davies, D. R. 223–224
Davies, Elwyn 69, 73, 75–76, 79, 82, 86–87
Davies, Gaius 13, 22, 25–31, 35
Davies, Rupert 302
Day, A. J. 45
Dearmer, Percy 40
Denney, James 66
Derham, Morgan 280, 283, 285–286
de Saussure, Jean 49, 51–52
Dever, Mark 323
Doctorian, Samuel 117
Donne, John 162
Douglas, J. D. 282, 286
du Plessis, David 117–118
Dyer, E. G. 254

Eaton, Michael 94, 115
ecumenism 12, 21–22, 32, 62, 73–76, 79–85,
    121–122, 189–191, 194, 198, 208, 215,
    233–234, 238–260, 269–292, 305–312
Edwards, H. W. J. 236
Edwards, Jonathan 14, 56, 66, 94–95, 108,
    110–111, 125, 127, 184, 296, 299, 309, 316,
    318, 320–321
Edwards, Lewis 181
Edwards, T. C. 182
Elias, John 181
English Churchman 47, 272, 276–277, 284
Erasmus 189, 282
Evangelical Alliance (EA) 89, 235, 241,
    243–244, 249, 269, 271, 280, 284–286, 323
Evangelical Fellowship in the Church in
    Wales (EFCW) 89

Evangelical Library 12, 53–54, 72, 118–120,
    135, 246, 264, 296–297, 310
Evangelical Magazine 9, 283, 291
Evangelical Magazine of Wales 73, 76, 81, 84–85,
    125, 144, 288
Evangelical Movement of Wales (EMW) 12,
    24–25, 36, 39, 62, 73–74, 76–90, 129, 136,
    145
Evangelical Quarterly 44, 49, 52–53, 57, 103,
    299
Evangelical Times 29, 130, 132, 141, 149–151,
    154, 253–254, 279–280
Evangelicalism Divided (2000) 21–22, 27
Evangelicals Now 21, 151–153, 155
Evans, Christmas 127
Eveson, Philip 36

Farncombe, C. J. 47
Farncombe, F. J. 47
Fellowship of Evangelical Churchmen
    44
Fellowship of Independent Evangelical
    Churches (FIEC) 31, 83, 130, 136, 243
Fellowship of Word and Spirit 22
Finney, Charles 125, 127–128, 320–321
Fisher, Geoffrey 245
Flavel, John 125, 127, 295
Forester, George 264
Forsyth, P. T. 66
Fountain, David 291
Fountain Trust 118, 121–122
Fox, George 295
France, R. T. 262
Francke, August Hermann 317
Free Church of England 43, 45, 51
fundamentalism 36, 44–45, 197–219

Gardner, David 265
George, C. H. 302
Gerstner, J. H. 194
Gillies, John 299
Gladwin, John 281
God's Ultimate Purpose (1978) 126–127

Goodwin, John 300
Goodwin, Thomas 125, 127, 295, 314, 316
Gospel Magazine 14, 47, 264, 286
Graham, Billy 21, 98, 137, 198, 323
Grier, W. J. 255
Griffiths, Peter Hughes 178
Growing into Union (1970) 27, 37, 255, 261, 287–289, 291–292

Hall, Basil 302, 306
Haller, William 302
Hammond, T. C. 54
Harper, Jeanne 120
Harper, Michael 115–121, 124, 134, 144, 155, 317
Harris, Harriet 217
Harris, Howel 60, 94, 99, 101, 107, 125, 181, 316
Harrison, Graham 141, 143–145, 195
Hart, Darryl 318
Havergal, Frances Ridley 26
Haykin, Michael 15
Helm, Paul 233, 288, 315
Henry, Carl 194, 212
Henry, Matthew 147
Henson, Hensley 162–163
Higham, Vernon 86
Hill, Christopher 302
Hillsborough, Viscount of 249
Hindmarsh, Bruce 297
Hinn, Benny 154
Hoad, Jack 195
Hodge, Charles 103, 299, 321
Hopkins, Evan 44
Horder, Thomas 12, 179
Horn, Robert 149–152
Houghton, A. T. 246
Houghton, Thomas 47
Howard-Browne, Rodney 137, 140
Howe, John 132, 295
Hughes, Philip 91–92, 110, 115, 179–180, 189, 291

Hughes, Trystan Owain 235
Hulse, Erroll 128–129, 132, 145, 150–151
Hunt, Paul 281
Hunt, R. C. P. 267
Hutchinson, Anne 315

Idle, Christopher 21, 29
International Fellowship of Evangelical Students (IFES) 12, 188, 244, 297
Inter-Varsity Fellowship (IVF) 12, 53–54, 56–57, 68, 72–73, 75–76, 220, 222, 244, 289, 293, 299
Inwood, Charles 102
Irving, Edward 149, 314
Islington Clerical Conference 117, 265

Jacob, Henry 311
James, John Angell 187
James, Peter 287
James, William 110
Jenkins, Omri 122, 287
John XXIII, Pope 245, 247
John Paul II, Pope 258
Johnson, Douglas 53–54, 56–57, 68
Johnston, Peter 266
Johnston, Raymond 263
Joy Unspeakable (1984) 17, 114, 120, 141–144, 146, 148, 150
Jones, Bryn 134
Jones, David Ceri 36
Jones, R. B. 68, 185
Joshua, Seth 183

Kay, William 36
Keele Congress, *see* National Evangelical Anglican Congress
Keller, Adolf 221
Keller, Tim 323
Kendall, R. T. 115, 135–140, 146, 155, 294, 303–304, 314–315, 324
Kennedy, G. A. Studdert 167
Keswick Convention 42, 44, 51, 68, 86, 102–103, 194, 295, 321

Keulemans, Michael 263
Kevan, Ernest 186
Kidd, Thomas 318
King, Martin Luther 322
Kirby, Gilbert 243, 245, 249, 286
Kirk, Kenneth 66
Knappen, M. M. 302
Knox, John 312
Knox, Ronald 236
Kuhlmann, Kathryn 154
Küng, Hans 236, 307
Kuyper, Abraham 47–50, 144, 322

Laing, John 77
Lamb, Roland 254
Lambert, Frank 320
Lamont, Daniel 42
Lane, Eric 263, 288
Lanphier, Jeremiah 106
Latimer, Hugh 124
Latourette, Kenneth 320
Laud, William 313
Lawrence, John 279
Lawson, Thomas 45
Lecerf, Auguste 39, 48–52
Legerton, H. J. W. 265, 276
Leigh Hunt, Stephen 50–51, 54
Leonard, Graham 255, 287
Letham, Robert 19–20
Lewis, C. S. 26
Lewis, Peter 91, 130–134, 143, 145, 150, 153, 155
Lewis, Vernon 65
Lewty, H. A. 42
Lillie, David 119
Linklater, Eric 40
Livingstone, John 124
Lloyd George, David 61
Lloyd-Jones, Bethan 14, 16, 64, 136, 140, 152, 206
Lloyd-Jones, Henry 61
Lloyd-Jones, Martyn 11–38, 56–362
Lloyd-Jones, Vincent 236

Llwyd, Morgan 300
London Bible College 31, 34, 128, 133, 176, 185–186, 188, 191–192, 286
London Theological Seminary 36, 183, 190–196, 256–257
Long, Kathryn 95
Lucas, Dick 22, 116–117
Lusk, William 42
Luther, Martin 26, 29, 54, 150, 189–190, 238, 244, 254, 260, 269, 282, 292, 304–308
Lythgoe, A. 45

MacArthur, John 21
McConnachie, John 222
MacDiarmid, Hugh 40
McGrath, Alister 19–21, 35, 272, 285
Machen, J. Gresham 187, 193, 272, 322
MacInnes, David 116
Mackay, J. R. 43, 49, 52
McKnight, R. J. G. 51
Maclean, Donald 49, 50, 52, 54–55, 57
Macleod, Donald 23–24, 35, 124, 127–129, 132, 150, 184, 194
Macleod, John 49
McQuilkin, James 106
Maguire, Frank 115, 117
Maiden, John 37
Manley, G. T. 321
Manning, Bernard 56
Manton, Thomas 132, 295, 300
Marchant, George 267
Marsden, George 303, 306
Marshall, Howard 53
Martin, Alexander 41
Martyn Lloyd-Jones Recordings Trust 13, 141, 151
Mascall, Eric 255, 287
Masters, Peter 146–147, 149–150, 154–155, 253
Matheson, George 307
Matthews, W. R. 244
Maurras, Charles 49
Metcalfe, Willis 151

Meyer, F. B. 102

Micklem, Nathaniel 55–56

Middleton, Roy 148

Milsom, Peter 33–34

Milton, John 300

Mohler, Al 323

Moody, D. L. 125, 127, 321

Montefiore, Hugh 283

Morgan, Campbell 12, 69–70, 136, 183, 247, 322

Morgan, Dafydd 105, 124

Morgan, D. Densil 16, 25, 33, 220, 224, 235

Motyer, Alec 262

Muller, Richard 304

Murray, Gordon 272–273, 276–277

Murray, Iain 13–16, 18, 20–23, 27, 30–31, 34–35, 63–64, 118, 129, 140, 144–145, 148, 155, 187, 233, 236, 249, 268–269, 271–274, 280, 283, 303, 314, 320–321

Murray, John 14

Musculus, Paul 51

National Assembly of Evangelicals (1966) 12, 22, 37, 81, 118, 152, 216, 251–253, 261, 267, 269–274, 276, 278, 283–284, 292, 307

National Evangelical Anglican Congress (Keele 1967) 37, 190, 233, 251, 253–254, 261, 278–282, 289, 292

National Evangelical Anglican Congress (Nottingham 1977) 190, 256

Naville, Edouard 44

Neill, Stephen 259

New, J. F. H. 302, 312

New Frontiers 133, 151

Newman, John Henry 307

Nichols, John 195

Nicol, J. 41

Niebuhr, Karl 190

Niebuhr, Reinhold 212

Nightingale, Thomas 234

Noll, Mark 33, 306–307

Nuttall, Geoffrey 302–303

Ockenga, Harold 57

Oden, Thomas 324

Old, Hughes Oliphant 161, 165

Owen, Glyn 135, 362

Owen, John 65, 125, 132, 238–239, 248, 295–296, 300, 311–312, 314, 316

Packer, J. I. 12, 19–22, 26–27, 29–30, 37, 58, 102–103, 110, 179–180, 186, 197, 214, 218, 250, 255–256, 262, 267, 269, 272, 274, 283–285, 287–292, 294, 296–297, 303, 307, 309–314, 324

Palau, Luis 85

Palmer, Phoebe 321

Parker, Joseph 40, 183

Pascal, Blaise 142, 303, 307

Paul VI, Pope 233, 250, 258

Peace and Truth 15, 45, 47, 50, 54, 288

Pearce, John 266

Pentecostalism, *see* charismatic movement

Phillips, Ieuan 59

Phillips, J. B. 26

Pink, A. W. 14, 42

Piper, John 114, 301, 323

Plato 50

Platt, Henry 46

Pollard, A. F. 53

Poole-Connor, E. J. 243

Pope, Robert 36

Popham, J. K. 43–44, 47, 53

Porter, Norman 255

Pouncy, A. G. 280–281

Powicke, F. J. 295

preaching 12, 36, 23–24, 105, 123–124, 156–175, 181–196

Preaching and Preachers (1971), 36, 105, 123–124, 158–159, 172, 187

Proclamation Trust 22

Prove All Things (1985) 17, 114, 120, 141–143, 146–148, 150

Puritan (Westminster) Conference 12, 17, 24, 37–38, 72, 93–95, 98, 100, 103, 108, 112, 118, 135, 186, 188–189, 238, 248,

255–256, 290–291, 297, 301, 304, 309–312, 322

Rabelais, François 50
Radcliff, Moshe 278
Ramsey, Michael 233, 250–253, 263, 280
Randall, Ian 36, 186
Ratzinger, Joseph 298
Rees, E. T. 63
Reformation Today 28, 128, 140–141, 144, 148, 151, 153
Renan, Ernest 50
Renewal magazine 124, 133, 138, 141, 154–155
revival 26, 36, 61–62, 64, 66–68, 74, 76–77, 82, 86, 91–113, 118, 123, 127, 133–134, 142, 147, 169, 194, 221, 240, 254, 271, 299, 303, 305, 310, 316–322, 324
Reynolds, Edward 295
Richards, Billy 115, 121–123, 126, 155
Richards, Wesley 123
Roberts, Evan 106–107
Robinson, John 262, 283, 286
Robinson, W. Childs 51
Roman Catholicism 21, 37, 81, 93, 101, 122, 153, 232–260, 279, 297–298, 305
Rookmaaker, Hans 322–323
Rosser, John 262, 281–282
Rowland, Daniel 11, 60, 94, 137
Rupp, Gordon 302
Rutgers, Victor 51
Ryle, J. C. 21, 42, 267, 269

Samuel, David 289
Samuel, Leith 31, 113, 194, 249, 272, 283
Sandfields Forward Movement Mission 12, 62–65, 168, 178, 182, 185
Sangster, W. E. 166, 195
Sargent, Tony 104–105, 115
Savonarola, Girolamo 142
Schaeffer, Francis 188, 306, 322–323
Scorer, C. G. 194
Scott, Thomas 42

Scripture Union 289–290
Searle, David 21–22
Sebestyén, E. 51
secession, *see* separatism
Selbie, William 244
separatism 18–19, 32, 36–37, 62, 72, 78–89, 109–110, 135, 146, 194, 214–217, 239, 242, 250–292, 307, 309, 316
Shedd, W. T. 299
Sheehan, Robert 195
Shields, T. T. 185
Shucksmith, Barry 262
Sibbes, Richard 127, 132, 295, 299, 316
Sinclair, J. S. 43
Sinden, William 46–47
Siviter, Isaac 44
Smith, Hannah Pearsall 321
Soper, Donald 286
Sovereign Grace Union (SGU) 45–47, 49–52, 55–58, 288
Spener, Philip Jakob 317
Sproul, R. C. 21
Spurgeon, Charles 14, 23, 29, 40, 87, 125, 131, 183, 192, 268–269, 295, 297, 322
Stacey, Nicolas 277
Stanley, Brian 244
Stephenson, George 46
Stibbs, Alan 21, 289–290
Stone, Jean 117
Stott, John 12, 21–22, 89, 116–118, 120, 197, 261, 267, 269, 271, 273–274, 280, 284–285, 289, 292, 307, 311
Stout, Harry 320
Strivens, Robert 36–37
Strong, Robert 126
Sweeney, Douglas 317
Swinnock, George 295
Sword and Trowel 146, 148
Sykes, William 47
Sylvester, Nigel 290

Tauler, John 142
Taylor, Jeremy 162

Tertullian 128, 142, 303
The Christian Warfare (1976), 125, 247
The Sons of God (1974) 124–126
Thomas Aquinas 56, 142, 307
Thomas, Geoffrey 20, 129
Thompson, D. A. 45
Thompson, Francis 307
Thornley, H. W. 43
Thornwell, James Henry 299
Tidball, Derek 34
Tinker, Melvin 21–22
Toplady, Augustus 47
Torrance, Thomas 52–53
Tozer, A. W. 316
Trapnel, Anna 300
Trueman, Carl 29–30, 35, 180, 231, 261, 272,
    285, 317–319, 324
Turner, Tony 276
Tyler, Henry 134, 155
Tyndale House, Cambridge 12, 179–180, 189,
    293, 298, 321

Unmack, E. C. 50

van Lonkhuyzen, Jan 47–48
Van Til, Cornelius 49, 55, 224
Vatican Council (Second) 245, 250, 259, 305,
    307
Vidler, Alec 244
Virgo, Terry 115, 133–134, 144, 155, 317
Vischer, Wilhelm 51
von Balthasar, Hans Urs 297–298

Wallis, Arthur 133
Warfield, B. B. 49, 52, 56, 66, 147, 184, 296,
    322
Warner, Rob 88, 285
Watson, David 115–116, 149, 151, 256
Watts, Isaac 111
Watts, Michael 156, 161
Waugh, Evelyn 236

Welsh Revival 36, 61, 67–68, 105–107, 152
Wencelius, Léon 51
Wenham, John 245
Wesley, Charles 111
Wesley, John 14, 22, 105, 110, 124–125,
    127–128, 274, 301, 321
Westminster Conference, *see* Puritan
    Conference
Westminster Fellowship 24, 77, 117, 122, 134,
    194, 278, 291–292
Westminster Theological Seminary 29, 123,
    158, 162, 173–174, 187, 192–193, 195
Weston, Keith 276
Whale, J. S. 56
Whitefield, George 23, 94, 105, 107, 124–125,
    299, 305, 315–317, 319–320
Wigley, Thomas 55
Wilberforce, William 305, 323
Wilkerson, David 300
Williams, Geoffrey 53, 296
Williams, Hugh 34–35
Williams, Roger 300
Williams, R. R. 268
Williams, Tom 67
Williams, William 60, 95, 97, 107, 111, 125,
    190, 316, 319
Wimber, John 114, 150
Winnington-Ingram, Arthur 40
Winter, David 271, 273, 284
Wood, Maurice 245, 266
Woodfield, Ralph 44
Woods, C. Stacey 297
Wordsworth, William 60
World Council of Churches (WCC) 72, 74,
    118, 242–243, 245–246, 251, 258–259, 274,
    279, 311
Wright, David 22
Wright, N. T. 324
Wycliffe, John 74

Zwingli, Huldrych 308

related titles from IVP

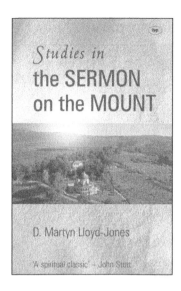

Studies in the Sermon on the Mount

D. Martyn Lloyd-Jones

ISBN: 978-0-85110-583-3
656 page paperback

With characteristic insight, Dr D. Martyn Lloyd-Jones here offers a detailed and comprehensive exposition of one of the best known but most frequently misunderstood passages of Scripture – the Sermon on the Mount.

The Sermon on the Mount, says Lloyd-Jones, is not a code of ethics or morals; it is a description of what Christians are meant to be. With his eye always on both Scripture and life, he explains and applies Christ's teaching for Christians struggling to live like Christ.

Originally delivered as sermons, the sixty studies in this devotional classic provide a fine example of clear, consecutive expository preaching from one of the greatest preachers of our time.

Available from your local Christian bookshop or **www.ivpbooks.com**

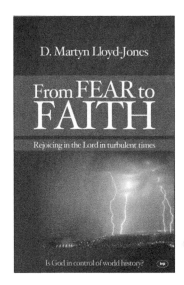

related titles from IVP

From Fear to Faith

Rejoicing in the Lord in turbulent times

D. Martyn Lloyd-Jones

ISBN: 978-1-84474-500-5
76 page paperback

Is God in control of world history?

The country was on the brink of a devastating invasion. Famine threatened. Violence and social injustice filled the land. Habakkuk the Old Testament prophet had every reason to sink into despair. Where was God in these turbulent times?

D. Martyn Lloyd-Jones was one of the twentieth century's foremost preachers and Bible teachers. The parallels he draws between the message of Habakkuk and the crisis-ridden West are still powerfully relevant to our own times. Here is the secret of the problem of history. No event, however catastrophic, fails to find a place in God's loving purpose for humanity. Habakkuk's great assertion of faith, in the midst of enormous personal upheaval and emotional strain, can be ours: 'Yet I will rejoice in the Lord ... The Sovereign Lord is my strength.'

Available from your local Christian bookshop or **www.ivpbooks.com**

related titles from IVP

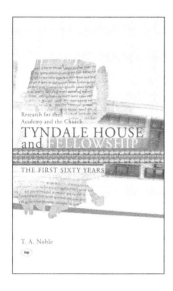

Tyndale House and Fellowship
The first sixty years
T. A. Noble

ISBN: 978-1-84474-095-6
336 page hardback

For more than sixty years, Tyndale House and the associated Tyndale Fellowship have made a unique and vital contribution to the healthy condition of contemporary biblical studies, and of historic Christianity in the United Kingdom and worldwide.

The House and Fellowship were founded in 1944, at a time when many conservative Christians failed to see any need for 'biblical and theological research', and when many academics were sceptical about whether committed Christians could engage in such research with intellectual integrity. The founders included such figures as F. F. Bruce, W. J. Martin, Douglas Johnson and D. Martyn Lloyd-Jones.

Thomas A. Noble traces the history of Tyndale House and the Tyndale Fellowship across the decades. His detailed narrative covers internal discussions and debates, progress through difficulties and discouragements, and eventual outward recognition, success and influence.

This valuable and informative volume will appeal to all who know Tyndale House and its work, members of the Fellowship and related institutions, and all with an interest in the history of Christianity in the twentieth century.

Available from your local Christian bookshop or **www.ivpbooks.com**

related titles from Apollos

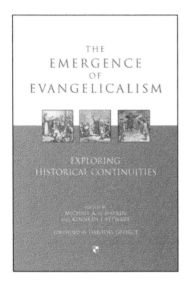

The Emergence of Evangelicalism

Exploring historical continuities

M. Haykin & K. Stewart (editors)

ISBN: 978-1-84474-254-7

432 page large paperback

David Bebbington's *Evangelicalism in Modern Britain: A History from the 1730s to the 1980s*, published in 1989, offered an intriguing hypothesis regarding the genesis of this movement. He argued that evangelical religion had emerged as a substantially new entity through transatlantic evangelical revival in the 1730s, and had taken a collaborative rather than antithetical stance towards the Enlightenment. In both respects, Bebbington distanced himself from older interpretations that had held the opposite view.

Now, after nearly two decades, the 'Bebbington thesis' has gained very wide international acceptance, and a review of its central contentions and implications is appropriate. In this stimulating volume, numerous scholars from arts and theology faculties on both sides of the Atlantic, representing several countries, and united by an admiration of Bebbington's work, take up various aspects of the 1989 volume and offer re-assessments. David Bebbington himself offers a substantial response.

Available from your local Christian bookshop or **www.ivpbooks.com**

Discover more great Christian books
at **www.ivpbooks.com**

Full details of all the books from Inter-Varsity Press – including reader reviews, author information, videos and free downloads – are available on our website at **www.ivpbooks.com**.

IVP publishes a wide range of books on various subjects including:

Biography

Christian Living

Bible Studies

Reference

Commentaries

Theology

On the website you can also sign up for regular email newsletters, tell others what you think about books you have read by posting reviews, and locate your nearest Christian bookshop using the *Find a Store* feature.

IVP publishes Christian books that are **true to the Bible** and that **communicate the gospel**, **develop discipleship** and **strengthen the church** for its mission in the world.

Printed and bound by CPI Group (UK) Ltd, Croydon, CR0 4YY

13/04/2025

14656474-0005